# HISTORY OF WORLD ARCHITECTURE

*Pier Luigi Nervi, General Editor*

# ANCIENT ARCHITECTURE
## MESOPOTAMIA, EGYPT, CRETE, GREECE

*Seton Lloyd, Hans Wolfgang Müller, Roland Martin*

*Harry N. Abrams, Inc., Publishers, New York*

*Produced under the supervision of Carlo Pirovano,
editorial director of Electa Editrice*

*Design: Diego Birelli*

*Photographs: Pepi Merisio and Bruno Balestrini*

*Drawings: Enzo Di Grazia*

**Library of Congress Cataloging in Publication Data**

Lloyd, Seton.
  Ancient architecture: Mesopotamia, Egypt, Crete, Greece.

  (History of world architecture)
  Bibliography: p. 397
  1. Architecture, Ancient — Near East. 2. Architecture — Near East.
3. Architecture, Greek. I. Martin, Roland. II. Müller, Hans Wolfgang.
III. Title
NA210.L58            722            73-2843
ISBN 0-8109-1020-9

# CONTENTS

PREFACE  *by Pier Luigi Nervi*                                      6

PART I  *by Seton Lloyd*
   Architecture of Mesopotamia and
   The Ancient Near East                                            7

PART II  *by Hans Wolfgang Müller*
   Architecture of Egypt                                           73

PART III  *by Roland Martin*
   Architecture of Crete, Greece,
   and the Greek World                                            191

SYNOPTIC TABLES                                                   383

SELECTED BIBLIOGRAPHY                                             397

LIST OF PLATES                                                    401

INDEX OF NAMES AND PLACES                                         409

LIST OF PHOTOGRAPHIC CREDITS                                      415

# PREFACE

*Architectural criticism has nearly always been concerned with the visible aspect of individual buildings, taking this to be the decisive factor in the formulation of value judgments and in the classification of those "styles" which appear in textbooks, and which have thus become common knowledge. But once it is recognized that every building is, by definition, a work subject to the limitations imposed by the materials and building techniques at hand, and that every building must prove its stability, as well as its capacity to endure and serve the needs it was built for, it becomes clear that the aesthetic aspect alone is inadequate when we come to appraise a creative activity, difficult enough to judge in the past, rapidly becoming more complex in our own day, and destined to become more so in the foreseeable future.*

*Nevertheless, what has struck me most, on studying the architecture of the past and present, is the fact that the works which are generally regarded by the critics and the general public as examples of pure beauty are also the fruit of exemplary building techniques, once one has taken into account the quality of the materials and the technical knowledge available. And it is natural to suspect that such a coincidence is not entirely casual.*

*Building in the past was wholly a matter of following static intuitions, which were, in turn, the result of meditation, experience, and above all of an understanding of the capacity of certain structures and materials to resist external forces. Meditation upon structural patterns and the characteristics of various materials, together with the appraisal of one's own experiences and those of others is an act of love toward the process of construction for its own sake, both on the part of the architect and his collaborators and assistants. Indeed, we may wonder whether this is not the hidden bond which unites the appearance and substance of the finest buildings of the past, distant though that past may be, into a single "thing of beauty."*

*One might even think that the quality of the materials available not only determined architectural patterns but also the decorative detail with which the first simple construction was gradually enriched.*

*One might find a justification for the difference in refinement and elegance between Greek architecture, with its basic use of marble —a highly resistant material, upon which the most delicate carvings can be carried out—and the majestic concrete structures of Roman architecture, built out of a mixture of lime and pozzolana, and supported by massive walls, to compensate for their intrinsic weaknesses.*

*Would it be too rash to connect these objective architectural characteristics with the different artistic sensibilities of the two peoples?*

*One must recognize, therefore, the importance of completing the description of the examples illustrated with an interpretation of their constructional and aesthetic characteristics, so that the connection between the twin aspects of building emerges as a natural, logical consequence.*

*This consequence, if understood and accepted in good faith by certain avant-garde circles, could put an end to the disastrous haste with which our architecture is rushing toward an empty, costly, and at times impractical formalism. It might also recall architects and men of culture to a more serene appraisal of the objective elements of building and to the respect that is due to a morality of architecture. For this is just as important for the future of our cities as is morality, understood as a rule of life, for an orderly civil existence.*

PIER LUIGI NERVI

*Architecture of Mesopotamia and the Ancient Near East  •  Seton Lloyd*

# THE ORIGINS AND THE PROTODYNASTIC PERIOD

The meaning of the word *architecture* is soberly defined in some dictionaries as "the science of building," though most people would agree that it has in our time acquired a more particularized connotation. It has in fact come to imply the notion of design and the deliberate contrivance thereby of certain aesthetic effects: something other than the mere technology of building construction. This secondary implication should be borne in mind by anyone wishing to study the earliest beginnings of architecture in the ancient world, since he will find himself seeking among primitive peoples the first symptoms of creative ingenuity manifest in the design of buildings. The relevance of this observation will become clear in the pages that follow, since they are concerned with that part of the world which may truly be said to have provided a setting for the birth of architecture. By far the earliest evidence we have of tentative experiments in architectural design is derived from Anatolia and the countries bordering the Syrian Desert; it is the results of archaeological research in this area that we have first to consider.

The incentive to build was initially an outcome of what has been called the Neolithic Revolution: a point of transition in the changing pattern of human behavior, at which the tribal organization of hunters and cave dwellers was discarded in favor of better-coordinated agricultural communities. Much study has in recent years been devoted to this important epoch in human evolution, and certain rather general conclusions have been reached. It is probable that the development began to take place soon after 10,000 B.C.; and it is certain that the geographical areas where it originated were the natural homes of wild grains, which provided the raw material of primitive agriculture, and of wild animals destined to become domesticated. The piedmont or semimountainous areas of the Near East answering to these requirements are those in which the remains of very early settled communities have been discovered, and among them evidence has been found of incipient agriculture. Here also we obtain a glimpse of a people in whose memories cave-dwelling must still have been very much alive, and who were now for the first time faced with the need to construct artificial shelters or dwellings.

Needless to say, the forms adopted for the earliest dwellings were dictated by purely practical considerations. Some of the earliest known houses at Jericho in Jordan, dating from the eighth millennium B.C., were circular in plan, with stone foundations and perhaps a clay upper structure. One feels that this may have been an imitation in more permanent materials of tents or other temporary shelters used during a period of nomadism intermediate between cave and village. The materials first used for such permanent dwellings are themselves interesting. Walls of undressed stone, perhaps the oldest and most obvious device, are found only in regions where stone is readily available. Elsewhere, sun-dried clay soon came into use and was universally adopted as the standard building material of the Near East. Tempered with straw, it could initially be built up in slabs in the manner suggested today by the words *pisé* or *adobe.* But at Jericho and elsewhere this clumsy method soon gave way to the use of prefabricated bricks, cast in a rectangular wooden mold and dried in the sun. With this material houses could be built with simple rectangular rooms and roofed with timber.

At a period in the seventh millennium known archaeologically as Pre-pottery Neolithic B, remarkable advances seem to have been made in brick building. One innovation is again seen at Jericho. Internal wall faces and floors are both neatly rendered in gypsum plaster, which could be stained red and burnished with a smooth stone. The jambs of doorways are carefully rounded to avoid damage to the corners. Even more important in this setting is the plan of a building which its excavator supposes to have been a religious shrine; here for the first time one sees that the design has been considered in relation to the ritual purpose of the building. The entry is through a portico, partly supported on wooden posts; two axially placed doorways lead to an inner sanctuary (Plate 1).

To observe an even more precocious elaboration of architectural ideas in this Neolithic phase of man's development (still in the seventh millennium), one must turn to the site of Catal Huyuk, near Konya in southern Anatolia. Here we are faced not with a village, but with a township covering fifteen or so acres. The houses, built of sun-dried brick, are closely contiguous, almost like the cells of a honeycomb, but each has several rectangular rooms similarly planned, and each is accessible only by a wooden ladder from its flat roof (Plates 2, 3). The roofs are, of course, intercommunicating and provide space for the communal life of the inhabitants. There are many strange features in these buildings. Some of them appear to be religious shrines and are elaborately ornamented with heads or horns of animals, either real or imitated in plaster (Plate 4). The walls are decorated with colored murals, repeatedly repainted after replastering, the designs closely resembling the cave paintings of an earlier cultural phase. As for the ordinary dwelling houses, the main living room has a raised platform to sleep on, and the fireplace is usually located beneath the entry ladder, so that smoke

1. *Jericho. Projected plan of Neolithic shrine*
2. *Catal Huyuk. Portion of town plan, Level VI B*
3. *Catal Huyuk. Perspective reconstruction of one section of town, Level VI B*

4. *Catal Huyuk. Reconstruction of interior of typical shrine-chamber*
5. *Catal Huyuk. Reconstruction of interior of typical house*
6. *Jericho. Remains of Neolithic tower*

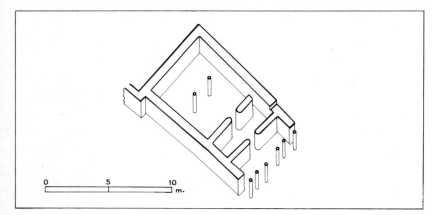

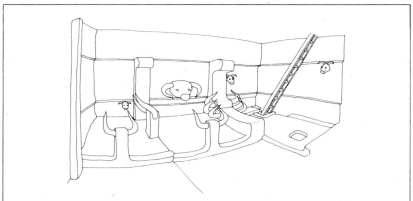

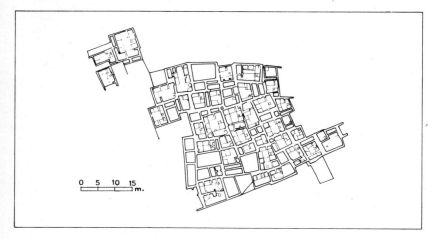

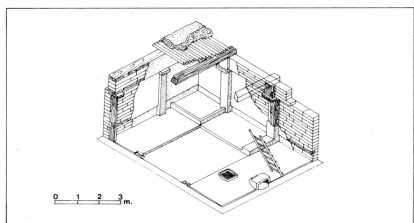

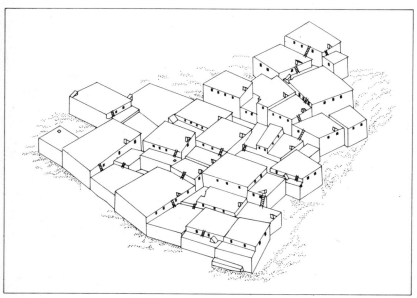

7. *Khirokitia (Cyprus). Reconstruction of Neolithic village*
8. *Hacilar. Isometric diagram of Fortress II A*
1) *Courtyard.* 2) *Granary.* 3) *Sentry post.* 4) *Pottery works.* 5) *Well.* 6) *Sanctuary*
9. *Hacilar. Isometric diagram of Neolithic house*

may escape through the open hatch above (Plate 5).

A new element appears in this settlement at Catal Huyuk, namely the necessity for peripheral defense, primarily against wild animals but also probably against the rivalry of other communities. Access to the communal rooftops from outside is again by removable ladders, and the outer house walls are without doors or windows. Returning for a moment to Jericho, one finds there a more familiar and probably more effective provision for defense. Here the excavators exposed the ruins of a huge circular tower built of stone, over twenty-six feet in diameter, and the contingent parts of a defensive wall (Plate 6). By comparison, it is interesting to note that a contemporary or slightly later settlement at Khirokitia on the island of Cyprus seems to have required no form of peripheral defense. Here the houses retain an archaic circular form and are roofed with mud-brick domes on a stone substructure (Plate 7). Inside there is an upper floor supported on stone piers and reached by a wooden ladder.

Elsewhere in southern Anatolia, at Hacilar near Burdur, one again sees examples of both these early developments: purposeful planning of buildings and communal defense. A settlement dating from the very end of the Neolithic period shows dwelling houses with a standard plan, in which a prominent domestic hearth between flanking wall-niches is axially placed opposite the entrance doorway (Plate 9). A little later (mid-sixth millennium B.C.), at the beginning of the so-called Chalcolithic period, houses on the periphery of the settlement were knit together to form an outer defense, their lower stories being strongly built with heavy internal buttresses (Plate 8). At this more advanced stage in cultural development it is not surprising to find, at Mersin in Cilicia, a perfectly planned little military fortress (Plate 10). Built of mud brick, again on a stone substructure, the exposed segment has a stone-paved gateway between flanking towers (the first example of a device later to become almost universal) and a stout enclosure wall. Built against the inner face of the wall is a continuous line of identical small buildings providing quarters for the garrison. Each dwelling is provided with two slit-windows in the outside wall, from which the approaches to the mound could be watched, and has a partly roofed yard where piles of sling-stone ammunition could be stored. A more spacious dwelling near the gate was perhaps for the commandant.

Our examples of incipient architectural design, evident so far only in planning, have been drawn from Anatolia and the Levant. In the early centuries of the Chalcolithic Age some of these building conventions had already spread to northern Iraq. The

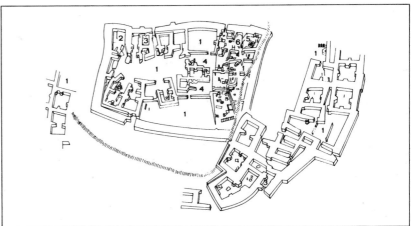

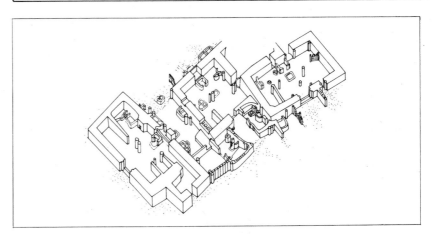

10. *Mersin. Isometric diagram of military fortress*
11. *Hassuna. Isometric reconstruction of farmhouse*
12. *Southern Mesopotamia. Modern Arabian reed-built structure*

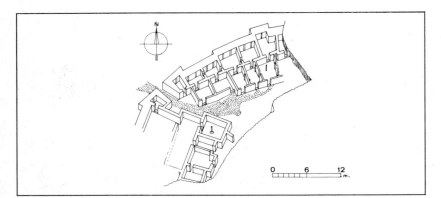

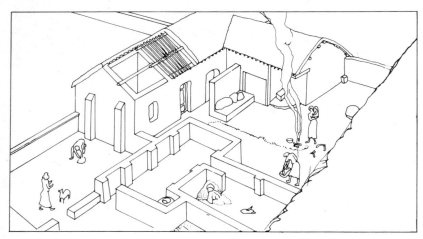

transition, for instance, from nomadic life to that of an agricultural village is well seen at Hassuna, west of the middle Tigris. Here campsites, with the relics of booths built from perishable materials, gave way first to small farmhouses built of pisé clay, then to mud brick (Plate 11). At Arpachiyah, near Nineveh, there seems to have been a reversion to an older pattern of building: circular houses known as tholoi with a rectangular dromos, closely resembling the Mycenaean beehive tombs of three thousand years later (see Plates 292, 293). But we must now turn to the alluvial plain of southern Iraq and the marsh country at the head of the Persian Gulf—a region of great importance, since here, in about 5000 B.C., the seeds of Sumerian culture were planted and the first formative elements of monumental architecture came into being.

Geographically, the first arrivals to southern Mesopotamia found a strange setting. Strangely also, the setting has remained unchanged for seven thousand years. Today it provides a background for the lives of the Marsh Arabs, who fish and tend their water buffalo from villages on low islands, in a landscape of interminable reedbeds. Their way of life, too, seems to have remained unchanged since prehistoric times, for they build their houses entirely of reeds, with tall and imposing guest chambers whose design provides an all-important clue to the forms taken by pre- or proto-Sumerian architecture (Plate 12). These forms are recognizable in the archaic imagery of the Sumerians themselves, particularly in the traditional representation of a temple (Plate 13). Nor can there be any doubt that when the settlers moved inland and more permanent building materials came to be used, the earliest mud-brick temples retained memories of reed construction in their design. The long and fascinating story of Mesopotamian temple architecture, which culminated in the giant ziggurats and palatial temples of Sumer and Babylon, had its beginning in this prehistoric age, and to the end retains suggestions of its reed-built prototypes.

We have then at the site of Eridu, traditionally the oldest holy city of southern Mesopotamia, a sequence of mud-brick temples repeatedly rebuilt during the late fifth and early fourth millennia B.C. It starts with a tiny chapel hardly ten feet square, which has already at least two of the primary elements of such buildings in later times: an altar in a niche facing the doorway, and a small offering table in front of the altar. Later generations elaborated the plan, retaining these elements but elongating the sanctuary and adding lateral chambers on either side (Plate 14). Each building was superimposed on the ruins of its predecessors, so that at an early stage the temple came to stand on a raised

13. *Proto-Sumerian alabaster trough, with traditional representation of Sumerian temple. London, British Museum*
14. *Eridu. Plan of temple, Level VII*
15. *Tepe Gawra. Perspective reconstruction of group of temples*

platform overlooking the surrounding houses, a development that was later carried to its logical conclusion in the construction of ziggurat towers.

Another feature with which we shall become familiar in observing later temples is the treatment of external facades. Their mud-plastered monotony was relieved by the use of alternating buttresses and recesses, a device whose origin may be traced to the reed buildings of earlier times. This persistent memory of an archaic prototype is equally recognizable in a contemporary group of temples at Tepe Gawra in northern Iraq, an area to which the proto-Sumerian culture had already extended by the end of the fifth millennium B.C. At Tepe Gawra a high elevation constituted from the remains of earlier settlements was crowned by some sort of acropolis, where three very interesting temples were set around an open courtyard (Plate 15). Only the plans of these temples have been recovered, but their somewhat similar arrangement shows facades that are deeply indented, for conventional reasons at which we can only guess. The walls themselves are of surprising fragility. The weight of their roofs must, in fact, have been carried by the more substantial piers with which they were strengthened at regular intervals, thus seeming to resemble the vertical bundles of reeds sustaining the framework of reed dwellings. However this may be, we shall observe from now onward that this type of buttressed facade becomes the most distinctive feature of all religious buildings in Mesopotamia, and is even copied in contemporary Egypt.

The planning of Mesopotamian temples takes an even more definitive form in the so-called Protoliterate period, which dates from the final centuries of the fourth millennium B.C. This was a time when the genius of the Sumerians seems to have reached its zenith, finding expression in some of the cardinal inventions that have contributed to our own civilization. In addition to monumental architecture, the art of sculpture now made its first appearance; the invention of writing foreshadowed the birth of literature and mathematics; and a new talent for social organization brought forth the archetype of the city-state. One Sumerian city whose fame predates the dynastic king-lists of later times was Uruk, the Biblical Erech. Here archaeology has revealed further steps in the evolution of temple architecture. Once again we are presented largely with ground plans, but there are two buildings of which more substantial remains have been found and of which reliable reconstructions can therefore be made. One of these is the so-called White Temple, whose foundations were laid forty feet above street level in the center of the city (Plates 16, 17). The platform on which the temple stood—once

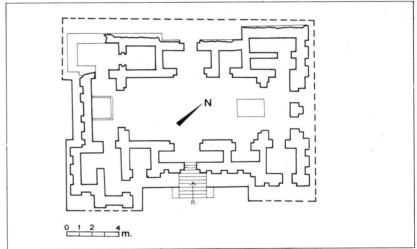

0 1 2 4 m.

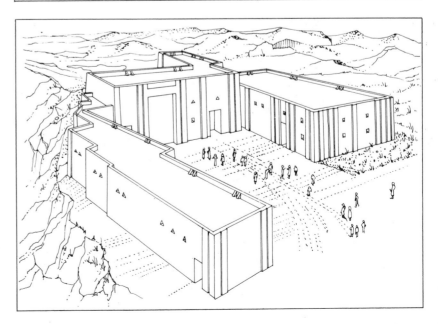

16. *Uruk. "White Temple"*
17. *Uruk. Perspective reconstruction of "White Temple"*
18. *Uruk. Integrated plan of ziggurat and "White Temple"*
*1) "White Temple." 2) Ramp. 3) Approach to ramp. 4) Terrace*

19. *Uruk. Temple plans, Level IV A, Eanna precinct*
*1) Temple C. 2) Temple D. 3) Edge of terrace. 4) Outer staircase. 5) Red Temple*
20. *Uruk. Temple plans, Levels V—VI, Eanna precinct*
*1) Temple B. 2) Temple on the terrace. 3) Courtyard of cone mosaics. 4) Atrium of pillars. 5) Limestone temple*

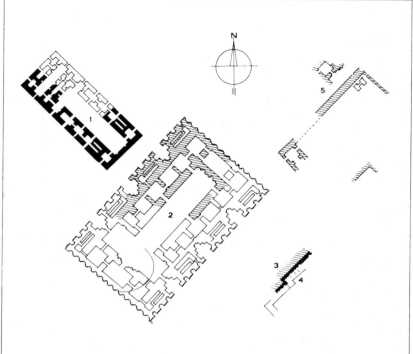

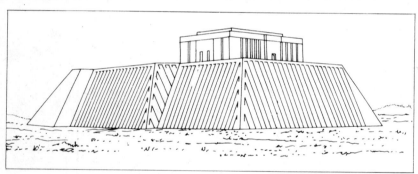

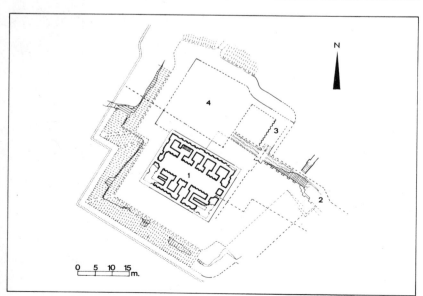

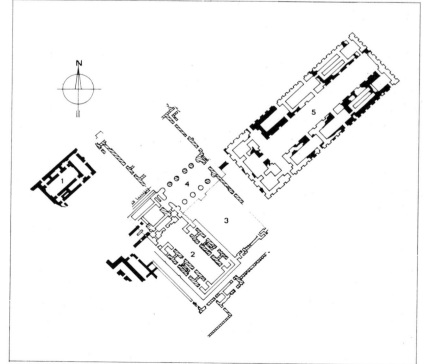

21. *Tell Brak. Plan of "Eye Temple"*
22. *Uruk. Cone mosaic courtyard, Eanna precinct*
23. *Eridu. Perspective reconstruction of Temple I*

more composed from ruins of earlier buildings—had sloping facades of paneled brickwork, and the wall faces of the temple itself showed traces of wooden ornament between the buttresses. The plan requires some explanation (Plate 18). The long sanctuary and lateral chambers had by now become an accepted convention; the entry for worshipers is through a side room, but there are imposing doorways at either end of the sanctuary itself, one of them displacing the altar from its axial position. Scholars have explained this by attributing to the "high" temple the function of a portal, through which a god could pass on his visits to earth. By contrast, they have postulated a category of "low" temples, in which the presence of the god would be symbolized by a cult statue. For examples of these one must turn to the neighboring Eanna precinct at the same site (Plates 19, 20). Here the plans of a half-dozen temples are presented to us, differing primarily from those hitherto studied only in the fact that the central sanctuary is occasionally cruciform—a peculiarity that is also to be seen in a contemporary temple at Tell Brak in northern Iraq (Plate 21).

It is also in the Eanna precinct at Uruk that we find our second instance of a better-preserved building (Plate 22). Here two groups of temples are connected by an astonishing portico, supported on colossal circular columns of mud brick and facing a broad open court, whose walls are ornamented with corresponding half columns. A novel and ingenious form of decoration now covers all the interior wall faces of the building. Set in a layer of clay is a mosaic of small terra cotta cones, their heads stained with varying colors to create a sequence of geometrical patterns. Here at last, color and texture are combined to produce a dramatic architectural setting, of the sort that would do credit to a modern decorator. We suspect that this device acquired an even more ambitious form in the last of the temples at Eridu (Plate 23). There, in the external facades, parapets and stringcourses were emphasized by bands of mosaic, sometimes composed of gypsum cones ten inches long whose ends were sheathed in polished copper. At Al 'Uqair in northern Sumer (Plate 25) painted murals were substituted for mosaics as internal ornament in a temple closely resembling the "white" building at Uruk. The subjects used for ornament appear to have been similar to those on the cylinder seals of the period, though the spotted leopards decorating the main altar are an unusual motif.

During the first centuries of the third millennium B.C. a new phase is reached with the founding of the first Sumerian dynasties. Where writing is concerned, primitive pictographs have

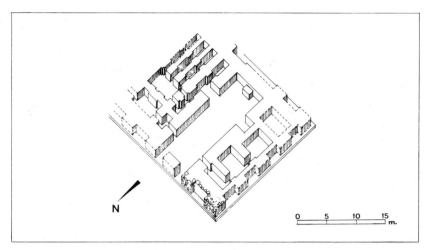

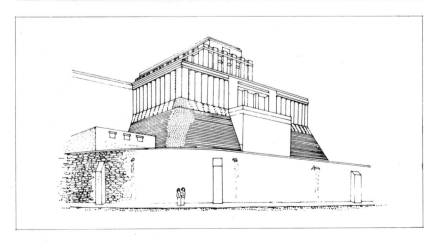

24. *Khafaje. Perspective reconstruction of Oval Temple*
25. *Al 'Uqair. Model of Protoliterate temple. Baghdad, Iraq Museum*

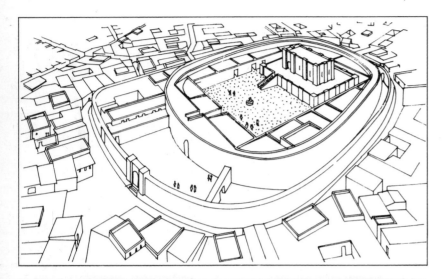

now been replaced by the cuneiform script, which provides a more convenient vehicle for the Sumerian language. The names of kings and certain political events are now historically recorded. Previously our knowledge of architecture has been largely derived from temples; but dating from the Early Dynastic period there are occasionally palaces to examine and a variety of more modestly planned private houses. The temples, to begin with, show a direct line of development from the Protoliterate buildings we have already discussed. Remnants of only two "high" or platform temples have been discovered, at Khafaje (Plate 24), east of Baghdad, and at Al 'Ubaid, near Ur of the Chaldees. In neither case have remains survived of the temple itself; but the platforms are of some interest, each one having been surrounded at some time by an oval outer wall enclosing a sacred precinct with some subsidiary accommodation. Judging from scanty remains at Ur and Kish, it seems certain that toward the end of this period such platforms had already acquired the stature of ziggurats; but unfortunately at both sites mentioned, later rebuilding has made their examination impracticable. The form also of the temple at their summit can only be surmised on the basis of Protoliterate precedents.

There is, however, one site at which ample evidence was provided, at least regarding the external embellishment of these elevated shrines during the Early Dynastic period. This is at Al 'Ubaid, where a rich collection of facade ornaments had fallen or been removed from the temple when it was intentionally or otherwise destroyed. The platform in this case was faced with kiln-baked bricks and was approached by a projecting stairway with stone treads. It was in the angle between the two that the objects were found, rather carelessly piled together. They included fragments of two freestanding columns, made from palm trunks sheathed in a mosaic of colored stone and mother-of-pearl. Perhaps these originally supported a huge lintel now in the British Museum, a relief panel of hammered copper depicting a mythical lion-headed eagle supported by two stags. There were also copper guardian lions from the doorway, freestanding copper oxen, smaller oxen in relief with projecting heads, and friezes of animals and birds, inlaid in shell or painted limestone against a background of black stone (Plates 26–28). There has been much speculation regarding the architectural composition of which these objects formed a part, but the tentative reconstructions that have been made lack conviction.

Turning to the "low" or ground-level temples, these are perhaps best represented at sites adjoining the Diyala River and its effluents, such as Khafaje. All founded in late Protoliterate

29. *Khafaje. Plans of Sin temples*
1) *Level I.* 2) *Level VI.* 3) *Level X*
30. *Tell Agrab. Plan of Shara Temple*

31. *Tell Asmar. Plan of Akkadian palace and contemporary buildings*
32. *Kish. Plan of "Palace A"*

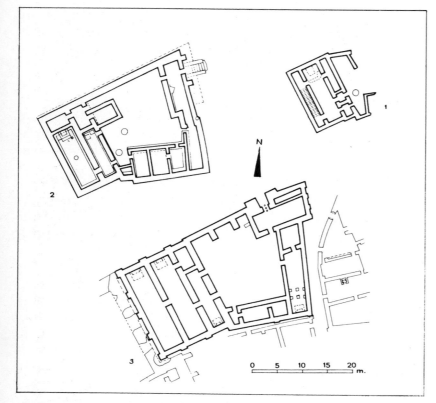

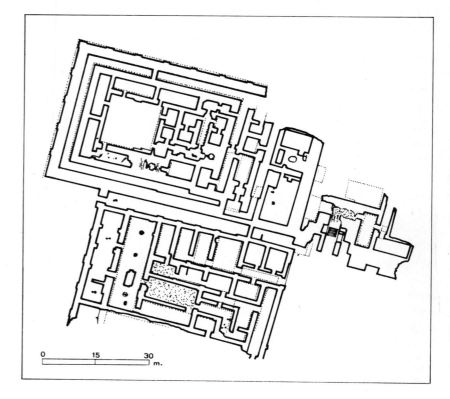

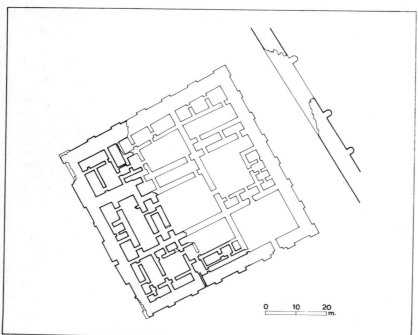

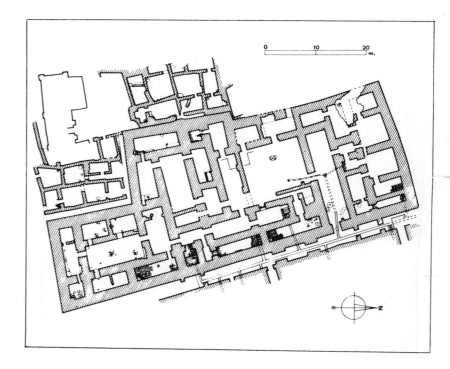

times, these have produced a number of temples whose development during the Early Dynastic period can be traced (Plates 29, 30). The old rectangular sanctuary, with its altar, offering table, and entrance on the cross axis, is still the basic element; but in addition to lateral chambers and staircases leading to the flat roof, it now acquires a forecourt surrounded by dependent buildings (Khafaje, Sin Temple), or becomes a symmetrically planned complex with buttressed outer walls, comprising minor sanctuaries in addition to the main shrine (Tell Agrab).

We must now turn to the more modest type of building in which Sumerian families actually lived. Among ruins of the Early Dynastic period, groups of private houses have frequently been found and studied. They are planned—as houses in Near Eastern cities have continued to be planned until quite recently—around a central court from which the surrounding rooms obtained light. Whether the court was occasionally roofed in and light obtained through clerestory windows is at present controversial. Windows were used only internally and then were sometimes protected by a pierced grille of terra cotta. Doorways were covered with wooden lintels or true arches of brickwork. Flat roofs were composed of palm trunks and reeds, covered with earth and plastered with clay. A word should be said about the technique of brick building at this period, since it applies equally to public buildings. Bricks were made in a four-sided wooden mold standing on a flat surface, but the surplus clay, instead of being removed, was merely rounded off with the hands, thus giving to the brick a loaf shape technically known as *plano-convex*. Such bricks are most ordinarily laid on edge, leaning diagonally against each other in alternate directions so that a herringbone pattern is created on the face of the wall. This habit makes a convenient criterion for identifying buildings of this period.

In the oldest quarter of the Sumerian city at Tell Asmar (Eshnunna) there is a mansion-sized dwelling house built around three separate courts; it can hardly yet be identified as a palace, though it was later rebuilt on a more pretentious scale (Plate 31). Failing here to find the distinctive features of a public building, we should perhaps turn to the complex known as Palace A, at Kish, where two semidetached edifices are enclosed in heavily buttressed outer walls (Plate 32). The larger of the two is again separated from this wall by a protective passage. It is planned around a square courtyard with careful symmetry, but the arrangement of the rooms unfortunately gives no clue to their purpose. The same may be said of the second building, which has two distinctive features: a long rectangular room

whose roof was supported on four circular columns of mud brick, and an open loggia, again with circular columns. Many fragments of figured inlay in mother-of-pearl and other materials have been found in these buildings, but their dimensions are hardly great enough to suggest architectural ornament.

So we reach the end of the Early Dynastic period, knowing a great deal more about temples than about buildings dedicated to other purposes. The universal material until now has been mud brick, which is understandable if one remembers the total absence of stone in the alluvial plain of southern Iraq; one does, however, find stone used sparingly at cities on the edge of the plain. At Eridu the whole mound is surrounded by a stone retaining-wall and the temple platform is revetted with stone. At Ur some of the tomb chambers in the Royal Cemetery are built of stone, which can be fashioned into corbeled arches and primitive vaults.

## THE DYNASTIC PERIOD

During the twenty-fourth century B.C. the Sumerian city-states were united under a Semitic dynasty founded by King Sargon of Akkad. Little is known about the architecture of this period, since Sargon's capital at Akkad has never been satisfactorily located. It is, however, certain that the Akkadian kings largely rebuilt or repaired the old Sumerian shrines, and two quite interesting secular buildings of this period have actually been excavated. One is the "mansion" house at Tell Asmar, which was now reconstructed on a more impressive scale (Plate 31). Three distinct units have been recognized; their purposes have been provisionally identified by the excavator as, first, the owner's suite with public reception rooms; second, a wing occupied by women; and third, quarters for servants. Each unit was provided with a number of lavatories and bathrooms having an elaborate system of drainage that discharged into a vaulted sewer running along one side of the building. These offices, however, have been differently identified by another authority, who surprisingly prefers to consider the building as a factory or a "guild" headquarters.

A less equivocal building of this period is the palace of Naramsin at Tell Brak in northern Iraq (Plate 33). Square and heavily fortified, it can be identified with some conviction as a military headquarters, with a wide central courtyard and long rectangular chambers grouped around several subsidiary courts. The plan, in its present denuded condition, is otherwise not self-explanatory.

After the fall of the Akkadian empire in about 2230 B.C. there

*33. Tell Brak. Plan of Palace of Naramsin*
1) *Court.* 2) *Reconstructed entrance*
*34. Ur. Plan of city at the time of Abraham*

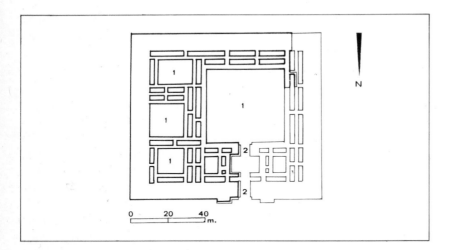

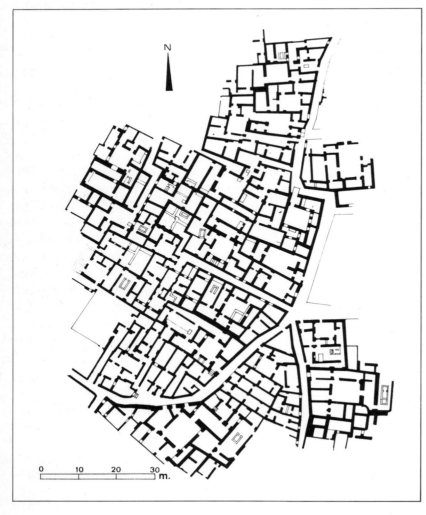

followed a striking revival of Sumerian culture under the Third Dynasty kings of Ur—old cities were again rebuilt and their shrines renovated. Architecturally most characteristic of the times is the layout of the city of Ur at this period (Plate 34). The shape of the walled city corresponded to that of the existing mound, whose sides were now revetted to support a powerful fortification. This great wall, of which little survives today, protected the main residential areas and also two enclosed harbors which gave access to shipping from the Euphrates. The principal public buildings—temples and palaces—were enclosed in an inner fortification, forming a sacred precinct surrounded by a double wall, with storage chambers in the interlying space.

The most conspicuous feature of this group was the great ziggurat standing on its own raised terrace (Plate 35). It was approached through a broad courtyard with tower-flanked gateways on all four sides.

This ziggurat is the best preserved and perhaps the best known of the "staged towers" that arose in almost every Sumerian city during this and the subsequent periods. It therefore merits a rather full description. Having evolved, as we have seen, from the raised temples of the Early Dynastic period, its design consists of three successive platforms, diminishing in size from the lowest upward and approached by a complicated system of broad stairways. The focal point of the whole structure was of course the temple at its summit; but since this has disappeared, the form it took remains a subject of speculation. For the rest of the building the reconstruction made by Sir Leonard Woolley, after excavation was complete, is based reliably on the most convincing evidence. His description of it reads as follows:

Ur-nammu's building, which also occupied the site of an older and smaller ziggurat, is a rectangle measuring a little more than two hundred feet in length by a hundred and fifty feet in breadth and its original height was about seventy feet. The angles are oriented to the cardinal points of the compass. The whole is a solid mass of brickwork, the core of crude mud bricks, the face covered with a skin, eight feet thick, of burnt bricks set in bitumen....The walls, relieved by broad, shallow buttresses, lean inwards with a pronounced batter, which gives a fine impression of strength, and it is noteworthy that on the ground plan the base of each wall is not a straight line but convex, from which again an idea of strength results.

35. *Ur. Ziggurat, Third Dynasty; northeast facade with flight of steps,
as presently restored*
36. *Ur. Royal Mausoleum, Third Dynasty*

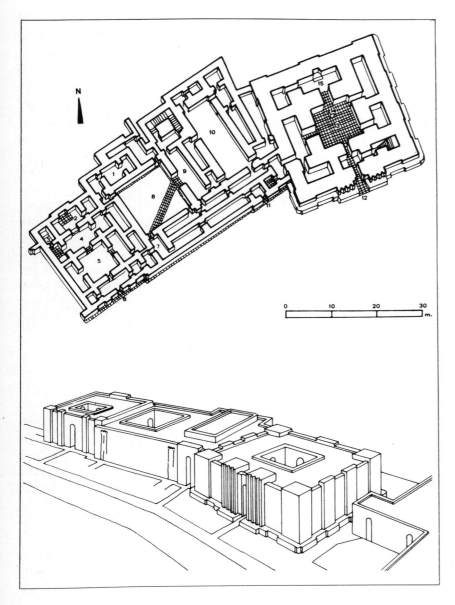

37. *Tell Asmar. Plan and reconstruction of Temple of Gimilsin and Palace of the Governors*
1) *Private apartment.* 2) *Chapel cella.* 3) *Toilet.* 4) *Antecella.* 5) *Chapel courtyard.*
6) *Main chapel entrance.* 7) *Ablution slab.* 8) *Palace courtyard.* 9) *Throne room.*
10) *Great hall.* 11) *Main palace entrance.* 12) *Main temple entrance.* 13) *Temple courtyard.* 14) *Altar.* 15) *Temple cella*

Woolley goes on to propose that this deviation was deliberately adopted for aesthetic reasons (though it might be equally attributed to the tumescent effect of so much brickwork). He also notices that the structure was reinforced at intervals with horizontal layers of reeds, sometimes resulting in a form of spontaneous combustion that damaged the fabric. Other refinements are the frequent weep holes intended to release moisture, and the vertical shafts for drainage of rainwater.

The remaining buildings within this central precinct at Ur are architecturally less revealing, since only their plans have been recovered. An understanding of them would require a greater knowledge of religious ritual and hierarchical organization than we now have at our disposal. The two largest are huge square edifices of a type that for want of a better term one might call temple-palaces. A third is clearly a residential palace, and a fourth, asymmetrically planned, has a raised platform accessible from the ziggurat terrace, with a "seat of judgment" facing an open courtyard. More interesting structural information is provided by the great mausoleum of the Third Dynasty kings, which lies just outside the limits of the precinct at its eastern corner (Plate 36). Here the burial chambers were sunk beneath ground level, so that their brick vaulting and pointed arches (constructed on a corbeled principle) are comparatively well preserved. They are surmounted by the ruins of funerary chapels whose elaborate ritual installations are again barely explicable.

More easily comprehensible from its plan is a group of buildings at the Diyala site, Tell Asmar, known as the Gimilsin Temple and Palace of the Governors (Plate 37). Historically, this complex is a bridge between the Third Dynasty of Ur and the subsequent regime at the beginning of the second millennium B.C., when Sumer was once more divided into conflicting principalities. It consists of a substantial temple, dedicated to a deified king of Ur, and a viceroy's palace with its own private chapel for the worship of a local deity. Here we at once observe that the standard planning of temples has adopted a new formula, which was destined to persist throughout the remaining history of Mesopotamian architecture. The whole building is now arranged on a single main axis, which passes through the center of the building, from the tower-flanked gateway across the central court to the sanctuary itself, terminating in the high altar with its cult statue. As for the adjoining palace, its interest is concentrated in the reception suite, a combination of features subsequently recognizable in all Babylonian palaces. A throne room is entered by a central doorway in one of its long sides, while smaller doors lead to a great hall or council chamber with adjacent retiring rooms and a staircase leading to the flat roof.

After the fall of Ur this group was repeatedly rebuilt by the independent governors of Eshnunna; but the dedication of the main temple had lost its relevance and its ruins were soon incorporated in the palace. In a well-known architectural reconstruction of its original form, some features of the upper structure are necessarily hypothetical. Little has till now been said on this subject, simply because so little is in fact known, but its discussion will be resumed in connection with buildings of later periods for which evidence is more plentiful. For the present, only bare facts can be mentioned. Walls, for instance, are built of large, prismatic mud bricks, faced with mud plaster within and without. Facades are still decorated with buttresses and towers, with multiple recessing in the form of vertical grooves. Kiln-baked bricks are reserved for pavements and, in conjunction with bitumen, for wall facing in settings where water is used.

The two earliest centuries of the second millennium B.C., which preceded the unification of Mesopotamia under Hammurabi of Babylon, have provided us with two unique examples of contemporary architecture, one a temple and the other a palace. The temple is a huge, complex building associated with the worship of a goddess called Ishtar-Kititum, at the Diyala site called Ischali (Plate 38). It is composed of three units, each a temple in its own right with its appropriate courtyards and dependencies, all skillfully united in a coherent and magnificent architectural composition. One-third of the complex stands at a higher level than the rest and contains the sanctuary of Ishtar herself, with a spacious treasury behind it. It can be approached either axially from the street outside or less directly from the enormous main courtyard by a flight of steps. One of the two subsidiary shrines can be entered from outside in the same way, but the other has reverted to an older tradition, with its approach at right angles to the true axis. All the main gateways are guarded by twin towers with grooved ornamentation. For the rest, the building requires little further comment, since its appearance is represented faithfully in the fine wash drawing by the late Harold Hill illustrated here.

The second building we have noted is in northern Iraq, on the middle Euphrates—the palace of Zimrilim, an independent ruler of the state called Mari (Plate 39). This building has been rather floridly described as "a jewel of archaic oriental architecture." If one considers its size—it has about three hundred rooms and covers an area of seventeen acres, rather more than the contemporary city of Troy—as well as its indications of interior dec-

oration, this description becomes less fanciful. As will be found in comparable buildings of later times, the life of the building seems to be concentrated around two major courtyards, one to which the public had access and another to which only the royal family and its immediate dependents were admitted. Facing the outer courtyard and reached by steps was an audience chamber with a throne emplacement, which must have brought the ruler into direct contact with his people. The kings of Mari were of Semitic origin, and it is tempting to see in this chamber, with its open-ended planning, a prototype of the vaulted *iwan,* which served the same purpose in Oriental palaces of the Moslem era. Turning to the inner courtyard, one finds two huge chambers, entered successively through a central doorway in the south wall, and one is first inclined to equate these with the throne room and great hall of the Babylonian reception suite, especially as the first chamber has a throne emplacement opposite the entrance. One finds, however, that there is a suggestion of religious ritual about this suite, for the larger chamber has at one end a raised sanctuary, approached by a flight of steps, toward which a throne at the other end faces.

A carefully segregated unit in the northwest corner of the building is easily recognizable as the ruler's own residential suite. Protected on the outside by double walls and a heavy filling of rubble, it has such amenities as bathrooms and mural ornament in the principal rooms. A smaller room, conveniently placed between this apartment and the inner courtyard, contained the now famous palace archive of cuneiform tablets, through which much has been learned about the history of the period. Also closely adjoining the royal suite is a school for scribes or a clerical department. In the surrounding labyrinth of chambers some, such as the treasury, storerooms, and domestic offices, can be positively identified; others remain anonymous.

Striking features of the palace's interior decoration are the figured mural paintings that once adorned the walls (Plate 40), notably in the audience chamber and on the south side of the inner courtyard, which was protected by a canopy roof supported on posts. The paintings themselves, in which the excavators detected traces of true fresco technique, show elaborate ritual scenes, such as a sacrificial procession or an investiture, and are of great archaeological interest. Much impressive sculpture was also found, but the fragments were scattered, and its place in the architectural decor remains uncertain.

At one point in the history of Mari the city was annexed and the palace occupied by Assyria, a newly prominent state with its capital at Assur on the middle Tigris. During the remaining cen-

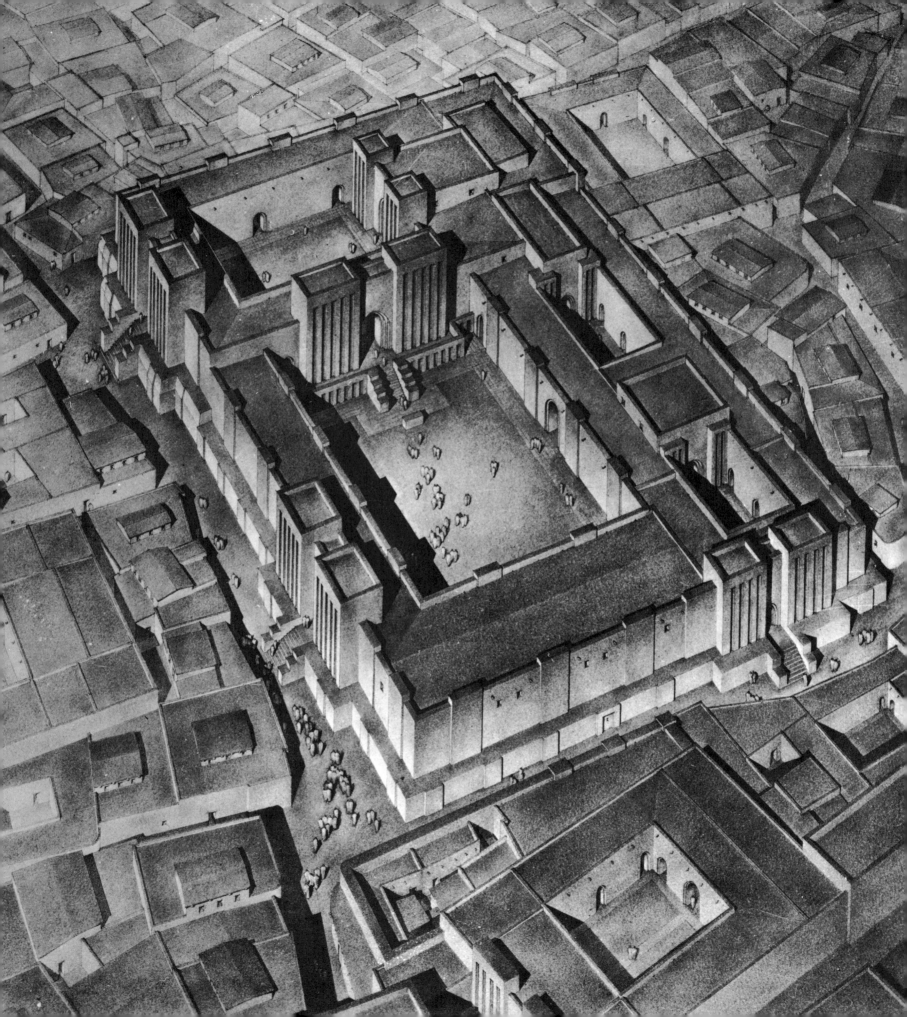

◄ 38. *Ischali. Perspective reconstruction of Temple of Ishtar-Kititum*

39. *Mari. Plan of Palace of Zimrilim*
*1) Well-preserved walls. 2) Poorly preserved walls. 3) Leveled walls. 4) Remains of brick paving. a) Main entrance. b) Large court. c) Painted court. d) Throne room. e) King's room. f) Scribes' school. g) Supervisor's quarters. h) Oven. i) Storerooms*
40. *Mari. Mural paintings from Palace of Zimrilim. Paris, Louvre*

turies of the second millennium B.C. Assyria played a leading role in the history of Mesopotamia. But before studying Assyrian architecture we should take one more look at contemporary events in Babylonia. In about 1600 B.C. southern Mesopotamia fell under the dominion of the Kassites, an intrusive Indo-European people from beyond the Zagros Mountains, and for almost four centuries Babylonia was ruled by a line of Kassite kings. The replacement of Hammurabi's dynasty by an alien aristocracy had surprisingly little effect on the basically Sumerian culture of the country, since its new rulers simply adopted the political and religious conventions they found there, repairing and often rebuilding the age-old monuments of the Sumerian cities. They did, however, found a new capital city at Dur Kurigalzu (Aqar Quf), whose ruins have been partially excavated (Plate 41). The denuded core of its huge ziggurat—heavy mud brick reinforced with matting and three-inch cables of twisted reeds — makes a striking landmark in the desert west of modern Baghdad. The temples and palaces surrounding it show some novel architectural features. One innovation, to be seen in the courtyard of a royal palace, is the use of mural painting to form an ornamental dado at the base of external walls, thus anticipating the relief sculptures used for the same purpose in later Assyrian buildings. A Kassite temple at Uruk again creates a precedent in facade ornament (Plates 42, 43). This takes the form of clay figures that were modeled in relief, cut into bricks before drying, and reconstituted after baking in a kiln. This technique, as we shall see, was further developed in Late Assyrian and Neo-Babylonian times.

To return now to the oldest Assyrian capital at Assur, we find a city strategically placed and heavily fortified. It stands on a prominent outcrop of limestone overlooking the Tigris, whose waters protect it on two sides (Plates 44, 45). Its defenses are completed by a powerful city wall, rebuilt at least once and extended to give greater living space. Its temples and palaces, which occupy the elevated northern quarter, have a complicated architectural history testifying in some cases to almost a thousand years of continual occupation. There are, to begin with, no less than three ziggurats, the largest dedicated to the city god, Assur. Two others, with a temple between them, are associated with the gods Anu and Adad (Plate 46B). A fourth, outside the city and again having its own "low" temple annexed to it, was dedicated to Assur by Tukulti-Ninurta I in the thirteenth century B.C. (Plate 46A). In all these towers the great triple stairway that we have seen at Ur is missing, and there is still some doubt as to how their summits were reached. Perhaps the approach was from the flat roofs of adjoining buildings.

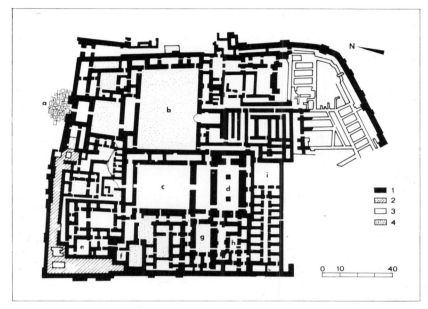

A good example of Early Assyrian temple planning is to be seen in the Ishtar temple at Assur (Plate 46C). Its first foundation was in Sumerian times and consisted of a single rectangular sanctuary, similar to those we have noted earlier in Sumer itself. By the thirteenth century B.C. it had acquired side chambers and a small subsidiary shrine at one corner, but both sanctuaries were still entered on the cross axis. A distinctively Assyrian feature, however, was the withdrawal of the main altar to an elevated alcove approached by a broad flight of steps, thus separating the worshipers from the shrine itself.

Having now reached the final centuries of the second millennium B.C., we are at last able to know something more about the facade treatment and general outward appearance of temples and palaces. We know, for instance, that the towers flanking entrance gateways, like those projecting at intervals from the city walls, rose to a greater height than the walls themselves, and were decorated with small windows, either real or false. We also know from representations on cylinder seals that both these towers and the walls themselves terminated in crenellated parapets, sometimes projecting slightly beyond the wall face. As for the mud-brick facades, the custom of creating vertical emphasis by means of recessed grooves or corrugated reeding had recently been elaborated to a surprising degree by the introduction of engaged or even freestanding columns, spirally carved or modeled to represent palm trunks. Examples of such ornament have been found in a Kassite setting at Ur, and again in a Middle Assyrian temple far to the north at Tell Rimah. Recent excavations at this last site have also removed once and for all any previous doubts about the proficiency of Mesopotamian architects at mud-brick vaulting. In a ziggurat temple at Tell Rimah surviving fragments have been found of elaborate vaulting, already based on a true-arch principle. Little more remains to be said about the decoration of internal wall faces. Orthostatic slabs of stone, such as were used in the Late Assyrian palaces, had not yet been adopted; but a similar feature, composed of painted and glazed terra cotta panels, has been found in the thirteenth-century palace at Kar Tukulti-Ninurta, near Assur (Plate 47). In a position higher on the wall, mural paintings were still used, for example in the Hurrian palace at Nuzi, near Kirkuk, where the ornamental motifs already suggest contacts with Egypt and Mycenae or Crete (Plate 48).

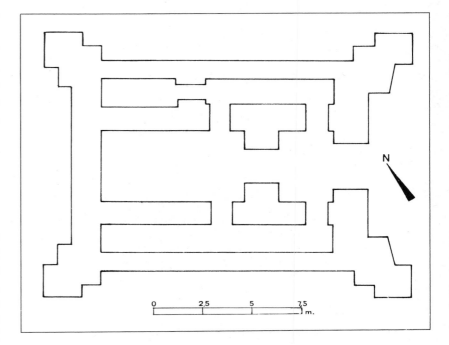

◄ 43. *Uruk. Molded brick ornament from facade of Temple of Kara-*
*indash. Berlin, Vorderasiatisches Museum*

44. *Assur. Perspective reconstruction of city, north sector*
45. *Assur. Plan of city*
*1) Portal. 2)New Palace. 3) Temple plaza. 4) Temple of Anu and Adad. 5) Temple of*
*Ishtar. 6) Temple of Sin and Shamash. 7) Old Palace. 8) Temple of Assur*

## Anatolia and the Hittite Domination

In our discussion of architecture in the Near East prior to the end of the second millennium B.C., our range of vision has so far been limited largely to the frontiers of Mesopotamia. If our attention is now turned to Anatolia—the great land bridge of Asia Minor that connects Mesopotamia with eastern Europe—we shall find ourselves faced with a notable time lag in the development of monumental building. Here, dating from the Early Bronze Age—which accounts for the greater part of the third millennium B.C.—few buildings have survived that have any pretension to be considered as architecture. One type in particular seems at this time to be conspicuously absent, namely, the temple. No building of this period has hitherto been positively identified as such; religious shrines amount to no more than semicomprehensible assemblages of ritual installations in buildings of a crude simplicity, which has led some scholars to identify them as mere private houses (Plates 52, 53). Where secular buildings and fortifications are concerned, we are on firmer ground, and in this respect the excavations of the city of Troy have exposed some of the best examples.

During its life span of almost two and one-half thousand years, from early in the third millennium B.C. to the time of Alexander the Great, the famous fortress at Troy was rebuilt repeatedly and often extended or replanned. Of the buildings thought to be contemporary with the Trojan War (Level VIIA) almost nothing remains, owing to the decapitation of the mound in later times; but below this level the fortifications at least are better preserved, and in one stratum (Level IIG), dating from the Early Bronze Age, the plan of almost the whole fortress has been more or less convincingly reconstructed (Plates 49, 50). The enclosure wall has a substructure of dressed stone, slightly battered or inclined to give it greater strength (Plate 51), and the single gate in use at this time is protected by a transverse tower structure with a narrow ascending ramp. From the layout of buildings within the walls the first inference to be made is that this cannot be described justifiably as a city. Excavations have shown that in Homeric times its area was slightly extended; but with a diameter of less than 150 yards the word *fortress* still seems more applicable. Apart from groups of rather carelessly planned private dwellings, and a "palace" on the western side—beneath which Schliemann unearthed the caches of gold jewelry that he called Priam's Treasure—the most conspicuous feature of the plan is the great building in the center with its rectangular hall, open portico, and enormous central hearth. This barnlike structure, with a breadth of almost twenty-five feet

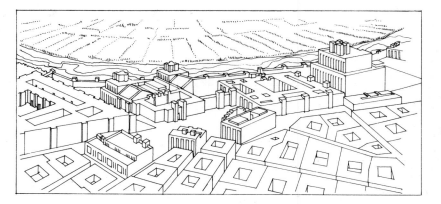

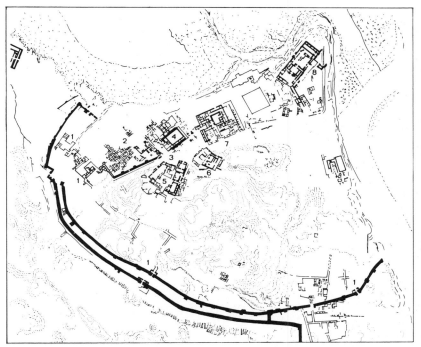

46. *Assur. Plans*
*A) Ziggurat of Tukulti-Ninurta I. B) Temple of Anu and Adad. C) Temple of Ishtar*
47. *Assur. Reconstruction of mural paintings, Palace of Kar Tukulti-Ninurta I*
48. *Nuzi. Fragment of mural paintings, Palace of Hurrian*

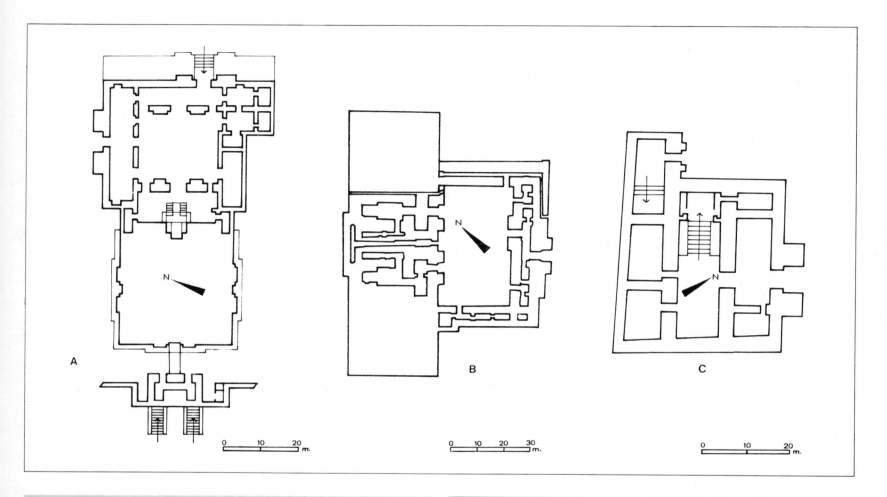

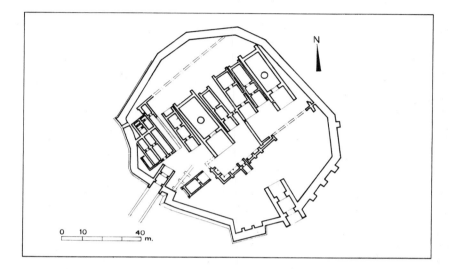

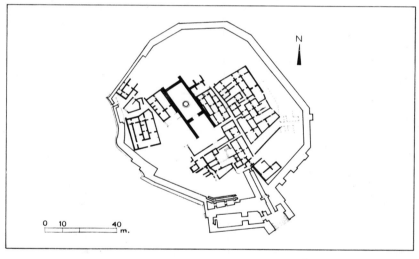

from wall to wall, is of special interest, as it represents an early example of the hall-and-porch plan that is later known to the Greeks as a *megaron* and that eventually reappears as the central element of the Classical temple. The origin of the megaron is buried in the prehistory of western Anatolia, where it appears from time to time as the basic plan for the Bronze Age dwelling house, until it is transmitted, probably by the Phrygians, to Greece. Its outstanding characteristics are the huge circular hearth, the "sleeping platforms" in the portico, and the occasional facings of stone or timber (parastades) on the outer ends of the projecting wings. One variant, incorporated as the central element of more elaborately planned buildings, is seen fully developed in the megaron halls of palaces at Mycenae and Tiryns (see Plate 281), but its counterpart is already found a thousand years earlier in an Early Bronze Age building excavated at Kultepe (the ancient Kanesh) in Cappadocia (Plate 54).

In Anatolia during the latter half of the second millennium B.C. architecture once more came into its own. A number of powerful states now contested the supremacy of the peninsula. Of these the Hittite kingdom is best known for the architectural monuments it has bequeathed to us, some surviving aboveground and others recovered by laborious excavation. Its territory, first confined to a province within the curve of the Halys River, was greatly extended by conquest during the fourteenth and thirteenth centuries B.C., when Hittite armies fought on equal terms with those of Egypt and Mesopotamia. During this time the Hittite capital was at Hattusas, now known to the Turks as Bogazkoy, where a four-mile circuit of powerfully built city walls dating from the fourteenth century B.C. can still be seen (Plates 55–57). The very size of the city testifies to the imperial greatness of the Hittite people. Strategically placed astride a rocky gorge, an inner enclosure—representing the earliest foundation—rises up toward the high citadel rock, Buyukkale. The greatly extended outer city was protected by a line of fortifications whose complexity anticipated the engineering accomplishments of much later times. The double walls, with their defensive towers and substructure of cyclopean masonry, stand on a stone-faced rampart of earth, itself protected by an outer apron wall of stone. Some of the many gates, with arched openings, are flanked by sculptured figures of lions or sphinxes, anticipating by five centuries the guardian sculptures of Late Assyrian buildings (Plates 58, 59, 61). Within the city, stone-built temples are once more in order; of the largest example, called Temple I, a plan is here reproduced (Plate 60). It will be

31

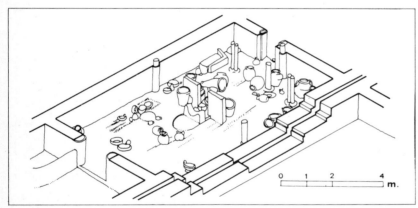

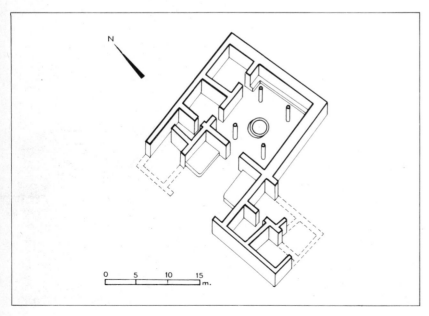

observed that the main sanctuary, isolated in a separate wing on the northeast side, and the great courtyard, with its pillared colonnade and small freestanding shrine in one corner, have nothing in common with the conventions of contemporary Mesopotamian architecture. The plan of another temple has also been recovered, near the entrance to the famous sculptured caves at Yasilikaya, outside the town (Plate 62). It is approached through an interesting freestanding propylon.

All these buildings, including the city walls themselves, had upper structures of sun-dried brick, of which few traces remain. In order to study this form of construction we must therefore turn to the houses of the rich Assyrian merchants at Kultepe (Kanesh I b) or to the Arzawan palace at Beycesultan (Plates 63, 64, 67). Both provide examples of a building principle already universally adopted throughout Anatolia at that time, which by modern analogy should be described as half-timbered construction. Above their stone foundations the walls consist of a stout timber framework with panels of brick filling in between. In the Beycesultan palace the stone substructure itself was founded upon transverse logs of wood, and the quantity of timber incorporated in the galleried upper story may be judged from the ample evidence of its destruction by fire.

It has been suggested that this long-surviving tradition of timber-frame construction—used to this day throughout Anatolia and in parts of the Levant—was originally devised and adopted as a precaution against earthquakes, affording as it does a certain elasticity to mud-brick structures. Rarely, if ever, to be seen in Mesopotamia, where earthquakes seldom occur, it extends into northern Syria and can be studied in two historic buildings of the second millennium excavated at Tell Atchana in the Plain of Antioch (Plates 65, 66). Both are the residences of local rulers, one called Yarimlim, who was a contemporary of Hammurabi in the eighteenth century B.C., and the other Niqmepa, who ruled some two and one-half centuries later. Neither building is very ambitiously planned, but both incorporate two architectural innovations, from now on increasingly characteristic of Syrian building. One is the basalt orthostats used in the Yarimlim palace as revetment for the lower part of the walls, which creates an important precedent. The other, seen at the approach to the main reception room in this building and again at the entry to Niqmepa's residence, is a screen of circular wooden columns on basalt bases, forming a portico of the sort which, as we shall see presently, will become the central feature of the so-called *bît-hilani* palaces of Iron Age Syria. One other feature of the eighteenth-century palace should also be noted. The most richly

55. Bogazkoy. *Plan of citadel of Buyukkale*
1) *Cistern.* 2) *Court.* 3) *Connecting structure.* 4) *Entrance building.* 5) *Pool.*
6) *Acropolis gate.* 7) *City gate.* 8) *Postern wall.* 9) *Modern road*

56. Bogazkoy. *Reconstruction and section of walls and gate*
57. Bogazkoy. *Lion Gate*

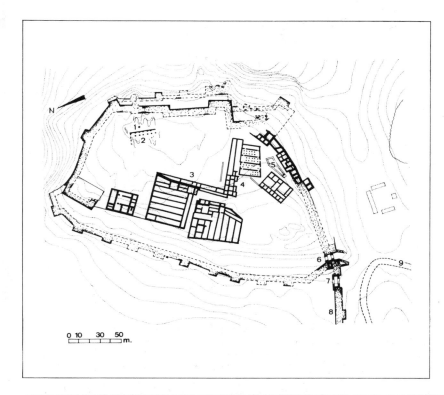

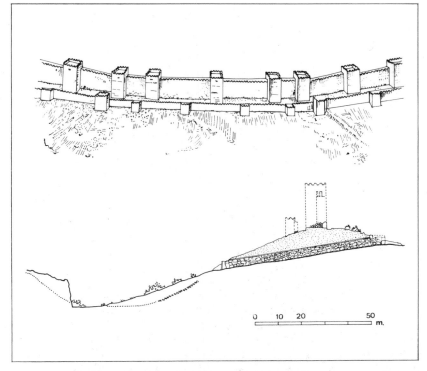

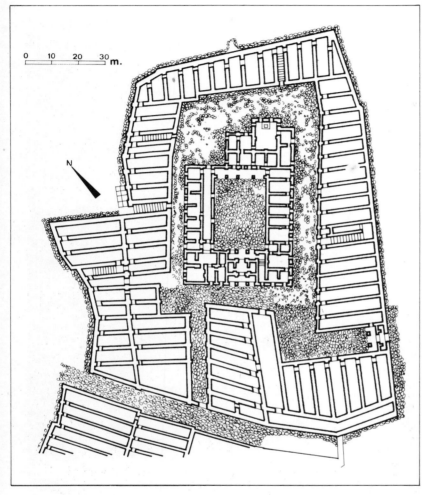

62. *Bogazkoy. Plan of rock shrine at Yasilikaya*
*1) Gate house. 2) Propylon. 3) Temple. 4) Court. 5) Entrance atrium to sculptured caves. 6) Sculptured caves*
63. *Kultepe. Reconstruction of Assyrian merchants' quarter*
64. *Kultepe. Examples of wall construction*

equipped residential rooms, those located southeast of the main courtyard, occupied an upper story, a so-called piano nobile, an arrangement also to be seen at Beycesultan in western Anatolia (Plate 67) and, too, at the palace at Knossos (Plate 266).

## The Neo-Assyrian Period

We must now return to Mesopotamia, and observe the prodigies of building activity achieved by the Assyrian kings during the earlier part of the first millennium B.C. This period, during which Assyria attained the status of a great imperial power, may be said to date from the reign of Assurnasirpal II (883–859 B.C.), who transferred his headquarters from ancient Assur to a newly built capital city at Nimrud (Calah), twenty-two miles south of modern Mosul (Plate 68). Later kings ruled from Nineveh, which lies on the left bank of the Tigris opposite Mosul itself (Plate 70), while Sargon II, like Assurbanipal, built his own capital at Khorsabad in the hilly country to the northeast (Plate 69). All three of these great cities have been excavated repeatedly during the past century, and successive generations of archaeologists have recorded their architecture. If we examine their planning and layout, they will be found to have much in common. In each case the site had been occupied already by a small town or village settlement, whose remains had created a useful elevation. The top of the existing mound could therefore be leveled and extended to create a raised platform on which the principal public buildings of the new city were placed. From either side of the platform, lines of protective walls extended to enclose a residential area adequate to the requirements of a capital city. At Nimrud the mound was skirted on two sides by the waters of the Tigris and of a major irrigation canal, so that the platform needed to be revetted with a stone quay wall. At the summit the palaces and temples built by successive kings were laid out with little coherent planning. The remains of a small ziggurat occupy one corner. The lower city also seems to have been irregularly planned, but its periphery measured almost five miles. Nineveh was even larger, covering an area of two and one-half square miles, and it had two palace platforms, Kuyunjik and Nebi Yunus, rather close together. A moat surrounded the walls not protected by the Tigris, and there were many towered gateways, some decorated with sculpture.

Sargon II's palace at Khorsabad is of particular interest because it was built on an open site, previously unoccupied except for the usual small mound representing the remains of an earlier village (Plates 69, 71, 72). From this a palace platform was created astride the city walls, which themselves enclose an area of

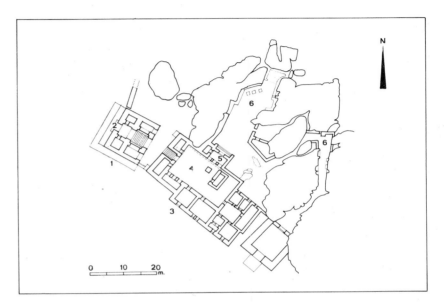

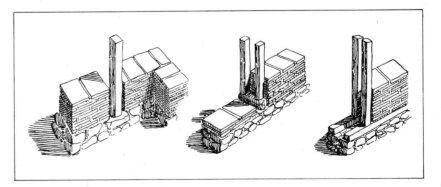

65. *Tell Atchana. Plan of Palace of Yarimlin*
1) *Entrance. 2) Rooms. 3) Reception hall. 4) Main court. 5) Staircase*
66. *Tell Atchana. Plan of Palace of Niqmepa*
1) *Entrance. 2) Main courtyard. 3) Chambers. 4) Bath. 5) State archives. 6) Storage and administration rooms*
67. *Beycesultan. Perspective reconstruction of Bronze Age palace*

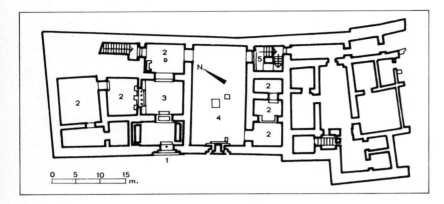

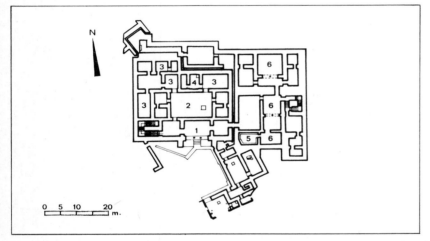

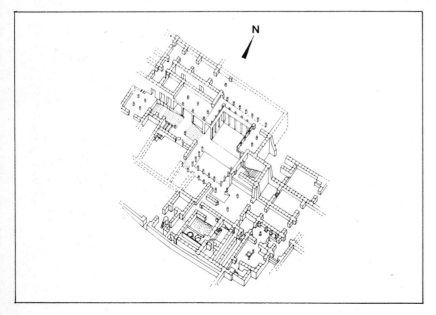

one square mile. Built of solid mud brick more than twenty feet thick, the walls have towered facades and seven monumental gateways. At the base of the palace platform inside the city there is a walled citadel containing several minor palaces and one important temple, dedicated to the god Nabu (Plates 69, 74). In a remote position near the southeast corner of the city there is a second raised palace, known as Palace F, of the type called *ekal mashati,* which was used for assembling military equipment and storing the spoils of war. This must be compared with "Fort Shalmaneser" at Nimrud, which occupies a site equally remote from the main citadel (Plates 72, 73). These primary public buildings at Khorsabad have been well excavated and deserve more detailed study; some initial comment on their architecture applies equally to their counterparts at Nimrud and Nineveh.

Our discussions of Mesopotamian architecture till now have been primarily concerned with the design of temples. In this Late Assyrian period greater emphasis came to be placed upon royal palaces, to which the temples appear subsidiary. Owing to their state of preservation and the circumstances of their excavation, far more is known about the planning and contents of these palace buildings than about their superstructure and architectural appearance. In this sense a major compensation has been the sculptures with which the lower parts of their walls were usually adorned (Plates 77, 78). The interior wall faces of the principal chambers were decorated with sculptured reliefs up to a maximum height of about nine feet, while the external doorways were flanked by guardian figures of human-headed bulls or lions sculptured in stone (Plates 75, 76). Built into the reveals and appearing to support the semicircular archways above, these are usually double-aspect figures with five legs, to be viewed either from in front or from the sides. A great deal has been written about Assyrian sculpture; as a document of Assyrian life the reliefs have proved an invaluable supplement to the written texts. Less is generally known about the technology of their installation. The bases of the largest portal figures measured almost twenty square feet and must have weighed approximately twenty-five tons. Roughly cut to the required shape, the stone was transported from the quarry, partly by rivercraft, and the sculpture completed in situ. The orthostat reliefs also had to be carved in situ—since the pictures on them overran from one slab to the next—and this was done before the mud-brick upper structure of the walls was completed (Plates 77, 78). The touches of color enlivening the sculptures may have been applied later.

The study of planning has been hampered by our comparative

**68. Nimrud. Plan of palace platform**
1) Temple of Ishtar. 2) Temple of Ninurta. 3) Northwest palace. 4) Serving room. 5) Well. 6) Palace of Adad-Nirari III. 7) Upper rooms. 8) Southwest palace. 9) Central palace. 10) Burned palace. 11) Temple of Nabu. 12) Governor's palace. 13) Houses

**69. Khorsabad. Plan of city**
1) Portal A. 2) Citadel walls. 3) Temple of Nabu. 4) Ramp. 5) Portal B. 6) Palace of Sinahasur. 7) Ramp. 8) Palace of Sargon. 9) City walls. 10) Ziggurat

**70. Nineveh. Plan of site**

**71. Khorsabad. Plan of Palace of Sargon II, including Temple complex (right); plan of temples in Royal Palace (left)**
1) Temple of moon god Sin. 2) Temple of weather god Adad. 3) Temple of sun god Shamash. 4) Temple of Ningal. 5) Temple of god of war and the hunt, Ninurta. 6) Temple of god of wisdom and the ocean, Ea

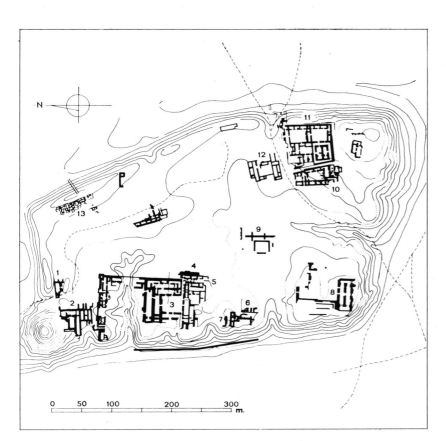

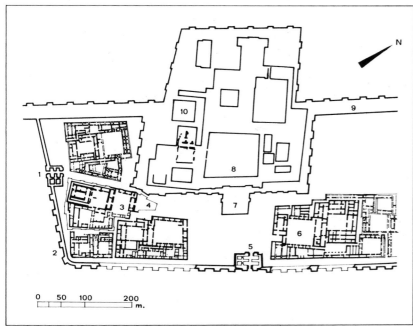

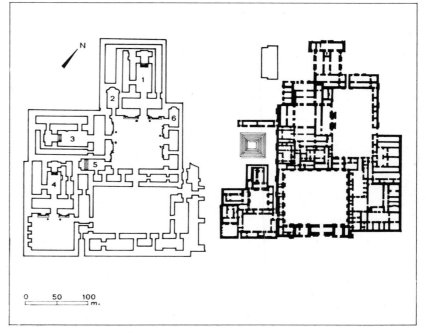

72. *Khorsabad. Perspective reconstruction of citadel with Palace of Sargon II*
73. *Nimrud. Plan of Fort Shalmaneser*
74. *Khorsabad. Perspective reconstruction of city, south from Ziggurat*

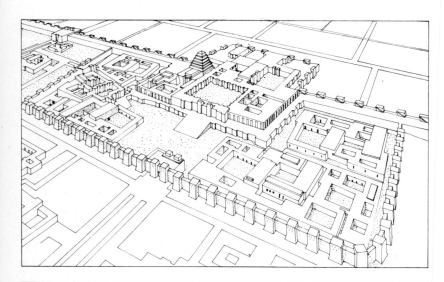

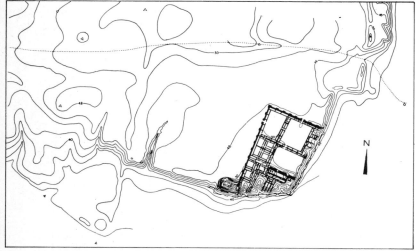

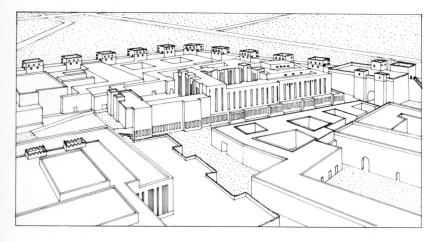

ignorance of secular ritual and domestic behavior in Assyrian times. Some aspects, however, of Sargon's main palace at Khorsabad are more or less comprehensible. The sculptured entrance to a huge public courtyard and the restricted access from this to a slightly smaller "court of honor" recall an arrangement already seen one thousand years earlier in the palace of Mari (see Plate 39). The long, rectangular throne room, with its stone emplacement for the throne at one end, is entered through triple doorways, decorated with a composition of sculptures comprising no less than ten winged bulls of varying sizes. Near it is a stairway leading to the flat roof, and behind it, an arrangement of residential and state compartments surrounding a smaller courtyard. Annexed to the palace on the south side is a religious complex consisting of three small temples and a miniature ziggurat, approached by a spiral stairway.

The throne-room unit is repeated on a smaller scale in the minor palaces contained in the lower citadel (Plates 69, 74). As one sees elsewhere, here the architectural planners have failed to profit from the unlimited space available. The buildings are awkwardly disposed and overcrowded. The Nabu temple, which is elevated to the height of the palace platform, has to be connected with it by a stone bridge, under which a street passes. Its plan, on the other hand, like those of the minor palace temples, is typically Late Assyrian. Approached through successive courtyards and vestibules, the sanctuary is entered on its long axis, which terminates in an alcove for the altar.

Something further may be said about Assyrian building construction. The fabric of the city walls consists of mud brick, laid without mortar after the clay had been only partially dried, and solidified by its own weight. The platform at Khorsabad has a heavy facing of dressed stone; stone is used sparingly elsewhere for pavements and the thresholds of important doorways. Kiln-baked bricks are in fairly frequent use, especially for the construction of arches; sometimes they are glazed to create designs in color for facade ornament (Plate 79). Interior wall faces in important chambers, like the throne room at Khorsabad, are covered above the stone reliefs with mural paintings, usually in formal designs. One such design, found in the lower citadel at Khorsabad, has been reconstructed (Plate 80). More freely figured mural paintings from minor Assyrian palaces at Til Barsip and Arslan Tash are now in the Louvre (Plate 81). These more closely reproduce the subjects of the stone reliefs, for which they were substitutes.

Much also has been learned about doors through the discovery in a country palace near Nimrud of the famous Balawat gates

75. *Khorsabad. Portal A of citadel, with guardian human-headed winged bulls*
76. *Khorsabad. Guardian human-headed winged bull (detail), from entrance to throne room, Palace of Sargon II. Paris, Louvre*

77. *Nimrud. Relief from palace, showing fugitives swimming with inflated skins. London, British Museum*
78. *Nineveh. Relief from palace, showing the sack of the city of Hamanu. London, British Museum*

(Plates 82, 83, 86–88). Mounted on a sub-pavement pivot stone and secured by a stone ring at the top, each gate is of wood, decorated with closely spaced horizontal bands of bronze. Though no more than ten inches high, these bands are ornamented in repoussé technique with miniature reliefs depicting in narrative form the campaigns of Shalmaneser III. They are annotated with cuneiform inscriptions and so once more constitute a priceless archaeological document. As for the buildings themselves, most architectural reconstructions are based on the assumption that only flat timber roofs were used; since no windows have been found, this would occasionally make clerestory lighting possible. The previously mentioned recent discovery at Tell Rimah of elaborate brick vaulting dating from the Old Assyrian period suggests a revision of our ideas on this subject.

The appearance of fortification walls and their gateways is known in part from their excavated remains and in greater detail from their representation in reliefs and on cylinder seals (Plate 85). The tops of the towers rose clear above the connecting walls, and both terminated in crenellated parapets. These projected beyond the wall face beneath, sometimes supported by corbeling or beam-ends, and they were often decorated with an openwork brick pattern. Rectangular windows, real or false, are sometimes shown in the face of the towers. Gateways were flanked by larger towers; the arched entrance between was often decorated with glazed brickwork above the guardian sculptures. The entrance was protected by transverse guardrooms, and a stairway led to the walkway above.

### The Phrygians

Little is known about the architecture of Anatolia during the "dark age" that followed the destruction of the Hittite Empire in about 1200 B.C. In this period the plateau was occupied by the Phrygians, but their earliest monuments date only from the ninth and eighth centuries B.C., by which time they had consolidated themselves into a powerful kingdom, with a capital at Gordion on the Sangarius River (now called the Sakarya). Something has been learned about their architecture from excavations made in comparatively recent years. The plans have been recovered of small fortified towns overlying the ruins of larger Hittite cities at such sites as Bogazkoy and Alishar. At Gordion the bastions of an impressive city gate have been brought to light, and in the town itself, public buildings of the megaron type with interesting timber-frame construction (Plate 89). Perhaps even more revealing are the rock-cut monuments of the period, which are concentrated around the principal Phrygian

*81. Til Barsip. Mural painting from Assyrian palace. Paris, Louvre*
*82, 83, Balawat. Bronze Gates (details). London, British Museum*

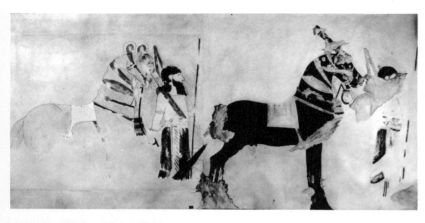

44

84. Balawat. Drawings of fortifications, in Bronze Gates
85. Nineveh. Relief from Palace of Sennacherib, showing Sennacherib
at the capitulation of Lakish. London, British Museum

86. Balawat. Bronze Gates (detail): Assyrian warriors; prisoners
brought from Sugunia. London, British Museum
87. Balawat. Bronze Gates (detail): Assyrian warriors; massacre of
prisoners. London, British Museum

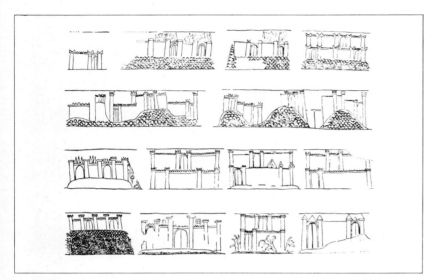

88. *Balawat. Bronze Gates (detail): Assyrian warriors; procession of women prisoners and animals. London, British Museum*

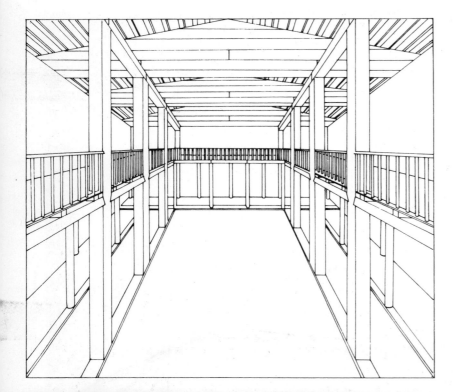

89. *Gordion. Reconstruction of interior of a megaron*
90. *Pazarli (Phrygia). Terra cotta relief, showing ibexes. Ankara, Museum*

91. *Yasilikaya (Phrygia). "Midas Monument"* ▷

cult center to the southeast of modern Eskishehir. The most striking one is the so-called Midas Monument (Plate 91): a tomb chamber framed in a rock relief representing the gabled facade of a building, whose details are realistically depicted. The building is clearly ornamented with architectural terra cottas and with glazed tiles or figured panels, actual examples of which have been found at other Phrygian sites (Plates 90, 92).

### The Urartians

During the final centuries of the Midas dynasty at Gordion the Phrygians were in contact with another newly created nation beyond their eastern frontiers. This was the state of Urartu, which began as a minor kingdom centered on Lake Van, but was later extended by conquest to include not only the eastern provinces of modern Turkey, but some parts of what are now Soviet Armenia and Iraqi Kurdistan. Interest in the general culture of the Urartians, and particularly in their architecture, has been greatly stimulated by the increasing number of archaeological excavations that have concentrated on Urartian sites in recent years. The results of these excavations create the picture of a prosperous and politically advanced state, which controlled a vast territory of mountainous country. From the ninth to seventh centuries B.C. its actual homeland continued to be the area around Lake Van; but in later years there were widely separated provincial capitals, and between them a well-contrived network of hill fortresses and fortress-cities, connected by good roads and supported by irrigation works. All this, combined with the alpine character of the country in which they lived, served to protect the Urartians from invasion by their neighbors, especially the Assyrians with whom they were continually at war. Their culture was nevertheless based upon that of Mesopotamia, and at one time historians saw in it only a provincial reflection of Assyrian art and architecture. Later discoveries have attributed to it a strong individuality and revealed in its architecture qualities that some consider superior to that of the Assyrians themselves. The monotonous mud-brick facades of the dusty Mesopotamian plain are replaced in Urartu by a pattern of stone towers and battlements adapted to the natural beauty of a rocky landscape.

A dozen of these Urartian fortress-cities have been or are at present being excavated. Built as a rule on a strategic hilltop or mountainside, guarding a pass or river crossing, they have a strong citadel at the summit and a residential walled city on the slopes beneath. Typical examples may be recognized in the ground plans of two provincial cities at sites near Erivan in

Soviet Armenia—Karmir Blur and Arin Berd (Plate 93). In the former of these, the staggering of the buttressed wall faces and projecting towers suggests a broken skyline, which must have been architecturally impressive, while the terminal treatment of the battlements, with their crenellated parapets, can be reliably reconstructed on the evidence of a small bronze model of such a building, discovered at another Urartian site, Toprakkale (Plate 95). Prominently placed in most citadel plans is a building recognizable as a temple, a typical example of which may be seen at Altintepe, near Erzincan (Plate 96). The plan is square, with a single compartment enclosed in immensely thick walls and corner buttresses; the centrally placed doorway opens onto a colonnaded courtyard. Early attempts to reconstruct such buildings were usually based on the representation of an Urartian temple facade in an Assyrian relief from Khorsabad (Plate 100). Of the metal facade ornaments shown in this illustration—giant spearheads, circular wall shields, and cauldrons within tripods—actual examples have been found. But where the elevation is concerned, the squat building with its gabled roof is now understood to be the sculptor's misleading adaptation of the shape of the building to the available space. The typical Urartian temple plan is undoubtedly that of a tower, and should be related to the temple towers of Achaemenid times in Persia (see Plates 123–25), for which it clearly provides a prototype. Another public building at Altintepe, with a roof supported by eighteen internal columns, also foreshadows the basic arrangement of Achaemenian palaces.

*The Syro-Hittites*

We have seen that in about 1200 B.C. the Hittites were swept from the Anatolian plateau by Phrygian invaders. During the lifetime of the Urartian kingdom, from the tenth to the seventh century B.C., they reappear as part-occupants of several small city-states in northern Syria and the Taurus area. The cities include Carchemish on the Euphrates and others such as Sinjirli and Malatya in the mountains to the northwest, where they shared political authority with indigenous Aramaeans and other peoples. A good deal is known about these Neo- or Syro-Hittites, as they are called, from the results of excavations made early in the present century. Their art and architecture were of a hybrid and slightly inferior character, much influenced in their later days by Assyria, to which the Syro-Hittites frequently became subject, but also by the Phoenicians of Syria and even by Egypt (Plates 98, 99). One notices, above all in their public buildings, the plentiful use of sculptured orthostats, sometimes

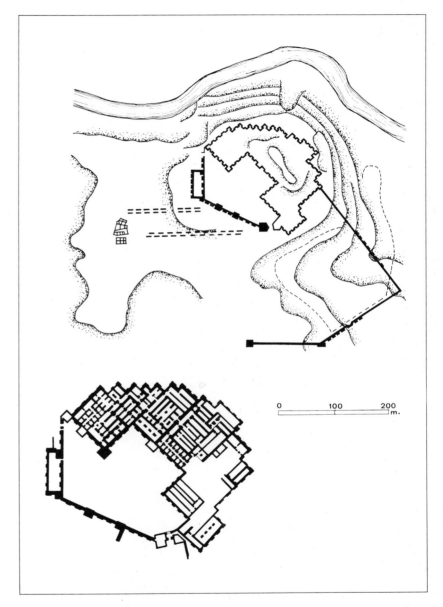

51

of coarse black basalt awkwardly alternating with whitish limestone (Plate 104). An innovation is the use of wooden columns with stone capitals and sculptured bases representing paired animals (Plate 101); monolithic statues, more than life-size, are another common feature.

Syro-Hittite cities vary in shape and size, but they are always well fortified. The walls of Sinjirli enclose an almost perfect circle one-half mile in diameter; in the center is a high, fortified citadel containing a complex of palaces and guardhouses (Plates 102, 103). The citadel at Carchemish is an ancient mound overlooking the Euphrates, and the enceinte of fortress walls has been extended twice (Plate 108). In all these cities the most conspicuous and characteristic features are the palaces built to an architectural formula known to the Assyrians as a *bît-hilani*. We have seen the early development of this formula in buildings of the second millennium B.C. at Tell Atchana (see Plates 65, 66). It consists of a columned portico, a long reception room with a staircase beside it leading to the roof, and a varying number of residential or retiring rooms behind. A striking example is the great Kaparu palace at Tell Halaf, near the source of the Khabur River (Plate 109). A purely Aramaean dynasty of princes ruled in this city in the ninth century B.C., and they decorated their palace with an almost barbaric array of sculptures, as in the portico columns composed of grotesque human figures and mythical beasts (Plate 111). The construction of Syro-Hittite buildings is usually of mud brick heavily reinforced with timber (Plates 105, 110). An exception to this generalization may be found at Carchemish; and one is reminded that this city lies in an area less subject to earthquakes.

### The Levant

Syro-Hittite monuments have been found as far south as Hama on the upper course of the Orontes. Here, in Syria, the Hittites are known to have been in contact with the Biblical Israelites; they must also have had trading relations with the Phoenicians, a Canaanite people whose homeland was a strip of the Levant coast reaching from Tartus to south of Mount Carmel. Our knowledge of both Phoenician and Israelite architecture is derived from excavations in Syria and Palestine, which for the most part have been concerned with fortified cities. A close study has been made of historical development in the design of city walls and gateways. One of the earliest examples, with a stone glacis and moat, has been exposed at Hazor in Galilee, and dates from the eighteenth century B.C. (Plate 112). By the time of King Solomon, in the tenth century, military architecture of this

95. *Toprakkale. Bronze model of a building. London, British Museum*

96. *Altintepe. Plan of Urartian temple*
97. *Altintepe. Reconstruction of a mural painting*

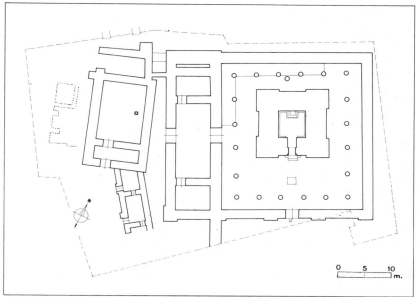

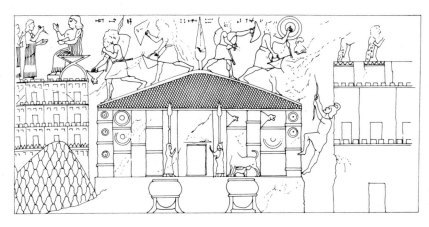

102. *Sinjirli. Plan of city*
103. *Sinjirli. Plan of citadel*

104. *Carchemish. Relief on orthostat, showing King Katuwas. London, British Museum*

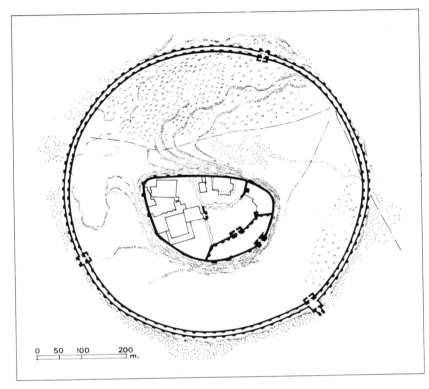

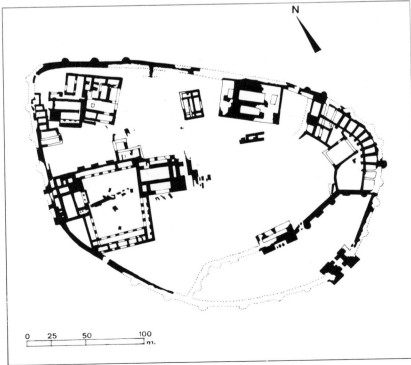

105. *Sinjirli. Wall construction, showing interior "paneling"*
106. *Tell Tayanat. Carved column base of palace*
107. *Tell Tayanat. Isometric diagram of palace and temple*

108. *Carchemish. Plan of city*
1) *West portal.* 2) *House.* 3) *Outer city.* 4) *House.* 5,6) *South gates.* 7) *Inner city*
8) *East portal.* 9) *Northeast fort.* 10) *Tower.* 11) *Acropolis.* 12) *River postern.*
13) *River portal.* 14) *Temple.* 15) *Wall with orthostats.* 16) *River wall*
109. *Tell Halaf. Plan of Kapara Palace*
1) *Scorpion Gate.* 2) *Portal of Kapara Palace.* 3) *Inner room*
110. *Tell Halaf. Wall construction of Kapara Palace, showing armature of wood*

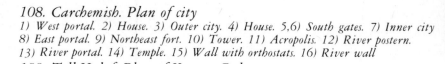

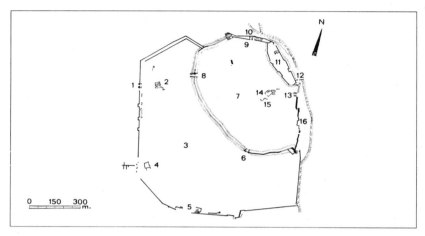

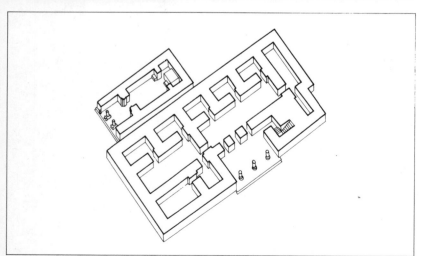

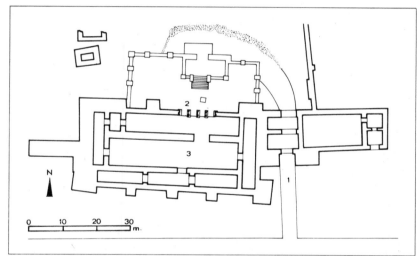

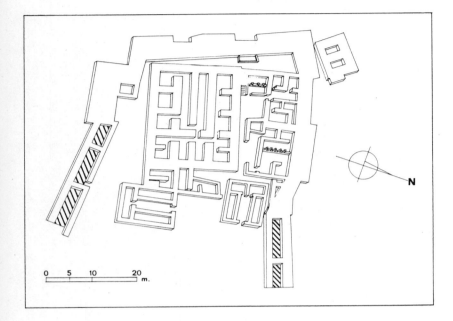

0    5   10        20
                    m.

sort seems to have been standardized, for at three cities—Hazor, Megiddo, and Gezer—walls and gates alike are almost identical. Walls are of the casemate type, with internal chambers for storage or the accommodation of the garrison. Gateways have become elaborate structures, their entry protected by flanking towers and consisting of three successive transverse chambers, to each of which in turn the attackers would need to gain access. It is thought that in the ninth century B.C. a new and improved battering ram must have been invented, against which the casemate wall proved an inadequate defense. It was accordingly replaced by a solid wall of equal thickness, sometimes with salients and recesses to give it greater stability.

Such remains as have been found of Canaanite temples date mostly from the late second millennium and are not very informative. Examples found at Hazor and elsewhere give at least an idea of the temple plan, which consists of a courtyard, main hall, and sanctuary, all on a single axis, with occasional side chambers. This convention must have survived at least into the tenth century B.C., because it is recognizable in the Biblical description of Solomon's Temple (I Kings 6–7), which was built by Phoenician craftsmen. A well-known though not altogether convincing reconstruction of this building (Plate 113) shows the three main compartments surrounded by narrow side chambers in three stories. On either side of the central doorway are the pair of "brazen pillars" mentioned in the Bible, a feature that also appears in the Hazor temple.

*The Neo-Babylonian Period*
One final chapter in the history of Mesopotamian architecture now remains to be studied. After the fall of Nineveh in 612 B.C. and the subsequent collapse of the Assyrian Empire, the center of power shifted from the upper Tigris to the lower Euphrates, and the city of Babylon was rebuilt on a magnificent scale by the kings of a Neo-Babylonian dynasty. Herodotus, who is thought to have visited Babylon in or about 460 B.C., said, "It surpasses in splendor any city of the known world"; and the long description of it that he wrote is interesting to compare with the results of the German excavations of 1899–1917. The excavations show that Herodotus' account of the fortifications at least was not greatly exaggerated (Plates 114, 115). The inner city is an irregular rectangle with a perimeter of almost exactly five miles, divided into two unequal parts by the bed of the Euphrates. The eastern part alone, on which the German archaeologists concentrated their attention, slightly exceeds in area Sargon's Khorsabad. It was defended by a double wall, with pairs of towers at

intervals of sixty-five feet, and by a navigable moat connected to the river. The moat was spanned by bridges leading to the six main gates. Nebuchadnezzar greatly extended the area of the city by building a triangular outer wall five miles long. This also had a moat, but the space between the double walls was filled with rubble to support a broad walkway behind the parapets. The main approach to the city was from the north, by a broad street known to us as the Processional Way; the entrance to the inner city was through the Ishtar Gate, a magnificent building that has been reconstructed in the Berlin Museum (Plates 116–18). Continuing southward, the stone-paved street skirted the broad temenos enclosure with its colossal ziggurat, Etemenanki; then, turning westward between these buildings and the "low" temple, Esagila, it crossed the river on a stone bridge to the western quarter of the town. The remainder of the inner city was filled with minor temples and large private houses (Plates 119–21), some of them terraced into the sides of the substantial mound, called Merkez, which represented the remains of earlier cities. The Ishtar Gate was an elaborate construction, with four towers and a huge rectangular gatehouse. Its facades and those of the Processional Way were faced with bricks covered in colored glaze and figured with lions, bulls, and mythical animals, mostly molded in relief. The labor of casting each brick in its appropriate wooden mold can be imagined, but the effect of these brilliant colors, in contrast to the ubiquitous mud brick of the surrounding city, must have been very striking. Of these buildings, all that remains today in situ are the foundations, which, according to some ritual formula, were carried down some twenty feet below pavement level in search of "clean" soil. They too are decorated with figures in relief, but are unglazed because they were not intended to be seen.

Curiously enough, the two buildings that the excavators were least able to reconstruct with any assurance were the ziggurat and the huge temple of Babylon's patron god, Marduk. The ziggurat had been almost completely quarried by brick robbers, while Esagila was buried beneath an almost impenetrable burden of later building remains. More completely excavated was Nebuchadnezzar's great palace to the west of the Ishtar Gate. Entered from the Processional Way, it is planned around at least four main courtyards. The throne room itself faces the third of these, with three doorways and a recess for the throne opposite the center door. The outer facade between the doorways was once more decorated with glazed bricks, and the designs here remind one that contact had by now been made between Mesopotamia and Classical Greece (Plate 122). Between

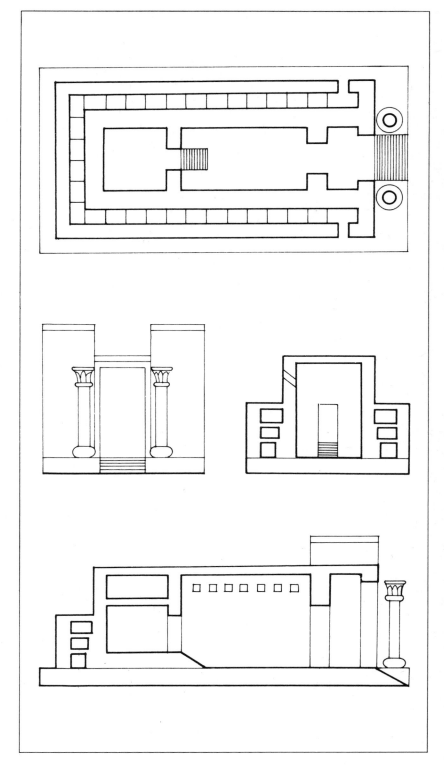

114. *Babylon. Plan of city*
1) *Euphrates River.* 2) *Lugalgirra Gate.* 3) *Temple of Belit Nina.* 4) *Temple of Adad.*
5) *Gardens.* 6) *Adad Gate.* 7) *New Town.* 8) *Mausoleum.* 9) *Temple of Shamash.*
10) *Shamash Gate.* 11) *Urash Gate.* 12) *Temple of Gula.* 13) *Temple of Marduk.*
14) *Esagila.* 15) *Ishtar Gate.* 16) *Temple of Nin-Makh.* 17) *Processional Way.*
18) *Temple of Ishtar.* 19) *Sacred Gate.* 20) *Temple of Ninurta.* 21) *Ninurta Gate.*
22) *Sin Gate.* 23) *Temple of New Year Festival*

115. *Babylon. Perspective reconstruction of city* ▷

the second and third courts there is a high-standing propylon, which recalls the reception unit of an Assyrian palace. A building in the northeast corner, comprising heavily vaulted storerooms, has been tentatively identified as an emplacement for the Hanging Gardens of classical tradition.

Little reference has till now been made to the architecture of private houses. At Babylon the ruins of some impressively large ones have been examined (Plate 121), but there is little to be said about them that does not equally apply to ordinary dwellings dating from any period in the history of the ancient Near East. For security reasons, there are no windows in their blank external facades, so that light must be obtained from open courtyards or roofed courts with clerestory openings. A main reception room, entered laterally from a court, is the most obvious feature; in early houses at Ur, Woolley detected evidence of a wooden gallery around this court, suggesting the existence of an upper story. Nothing of this sort was found at Babylon, which suggests that Herodotus' account was in this respect at fault. The planning of such houses was often hampered by the irregular shape of the site available in a frequently rebuilt crowded quarter. This fact has some relevance to the subject of Mesopotamian town planning in general, about which no scholar has ever ventured to write at any great length. To be truthful, planning as we know it today—that is, the conscious design and disposal of buildings in relation to each other—was practically nonexistent in the cities of the ancient Near East. Apart from private dwellings, the public buildings themselves were designed, as it were, from the inside outward, and little thought seems to have been given to their interrelation or overall composition. We have seen, for example, the citadel at Khorsabad, the palace platform at Nimrud, and the walled city of Ur, with their individual palaces and temples placed haphazard in apparently unrelated positions. Except for the Processional Way at Babylon, it would be hard to find any trace of a preplanned civic layout of the sort that becomes familiar in later times. Such things had to await the advent of Greek influence, which after the final conquest of Mesopotamian lands by the Persians soon began to be in greater evidence.

## ACHAEMENIAN ARCHITECTURE

The development and history of Mesopotamian architecture must be considered to end with the conquest of Babylon by Cyrus the Great in 539 B.C. Some account must now be given of subsequent events in Persia under the Achaemenid dynasty, of

116. *Babylon. Perspective reconstruction of Ishtar Gate and Processional Way*
117. *Babylon. Line reconstruction of Ishtar Gate*

118. *Babylon. Reconstruction of Ishtar Gate. Berlin, Museum*
119. *Babylon. Plan of Nin-Makh Temple*
1) Altar. 2) Well. 3) Courtyard

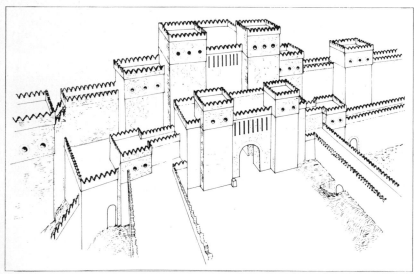

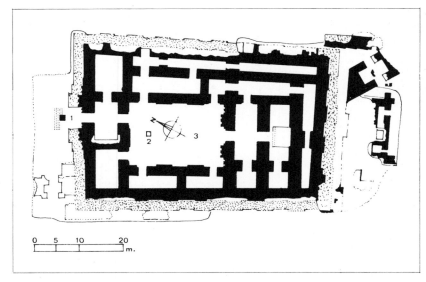

120. Babylon. Plan of the Great Palace
1) Hanging Gardens. 2) Ishtar Gate. 3) Temple of Nin-Makh. 4) City walls.
5) Fortress on Euphrates River
121. Babylon. Plan of largest private house
1) Courts. 2) Principal room

122. Babylon. Glazed brick facade of throne room, from Palace of Nebuchadnezzar. Berlin, Museum

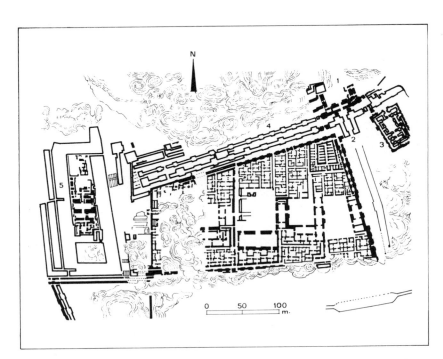

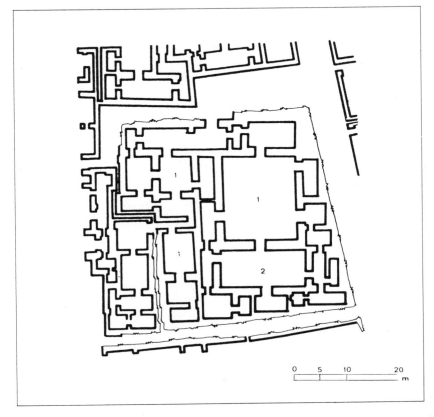

which Cyrus was the founder. With this purpose in view, it will be well first to recollect the historical background against which Achaemenian art and architecture came into being. The country that we now call Iran had for some centuries been withdrawn from the mainstream of cultural development in the Near East. Its most recent rulers were the Medes, whose tribal dispensation had afforded little encouragement to the refinements of civilization. Now, with the sudden elevation of the Persians to an imperial power and the sweeping success of their conquests, an unprecedented situation had been created. It was as though civilization had suddenly fallen to a tribe of seminomadic horsemen, who were in a position either to accept or to destroy the cultural heritage they had acquired. Certainly, where architecture was concerned, the Persians not only accepted this heritage but enhanced it with their own peculiar genius.

The earliest stages in the evolution of Achaemenian architecture are to be seen in the rather scanty remains of Cyrus' capital city at Pasargadae (Plate 126). The style is understandably derivative, combining Median and Urartian with Assyrian elements. The layout still retains the character of a nomadic encampment: widely separated buildings—consisting of gatehouse, residential palace, and audience hall—standing in a vast park, surrounded by a wall thirteen feet thick. Only the audience hall provides an example of a formula in design later to become a criterion of Achaemenian architecture: a hypostyle hall with corner towers and external colonnades between them, called by the Persians an apadana.

The full flower of Achaemenian architecture is to be seen at Persepolis, to which Darius transferred the state capital in 518 B.C. Two new sources of influence are now in evidence. One is the traditional architecture of Elam, which had thrived from the second millennium B.C. onward and whose true character has only recently been revealed by the excavation of a great ziggurat and temple complex at Choga Zambil (Plate 127). The other—a far more significant development—is the knowledge of Greek architecture and the great army of Greek craftsmen that Darius had brought back from his wars in the Aegean. It is to these influences, combined with the creative talent of the Persians themselves, that the truly novel features of Achaemenian architecture must be attributed. Its links with the past on the other hand were supplied by Mesopotamia. Achaemenian palaces, like those of Assyria, were built on artificial terraces (Plate 128); their gates were guarded by winged demons and human-headed bulls; their walls were built of mud brick and decorated with panels of polychrome glazed tiles or relief sculptures in stone

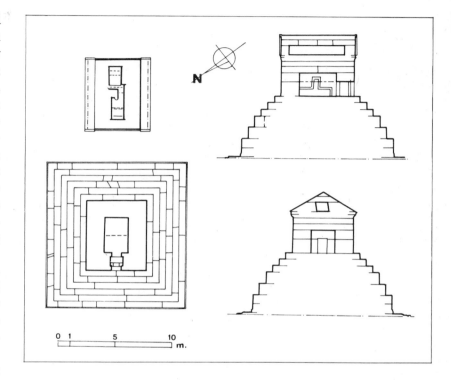

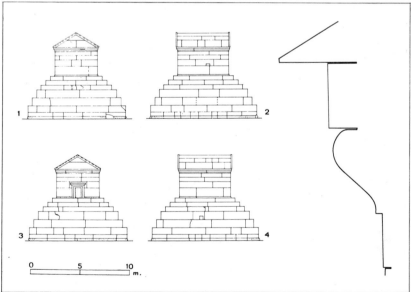

126. *Pasargadae. Residential Palace, from southwest*
127. *Choga Zambil. Perspective reconstruction of ziggurat*
128. *Persepolis. General view, from east: foreground, Hall of One Hundred Columns (throne hall of Xerxes); behind, audience hall of Darius I (apadana); left, tripylon* ▷

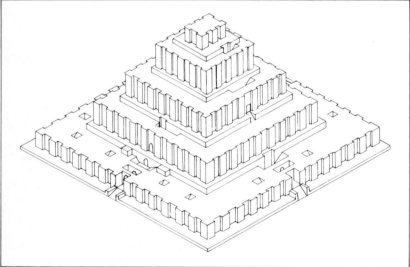

129. *Persepolis. North staircase of audience hall of Darius I (apadana), front view of outer ramps*
130. *Persepolis. Palace of Xerxes, from northeast*
131. *Persepolis. Reconstruction of Hall of One Hundred Columns (throne hall of Xerxes)*

132. *Persepolis. Audience hall of Darius (apadana), ramps of north staircase* ▷

(Plates 133–35). But in other ways, striking innovations may be recognized in the lavish use of wooden columns with elaborately carved stone capitals, in the sculptured stone frames of doors and windows, in the monumental stairways ornamented with figured reliefs, and in the tendency to plan important buildings around a square central unit (Plates 129–32, 136).

At Persepolis the most striking effects of Greek craftsmanship, imposed on the native tradition of Persian art, are best seen in the sculptured reliefs themselves, whose major contribution to the appearance of the buildings is immediately apparent (Plate 129). The straightforward relief technique of the Assyrians, with its engraved detail and lack of modeling, has been retained as a basis for the new style, but the employment of Ionian sculptors results in a complete break with Mesopotamian tradition. Relief carving in Assyria had maintained until the end its linear character, with modeling playing a very subordinate part; the surface of the figures stood in front of the background as in a parallel plane, almost without three-dimensional treatment. These limitations were distasteful to the Greek sculptors, for whom sculpture in the round and sculpture in relief were closely related, so that a fuller plastic rendering of human and animal subjects now became the rule. In the Greek manner, it is carried to extremes in the modeling of drapery, through which are perceptible the contours of the body. The outcome of these innovations produces a form of sculpture whose elegance and precision is probably unrivaled in the whole history of art. If any criticism is to be made of the Persepolis reliefs, it is in regard not to the details of the carving, but to the poverty of imagination in the subjects depicted. The interminable processions of almost identical figures tend to become monotonous, and one remembers by contrast the spirit and variety of the Assyrian narrative scenes. However, these Persian reliefs fulfill a totally different function in the decoration of a building: the Assyrian palace reliefs were used internally and confront the spectator at close quarters, whereas the Persian reliefs are used as ornament for the outside facades of artificial terraces on which the buildings stood. Dominated by the walls and roofs above, which have now disappeared, they were intended merely to give decorative emphasis to the most important external features of the architecture—the stairway approaches to the palaces.

If we now consider individual buildings on the palace platform at Persepolis (Plates 128, 137), we shall find the great apadana of Darius obviously the most impressive. It is 250 feet square with a height computed at fifty feet, and it is said to have accommodated ten thousand people. The towers at each of the

133. *Persepolis. Reliefs showing bearers of gifts, on north staircase to audience hall of Darius (apadana)*

134. *Persepolis. Relief showing lion attacking a bull, on staircase to tripylon*

135. *Susa. Glazed brick reliefs: archer of royal guard. Paris, Louvre*

136. *Persepolis. Bull capital (detail) ▷*

137. Persepolis. Plan of site
1) East fortifications. 2) Treasury. 3) Harem. 4) Guard room. 5) Ruined buildings. 6) Tripylon. 7) Palace of Xerxes. 8) Ruined buildings. 9) Unidentified palace. 10) Palace of Darius. 11) Audience Hall of Darius. 12) Gate house of Xerxes. 13) Staircase to terrace. 14) Throne hall of Xerxes (Hall of One Hundred Columns). 15) Gate to court of throne hall. 16) Outbuildings. 17) North fortifications. 18) Royal Tomb. 19) Cistern. 20) Street between harem and treasury

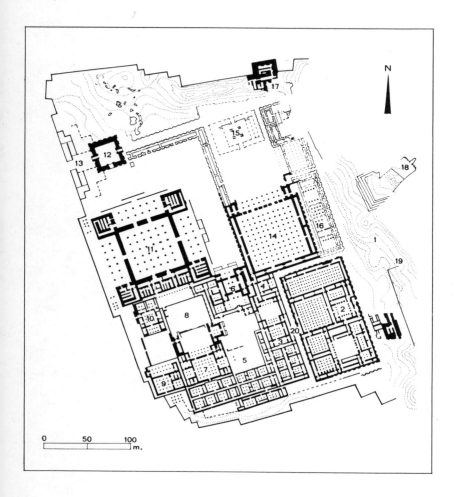

four corners may have contained guardrooms and stairs. From the western portico there was an open view of the countryside, and perhaps also of the sunset in the evening, since a low parapet here replaced the fortress wall that surrounded the rest of the terrace. The private terrace on which the apadana stood was cut from living rock, and the great stairways leading up to it bore the famous reliefs of tribute bearers. Next comes the throne hall or Hall of One Hundred Columns, begun by Xerxes and finished by Artaxerxes I. The portico on its north side was supported by sixteen pillars and had at either end two huge guardian figures of bulls, which were built into the walls of the towers. The wall between hall and portico contained seven stone window frames; the short walls had niches instead of windows. The reveals of the doorways were also carved in relief.

The identity of the majority of other buildings on the main terrace is hypothetical. The "Harem" is to some extent self-explanatory, while the character of the "Treasury" is evident in the fact that it is accessible only through a single small doorway. In common with all these buildings, its columns were of wood, heavily plastered and painted in bright colors. They are fluted in the Classical Greek manner, while the more elaborate bases and capitals show a floral treatment that is half Greek and half Egyptian (Plates 132, 136). Examples have been found at Persepolis and elsewhere of the double-figure impost block (bulls, bull-men, or dragons), a feature that is peculiar to Achaemenian architecture.

*Architecture of Egypt* • *Hans Wolfgang Müller*

## THE PREDYNASTIC PERIOD

Egyptian architecture did not develop from homogeneous principles and traditions. Upper and Lower Egypt remained geographically and culturally distinct, even when joined politically in the Kingdom of the Two Lands. They had different peoples with their own customs, characteristic dwellings, and modes of burial, with different ideas about the divine powers and about the kind of life that followed death. In both regions the cultivation and storage of crops had long been the basis of existence. Settled farmers tend to build permanent dwellings with provision for their grain, cattle, and tools, but in Upper Egypt the farmers shared the land with a nomadic people who had migrated to the Nile Valley from the increasingly arid steppes. Hunters and herdsmen, roaming to find well-stocked hunting grounds and fresh pastures, have always built dwellings that are easily erected and taken down wherever they choose to camp; thus these lived in lightweight tentlike structures with roofs and walls of skins or matting stretched over a rigid frame.

Each region also had its own distinctive burial practices. The inhabitants of Upper Egypt, to the south, buried their dead away from the settlements, in the dry sand at the edge of the nearby desert, and formed a mound or tumulus over the grave. The deceased had to be provided with everything they might need—weapons, adornments, food and drink—for their continued separate existence. But in the north, in Lower Egypt, which was flat and wet, the dead received the protection of the villages on higher ground, and were buried under the floor of the houses; thus they remained within the sphere of the living. Each of these modes of burial presented a different conception of the nature of the afterlife and of the necessary ritual provisions for a continued existence.

Even in Predynastic times the typical settler lived in a rectangular one-room peasant hut of sun-dried Nile mud. A model of such a hut, found in a tomb, plainly shows the inward sloping walls, the door, and the tiny window openings set high for ventilation more than to let in light. The roof has not survived, but it was flat and may originally have consisted of palm trunks laid side by side: this type of roof was sculpturally reproduced on the ceilings of later stone-built tombs. The slope of the walls later became a characteristic feature of monumental stone architecture: tombs, temples, gate towers (pylons), and enclosure walls. It goes back to the early architectural experience with primitive mud-walled structures.

From the very beginning the inhabitants of the Nile Valley

*138. Hieroglyphs representing primitive forms of Egyptian temples a) Lower Egyptian sanctuary of the goddess Neith of Sais (First Dynasty). b) Buto heron sanctuary (Narmer mace, Hierakonpolis, First Dynasty). c) Upper Egyptian sanctuary (after Third Dynasty hieroglyph). d) Lower Egyptian sanctuary (after Fifth Dynasty hieroglyph). e) Reed hut beneath awning (after Fifth Dynasty hieroglyph)*

139. *Walled Lower Egyptian city, from Palette of Menes (Narmer). Unification period, c. 3000 B.C. Cairo, Egyptian Museum*
140. *Abydos. Funerary stele with the "Horus name" of King Zet; below, representation of palace facade. First Dynasty, c. 2900 B.C. Paris, Louvre*

141. *Abydos. Reconstruction of royal tumulus tomb with steles. First Dynasty*
142. *Abydos. Plan of Temple of Khentiamentiu. First Dynasty*

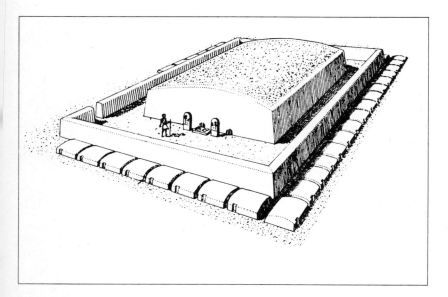

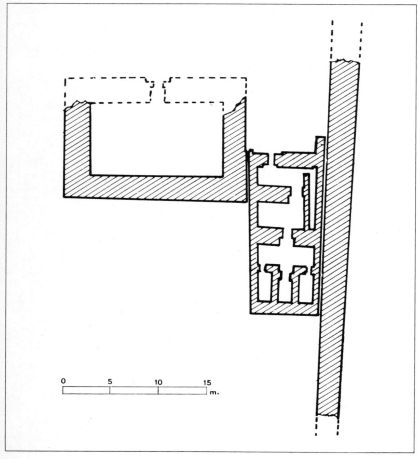

and the Delta had made shelters and huts from reeds and rushes. Reeds and papyrus stems, tied or woven together to form walls and bundled together to form light supports for the roofing, are the oldest building materials in Egypt. Ancient hieroglyphs represent various types of huts in simplified outline. These huts made of perishable material, together with the primitive mud houses, served as prototypes for the later monumental architecture. In hieroglyphic writing the two "royal sanctuaries" of Upper and Lower Egypt are distinguished by huts of two kinds (Plate 138c–d). A hut with a semicircular roof, above which two corner posts appear to project, must be interpreted as a structure consisting of bundled reeds and matting on the basis of its green or yellow color in the writing. In the oldest representations this hut form also denotes the holy places of Buto, the capital of a prehistoric Delta kingdom (Plate 138a–b); in the writing, the "royal sanctuary of Lower Egypt." Translated into three dimensions, this type of hut reveals its basic structure: a building with a roof vaulted longitudinally, between elevated transverse walls.

The reed hut of Lower Egypt corresponded to the Upper Egyptian tent of the nomad chieftain, a frame building designed to resemble an animal, with horns projecting from the front and sometimes a fence around the main entrance; at the back hung down an animal tail. The imprints of ancient cylinder seals have transmitted this aboriginal building type; in the developed hieroglyphic writing the animal features have been toned down (Plate 138c). The nomad chieftains, who first brought the two kingdoms under their own rule and created the united Egyptian state, had long been settled in the Nile Valley but continued to live in tents, stretching colored matting over the structural skeletons. After Memphis was founded as the permanent residence of the kings of Upper and Lower Egypt, the palace of reed matting remained a model for the palace of the king as ruler of Upper Egypt and for the shrines of Upper Egyptian gods; but it was now constructed—like the reed hut, its Lower Egyptian equivalent—of solid brick and timber. Both of these building types testified to their particular origins and significance within the new political order, and accordingly their characteristic structural features had to be strictly preserved in the more permanent monumental form.

Another building type known from hieroglyphs was also composed of vegetable material. The tall rectangular front of this hut was of matting construction with the corners and eaves stiffened and reinforced with bundles of plant stems bound together. The concave cornice, highly stylized, probably represents the free ends of the rushes that tied the upper edges of the mat-

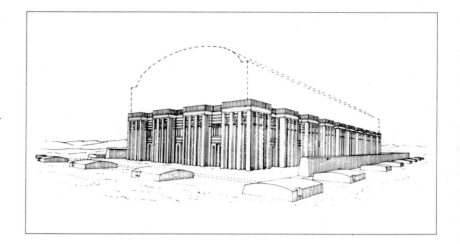

ting walls to the top stiffener. As a hieroglyph this hut means "hut of the god," and in monumental architecture it is perpetuated in the exterior design of a chapel held together with round fillets and crowned by a concave cornice. In the older writing it also appears in another special form, namely, a hut beneath an awning supported on wooden posts (Plate 138e). In monumental architecture this form became the prototype of the later "baldachin temple" (see Plates 182, 190), erected for the celebration of special rites and as a "way station" or resting-place for the images of the gods and their sacred barge during the processions through the precincts of large temple complexes. The "birth houses" of the late temples were also modeled after the hut shaded by an awning (see Plates 228, 237).

## THE THINITE PERIOD AND THE OLD KINGDOM

Menes (Narmer), who unified Upper and Lower Egypt, built his residence in Lower Egypt on the site where later the capital city of Memphis was erected. The name of the palace, "white walls," suggests a brick enclosure, and within it were the residences of the king, the shrines of the gods, and the government buildings of the Two Lands, all these in the styles of Upper and Lower Egypt, respectively. Walls reinforced with projecting buttresses were characteristic of the conquered Lower Egyptian cities, as seen in representations of the triumphs of Menes (Narmer) (Plate 139), this Lower Egyptian tradition being adopted by the conqueror from Upper Egypt for his stronghold in the Delta.

### The Palace Facade

In the combination of the two different building forms—the tent palace of the Upper Egyptian king and the niched enclosure wall of his Lower Egyptian residence—is an artistic translation of the "Horus name" that thenceforth constitutes the first part of the royal title for the united Egypt (Plate 140): within an upright rectangle is enclosed an artfully composed facade with two gates, the whole surmounted by the ruler as the Horus-hawk. Preserved painted representations of decorative matting and wood framing on the projecting and recessed faces of these articulated walls have been taken as evidence that their niche-modeled surface was derived from wood construction—and from Mesopotamia, where contemporary finds include similar buildings depicted on cylinder seals. However, subsequent monuments make it clear that the wall articulated with niches belongs to a quite different mode of construction from the matting stretched over a wood frame; both were purely Egyptian in origin and, heraldically merged in the "palace name," came to-

gether in the Memphis residence. A better idea of what Upper and Lower Egypt contributed to the building forms in and around the royal residence can be obtained from the tombs that were built by the unifiers of the country (Plates 141, 143) and their successors, especially the limestone tomb precinct of King Zoser (Plates 146–55).

The unification of Upper and Lower Egypt stimulated the development of a true architecture with quite new tasks, and foremost among these was the building of monumental tombs for the kings of the unified country. Toward the end of the Predynastic period the wood frame for molded mud brick was invented, which was a technical step forward.

### Tomb Complexes of the Early Kings

The form of tomb structures grows from the dual nature of the Egyptian kings as "rulers of Upper and Lower Egypt"; this required two separate burials, one in each half of the country. The prehistoric burial customs that had evolved—cemetery burial in a tumulus grave in Upper Egypt and house burial in Lower Egypt—were incorporated into the architecture of the royal tomb complexes. In Memphis the Lower Egyptian idea of house burial led logically to the tomb being designed and equipped as a "residence"; in the Upper Egyptian cemetery at Abydos, on the other hand, the grave mounds were merely enlarged and developed into abstract geometric shapes. The cult arrangements within each mode of burial led also to particular formations.

### The Royal Cemetery at Abydos

At Abydos the subterranean burial chambers of the royal tumuli were walled with brick, the floors and walls faced with imported softwoods, and the burial pit roofed over with timbers. However it is known that during the First Dynasty one of these tombs was given a floor and walls of granite blocks that herald the transition to a stone architecture. The tumulus, a heap of sand, rose above the timbered roof that covered the tomb chamber and the lateral rooms for grave furniture; it was contained by a brick wall and probably covered by a shallow brick dome. In front of the east side of the tumulus two freestanding name steles were set up to indicate the offering place (Plate 140). The entire precinct was surrounded by a low wall, outside of which the members of the king's family and court were interred (Plate 141). The royal cemetery, which lies in flat desert country about a mile from the Nile Valley, stood under the protection of Khentiamentiu ("Foremost of the Westerners"), a god of the dead who had a temple at the edge of the valley. This was a brick building whose foundations are preserved, the only example of an Early Dynastic temple (Plate 142). It was elongated in plan; on the short side, two outer chambers with offset entrances led into a third room where the shrine for the cult image was built against the rear wall. As the oldest representations show (Plate 138a–b), the shrine was originally a construction of reeds standing free within an enclosure; when translated into brick it became solidly incorporated in the structure of a closed building, and was moved back against the rear wall.

## The Royal Tombs at Memphis

The first rulers of the united country and their successors, as kings of Lower Egypt, lie buried on the western desert plateau across from their capital at Memphis; their tombs are of a type adapted from the burial practices of Buto, once the capital of a Lower Egyptian kingdom. These Memphite tombs have imposing mud-brick superstructures whose multilayered exteriors form a series of buttresses and niches (Plates 143–45). They demonstrate the Lower Egyptian palace in the characteristic aspect of its articulated enclosure walls (see Plate 167). The articulation has now become an aesthetic system: on the projecting and recessed faces are painted colorful carpet patterns that link the idea of the tomb as a "Lower Egyptian residence" with that of the tent palace derived from Upper Egypt, and thus symbolically express for each king the guaranty of the unified kingdom. The "palace tombs" are also surrounded by low walls, and outside these, as at Abydos, the subsidiary graves are ranged (Plate 141). The offering place of the palace tomb was located in front of a niche in the exterior of the east wall. Detached from its structural context, this niche later became incorporated as a "false door" in the royal and private tombs of the Old Kingdom, a Lower Egyptian element symbolically linking the worlds of the living and the dead. In this isolation of its form and function the false door is frequently edged with beading and crowned by a concave molding. It persisted in three-dimensional or in painted form into the later dynasties and even found its way into temples and palaces, occurring wherever a deceased person, a god, or the king was to appear.

## King Zoser's Funerary Precinct at Memphis

To revitalize and consolidate the idea of a unified kingdom, King Zoser, the founder of the Third Dynasty, combined the two separate cemeteries and their funerary institutions into a single giant precinct near his capital of Memphis (see Plates 146–55). The sanctuary was surrounded by niched walls of white limestone over thirty feet high; these represented the "white walls" of the residence. At the focal point of the entire precinct stands the 200-foot stepped tomb (see Plates 147, 155), combining an exaggerated monumental stone tumulus in the Upper Egyptian tradition (mastaba) with the idea of a gigantic stairway to heaven. It is still possible to distinguish the various stages in the history of this structure—from the original flat mastaba to a small pyramid, then to the final large step pyramid. The king's Lower Egyptian tomb is a massive stone structure attached to the south wall of the sanctuary; its arched cornice and niched facade correspond to the royal tombs of the unifiers at Memphis. In a consistent development of the Lower Egyptian-Memphite concept of the "house tomb," the other buildings within the precinct are patterned after the Memphis residence, including the king's palace, the government buildings of the Two Lands, and the shrines of Upper and Lower Egyptian gods. In the courts of the tomb complex the royal existence in the hereafter was affirmed and perpetually renewed by ritual reenactments of the "jubilee festival" in the presence of the gods.

The various building types in King Zoser's burial precinct were shown three-dimensionally in stone in their Upper and Lower Egyptian forms, with architectural elements appropriately painted for their cult requirements. Airy wood-framed structures covered with reed matting in the nomadic manner of Upper Egypt (Plates 148–50, 152) are recognizable by their arched roofs, fluted masts, and the mats stretched between cross battens or rolled up over doorways. The Lower Egyptian chapels (Plate 153) reproduce the forms of the ancient hut of bundled and woven reeds; as independent decorative elements, the round fillet and concave upper molding have their origin in the translation of primeval reed forms into stone. Brick buildings are identifiable from the flat roof and interior ceiling construction, which simulates round timbers resting on architraves supported by fluted wooden posts (Plate 154). Wooden door leaves are reproduced in stone in a half-open position (Plate 155). The fluting of the posts as an artistic form probably goes back to the dressing of softwood trunks with the rounded cutting edge of the Egyptian adz. In connection with the roof construction of the tent buildings it should be noted that the fluted masts support on brackets the ribs of the arched roof; these brackets are missing from the posts in brick buildings, and here they take the form of lateral overhanging plant leaves (compare Plates 152, 153). At the top of the masts are reproduced sawn-off branches in stylized form. The mortises probably served for the insertion of horns, like those on the old tent palaces of the nomad chieftains (see Plate 138c).

146. *Saqqara. Mortuary precinct of King Zoser, re-erected enclosure wall with niche articulation and step pyramid. Third Dynasty, c. 2650 B.C.*

147. *Saqqara. Plan of mortuary precinct of King Zoser*
*1) Step pyramid derived from square-plan mastaba. 2) Funerary temple of Zoser. 3) Court with Serdab. 4) Large court with altar on two B-shaped stones. 5) Entrance portico. 6) Heb-Sed court. 7) Small temple. 8) Court before South Palace. 9) Court of South Palace. 10) South tomb*

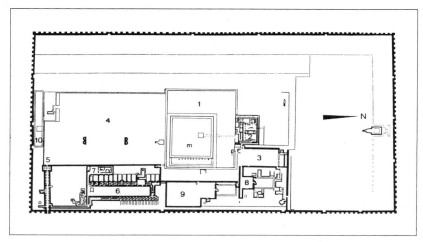

148. *Saqqara. Mortuary precinct of King Zoser, reconstruction of Upper Egyptian tent building for the government of Lower Egypt*
149. *Saqqara. Mortuary precinct of King Zoser, remains of Upper Egyptian tent building for the government of Lower Egypt*

150. *Saqqara. Mortuary precinct of King Zoser, detail of building for government of Lower Egypt: fluted masts, stretched matting in lower section, entrance with rolled-up mats. Third Dynasty, c. 2650 B.C.* ▷

Most of the structures within the burial precinct are simply solid sham-buildings that have mere niches or short passageways for cult images or ritual processions. The only ones with interior rooms are the lengthy entrance hall, the "sacristy" (Plates 154, 155), and the living quarters of the king which are built onto the north side of the step pyramid. The disposition of the various buildings within the precinct and their interconnection by means of real passages or false doors did not have to correspond exactly with the residential prototype, but were determined by special requirements of the burial rite and the cult of the dead. For example, the triple-aisled hallway through which the funeral procession entered the sacred precinct had assumed the role of "palm grove of Buto"; thus the stone columns are decorated with a fringe of palm fronds.

This first stone-built mortuary complex, whose architectural organization and formal design already indicate a high level of accomplishment, has been identified from inscriptions as the work of the king's chief architect Imhotep, who simultaneously served as high priest of Heliopolis.

### The Pyramid Complexes of the Fourth and Fifth Dynasties

The transition from the Third to the Fourth Dynasty was accompanied by a fundamental change in the planning and design of the royal tombs. The Lower Egyptian or Memphite concept of the tomb was abandoned; no longer was it a residence for the afterlife, nor the funerary precinct a realistic open-air stage setting for ritual performance. Probably under the influence of the myth of the death and resurrection of the god Osiris, the death of the king now became a mythical fate, whose "mysteries" permeated the burial ceremonies and cult practices and established the principal theme of the new royal tomb architecture. Subsequently the cult area was organized in the form of a "processional stage" along an architecturally defined "sacred way" that began at the edge of the desert and ended in the tomb chamber; therefore the rites were performed and the utterances recited in a succession of rooms, passages, courts, gates, and pillars.

The impetus for change came from Abydos, in Upper Egypt; there the procession led from the temple of the cemetery god through the flat desert valley to the royal burial ground in the west. The Upper Egyptian character of the new trend is also expressed in the development and exaggeration of the king's tomb into a pyramid. King Zoser's step pyramid had a rectangular plan; the next phase, the square plan of the step pyramid at Medum (Plate 157), came with the accession of the Fourth Dynasty, and after that the increasing abstraction led to the

151. Saqqara. Mortuary precinct of King Zoser, east side of building for government of Lower Egypt: papyrus stalks as half-column supports. Third Dynasty, c. 2650 B.C.
152. Saqqara. Mortuary precinct of King Zoser, Jubilee Court with re-erected chapel of Upper Egyptian tent-building type. Third Dynasty, c. 2650 B.C.

◄ 153. *Saqqara. Mortuary precinct of King Zoser, chapel of Lower Egyptian type: in foreground, podium for royal baldachin (on side, steps leading to statue niche of older chapel). Third Dynasty, c. 2650 B.C.*

154. *Saqqara. Mortuary precinct of King Zoser, great court on south of step pyramid and "sacristy." Third Dynasty, c. 2650 B.C.*
155. *Saqqara. Mortuary precinct of King Zoser, "sacristy," half-open wooden door simulated in stone. Third Dynasty, c. 2650 B.C.*

crystalline geometry of the true pyramid (Plate 158). The step pyramid at Medum next took over—again evidence of its origin in the Upper Egyptian tumulus—an offering temple on the east side. This, however, was still a primitive affair, a modest flat-roofed building with two parallel antechambers (Plate 156) before a small court with two steles. From a "valley temple" at the edge of the desert a walled causeway led up to the pyramid precinct. In the arrangement of this royal burial area at Medum—valley temple, causeway, and offering temple—the future theme and plan of the Memphite pyramid complexes are first stated.

The new ideas about divine kingship and the burial rite were most fully realized in the pyramid complexes built during the Fourth Dynasty by Chephren and Cheops at Giza, where these ideas are manifest in the enormous masses and in the use of hard stones, granite and basalt, and alabaster as building materials (Plate 158). Chephren significantly enlarged the valley temple and roofed over the causeway; his offering temple at the foot of the pyramid was preceded by a huge "veneration temple" with a row of statuary shrines as the "sanctuary" (Plate 160). An immediate impression of this architecture can now be gained only from the valley temple, a square building with smooth sloping exterior walls. The masonry consists of a core of local limestone faced on both sides with massive slabs of granite. Also of granite are the pillars inside, and the architraves and roof beams, all monoliths. The floors are paved with white alabaster slabs.

The funeral procession arrived from the east, from the Nile Valley, first landing on the west bank in front of the valley temple; it split into two groups and entered the narrow antechamber through two portals bordered only by bands of inscriptions; reunited, it passed through a central doorway into the inverted T-shaped hypostyle hall with its square granite pillars (Plates 159, 161–62). Ranged around the walls were twenty-three statues of Chephren enthroned, which figured in the ceremonies of the "Opening of the mouth." The thin light that found its way through the slit windows in the roof was reflected from the bright alabaster floor. These early monumental interiors are otherwise unadorned, and they achieve their effect exclusively from the interrelated masses, the construction, and the color and durability of the materials. The procession left the valley temple through a narrow passage and ascended for nearly one-third of a mile the covered causeway to the pyramid temple (Plate 160).

The pyramid temple was also completely sealed off from the outside world and shielded from profane eyes by its smooth sloping walls. In its design the two parts stand out plainly, the

156. *Medum. Offering temple and two steles on east side of step pyramid; remains of enclosure wall and upper portion of causeway. Third–Fourth Dynasty, c. 2600 B.C.*

157. *Medum. Step pyramid, from east; in foreground, site of former valley temple and causeway. Third–Fourth Dynasty, c. 2600 B.C.*

outer temple and the veneration temple. The spaces of the outer temple occupy the hollow core of the otherwise solid mass of stone; they repeat the arrangement of the valley temple except that here the constriction of a passageway separates thematically the crossbar from the stem of the T-shaped hall. A court surrounded by granite pillars introduces the veneration temple; there is evidence that the indentations in these pillars contained enthroned images of the king. Beyond and side by side are the five deep shrines that composed the sanctuary proper, directly behind the five bays of the western row of pillars. The offering place of the Abydos type with its two steles probably occupied the space between the rear wall of the veneration temple and the foot of the pyramid. The procession followed a narrow passageway leading from the northwest corner of the pillared court directly into the walled pyramid precinct—bypassing the sanctuary—and continued to the passage on the north side of the pyramid that ended in the tomb chamber.

Already under Chephren's predecessor Radedef, the sun cult of Heliopolis had begun to exert an influence on the dogma of divine kingship and life in the hereafter, and the arrangements of the tomb were correspondingly affected. The Lower Egyptian heritage began to assume greater importance. In the mortuary temple of Radedef's tomb complex, north of Giza near Abu Roash, a system of columns with plant motifs replaces the more abstract architecture of pillars. These religious influences are unequivocal in the tombs of the late Fourth Dynasty. The pyramid shape was sometimes abandoned in favor of the "house tomb" form as, for example, in the tomb of Queen Khent-kaw-s in the necropolis of Giza with its "palace" rising above niched walls (Plate 167).

With the advent of the Fifth Dynasty sun worship became the state religion. In the choice of their tombs these kings reverted to the classical pyramidal form and adapted the Memphite mortuary temple to the demands of the new cult. The founder of the dynasty, King Weserkaf, shifted the mortuary temple to the south side of his pyramid at Saqqara in order to include the entire path of the sun in a ritual performed within a pillared court. His successors returned to the traditional axial arrangement with the temple on the east side of the pyramid; the stern blankness of the temple exteriors was relaxed, however, and colonnades were introduced to open up the valley temple, and sometimes the veneration temple, to the outside world (Plates 168, 169). Columns in the form of palm trees and bundles of papyrus and lotus stalks (see Plate 183) supported the roofs of the porticoes; these ultimately derive from the early reed architecture, in

158. *Giza. Pyramids, from east; right to left, Cheops, Chephren, Mycerinus. Fourth Dynasty, 2550–2480 B.C.*

◁ 159. *Giza. Valley temple of Chephren's pyramid complex; passage leading from antechamber to T-shaped hypostyle hall. Fourth Dynasty, c. 2520 B.C.*

160. *Giza. Plan of temples in Chephren's pyramid complex: above, veneration temple adjoining pyramid; below, valley temple*

which bundled plants were used as structural supports, and in their stone form they stand for the sun god, the divine myths, and the burial practices of Buto. On the axis of the sanctuary, at the base of the pyramid, another cult edifice with a vaulted ceiling was introduced; its false door, a Lower Egyptian element, displaced the Upper Egyptian offering place with steles that had originated at Abydos.

The decoration of the interior gives "cosmic" significance to the chambers of the Fifth Dynasty temples. Ceilings are painted blue with golden stars to represent the night sky; floors of black basalt represent the dark earth from which sprout plants in the form of columns.

The creative development of monumental tomb architecture came to an end with the close of the Fifth Dynasty. The mortuary temples of the kings of the Sixth Dynasty adhere strictly to the established plan and return to the closed structure and abstract pillars of an earlier period.

This change in the architectural organization and design of the royal tomb complexes of the Old Kingdom is not to be understood as a "stylistic mutation." Each complex shows individual planning. Upper and Lower Egyptian influences are interwoven as principal themes; in the course of development the relationships among chambers, halls, and passages are dissolved and the elements reshuffled. The architectural historian must take these complexes "apart again at the joints" and explain them as changes in "thematic functions." These functions are recognizable in the Pyramid Texts that first appear on the walls of the passages and tomb chambers in the pyramids from the late Fifth Dynasty. In their arrangement, progressing from the entrance to the heart of the pyramid, they correspond to the successive features of the valley temple, causeway, and pyramid temple. Thus the architectural development of the pyramid complexes becomes a sublime manifestation of continually changing rites and eschatological beliefs, and in these one can discern the spiritual tensions of the epoch and the clashes of contending principles and forces.

*Temples of the Old Kingdom*

Of the Old Kingdom sanctuaries of the gods at Memphis, nothing has survived. The only sanctuary of that period still standing is the temple of Qasr el Sagha, north of the Faiyum. On the basis of its construction of massive limestone blocks it probably belongs to the Fourth Dynasty; its plan is scarcely distinguishable from that of the sanctuaries of the pyramid temples. The seven shrines of the gods once worshiped here stand side by

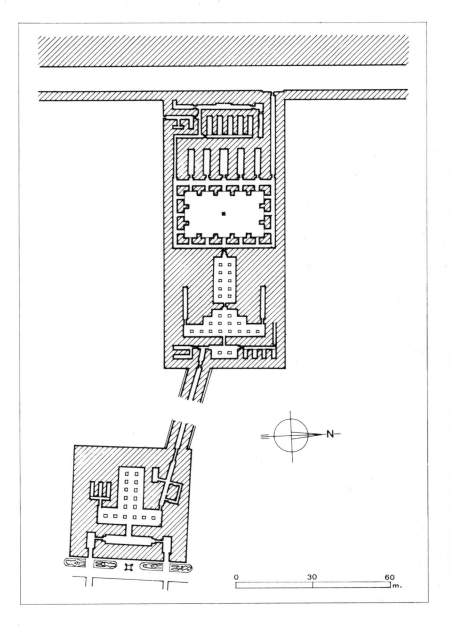

161. *Giza. Valley temple of Chephren's pyramid complex; transversal area of T-shaped hypostyle hall*

162. *Giza. Valley temple of Chephren's pyramid complex; longitudinal area of T-shaped hypostyle hall (statues of the king once stood against the walls)* ▷

163. *Giza. Pyramid of Chephren, Great Sphinx of Chephren, and pyramid of Cheops, from southeast* ▷

side on a raised platform. Each shrine concealed a cult image behind doors that could be opened and closed, and is bordered by a molding and crowned by a concave cornice. The row of shrines opens on a narrow passage bounded on the other side by the thick front wall of the building. In the middle of this wall, opposite the large central shrine of the principal deity, is the entrance to the temple. Small rooms on the two short sides of the sanctuary probably served for storing ritual accessories. No inscription reveals the names of the gods to whom this temple was dedicated.

### The Sun Sanctuaries

It is possible that in the Old Kingdom the national gods had their shrines in the imposing mortuary temples of the kings and were included in an established cult. The growing influence of the sun god has already been mentioned, and the sun sanctuaries closely connected with the royal tombs are, in the area of the capital, the only temples of which enough is preserved for a plausible reconstruction. For these temples, too, in which the day star was worshiped, there was no established architectural composition; it was determined by the evolving theological system of the sun cult.

Just north of Chephren's valley temple at Giza lie the remains of a monumental temple on the axis of the Great Sphinx immediately to the west (Plates 164–65). This temple of the Sphinx was dedicated to Harmakhis, or "Horus at the horizon," according to a New Kingdom inscription. The massive structure with sloping walls and concave cornices is accurately aligned with the four points of the compass. The outer and inner walls and the pillars of the inner court are faced with granite blocks, the smaller pillars and roof beams surrounding the court are granite monoliths. As in Chephren's valley temple, two entrances from the east lead into the building, emerging in the north and south pillared halls of the court, which is narrow and on a precise north-south axis. In front of the broad pillars surrounding the court extant remains indicate that seated figures of Chephren were placed there. The design of this unique building showed on the long east and west sides of the court a several-stepped niche, provided in each case with a row of six pillars and, nearer, a row of two. The ambulatories on the short north and south sides, in a modification of the original plan, were widened by another row of six pillars each.

The niche in the west wall is aligned with the Sphinx behind, which as "Horus at the horizon" equates the dead king with the evening sun; the eastern niche indicates due east, toward Horus

164. *Giza. Pyramid complex of Chephren: plan of Harmakhis temple, valley temple, and Sphinx*
1) *Terrace of Sphinx.* 2) *Temple of Amenhotep.* 3) *Rock-cut tomb.* 4) *Temple of Harmakhis.* 5) *Valley temple of Chephren*

165. *Giza. Great Sphinx of Chephren and remains of Harmakhis temple, from east (behind, left and right: pyramids of Mycerinus and Chephren)* ▷

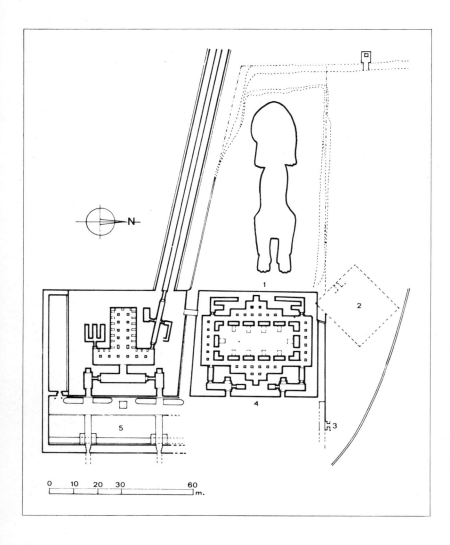

166. *Giza. Pyramid complex of Chephren: Great Sphinx, from northeast*

167. *Giza. "Buto type" tomb complex of Queen Khent-kaw-s. End of Fourth Dynasty, c. 2450 B.C.*

168. *Abusir. Pyramid complex of Sahura, valley temple in foreground. Fifth Dynasty, c. 2440 B.C.*

169. *Abusir. Plan of pyramid complex of Sahura*
*1, 2) Arrival points at valley temple. 3) Covered passage. 4) Entrance. 5) Court.*
*6) Statue room. 7) Sanctuary. 8) Entrance to funerary chamber in pyramid.*
*9) Subsidiary pyramid*

170. *Abusir. Reconstruction of sun sanctuary of Ne-user-ra. Fifth Dynasty, c. 2370 B.C.*

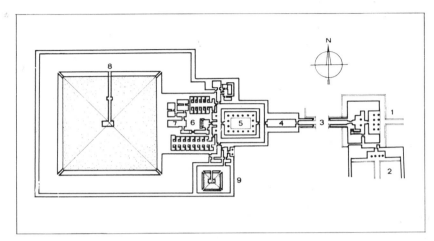

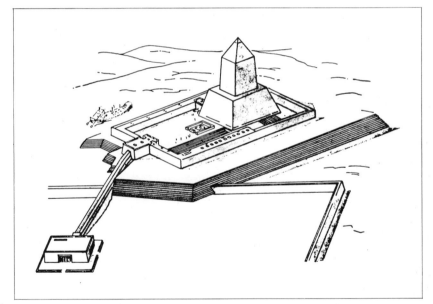

171. *Aswan, west bank of Nile. Tomb complexes, including causeways and double tomb of nomarchs Sabni and Medhu. Sixth Dynasty, c. 2250 B.C.*

reappearing as the morning sun. The twenty-four pillars in the four ambulatories constitute an allusion to the sun's daily journey. The two pairs of pillars in the niches probably represent the four pillars of the sky. The Harmakhis temple is therefore a monument and holy place of the sun god in the person of Horus, with whose disappearance in the evening the king was identified in the Sphinx and upon whose cyclical return every morning the king based his hopes of continued existence through eternity.

On the rim of the western desert, just north of their pyramids at Abusir, the kings of the Fifth Dynasty built sun sanctuaries of which two have so far been cleared. They were "monuments of the living king to his father Ra," and, after the death of their builders, probably served for the worship of that god, source of the perpetual renewal of both nature and the kingdom. As an architectural type, these temples constitute a special form that would seem to go back to the sanctuary of the sun god Ra in Heliopolis; the original model was probably a "primeval hill" with a monumental pillar, the benben stone. The first of these sanctuaries of the sun, built by the founder of the Fifth Dynasty, King Weserkaf, was made of brick; King Ne-user-ra built his of limestone (Plate 170). It had an obelisk about 120 feet tall, constructed of white limestone blocks, and this stood on a sixty-foot-high granite-faced base with sloping walls on the west side of the court. The walled court was surrounded inside by a walled corridor. From the entrance on the east the portico ran along the south wall to the base of the obelisk, and from there interior ramps led to an upper platform in front of the east side of the base. In the court, in front of the obelisk base, open-air sacrifices were offered on a big altar built of massive alabaster blocks; north of the altar was an area where the sacrificial animals were slaughtered. Outside the sanctuary, to the south, are the brick foundations for a solar boat. The situation of the sun sanctuaries on the desert plateau made it necessary to build a valley temple with a causeway leading to the high ground, like those associated with the royal tombs.

The hieroglyphs for the names of the individual sun sanctuaries of the earlier Fifth Dynasty show only the base, whereas the later ones include an obelisk as well. In the Old Kingdom the obelisk is relatively thick in shape; in the Middle Kingdom and particularly in the beginning of the New Kingdom it became more slender and was made a feature of the architecture, generally paired in front of the pylons of the temple. It is derived from the Heliopolitan monumental pillar, the benben stone, the resting place of the sun. In the Old Kingdom, under the influence of the same abstracting tendencies that led to the true

172. *West Thebes. Tomb complex of Djar, broad court and pillared vestibule in manner of older princely tombs. Eleventh Dynasty, c. 2050 B.C.*

173. *Deir el Bahari (West Thebes). View from east: left, mortuary temple of Neb-hepet-ra Mentuhotep (Eleventh Dynasty, c. 2050 B.C.); right, funerary temple of Hatshepsut.(Eighteenth Dynasty, c. 1480 B.C.)* ▷

174. *Deir el Bahari (West Thebes). View from southeast: foreground, mortuary temple of Neb-hepet-ra Mentuhotep (Eleventh Dynasty, c. 2050 B.C.); beyond, newly excavated mortuary temple of Tuthmosis III (Eighteenth Dynasty, c. 1470 B.C.); toward right, funerary temple of Hatshepsut (Eighteenth Dynasty, c. 1480 B.C.* ▷

pyramid, it acquired the geometrical shape of a square tapering pillar with a pyramidal apex. Today of the Heliopolitan sanctuary only the sixty-five foot granite obelisk of Sesostris I still stands (see Plate 181). However, we shall have occasion to mention Heliopolis again in connection with the planning of the temple of Amon-Ra at Karnak during the New Kingdom and, above all, the temple complexes at Amarna of the sun worshiper Akhenaten.

*Tombs of the Royal Officials and Provincial Tombs*

Just as the smaller graves of the courtiers were disposed around royal tombs (see Plates 141, 143) in the cemeteries of the unifiers of Upper and Lower Egypt and their successors, at Memphis and Abydos, so in the later epochs the high state officials were buried near the tombs of their masters. In the Old Kingdom these dignitaries were typically buried in "mastabas," monumental tumulus tombs with sloping exterior walls, first built of brick but before long of squared limestone blocks. In the interior of this mass were first created—starting with the "door niche" as the offering place (false door)—narrow cult places, which were gradually widened into cult chambers; by the end of the development, in the tombs of the viziers of the Sixth Dynasty, these took over the entire core of the mastaba. During the Old Kingdom the offering place with the false door underwent many changes. The mastaba was also influenced by domestic architecture, as exemplified by the narrow pillared halls at the entrance or around the courts that preceded the tomb. Certain elements, such as the statuary shrines for the statue cult, were clearly borrowed from the royal tombs. In its spatial planning the mastaba has an evolution parallel to that of the royal mortuary temple during the Fifth and Sixth Dynasties; the plan was continually being revised and adapted to conform to changes in the requirements of the cult.

Tomb-building practices outside the capital, in the nomes of Middle and Upper Egypt, had a decisive effect on the course of Egyptian monumental architecture. They were controlled by the local governors or nomarchs, a feudal nobility, who, starting as mere servants of the king, had become increasingly independent with the weakening of centralized power. In Middle and Upper Egypt the boundary between desert and fertile land is often marked by sharply rising ground; sometimes steep cliffs actually form the bank of the river, and the provincial tombs are mostly carved out of the living rock high up the cliff face (Plate 171). Their cult chambers and furnishings were patterned after the prototypes at the royal capital. The sequence of a forecourt in

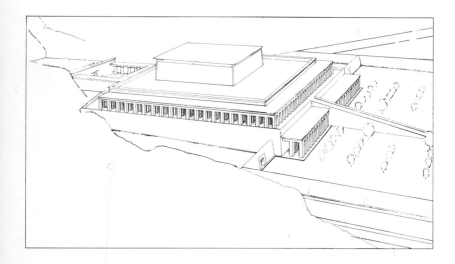

175. *Deir el Bahari (West Thebes). Reconstruction of mortuary temple of Neb-hepet-ra Mentuhotep*
176. *Deir el Bahari (West Thebes). Mortuary temple of Neb-hepet-ra Mentuhotep, from northwest*

front of the rock-hewn tomb facade, a screened entrance hall supported by pillars, and a causeway was dictated by the physical nature of the site; in the provinces the burial arrangements may show many variations.

At Thebes, loose sediments form low hills between the river and the western cliffs. Here, as part of the tomb complexes of the local princes, huge courts could be excavated on an east-west axis: before the narrow west end of the court an open hall of stout pillars was carved out of the poor rock nearby (Plate 172); from the center aisle of this hall a level passage was tunneled westward to a cult chamber; the shaft went from here to the sarcophagus chamber. The retinue of the Theban prince was buried in separate graves in the side walls of the court.

## THE MIDDLE KINGDOM

### Neb-hepet-ra Mentuhotep's Mortuary Temple at Thebes (Deir el Bahari)

The collapse of the Old Kingdom was followed by a lengthy period of turmoil and internal disorder, during which no monumental buildings were erected. About 2050 B.C. Neb-hepet-ra Mentuhotep, a member of one of the princely houses of Thebes, succeeded in reuniting the Two Kingdoms. Thebes became temporarily the royal capital. On the east bank of the Nile, near the principal sanctuary from which later grew the temple complex of Karnak (page 127), lay the city with its palace, administrative buildings, and residential quarters. On the opposite (west) bank the dead had been buried since time immemorial at the foot of impressive cliffs.

King Mentuhotep, founder of the Middle Kingdom, chose for his mortuary temple and burial place the edge of a valley leading into these western cliffs and ending in a sheer wall of solid rock (Deir el Bahari; Plates 173–76). This deep basin was probably already sacred to Hathor, goddess of the dead. Mentuhotep's mortuary temple is the first known monumental building in Upper Egypt and in Thebes. As a royal tomb and center for the worship of the king and the Theban gods, it had to give prominence to the new dynastic order under the leadership of Thebes. The fabric of the temple has suffered severely from subsequent exploitation as a stone quarry and from rockslides. The design was strongly axial, leading from the edge of the fertile land to the tomb chamber of the king deep within the cliff. The facade faced east, toward the sanctuary of Karnak, where the cult of Amon can be traced back to the rise of Thebes. As in the royal mortuary complexes of Memphis, here too a valley temple (not

preserved) gave access to a walled causeway that ascended to a broad walled court, terminating in the temple area abutting the western cliff. The final stretch of the approach to the temple was flanked by sycamores and tamarisks.

The temple itself stood on a raised terrace carved from the living rock; access from the court was by a massive central ramp. The base of the terrace was fronted with double porticoes on either side of this ramp. On the terrace was a broad freestanding building, square in plan, and upon it an elongated structure that extended west into the cliffside. The square structure had a massive core with sloping walls, pillared galleries ("ambulatories") on all four sides, and an outer ring of thick battered enclosing walls. Like the east face of the terrace, these walls were fronted by porticoes on east, north, and south. The openness of this architecture probably goes back to the earlier Theban princely tombs.

The western part of the temple was primarily dedicated to the worship of the dead ruler. Here was the entrance to the tomb chamber, in the floor of a small columned court that separated the "fore-temple" from the mortuary temple proper. The latter consisted of a wide hall, whose flat roof was supported by ten rows of eight columns, the oldest known hypostyle hall of any size in Egyptian architectural history. The holy of holies was a rock-cut chamber opening off the west side of this hall.

The design of the mortuary temple of King Mentuhotep is one of the most independent in Egyptian architecture. Since it was first discovered the assumption has been that the massive core structure at the east end of the terrace was once topped by a pyramid that rose above the flat roofs of the ambulatories and the outer walls, and this is the reconstruction found in all the histories of Egyptian art and architecture. Only recently, through the efforts of D. Arnold, has the underlying religious and lordly conception of the temple become apparent. According to Arnold, the core structure is a reflection of a primitive sanctuary excavated beneath the Monthu temple of Medamud (near Thebes), interpreted as the primeval abode of the deity Monthu-Ra worshiped in the Theban region and thus as a monumentalized "primeval hill." In the exercise of his authority on earth and in death the king had close ties with this local creator god. Mentuhotep's hypostyle hall carved out of the western cliff was devoted to the cult of the king, living and dead, and of the god Amon-Ra of Karnak; this is the first hint of the intimate relationship between the ruler and Amon-Ra that was to play so large a part in the New Kingdom mortuary temples at Thebes.

Beneath the core structure lies the dummy tomb of the king,

178. Beni Hasan. Cult chamber of rock tomb of Prince Kheti. Eleventh Dynasty, c. 2000 B.C.
179. Aswan, west bank of Nile. Rock tomb of Prince Sirenpowet II. Twelfth Dynasty, c. 1870 B.C.

180. Beni Hasan. Triple-aisled cult chamber, rock tomb of Prince Amenemhat; from statue niche toward entrance. Twelfth Dynasty, c. 1950 B.C. ▷

reached from the forecourt (Bab el Hosan), an Osiris tomb with which the plantings in the court were presumably related. The statues of the king in long festive robes, found in the broad temple courtyard, signify the earthly and eternal celebration of his royal jubilee and the perpetual rebirth of the ruler and the dynastic order that he embodied.

In Arnold's interpretation, which is consistent with the surviving fragments of the wall reliefs, Mentuhotep's mortuary temple was newly shaped by a theology and a conception of kingship that had developed from local Theban traditions. It was a unique creation representing influences that emerged in modified form in the terracing of the Twelfth Dynasty princely tombs of Qaw el Kebir and, some five hundred years later, in Hatshepsut's temple complex, its close neighbor to the north.

### The Pyramid Complexes of the Twelfth Dynasty Kings

The kings of the Twelfth Dynasty also came from Thebes, but for political reasons they transferred their residence back to Memphis. At the same time, they retained a particular affection for Thebes and adorned the nome with temples; after Memphis, Thebes became the most important religious center. South of Memphis, near Lisht and Dahshur, and farther south at Lahun and Hawara, on the edge of the Faiyum (an area that the kings of the late Twelfth Dynasty opened up for farming), lie the royal tombs built again in accordance with Memphite tradition, in the form of pyramids with mortuary temples. Only the tomb monument of Sesostris I near Lisht has enough architectural and sculptural remains to permit a plausible reconstruction. The plan of the mortuary temple is reminiscent of the pyramid complexes of the later Old Kingdom during the Sixth Dynasty. The pyramids of the Middle Kingdom have neither the height nor the solidity of those built of squared stone blocks in the Old Kingdom. The position of kingship had changed, and confidence in the massiveness of tombs as a means of ensuring the continuance of eternal existence had been shaken by the political upheavals of the First Intermediate Period; also social changes had occurred that meant the labor resources of the entire country were no longer at the disposal of the Twelfth Dynasty kings.

Amenemhat I, founder of the Twelfth Dynasty, plundered the mortuary temples of Cheops and other kings of the Old Kingdom for granite blocks to build his own pyramid. All the pyramids of this period exhibit new techniques that are saving of both labor and materials. Their cores consisted either of sand and rubble, the mass held together by a radiating system of rub-

ble walls, or entirely of sun-dried brick. Only the outer sides of the pyramids were carefully faced with white limestone slabs, and the apex was sometimes of dark granite. On the other hand, as compared with the Old Kingdom, greater resources were diverted toward safeguarding the royal tomb itself by the most solid possible construction for the sarcophagus chamber, sometimes hollowed from an immense monolith, and by blind corridors to defeat tomb robbers.

The most important of the mortuary temple complexes, that of Amenemhat III at Hawara, was known to the Greeks as the "labyrinth." Herodotus (*Histories,* II, 148) and Strabo (*Geography,* XVII, 1, 37) are among the ancient authors who have left descriptions of this enormous structure, of which almost nothing now remains. Attempts to reconstruct it exclusively on the basis of these accounts have been only partially successful.

## Provincial Burials of the Twelfth Dynasty Nomarchs

Apart from its kings, the Twelfth Dynasty also had its feudal nobility, the princely families of Middle and Upper Egypt who constituted an influential and largely independent power. Near their provincial capitals on the gently or steeply sloping flanks of the hills that fringed the Nile Valley they also built rock tombs, some of which vied in lavishness, spaciousness, and independence of design with the mortuary complexes of the kings. Because of their excellent state of preservation they add greatly to our understanding of the tomb architecture of the period.

The rock tombs at Beni Hasan in Middle Egypt reflect the Lower Egyptian concept of the tomb as a representative eternal "abode" and "residence" of the dead. The rock chamber of one of the older tombs is furnished with papyrus-bundle columns (Plates 177, 178), and represents a "festival hall" that may have existed—built of less permanent materials—in the palaces of the princes. The entrances often lie beneath an open porch of a kind also found in the contemporary houses of the nobility. In the later princely tombs at Beni Hasan a stricter emphasis on cult requirements and royal prototypes produced a deep, axially oriented, three-aisled rock chamber (Plate 180). The sections of ceiling between the longitudinal architraves are flat vaults, and rest on polygonal pillars; exactly opposite the entrance in the rear wall of the middle aisle stands a niche containing the statue of the owner of the tomb. The vaulted ceilings over the three aisles are painted with elements characteristic of the tentlike festival halls, colorful carpet patterns and simulated wooden ribs, whose perishable counterparts have not survived.

Upper Egyptian ideology, on the other hand, corresponds to the abstraction of architectural forms, and serves only the ceremonial fulfillment of the cult along a strong axially directed spatial sequence. The tomb of Prince Sirenpowet II on the west bank near Aswan (Plate 179) is a grandiose example of the axial plan oriented strictly east and west. From the lofty three-aisled entrance hall, with its flat ceiling and square pillars, one continues westward over low steps that lead to a long passageway with a low-vaulted roof, ending in the cult chamber. The floor of this passageway sinks by imperceptible degrees to permit sunlight to pass through the tall entrance door into the cult chamber and fall on the richly painted sanctuary with the statue of the deceased. In their architectural plan and articulation, the most highly developed of the princely tombs are those at Qaw el Kebir (east bank, south of Assiut). From a broad columned forehall built of brick at the foot of the hill a covered causeway led up to the mortuary complexes; these are in many stories that overlap the slopes, and through open stairways the cliff spaces are linked with screened forecourts, pillared halls, and sanctuaries in wide hollowed-out halls. This is the articulation of the royal mortuary temple adapted to the exigencies of a hillside site. The resemblance, moreover, is not merely external; the thematic correspondence of the sequences of rooms and the furnishings with those of the royal tombs extends even to the details.

## The Temples

From the Middle Kingdom there are more important remains of temples than from the Old Kingdom. They were frequently, even in the Twelfth Dynasty, still constructed of brick, and through later renovations in stone their remains, though widely scattered throughout the land, are scanty indeed and often insufficient to permit an intelligible reconstruction of the plans. Nonetheless, it is clear from the little that survives that the architecture of the Middle Kingdom put into effect certain new ideas that were to have a decisive influence on the future organization of the sanctuaries of the gods. One might mention the sanctuaries that now appeared for the first time in temples in the neighborhood of Thebes, at Medamud (northeast of Karnak) and Tod (south of Luxor): these had closing doors at front and rear and were approached through a broad hall of pillars or columns. They served, like later examples from the Eighteenth Dynasty, as permanent or temporary repositories for the images of the gods and their barges, and indicate that these images were carried in procession to other sanctuaries inside and outside their own temple. An unusual feature of the small temple built by Amenemhat III and IV on the edge of the Faiyum at Medinet

Madi is the antechamber supported by two papyrus-bundle columns between side walls extended to the front to protect the entrance. Inside, the arrangement of the three shrines for the statues of the gods honors a tradition going back to the time of the pyramids.

The two-towered "pylon," so characteristic of the monumental entrances of the walled temples after the beginning of the New Kingdom, has its origins in the Middle Kingdom, as excavations at Hermopolis have shown. The pylon towers were probably the end result of a process of thickening and raising the front walls of large courts on either side of a lower entrance gate. The gate towers ("pylons") have battered walls on all sides, beaded fillets at the corners, and an encircling concave cornice at the top. In the front walls are narrow recesses, varying in number, and on holidays these contained tall masts with colorful pennants (see Plate 216). The masts were steadied by wooden braces projecting from narrow window openings high above the recesses. Inside the pylons stairs led to the upper rooms and the flat roof. Between the two gate towers was sandwiched the lower main portal of the temple, also crowned with a concave cornice. In late texts the pylons are designated as the "hills of the horizon," between which the sun rises. The late identification of the two gate towers with the goddesses Isis and Nephthys probably derives from the mythological concept that these two goddesses bear up the rising sun in their arms.

The pylons give the temple facade and its entrance portal a strong accent and unique monumentality. At the same time, their fortress-like aspect clearly expresses the idea of the defense of the temple entrance against all hostile powers. Accordingly, from the Nineteenth Dynasty on, the kings recorded their victorious battles, or the god's bestowal of a victory-promising weapon, on the outer walls of the pylons (see Plate 230). Against the two narrow sides or the rear of the pylons abutted the walls that enclosed the temple.

In the New Kingdom paired obelisks were often erected in front of the pylons, one on either side of the temple entrance (see Plate 213). A single obelisk, originally symbolizing the resting place of the sun god, was first erected of limestone blocks in the Fifth Dynasty sun sanctuaries (page 102). Since the Old Kingdom the center for the worship of the sun god Ra had been the sanctuary at Heliopolis, the site of the "primeval hill" with the benben stone, which had established the pattern for the Old Kingdom sanctuaries of the sun (see Plate 170). At the beginning of the Twelfth Dynasty Sesostris I had a rectangular temple built over the low roundish sacred primeval hill of Heliopolis.

Of this building one of the two sixty-five-foot rose-granite monolithic obelisks that once flanked the main entrance is all that still stands (Plate 181). This pair of obelisks also suggests an entrance portal between gate towers, of which, however, nothing at Heliopolis has survived. Excavations there have merely established the east-west orientation of the temple and an avenue of sphinxes that led from the bank of the Nile to the main gate. A few clues to the former appearance of Heliopolis, this important sanctuary and theological center, are supplied by the fragments of a stone tablet of the seventh century B.C., now in the Museo Egizio in Turin, bearing traces of an incised temple plan. The reconstruction shows an axial succession of three courts, each entered through a portal between gate towers. Tall flagpoles rise above the pylons of the first court, while those of the third court may have been preceded by a pair of obelisks. In the second court pillared galleries are indicated along the side walls; an adjacent sanctuary on the right has been included in the court for lack of space at the right edge of the tablet. In the third court a transverse row of pillars cuts off a narrower area in the front where, against the side wall on the right, a mighty altar is built, reached by two short flights of steps.

Open courts entered through a portal between gate towers are also characteristic of the temple of Karnak, dedicated to Amon-Ra, whose expansion dates from the beginning of the New Kingdom. This is particularly true of the core of the sanctuary, which Tuthmosis I enclosed with walls, and of the south axis of the temple developed by his successors. An altar in an open court for the worship of the Heliopolitan sun god Ra-Harakhte has been preserved on the north side of the upper terrace of Queen Hatshepsut's temple at Deir el Bahari; there was another at Karnak. The sanctuary of Heliopolis was most faithfully copied under Amenhotep IV (Akhenaten), introducer of the exclusive cult of the day star (Aten), in the Aten sanctuary at Karnak and, above all, in the Aten temples of the new capital Akhetaten (Tell el Amarna).

An early Twelfth Dynasty sanctuary, richly adorned with delicate reliefs, was dismantled into blocks and used as fill in the building of the third pylon of the temple of Karnak. The parts have since been fully reconstructed; it is the "White Chapel" of Sesostris I, which the king built on the occasion of his jubilee for Amon of Thebes and Min of Coptos, the fertility god assimilated by Amon. This almost square pavilion (Plate 182) stands on a low podium accessible at either end by ramps between low stairsteps. The building rests on four angle pillars with round fillets at the outer corners, and on two intermediate pillars on each side;

these support architraves and a flat roof crowned with a concave cornice. Between the pillars the spaces, except for the two entranceways, are bridged by low parapets rounded on top. Inside, a small rectangular space is formed by four pillars, and in the center is a granite pedestal on which stood an image of the king or the god. The "White Chapel" may be regarded as the oldest surviving example of a "baldachin temple" (page 79), representing in stone and in monumentalized forms the ancient shrine beneath an awning.

The Middle Kingdom also shows the first appearance of "Osiris statues" in an architectural context. In these the ruler is portrayed in a standing position, entirely swathed in a close-fitting garment that even covers the feet and leaves only the hands free to clasp the scepters in a crossed position over the breast; Osiris, the god of death, is similarly portrayed in his cult images and other representations. At the mortuary temple of Sesostris I at Lisht such approximately lifesize statues flanked the probably unroofed approach to the temple, and thus they represented the king, with the crown of Upper or Lower Egypt on his head, as Osiris "risen." A colossal statue of the same king and the same type stood within the temple precinct of the god Osiris at Abydos; it was probably propped against a pillar and belonged as architectural sculpture to an open court of that temple. In the New Kingdom, after the beginning of the Eighteenth Dynasty statues on the same colossal scale appeared in front of interior walls, or before pillars of open halls around the wider courts, to provide architectural accents as well as to illustrate the functions of the building. They relate to the jubilee festival that the king usually celebrated at the end of the thirtieth year of his reign—that is, as an aging ruler. In these ceremonies were renewed the king's powers over the stage of a ritual death as Osiris, to permit his rebirth as Horus.

The architecture of the Middle Kingdom contributed many new forms to the design of sanctuaries, despite the paucity of its remains, and these the much more important architecture of the New Kingdom was quite willing to exploit.

## INTERIOR SPACES AND SUPPORTS

Egyptian stone architecture began with imitative building forms, with three-dimensional representations of constructed types developed to serve the royal cult of the dead at the time of the first unification of Upper and Lower Egyptian traditions. The dummy buildings of King Zoser's mortuary precinct, translations into stone of tents and structures of matting and brick that were furnishings of the Memphis residence for use in the afterlife, can be converted back into the original building method according to their construction features. In Zoser's capital tent and matting buildings had already been translated into more durable brick while preserving their typical outward appearance. The "sacristy" in the king's mortuary precinct, as an imitation brick building with interior spaces, shows the characteristic spatial division of a brick house: the rooms are narrow, based on the spans and carrying capacity of the palm trunks which formed the flat roof. Posts are used sparingly.

In granite block construction the mortuary temple complexes of the pyramids had, since Cheops, been characterized by roofed multi-aisled halls from which opened courts and antechambers, whose flat stone ceilings were supported on square pillars. The monumental halls, passages, and courts were intended for rites celebrated at "way stations" on a processional route within the massive walls of the valley and pyramid temples. This arrangement of wide spaces articulated by rows of pillars, and courts with colossal royal statues placed before the pillars, is far removed from the old idea of a "residence." Granite block construction imposes its own imperatives of building statics and mathematics. But what origin has this conception of space?

Obviously, it was the system of supports of the tent palace, monumentally reproduced in brick and wood, that first prompted the unlimited increase of piers supporting the roof to create broad spaces in stone construction. The flat roofs of the stone buildings go back to the typical system of the brick house, palm trunks laid across architraves supported on wood posts.

Flat terrace roofs are characteristic of Egyptian monumental architecture, from the Old Kingdom to the buildings of the last Pharaohs. The roofs were reached by stairs from the inside of the building and were also often involved in the cult ritual. This type of roof, screened from view by continuing the exterior walls upward to form a parapet, was made possible by the minimal rainfall of the climate, even in the north of the country, but some provision had still to be made for drainage. The roof was given a slight pitch to deflect water from the occasional rainstorms into a system of gutters and outlets in the parapet walls; from the Fifth Dynasty until the end of the Late Period the waterspouts took the form of the foreparts of a lion. These lions were supported on regularly spaced blocks projecting far out from the face of the wall at roof level and the water flowed from between their outstretched paws (see Plate 234). As an integral part of architectural sculpture, these Egyptian lions are the equivalent of the lion-head waterspouts on Greek temples—probably borrowed from Egypt. The Egyptians saw a close connection between the lion, as lord of the desert, and the storms that blew in from the desert to strike the Nile Valley, and it also represented an apotropaic power, warding off evil from these indispensable openings in the temple walls.

In the Old Kingdom the pillar occurs in its original abstract square form without base or bearing slab (abacus). Not until the early Middle Kingdom were the edges shaved off to make it an eight- or sixteen-sided shaft, standing on a flat round base and supporting the architrave on an abacus. Thus the polygonal pillar is an approximation of the column form. Eventually the narrow vertical faces of the sixteen-sided pillar were fluted, thus continuing the tradition of the fluted supports in King Zoser's tent- and brick-style buildings, traceable to wood prototypes.

Occasionally in the Fourth Dynasty and more commonly in the Fifth, "plant columns" of various kinds began to be used in stone architecture for the support of beams. Within the royal mortuary temples they not only took over the functions of the abstract pillar but had their own thematic significance in the architectural scheme, now modified by the new solar religion; they also had their particular message recalling the prototypes in Egyptian mythology.

The idea of using bundled plant stems as supports goes back to prehistoric construction of light mat-buildings, a technique by which herdsmen and birdcatchers build their huts even in historic times.

Plant columns came to be the most usual type of support in Egyptian monumental architecture, and not only in sacred buildings of stone but also in houses and palaces, where, with no mythological reference, they are cut from wood and stand on stone bases, supporting wooden ceiling beams. Finally, plant forms must also be the origin of the fluted masts in the facade of the stone reproduction of a tent building in Zoser's mortuary precinct, and certainly of the leaflike form at the top on either side of the roof rib (see Plate 148). Apotropaic horns were inserted in the fronts of these masts (see Plate 138c). The two round bosses near the top of the masts, to be interpreted as stylized sawn-off branches, show that the memory was still fresh of the plant stems of the prehistoric tent structures, and of their translation into pine poles in the monumental royal tent.

The three-sided papyrus-topped stalks with open bell-shaped flowers (see Plate 151), that represent supports in the facade of the building branching off the tent hall at right angles, may likewise have originated in wood construction. They are symbolical in character. In stone construction, as plant columns without a plinth, they represent the heraldic plant of Lower Egypt,

comparable in this function to the granite heraldic pillars in Tuthmosis III's "hall of annals" in the temple of Karnak (see Plate 196), the northern pillar decorated with three papyrus stems in painted high relief, while the southern one bears the lily-like plant of Upper Egypt.

Columns in the shape of an individual papyrus plant, with rounded shaft and an open bloom for the capital, appear for the first time in the Eighteenth Dynasty under Amenhotep III in the long entrance hall of the temple of Luxor (see Plate 214). Like all Egyptian plant columns they carry the heavy architrave on an abacus (Plate 183), but in the case of the papyrus column with an overhanging bell-shaped flower capital, and similarly in the palm-tree column, the abacus is so small in proportion that it almost disappears behind the spread of the capital. The free-growing plant with its mythological connotations determined the form, not its supporting function within the structure.

The palm column (Plate 183a) does not actually represent the tree; around the top of the circular, only slightly tapering shaft are bound eight palm fronds. The turns of the binding, with the loop end hanging down, are unmistakably reproduced. The tips of the individual fronds are rounded and curve gently outward. The abacus, so small that it cannot be seen from below, nestles in the center of the cluster of fronds. The palm column, too, stands on a flat round base. The form unites several different ideas in its meaning. In early representations palms surrounding a designated place indicate the buildings of the Lower Egyptian prehistoric royal cemetery at Buto. In ancient times stakes driven into the desert soil, and probably bound around with palm fronds, represent the holy place as the setting for burial ceremonies in front of royal Memphite tumuli. The palm, however, is also the seat of the sun god, and in the mortuary temples of the Fifth Dynasty it alludes directly to the mythical relationship between the tree and the god. It was also reserved as a heraldic plant of Upper Egypt, and for this reason palm columns were used in the royal palaces and in temple chambers set apart for the royal cult.

The lotus column (Plate 183c) likewise makes its first appearance in stone form during the Fifth Dynasty. It represents the stylization of a bundle of six lotus stalks that spring without swelling or shrinking from the round base to the flower capital, beneath which they are tied together. Six buds, only slightly open, stretch steeply upward to form the capital, on which rests a sturdy-looking abacus. Six small stalks with opening buds are inserted into the binding between the main stalks. In the realm of myth the lotus, too, was closely related to the sun god, who

## 183. Principal forms of Egyptian columns
*a) Palm column. b) Papyrus-bundle column. c) Lotus column. d) "Tent pole" column.*
*e) Papyrus column with open bud*

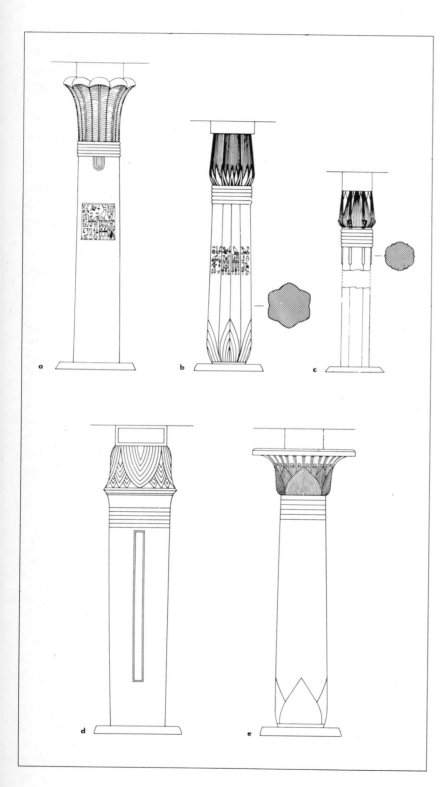

emerged from the primeval flood on a lotus blossom and rejoiced in its fragrance.

The papyrus-bundle column (Plate 183b) occurs much more frequently, and is related in form to the lotus column. Its first examples in monumental stone are also in the Fifth Dynasty. Eight three-sided stalks swell from their sheaths at the base of the column and taper up to the bands beneath the capital, consisting of eight closed buds that support the abacus as in the lotus column. Here, too, smaller stalks are tucked into the binding between the main stalks. From early times until the Eighteenth Dynasty each papyrus stalk was modeled to display its triangular front edge (see Plate 214); under the Ramessids the column shaft was unified by suppressing the stalks (see Plate 206).

Papyrus-bundle columns in the halls of the temples represent, according to a late temple inscription, the primeval landscape of the Nile Valley, "a papyrus thicket" in which the god walked. As elements of the world created by the gods, all the plant columns belong to the "cosmic" theme of the temple. They sprout from their low round bases like plants from the "primeval hill"; above them spreads the flat roof painted with golden stars on a dark blue ground to represent the night sky. Plant designs on the lower strips of the temple walls complete the meaning of the temple as an untouched divine creation where the gods could be thought to dwell. Likewise the closed bud capitals of the lotus and papyrus columns may symbolize the night, from which the temple and its inhabiting god are aroused in the morning rites.

A column of a special sort is the Hathor column, of Middle Kingdom origin. It was restricted to sanctuaries of the goddess Hathor and goddesses associated with her, and represents the goddess' rod-shaped fetish which was also carried in procession on festival occasions. The round shaft bears as its capital the masklike face of the goddess, her long hair framing her features and the lower ends curling behind her bovine ears; on her head she bears the "sistrum," a musical rattle that was sounded in her worship. The face of Hathor with its sistrum crown often decorates both front and back of the capital or even all four sides (see Plate 244).

The stone "tent pole" column (Plates 183d, 200, 201) is known only from the great festival hall of Tuthmosis III in the temple of Karnak. In it are copied the slim wooden poles that supported the canopy over the royal throne, translated into stone forms. Tuthmosis III, to mark his jubilee, set up columns of this type in a court surrounded by pillared galleries to transform the area into a tentlike festival hall (page 130).

To these supports should be added the eight- and sixteen-

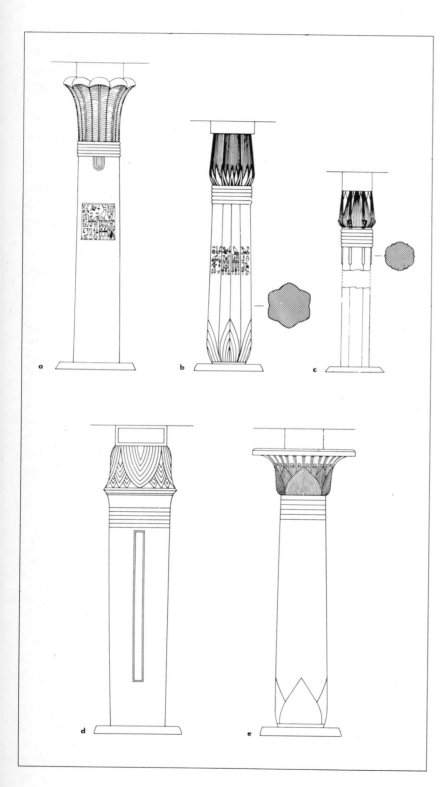

sided "pillars" which, having a flat base and abacus, are also classed as columns (see Plates 180, 185).

Starting with the Amarna period the classical forms of the plant column, above all the palm column, underwent substantial changes, particularly in relation to the capitals; this arose from their use as supports in the official reception halls and audience chambers of the royal palaces. (Since these columns were made of wood, they survive only in fragmentary form.) From these models come the numerous forms of the "composite capital" in the stone temples of the Late Period (Plates 183e, 232, 233).

Because the tomb was regarded as the "abode" of the deceased, and the temple as the "castle," "palace," or dwelling of the god, the succession and design of spaces and the architectural construction of the royal palaces and the residences of the nobility exerted influence over the monumental sacred architecture. Open porticoes and halls articulated with rows of supports, as in the rock tombs of Beni Hasan (see Plate 180), furnish decisive evidence about royal palaces and noble houses. As originally conceived, these were most probably derived from the arrangement and construction of the tent palace, transformed in the course of a long period of settled existence into structures of sun-dried brick with timber roof and posts. From the earliest times to the end of pharaonic civilization, Nile-mud bricks and wood were regarded as the prime building materials for residential construction, being well suited to the hot Egyptian climate. The brick walls and earthen floors were plastered over and painted. The ceilings, supported on wooden columns, consisted of beams of imported pinewood over which matting was stretched, then plastered and painted. The wooden columns were also gaily painted, and stood on flat stone bases. The sills and frames of the main doorways, which had to carry the weight of the wooden doors, were made of limestone blocks. On the uprights were bands of inscriptions, and on the broad lintels were inscriptions and figured compositions; inlays of glass paste and faience were sometimes used instead of painted relief.

The foundations of settlements with the modest dwellings of Old Kingdom artisans and laborers are now preserved near the Giza necropolis. At Lahun, on the edge of the Faiyum, the remains of an entire town, built on a unified plan, have been cleared; its buildings housed the workers and superintending officials employed at the nearby site of the pyramid of Sesostris II. A palace, now almost vanished, was built on high ground north of the town, apparently for the occasional use of the king. The town is entirely surrounded by thick walls and divided internally into several rectangular quarters by other walls. The streets are parallel and straight. Within each quarter the houses, compressed together cheek by jowl, are identical in size and spatial division. The spacious premises of the officials are ranged along the north wall of the town. Within each estate is a complicated arrangement of corridors and connecting rooms between the quarters for women and servants, kitchens and pantries, that always surround the inner courts; the typical suite occupied by the master of the house can be readily distinguished by its clearly discernible plan. The apartment faces north and consists first of a patio on whose south side stood a portico open to the cool north wind; through the portico is a broad antechamber leading to the central hall, a reception room whose ceiling rests on four columns. Beyond is the small private living room, as well as bedroom and bath. This suite is the core of the official house, and the same clear scheme is found in the royal palaces of Amarna, large and small, and in the houses of the officials.

Great triple-aisled columned halls with a dais for the throne that faced the entrance in the opposite wall, and wide columned halls that formed entry rooms to smaller audience chambers, are clearly recognizable in the plan of Amenhotep III's palace at Malkata, west of Thebes. Along either side of the great central columned hall were the suites for the ladies of the royal harem, also divided into a small antechamber, a throne room, and a connecting bedroom and bath.

At the end of the Eighteenth Dynasty the royal capital was transferred to the east Delta; Thebes remained only as the center of worship of the god Amon-Ra and the burial place of the kings. Accordingly small palaces, apparently occupied only briefly by the ruler during the great festivals, were annexed to the royal mortuary temples on the west bank. These were always built against the south wall of the first court, and were connected with it by the "window of appearances." The best-preserved palace of this kind is that of Ramesses III at Medinet Habu. Immediately adjacent to the wall of the temple court is a room containing two columns, and steps which lead up to the "window of appearances." From here the king participated in the solemn ceremonies performed in the first court, and received and rewarded deserving officials. The main room of the palace is the great hall, divided into three aisles by six columns, with a dais on which stood the king's throne and beyond it a smaller throne room for more intimate receptions. Smaller suites on the south of the main temple, from which they are separated by a corridor, each contain a bedroom and bath for the king and his retinue.

The roofs of the palace retain clear marks of their original

*184. Deir el Bahari (West Thebes). Funerary temple of Queen Hatshepsut, from east. Eighteenth Dynasty, c. 1480 B.C.*

form, where they were added to the stone outer wall of the first temple court. The reception rooms had longitudinal vaults resting on architraves supported by palm columns. The central block containing the royal halls was considerably taller than the apartments on either side and was lit by small stone-grilled windows in the clerestory.

In the permanent residences, which also included government buildings, temples, and quarters for the officials—for example, in the palace complexes of Amenhotep III in West Thebes and Amenhotep IV (Akhenaten) in Amarna—all the arrangements and especially the royal rooms were much more spacious. In both instances the painted decoration that filled the rooms has been preserved. The floor painting stretches from portal to portal representing the "royal way," decorated with bound and prostrate figures of Egypt's neighbors. Other floor paintings represent the primeval Egyptian landscape with swampy thickets where calves scramble and birds flutter overhead, thus hinting at the king's mythical role as "god of creation" and guarantor of world order, as well as his duty to beat off and destroy the nation's enemies.

185. *Deir el Bahari (West Thebes). Funerary temple of Queen Hatshepsut, first terrace: right, entrance hall to Anubis chapel; left, north portico of facade ("birth room"). Eighteenth Dynasty, c. 1480 B.C.*

## THE NEW KINGDOM

Following the collapse of order at the end of the Middle Kingdom the "Hyksos," mercenary leaders from the Near East, established themselves in the east Delta and gradually extended their rule to Memphis and Middle Egypt. Upper Egypt remained virtually untouched by the invaders. It was again the princes of Thebes who had to expel the foreigners and found a new united kingdom, thus preparing the way for the most brilliant era of Egyptian civilization. By pursuing the Hyksos into their Palestinian homeland, and by other conquests in the north and in the south, deep into the Sudan, there arose a powerful Egyptian empire that lasted, with Thebes as its capital and religious center, for two hundred years.

One of the prerequisites of this renaissance was a renewal of the conception of kingship. According to the new official dogma the legitimate ruler was begotten by the god Amon-Ra and the sister-consort, now exalted to "consort of the god," of the ruling king. In death the ruler entered into the being of his divine father Amon.

At the beginning of the New Kingdom Thebes was still a young city whose historical traditions did not extend beyond the local nomarchs, from whom Neb-hepet-ra Mentuhotep, founder of the Middle Kingdom, had stemmed (page 110). The new capital had to establish its visible supremacy through the superiority of its system of gods and a display of monumental sanctuaries. In the Middle Kingdom Thebes had become the abode of Amon, the creator god, who, by appropriating nearby cults such as that of the primeval fertility god Min of Coptos and finally the sun god Ra of Heliopolis, had developed into a universal divinity and "king of the gods." The military victories had been won in Amon's name and into his sanctuaries streamed most of the booty, and the tributes of the conquered peoples. Amon-Ra became the national deity. He acquired the Theban goddess Mut as his consort and the moon god Khonsu as their son. From now on this family of gods formed a triad, with coordinated sanctuaries at Karnak. Each member of the triad possessed near his cult image a sacred barge, and in these the images could be taken to visit one another within Thebes. Apart from these principal Theban gods, the cults of other important deities, such as Ptah of Memphis, had already found their way to Thebes during the Middle Kingdom; these sanctuaries were also expanded under the New Kingdom rulers.

The active construction of temples for the gods and of royal mortuary temples began immediately under the first kings of the

*186, 187. Deir el Bahari (West Thebes). Funerary temple of Queen Hatshepsut, first terrace: left, "birth room"; center, Anubis chapel; right, north colonnade. Eighteenth Dynasty, c. 1480 B.C.*

188. Deir el Bahari (West Thebes). Funerary temple of Queen Hatshepsut, south end of first terrace: Hathor chapel, interior of rock-cut sanctuary. Eighteenth Dynasty, c. 1480 B.C.

Eighteenth Dynasty, and it aimed at giving monumental expression to the various theological systems newly drawn together; their arrangement turned the entire area of Thebes into "Amon's city."

The district of the capital city of Thebes extended along both banks of the Nile. On the east bank stood the royal palaces, with the government buildings and residential quarters between the boundaries of the principal sanctuary of Karnak on the north and the sanctuary of Luxor on the south, both dating from the Middle Kingdom. On the edge of the west bank, confined by its cliffs, lay the necropolis, which had as its first monumental center the tomb complex of the founder of the Middle Kingdom in the valley at Deir el Bahari (see Plate 174). Here lie buried also the kings of the New Kingdom, but for reasons of security the royal tombs were tunneled into the rock in the lonely Valley of the Kings in the western hills, physically separated from the temples for the worship of the dead. The royal mortuary temples were ranged at the foot of the cliffs that run in a line north and south, facing the fertile land and the sanctuaries on the east bank: they were memorial temples in the true sense of the word, serving not only for the cult of the king and his followers but also for the worship of Amon-Ra and other gods. Also on the west bank, further to the south and beyond the limits of the original city there has been found a "primeval hill" that was probably already extant in the Middle Kingdom (page 115).

The sanctuaries of the gods of Thebes were certainly independent buildings that were erected for specific reasons and especially in connection with jubilee festivals as "memorials of the kings for their father Amon," but their planning played an important role for the neighboring cults.

### The Temple of Amon-Ra at Karnak

The remains of the oldest sanctuary of Karnak, rebuilt in the Twelfth Dynasty, are so scanty that the ground plan can no longer be established with certainty. It formed the core of all later expansions. Its east-west orientation was determined by the Nile from which a canal probably led to the forecourt of the temple at an early date. Because the temple was expanded continually toward the west the landing place, with its small obelisks and an avenue of ram-sphinxes leading to the later main entrance of the sanctuary, was likewise shifted westward, and its existing remains date only from late in the New Kingdom (Plate 195). The history of the sanctuary is complicated by repeated expansions and by razing old shrines and constructing new ones, in the principal east-west directions and toward neighboring cults

189. *Deir el Bahari (West Thebes). Funerary temple of Queen Hatshepsut, north wall of second terrace: interior of Chapel of Tuthmosis I. Eighteenth Dynasty, c. 1480 B.C.*
190. *Medinet Habu (West Thebes). Reconstruction of Queen Hatshepsut's baldachin temple, in original state*

191. *Medinet Habu (West Thebes). Section and plan of Queen Hatshepsut's baldachin temple*
192. *Medinet Habu (West Thebes). Remains of Queen Hatshepsut's baldachin chapel, from south. Eighteenth Dynasty, c. 1470 B.C.*

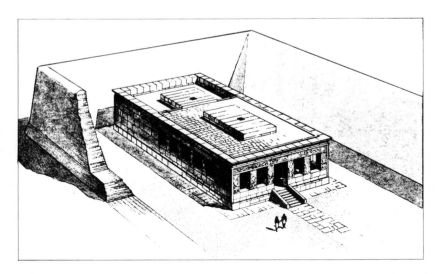

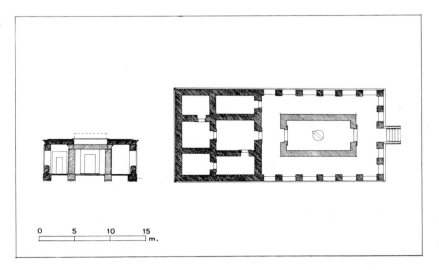

on north and south, a process that lasted from the beginning of the New Kingdom into the Late Period. Only traces are left of many of the buildings. Accordingly we can only discuss the basic conception of the architectural layout with reference to the more important elements of the temple, and describe the most notable sites.

So many cults gathered around the main temple of Amon-Ra, the king of the gods, that Karnak had the name "Collector of Holy Places" (Plate 197). The decisive influence on planning during the Eighteenth Dynasty was Amon's taking over of the essence of the sun god. The connection with the Heliopolitan place of worship of Ra, with its pylons, obelisks, and wide courts, was thus supplied by the essence of the national deity. King Tuthmosis I was responsible for a considerable widening of the boundaries of the Middle Kingdom sanctuary, which he enclosed with stone walls on north, south, and east; on the west, toward the Nile, he built two monumental portals in close succession, between gate towers. Inside the giant court, against the enclosure walls, he set up statues in the form of Osiris, symbolizing the perpetual renewal of the kingship within the dynastic order: here began the furnishing of buildings with sculptures closely associated with the architecture. On either side of the gateway in the broader and taller front pylon (present pylon IV) Tuthmosis I erected sixty-five-foot obelisks of rose granite, of which the southern one still stands (Plate 207). Between the two pylons (IV and V) was inserted a splendid hall with papyrus-bundle columns and colossal standing figures of the king. The central precinct of the temple was thus permanently fixed. Here, within the zone of the Middle Kingdom sanctuary, Queen Hatshepsut built a red quartzite chamber for the processional barge and the cult image of the national god. Open to east and west, it was flanked by subsidiary chambers for religious implements. In the narrow court intervening between her father's pylons (IV and V) the queen raised two obelisks almost one hundred feet high, of which the northern one still stands (Plate 203). At the same time she took in hand the south axis, that led from the forecourt in front of pylon IV to the temple of Mut and thence to the sanctuary of Luxor, and built pylon VIII, placing before it enthroned statues of colossal size. Her successor, Tuthmosis III, replaced the queen's red quartzite shrine with a new one in rose granite and in front of it he erected a small pylon (VI) as the entrance to his "hall of annals"; the ceiling rested on two slender square pillars decorated in painted high relief with the heraldic plants of Lower and Upper Egypt, the papyrus on the north pillar and the so-called lily on the south

(Plate 196). In the hall of annals the conqueror recorded the details of his victorious campaigns against Palestine and Syria. Finally, Tuthmosis III erected two larger obelisks in front of the pair built by Tuthmosis I, but these have not survived.

The area enclosed by Tuthmosis I was extended to the east by Tuthmosis III when he added a self-contained temple whose principal element was the great "festival hall" for the celebration of the king's jubilee (Plates 198–201). It consists of a court laid out at right angles to the main axis of the temple and ringed beyond by entrance halls supported on square pillars. In the middle of the eastern wall of the hall of columns lies the entrance to the holy of holies, which extends toward the east. Into this hall the king introduced two rows of tall columns, bearing a flat roof that is higher than the roofs of the surrounding halls; between the necessary supports the zone remained open, so that the interior suggests in cross section the appearance of a "basilica" with a clerestory. The orientation of the building, the mode of construction, and the form of the columns lining the central aisle, which resemble stone "tent poles" (see Plate 183d), reveal that here two elements, a court with a festival tent erected in it, have been skillfully combined. Against the outside of the east wall of this jubilee hall the king built a small sanctuary facing east, and in front of it he erected a huge single obelisk, now standing before the Lateran Palace in Rome.

Tuthmosis III also developed the south axis of the temple, adding another pylon (VII) with colossal statues of the king on the south side. On the east side of the court formed between pylons VII and VIII he erected a small repository chapel that also leads to the "sacred lake" of the Karnak area. Sacred lakes were permanent features of Egyptian temples. They were the source of the holy water used in the ritual and, on festival occasions, the scene of excursions of the sacred barge. Along the banks there were also enclosures with birds flying about in them, later to be used in ritual sacrifice. The pylons further along the south axis (IX and X) were built at the end of the Eighteenth Dynasty, pylon X serving also as the monumental southern entrance to the temple precinct. An avenue of sphinxes led south from here to the nearby temple of the goddess Mut, partially surrounded by its own horseshoe-shaped sacred lake.

The main temple was also enlarged westward, in the direction of the Nile, by the addition of further pylons. Sety I began the building of the great hypostyle hall at Karnak, in the courtyard between the pylons of Amenhotep III (III) and of Ramesses I (II); the enormous structure was completed by Ramesses II (Plates 202–7). It is of particular historical interest as the first

193. Karnak. Temple of Amon-Ra, sacred lake, from south. Left to right in background: pylon VII, pylon I, great hypostyle hall, obelisk of Hatshepsut

194. Karnak. Temple of Amon-Ra, view toward south from pylon I: great court with kiosk of Taharqa: facade of temple of Ramesses III; pylons VIII and IX on south axis

true example of a building of the "basilica" type, that is, a long multi-aisled hall with a tall central aisle and much lower side aisles. The central aisle supports a ceiling on two rows of papyrus columns nearly eighty feet high with open bell-shaped blossoms as capitals (see Plate 183e). The two lower side areas containing the aisles have each sixty-one close-set papyrus-bundle columns forty feet high, of the smooth unified type introduced in the age of the Ramessides. The important clerestory zone between the roofs of nave and aisles consists of the supporting pillars and stone grilles between, which could have only dimly lighted the central aisle. The bands of inscriptions on the wall surfaces of this hall indicate that it served not as a real place of worship but as an assembly place for the sacred barges of the Theban triad at the time of processions. The barges were brought there from their sanctuaries "when Amon appeared at the festival to behold the beauty of the Theban region." Other "basilican" structures of this type, though on a much smaller scale, are found in the mortuary temple of Ramesses II (Ramesseum) on the west bank at Thebes, and the contemporary remains of the main temple of Ptah of Memphis.

At right angles to the main axis of the temple were built repository chapels, large and small, that served as resting places for the sacred barge during the processions. Other individual temple buildings were on north or south according to their relationship to the neighboring sanctuaries. The most important of these is the temple of the moon god Khonsu (Plates 208-11), child of Amon and Mut. It faces south toward the temple of Luxor, with which it was connected by an avenue of sphinxes well over a mile long. Its builder was Ramesses III. It is historically important for its good state of preservation and also for its systematic layout; in its succession of halls and their arrangements it continued to serve as a model until the temples of the Late Period. Passing through a portal between gate towers, one enters a court flanked by double porticoes. At the end of the court stands the temple porch at a slightly higher level. Next comes a broader hypostyle hall with a tall central aisle and lateral windows. The columns of the central aisle, like those of the great hypostyle hall at Karnak and the Ramesseum, have open papyrus blooms as capitals. Beyond this hall lies a square room with the barge chapel of the god in the middle. In the rear part of the temple is a broad low-pillared hall with chapels on three sides. These characteristic features, which were already prepared for in the Eighteenth Dynasty in the layout of the temple of Luxor, have been organized into a logical schema in the temple of Khonsu. From one chamber to the next the floors are

◁ 196. Karnak. Temple of Amon-Ra, heraldic pillars in hall of annals of Tuthmosis III. Eighteenth Dynasty, c. 1450 B.C.

197. Karnak. Plan of Temple of Amon-Ra
1) Temple of Osiris. 2) East gate. 3) Enclosure wall. 4) Kiosk of Taharqa. 5) Temple of Ramesses II. 6) "Lateran" obelisk. 7) Buildings of Tuthmosis III. 8) Sacred lake. 9) Buildings of Psamnut. 10) Temple of Amenhotep II. 11) Temple of Ptah. 12) Great court. 13) Temple of Khonsu
198. Karnak. Temple of Amon-Ra, great festival hall of Tuthmosis III, from west. Eighteenth Dynasty, c. 1460 B.C. ▷

slightly raised, the ceilings become lower in the same rhythm and the passages narrower. As one advances through the first pillared hall into the interior of the building the light becomes steadily dimmer, first admitted through lateral windows and then through mere slits in the roof. The sanctuary lies in total darkness; it hides with its cult image the "secret" of the temple.

### The Temple of Luxor

The temple of Luxor, on the south side of Thebes like the principal sanctuary of Karnak, also goes back to the Middle Kingdom. Under Hatshepsut and Tuthmosis III a granite chapel stood there with well-proportioned papyrus-bundle columns, incorporated by Ramesses II with the great court he added on the north. The Luxor temple itself was the work of Amenhotep III and was built according to a uniform plan and on a much larger scale than the older sanctuary (Plates 212–17). It lies close to the Nile bank facing north and was the "southern harem" of Amon, who was worshiped here as the god of procreation. It thus had a particular significance for the king, whose divine conception and birth are represented in the "birth room" on the east side.

Unequaled in Egyptian architecture is the lofty elongated passage, with its two rows of fifty-foot papyrus columns with open flowers for capitals, that leads into the great court of the temple (Plate 212). No pylon towers emphasized the entrance to this huge hall; no side aisles expanded it, as in the great hypostyle hall at Karnak. It formed a monumental reception hall for the king and the sacred barges, which paused here before crossing the wide courtyard leading to the inner temple. The square open court with its double rows of well-proportioned papyrus-bundle columns merges on the south into the main entrance hall having columns of the same form (Plate 214). Crossing the "hall of offerings" one enters the barge sanctuary which, built within an ambulatory, is distinguished as an independent structure by fillets at the corners and crowning concave cornices. The rearmost chambers of the temple are accessible only from the sides through a transverse columned hall. They consist of a row of three chapels, the one in the center being the holy of holies where the cult image of the sacred triad stood on a pedestal.

In front of Amenhotep III's long entrance passage Ramesses II added the already mentioned spacious court; its entrance, on the north, is guarded by a pylon and obelisks (Plates 215, 216), and the facade faces toward Karnak, linked by an avenue of sphinxes with Amon's main sanctuary.

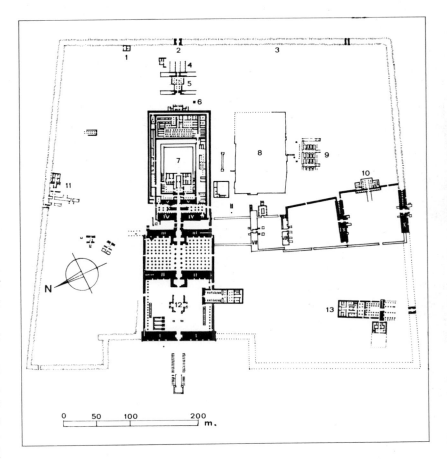

199. Karnak. Temple of Amon-Ra, longitudinal section of great festival hall of Tuthmosis III

200, 201. Karnak. Temple of Amon-Ra, great festival hall of Tuthmosis III, with tent pole columns, from south. Eighteenth Dynasty, c. 1460 B.C. ▷

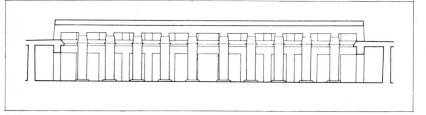

202. Karnak. Temple of Amon-Ra, great hypostyle hall from north, and obelisks of Tuthmosis I (left) and Hatshepsut (right)

203. Karnak. Temple of Amon-Ra, transverse section of great hypostyle hall

204. Karnak. Temple of Amon-Ra, south side of great hypostyle hall. Nineteenth Dynasty, c. 1290 B.C. ▷

205. Karnak. Temple of Amon-Ra, view toward south, through aisle of great hypostyle hall with ancient grille preserved. Nineteenth Dynasty, c. 1290 B.C. ▷

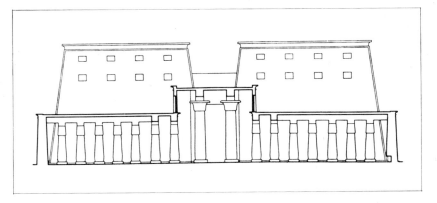

206. *Karnak. Temple of Amon-Ra, view toward central aisle of great hypostyle hall. Nineteenth Dynasty, c. 1290 B.C.*

207. *Karnak. Temple of Amon-Ra, obelisk of Tuthmosis I and central aisle of great hypostyle hall, from east* ▷

*209. Karnak. Temple of Khonsu, inner face of access portal. Ptolemaic period, c. 220 B.C.*

## The "Primeval Hill" at Medinet Habu

In addition to the temples of Karnak and Luxor on the east bank of the Nile at Thebes, there is on the west bank a small but important sanctuary at Medinet Habu, south of the original city limits. As the "true center of primordial creation" this little temple could claim to be one of the holiest places of Thebes. Hatshepsut began its construction, over an older sanctuary, and it was revised and completed by her successor Tuthmosis III (Plates 190–92). The elongated rectangular building, whose ground plan is also recognizable in sanctuaries elsewhere, has rounded moldings at the four corners and is crowned above an upper encircling molding by a concave cornice. The whole stands on a moderately high podium reached by a small flight of steps on the east front. A canal branching from the Nile probably ended in front of the temple forecourt.

The building is divided into two different areas. In front of the customary sanctuary is a barge chapel of the "baldachin temple" type with pillars on three sides and waist-high walls between them; in the middle stands a long shrine for Amon's barge. Originally the ceiling of this shrine—evidently the archetypal sacred hut beneath an awning—was lower than the roof of the surrounding column structure. The rear part of the temple is enclosed by outer walls, and here the ceiling height is lower than in the front part. The structure contains several small chambers: on the central axis is a square room, the main chamber, for its ceiling is somewhat higher and has a light-slit directing a feeble beam of light onto a statuary group representing the god Amon and the king, of which remains have been preserved. The rooms lying south and west of the main chamber served the cult of Amon; the room on the north, accessible only from the barge chapel, served the cult of the king.

This sanctuary on the "primeval hill of Djeme" (Thebes) maintained close relations with the temple of Luxor on the east bank. At the beginning of each decade Amon was transported by barge, from his "southern harem," across to the temple on the west side of the river to make offerings to the "primordial gods." In the Twentieth Dynasty Ramesses III chose the immediate vicinity of this hallowed place to build his huge mortuary temple. He enclosed the ancient sanctuary within the fortress-like walls of his own temple area (Plates 218–19). The cult was maintained into the Ptolemaic era and during all this time the small Eighteenth Dynasty temple remained substantially untouched. Late inscriptions refer to the sanctuary as the "tomb of the eight original gods and the primeval snake Kneph," and accordingly various additions were made in the Thirtieth Dynasty and under

210. *Karnak. Temple of Khonsu, outer face of access portal. Ptolemaic period, c. 220 B.C.*
211. *Karnak. Temple of Khonsu, reliefs in access portal. Ptolemaic period, c. 220 B.C.* ▷

212. *Luxor. Temple of Amenhotep III, from north; colonnaded passage and great court. Eighteenth Dynasty, c. 1370 B.C.*

the Ptolemies: entrance buildings, a hypostyle hall, pylons, and a small pillared entrance hall where the processions were ceremonially received.

### The Mortuary Temple of Queen Hatshepsut

For Thebes, the early Eighteenth Dynasty was a genuinely creative period in architecture. The most important building of this period—surpassing all others in originality and boldness of conception, in the balance of its masses, in its climactic progress from entrance to holy of holies, and in wealth of statuary and reliefs—is the terraced temple of Queen Hatshepsut (Plate 184) on the cliff valley at Deir el Bahari (the place takes its name from the Christian monastery called "northern monastery" that once nestled among the ruins). Hatshepsut has already been mentioned as a builder of the temple of Karnak. The temple at Deir el Bahari served not only for her own funerary cult and that of her father Tuthmosis I and of her husband Tuthmosis II, who died young, but was also dedicated to the cults of Amon, her divine begetter, and of other gods. In choosing the site the queen acknowledged the first political rise of Thebes in the Eleventh Dynasty, the proximity of Mentuhotep's mortuary temple (see Plates 173, 174), and the neighboring sanctuary of the goddess Hathor, guardian of the necropolis. The huge temple complex is the work of the architect Senmut, the queen's favorite, and it shows a solution that takes over from the earlier model only the outward-directed effect of its open galleries and additional influences from Twelfth Dynasty architecture of the Upper Egyptian nomarchs' tombs, with their numerous terraces clinging to the cliffs (see Plate 171). All of these prototypes are wholly surpassed, and in the grandeur of the site, with its backdrop of majestic vertical cliffs, is proclaimed a totally new concept of the dignity of divine kingship.

The long sphinx-lined causeway leads from the rim of the cultivated land to the entrance portal, flanked by trees. The court extended, as with Mentuhotep's mortuary temple immediately to the south, in its full width of over 300 feet right up to the sanctuary, which rises in two giant steps and facing colonnades to the cliffs behind. These cliffs, soaring 350 almost vertical feet to a pyramidal peak, assumed the role of the missing pyramid. Into the other side of this mass of rock, from a spur of the Valley of the Kings, was tunneled the shaft leading to the tomb chamber of the queen, a distance of several hundred yards.

The broad court was planted with palm trees and grapevines. In front of the main structure ponds fringed with papyrus were laid out on either side of the center axis. Central ramps lead to

213. *Luxor. Plan of temple of Amenhotep III*
214. *Luxor. Temple of Amenhotep III, papyrus-bundle columns at northeast corner of great court. Eighteenth Dynasty, c. 1370 B.C.*
215. *Luxor. Temple of Amenhotep III, pylon and exterior wall of north court (colonnaded passage beyond). Ramesses II, Nineteenth Dynasty, c. 1250 B.C.*

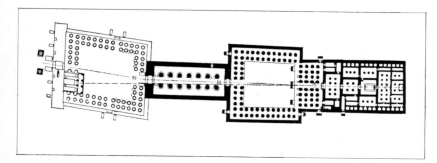

the first and second terraces, and the buttressing walls are faced with colonnades of square pillars. Those of the lower colonnade, closing the court on the west, are decorated with the "Horus name" of the queen; this motif is continued on a giant scale along the outside of the niched buttressing wall that supports the second terrace on the south. The lower colonnade terminates at north and south in huge Osiris statues of the queen. The architectural decoration of the lower-story structures proclaims the royal name; on the next level the holiness of the precinct correspondingly rises, and on the outside faces of the pillars of the second colonnade the queen is shown before Amon. The sphere of the gods has begun; the second colonnade ends at the south in the chapel of the goddess Hathor, at the north in that of Anubis, god of the dead (Plate 185).

The Hathor chapel could also be reached by way of a separate ramp along the south buttressing wall. Its facade is formed by a row of square pillars between short end walls, identified as an independent building by its crowning cornice and rounded corner moldings. Inside, round columns with Hathor-head capitals divide the anteroom of the chapel into several aisles, and through the aisle between the central row of columns was accessible the holy of holies, carved out of the rock at the end (Plate 188). Even this rock-cut sanctuary of the goddess Hathor is identified as a separate building by the relief decoration on its entrance portal, in this case a tentlike Upper Egyptian shrine. The slender fluted supports with small Hathor-head capitals and apotropaic horns, which bear a flattened vaulted roof, and the decorative loops of the matting walls of a tent structure, recall a type similar to the dummy buildings in King Zoser's burial precinct (see Plates 148–50). The Anubis chapel at the north end of the upper colonnade is also treated as an independent building. On the facade of the anteroom and within, the sixteen-sided fluted columns on low round bases stand out from the square pillars of the main colonnade (Plates 185, 186). In this chapel, too, the holy of holies is carved out of the same cliffs; the walls and vaulted ceiling, as in all the rock-cut chambers, are faced with stone slabs and richly decorated with painted reliefs. The vault is painted with golden stars in a night-blue sky.

The curve of the vaulted ceilings, employed in Egyptian stone architecture since the Fifth Dynasty pyramids, was obtained by cutting off the projecting edges of layers of stone, and these ceilings seem to have signified the crossing over from this world to the next. Brick barrel vaults and domes over small square chambers were already familiar to the builders of the Fourth Dynasty, who used them in the annexes to stone mastabas. The segmental

218. *Medinet Habu (West Thebes). Reconstruction of High Gate, southeast precinct gate of mortuary temple of Ramesses III. Twentieth Dynasty, c. 1150 B.C.*

219. *Medinet Habu (West Thebes). Interior face of High Gate, southeast precinct gate of mortuary temple of Ramesses III. Twentieth Dynasty, c. 1150 B.C.* ▷

arch first appears in stone architecture in the eighth century B.C. But apart from its use in the inner chambers of sanctuaries in the specified Old Kingdom pyramid temples, and in the rock-cut chapels and a few other rare instances, the vault played no part in Egyptian sacred architecture; where it was used it could never be discerned from the outward appearance of a sacred building.

At the northeast corner of the Anubis chapel the cliff makes a sharp turn forward and forms the northern boundary of the terrace. Here too a shallow colonnade makes a facing for the cliff wall (Plates 186, 187).

The second ramp leads to the uppermost terrace, the culmination of the sanctuary. A long solemn row of identical Osiris statues of the queen forms the facade fronting the square pillars of the main hall. In the center of the facade a granite portal leads into a narrow open court that is ringed by deep colonnaded halls. Recent examinations of this structure, which is in an advanced state of ruin, indicate that the row of pillars bordering the court was somewhat raised above the others. Immediately to the north of this courtyard area is a small open court where the sun god was worshiped at a great open-air altar that faced the rising sun; across from this sun sanctuary, to the south, is a group of vaulted chambers for the funerary cult of the queen and her ancestors (Plate 189). The holy of holies, dedicated to the god Amon, was carved out of the western cliff, exactly on the main axis of the temple and reached from the central court. Originally there were two chambers, one behind the other, but under the Ptolemies a third was added for the worship of two great mortals: Imhotep, King Zoser's architect, inventor of stone architecture and author of a treatise on the planning of temples; and Amenhotep, son of Hapu, the architect of Amenhotep III. For their wisdom, these architects were worshiped as gods: Senmut, architect of the terraced temple and favorite of Queen Hatshepsut, was long forgotten.

The terraced temple of Deir el Bahari is a remarkable example of the aesthetic adaptation of a building to its natural setting. Architecture, however, is always the product of a shaping intelligence and must assert its forms against the chaotic formlessness of nature. Small as compared with the towering crags against which it is built, Hatshepsut's temple occupies only the lower zone of the wall of cliffs. Yet the crisp horizontals of its terraces and the strict verticals of its colonnades differentiate it sharply from the rugged terrain, with which it is nonetheless intimately, though not visibly, connected by the sanctuaries hewn out of the living rock. The natural grandeur of the landscape has been incorporated with the temple's thematic function as the

eternal seat of the godhead and as the burial place of the queen deep within the mountain.

## The Amarna Period

The principle for the planning of the national sanctuary of the universal god Amon-Ra at Karnak, at the beginning of the Eighteenth Dynasty, was based on the worship of the sun god in open courts guarded at front and back by pylons and obelisks, as exemplified by the scant remains of the temple at Heliopolis. This principle can be recognized in the ancient core of the Karnak temple complex, as well as in the later additions on the south and west. The perpetual renewal of the kingship through the jubilee festival had a close association with the sun god—already confirmed in the Fifth Dynasty sun sanctuary, in the rich relief cycles of a "jubilee chamber" south of the great obelisk (see Plate 170); and the idea of legitimate dynastic continuity, in the sense of the renewed conception of kingship, provided the stimulus for continual expansion through developing, enlarging, and improving the efficacy of the national shrine.

Thus, it was not in itself surprising that Amenhotep IV, successor of Amenhotep III, should have built, still under his original name, two separate temples for Ra-Harakhte, the sun god of Heliopolis, one east of Karnak, the other near Luxor. To judge from the partially cleared remains at Karnak—those at Luxor have not yet been excavated—these temples, too, appear to have consisted of large courts for the open-air worship of the day star. Amenhotep IV resided for about five years in the capital city of Thebes, before his personally propagated theology of the sun as "Aten" (the solar disk) took a turn so one-sided and so hostile to Amon that the king changed his own name from Amenhotep ("Amon is satisfied") to Akhenaten ("In the service of Aten"). He deserted Thebes, and banned and persecuted the cult of Amon. On virgin land in Middle Egypt, untrammeled by religious traditions of any kind, he founded his new capital, Akhetaten ("The horizon of Aten"), on the east bank of the Nile opposite the ancient site of Hermopolis. After a mere twelve years this royal residence and exclusive cult center of the sole god proclaimed by the king fell into decay, following the collapse of the new belief and the king's death, and shortly it was razed with all its buildings and sanctuaries to obliterate all memory of the "heretic." Excavations at the site thus reveal little more than the foundations of the palaces, temples, and living quarters, whose original buildings have been to some extent reconstructed with the aid of contemporary reliefs discovered in the tombs nearby.

Like the visage of the new god, the planning of his temples at Akhetaten can be linked with the Heliopolitan model. The common theme was an axial succession of pylon-fronted courts, where on innumerable altars in the open air the king and his family offered sacrifices to the sun. Statues of the king placed against pillars, as in the open areas of the temple of Karnak, stood around the courts as witnesses to his presence and to the perpetual renewal of his claim to kingship. The architects of the Amarna period consistently translated the religious ideas propounded by the king himself into a succession of new architectural forms. These include many appurtenances of the temples (whose thematic significance is still not clearly understood), the erection of columns in front of pylons to form vestibules flanking the entrances, and especially the temple gates to the sanctuaries. In the theology of the new sun cult, the display of the gloom of the Underworld had no longer a place, and now even shadow was to be shunned. The temple gates had lintels broken back in the middle and cropped on either side, so that the king could pass through in unbroken sunlight. Temple approaches continued to be treated in this way to the very end of Egyptian architecture (Plates 233, 236); they made it possible to carry the emblems of the gods in procession into the interior of the temples without lowering them at the entrance.

After the collapse of Amenhotep IV's religious reformation, Thebes ceased to be the country's political capital; however, it remained the religious center of the restored cult of Amon and, until the end of the New Kingdom, the burial place of the kings. The royal mortuary temples, the kings' "houses for millions of years," were ranged at the foot of the western hills, but the great experiment of Hatshepsut's terraced temple was nowhere adopted. Of the mortuary temples of the queen's immediate successors only that of Tuthmosis III has been thoroughly explored (see Plate 174); although it is on a more modest scale, the two share certain features, for example, a Hathor chapel on the south side. From Amenhotep III's huge mortuary complex, all that remains are the enthroned colossi, sixty-five feet high and made of quartzite that the king's architect, Amenhotep, son of Hapu, ordered from the quarries near Heliopolis, some 300 miles north of Thebes. At one time they flanked the monumental entrance with its massive pylon towers. The later mortuary temples (insofar as they still stand)—of Sety I in the northern section of the necropolis, of Ramesses II (Ramesseum), and of Ramesses III at Medinet Habu—appear to have been planned according to the principle of successive spaces at the temple of Luxor. The temple is usually approached through two sets of pylons, each leading into a broad court. A vestibule on the west side of the second court leads to the hypostyle hall, which may be followed by various smaller pillared halls, and finally to the sanctuary. A separate chapel is reserved for the royal ancestors. The main sanctuary is solely for the cult of Amon and the king. The sun god also has a private chapel within the temple. Along the main axis the sequence of rooms is fixed; the side rooms and the arrangements at the rear of the temple follow the cult requirements imposed by the royal builder.

In the back area of the Ramesseum huge brick-built storerooms and offices for the administration of the temple have been preserved. Each chamber is covered by a barrel vault. After the end of the Eighteenth Dynasty, when Thebes was no longer a royal residence, a small palace was built on the south side of the first court of the ruler's mortuary temple for his occasional visits at the time of the great festivals.

As cult places for the king and the gods, the mortuary temples were enclosed by high walls like the sanctuaries of the gods, with pylons forming the monumental front entrance. Ramesses III, developing the idea of the temple as a "fortress of the god" but certainly also mindful of the internal political difficulties of the Twentieth Dynasty, enclosed his funerary temple within double battlemented walls with massive tower-like fortress gates on east and west (Plates 218–19). In front of the east gate was a landing place for a canal leading from the Nile. Despite its fortified aspect, emphasized by the triumphal reliefs decorating the exterior, the upper chambers of the towers served as a "pleasure pavilion" for the king and his daughters, who are represented on the walls in reliefs of intimate scenes.

### The Cliff Temple of Abu Simbel

Nubia had been an Egyptian province since the beginning of the New Kingdom. Temple buildings in a purely Egyptian style secured the land in the name of Egyptian gods and kings. The most important of these temples was that built by Ramesses II on a bend in the Nile at Abu Simbel. On the west bank the high ground runs directly down to the river, forming a steep cliff. As at Deir el Bahari on the west bank at Thebes, here too the cliff itself was sacred. Ramesses transformed it into a temple. Within a trapezoidal area are four colossal statues of the enthroned king, the whole carved from the wall of sandstone cliffs to resemble the front of a pylon. The paired statues flank the entrance portal, which is oriented precisely east toward the sunrise (Plates 220–22). Above the portal in a niche is the figure of Ra-Harakhte of Heliopolis, the falcon-headed sun god. The upper termina-

tion of the "pylon" front is formed by a row of baboons, their arms raised to hail the rising run. The arrangement of the inner rooms, which penetrate deep into the side of the cliff, corresponds to the plan of the Theban temples (page 132). The great rock-cut hall that one first enters after passing through the entrance portal (Plates 223–25) is the counterpart of the temple court. Standing figures of Ramesses II in festival attire are ranged in front of the pillars. Next follows a square hypostyle hall and a wider chamber, with the holy of holies beyond the center of its innermost wall. The shrine, moved now to higher ground, contains a group of four seated statues representing Amon-Ra of Thebes, Ra-Harakhte of Heliopolis, Ptah of Memphis, and the king himself, all of whom were worshiped here.

An unusual feature of this temple is the presence of narrow compartments at right angles on either side of the main halls. These were probably treasure chambers, repositories for Nubian gold.

### The Temple and Cenotaph of Sety I at Abydos

Egyptian architecture was chiefly preoccupied with the expression of eternal verities in material form, and the unusual temple of Sety I at Abydos (Plates 226, 227) illustrates this concern impressively. Abydos, the Upper Egyptian burial place of the early kings, had become in the Old Kingdom the home and sanctuary of the god Osiris. As vegetation god and divine ruler of the mythical past, Osiris was closely associated with the question of legitimate succession. In death the king suffered the fate of the god, to be summoned like him to rule over the world of the dead; the king's son and heir, identified with Osiris' son Horus, was the earthly ruler. Osiris, who came originally from the Delta (Busiris), had since the Old Kingdom taken over the seat of the god of the dead and the cult place of the "Foremost of the Westerners." His burial place was believed to have been found at Abydos in what was, in fact, the tomb of a First Dynasty king, and his death and return to life were dramatically celebrated in mystery plays enacted along the path that stretched from the city temple to the ancient royal necropolis. Abydos became a center of pilgrimage; kings and private individuals built cenotaphs along the processional route of the mystery plays to ensure themselves a share in the blessings of this holy place.

Like all the kings of the New Kingdom, Sety I had his burial place at Thebes, in the Valley of the Kings, although for strategic reasons he had established his residence at Kantir in the eastern Delta. His mortuary temple, in part well preserved, is the northernmost of those on the Theban west bank. In the Theban mortuary temples the worship of Amon-Ra as the universal god, and the dogma of his having fathered the king, had driven the older god Osiris into the background. The Nineteenth Dynasty first brought back shrines dedicated to the god of the dead, of vegetation, and of the rulers.

Thus Sety I returned to earlier beliefs when at Abydos he built an important westward-oriented temple with two pylons, two courts, and an interior laid out according to the Theban plan (Plate 226). The aisles through a rising sequence of pillared and columned halls lead to seven chapels; the central one, dedicated to the national god Amon-Ra, is flanked by those of Ra-Harakhte and Osiris. The south wing contains the chapels of the king and the Memphite god Ptah, the north those of Isis and Horus, wife and son of Osiris. These elongated chapels, except for that of Osiris, had vaulted ceilings. A false door was represented in the westward-facing rear walls; false doors signified that behind them lay something involved in the cult. Only the Osiris chapel has a real door. This leads to chambers, dedicated to the cult of the god and his family, that form a narrow transept at the back of the seven chapels.

Reliefs on the temple walls depict the shrine, barge, and cult images, and the rites performed by the king; they are invaluable for recreating the former appearance of the temple and determining the functions of its various parts. The unusual annex on the south side of the main building contained chapels for other gods and the shrine of Sety's ancestors, who are listed by name, from Menes (Narmer), the founder of the kingdom, to the builder of the temple himself.

The cenotaph of Sety I lies just to the southwest on the axis of the main temple; it is important for the architectural history of this complex. A structure sunk deep in the ground, its roof lay below the floor level of the main temple and its core was built entirely of massive granite blocks. Originally it was an isolated building; there is a separate access at the northeast end which, however, is interrupted by a deep shaft. The core of this cenotaph forms a rectangular chamber (Plates 226, 227) with a platform occupying the middle, surrounded by a moat that was filled with water by the annual Nile floods. On the short sides there are steps leading down to the level reached by the water. In the middle of the "island" two recesses for the sarcophagus and the canopic shrine are still visible. Two rows of stout granite pillars on the long sides support giant longitudinal architraves on which rested the ceiling blocks of the roof; these were probably corbeled toward the center, forming a barrel vault above the center of the platform. The walls surrounding this entire space

221, 222. *Abu Simbel. Facade of great rock temple and four colossi of Ramesses II (as relocated). Nineteenth Dynasty, c. 1250 B.C.*
223, 224. *Abu Simbel. Interior of great rock temple of Ramesses II, longitudinal and lateral views of royal statues before pillars. Nineteenth Dynasty, c. 1250 B.C.* ▷

◁ 225. *Abu Simbel. View toward entrance of great rock temple of Ramesses II. Nineteenth Dynasty, c. 1250 B.C.*

226. *Abydos. Plan of temple and cenotaph of Sety I*
1) Entrance pylon. 2) First court. 3) Pylon. 4) Second court. 5) Main entrance. 6, 7) Hypostyle halls. 8) Royal gallery. 9) Room of Osiris. 10) Cenotaph of Sety I. 11) Storerooms

227. *Abydos. Cenotaph of Sety I, from northeast. Nineteenth Dynasty, c. 1290 B.C.*

contain niches whose significance is still uncertain. The use of undecorated massive granite blocks recalls the architecture of the Fourth Dynasty mortuary temples at Giza (see Plate 159).

The location and organization of this building leave no doubt that it was a cenotaph of the builder at the place most sacred to Osiris. The inner "island" symbolizes the "primeval hill" emerging from the waters of chaos to indicate the beginning of self-perpetuating creation. Simultaneously the island tomb equates the king with the god Osiris; according to ancient belief Osiris lay buried on an island which, on the one hand, represented the "pure" and "unapproachable," and on the other, symbolically linked his death and resurrection with the cyclical rise and fall of the Nile. Later representations show a sacred grove planted over Sety's subterranean building so that its shadow would envelop the soul of the dead king while its plants simultaneously honored Osiris as the creator of vegetation.

## THE ARCHITECTURE OF THE LATE PERIOD

The end of the New Kingdom was followed by political debility, domestic turmoil and impoverishment, pressures from without, and foreign rule, and during these times the opportunities for Egyptian architecture diminished. There were frequent shifts of the capital, mostly within Lower Egypt. Memphis rose repeatedly to prominence, but there and throughout the Delta virtually nothing has survived to supplement the buildings of the Late Period that still stand in Upper Egypt.

The occasional partitioning of the country and the frequent changes of dynasty weakened and secularized the kingship. No extensive royal tombs survive, not even those of the native kings from Sais, Mendes, and Sebennytos in the Delta. According to Herodotus, the kings of the Twenty-Sixth Dynasty, like those of the Twenty-First Dynasty at Tanis, were buried according to ancient Lower Egyptian custom within the temple precincts of the local deity. The Egyptianized Ethiopian kings of the Twenty-Fifth Dynasty, in their capital of Napata below the fourth cataract, were buried in small, very steep pyramids with a mortuary chapel on the east side.

The kings of the Ptolemaic dynasty, the successors of Alexander the Great, resided in their newly founded, purely Hellenistic capital of Alexandria, where they were buried in tombs of which nothing has been preserved (page 380).

Throughout and after the first millennium B.C. native and foreign rulers alike continued to assume the ancient role of the Pharaohs. The basic Egyptian concept of the king ruling with the god in the interests of world order continued to be preserved,

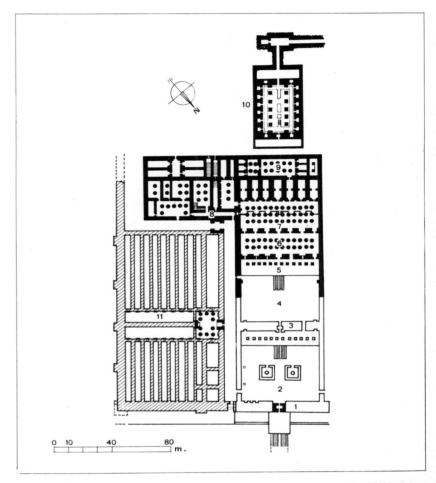

228. *Edfu. Birth house in front of Temple of Horus. Ptolemaic period, 237–57 B.C.*

at least as a fiction. The maintenance and embellishment of the famous old sanctuaries and the erection of new temples continued to be a royal obligation. Wearing pharaonic regalia Ethiopians, Persian kings, Macedonians, and Roman emperors appear in reliefs and inscriptions venerating the Egyptian gods and confirming the god-given cosmic order in the prescribed rites. Pomp and ritual establishes inwardly and outwardly their legitimate royal claim by way of the old forms of architecture, reliefs faithfully reproduced, and statues following the Egyptian canon.

The building activities in the Nile Valley of the Ethiopians, the Saitic dynasty, and the Persians are hardly noteworthy. Large-scale building throughout the country was resumed only under the kings of the Thirtieth Dynasty. The Ptolemies completed temples already begun, such as Nectanebo II's temple of Isis built all of granite in the Delta—the celebrated Iseum of Roman times, later destroyed by an earthquake and today only an imposing heap of ruins. The Ptolemies and Romans built temples throughout Egypt, including Nubia; preference was given to places that had special political and religious importance in maintaining the accustomed order and legitimate rule. The large temples of Upper Egypt stand on hallowed ground and, appealing to the oldest traditions, were rebuilt over ancient sanctuaries which they far outstripped in size and splendor. The most important and best preserved are at Dendera, Esna, Edfu, Kom Ombo, Philae, and, among the Nubian temples, Kalabsha. Architecturally each temple has a marked individuality determined by the local tradition of its principal deity and subsidiary cults, and each makes an appeal through inscriptions to a venerable history reaching back to the age of myth and the days when the country was first united.

The orientation of the temples is determined by their particular location on the east or west bank and by the usually north-south course of the river. The clear axial arrangement and spatial succession, extending from entrance portal to holy of holies, divides the temple into two halves, one on the north, one on the south, whose plan and arrangements correspond to one another in their inscriptions. There is regularly a canal leading from the Nile to the temple precincts furthest inland. The traditional festivals, in which, for example, Hathor of Dendera visited Horus of Edfu in his temple almost one hundred miles up the Nile, required these waterways for transporting the cult image on the sacred barge.

The temple precincts were always sheltered from the impure world outside by high brick walls and were entered through monumental stone portals. One such portal, dating from Ptolemaic times, has been preserved at Karnak (see Plate 195). The sacred enclosure included the temple of the principal deity, the sacred lake, a well (whose water level simultaneously indicated the state of the Nile), the smaller sanctuaries of lesser gods, and, after the fourth century B.C., the "birth house," usually situated to one side of the main entrance facing the approaches to the temple (see Plates 228, 237).

A new, lively, and especially versatile element, characteristic of the temples since the fourth century B.C., is the column capital. From the older plant-form columns late temple architecture retains only the palm and lotus columns in their original form (see Plate 183); no use is made of the various older forms of pillars. The new capitals all develop from the papyrus plant in bloom. Two basic forms may be distinguished: first, the full-blown bell-shaped papyrus capital decorated with vertical plant ribs, leaves, and floral ornament in finely graded relief; second, large semicircular papyrus blooms arranged to form a circle in the upper part and interlaced below with smaller blooms, composing a sort of bouquet. These forms have many variants and the capitals may change within the same building or even from column to column within the same row (Plates 232, 233).

## The Temple of Horus at Edfu

To describe the oldest and largest of these Ptolemaic temples, the temple of Horus at Edfu, is in a sense to describe them all (Plate 228). The construction took about 180 years (237–57 B.C.). The massive pylons and main gate of the temple face south (Plates 230, 231). High stone walls with concave and roll moldings on the outside abut against the backs of the pylons, form the side walls of the great court, and enclose the temple structure on the other three sides (Plates 233, 234). The court, "the hall of the masses," was open to the people. Porticoes, their architraves surmounted by concave and roll moldings, surround it on east, west, and south (including the side backing the pylons), stopping just short of the actual temple.

The main temple building is divided clearly into two parts, differentiated by unequal height, width, and depth. Fronting on the court is the great hypostyle hall, a broader and taller "antechamber" to the closed, elongated sanctuary behind (Plate 232). The intercolumniations of the facade, apart from the central portal with its cropped architrave and doors that could be closed, are filled by stone screens half the height of the column shafts and preventing a view of the interior. These screens are edged with fillets and crowned by a concave molding with a uraeus frieze; their outer faces are decorated with reliefs. They

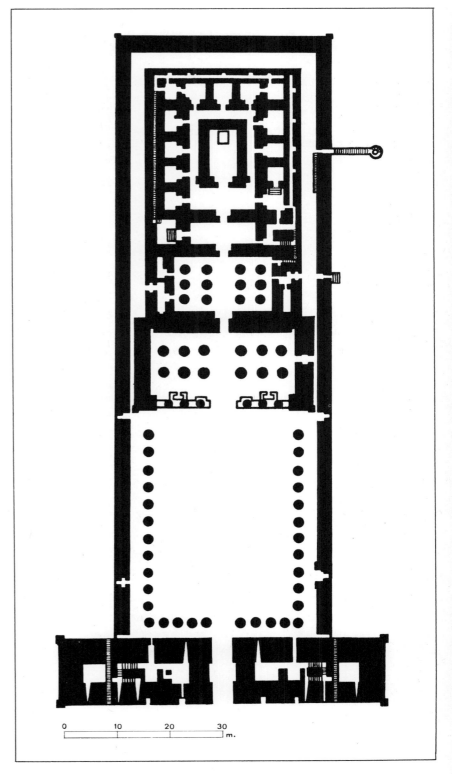

are derived ultimately from the mats stretched between the fluted posts of tent structures, reproduced in stone in King Zoser's mortuary precinct (Plate 233; see Plate 148). As an architectonic element with concave and roll moldings they are first represented in the small chapel in a New Kingdom tomb, and they appear in stone construction in the Twenty-Second Dynasty temple of Amon, built at el-Hibe in Middle Egypt.

The great hypostyle hall, like an independent building, has torus moldings at the four outer corners, at the top of the outer walls, and above the architraves in the facade, and the whole is crowned by a massive cornice. Its floor is one step above the level of the court. Built onto the back of one of the screens of the front colonnade is the library, whose catalogue of papyrus rolls is recorded on the inner walls of the small chamber. The hypostyle hall is a special feature of the temple; at Dendera (see Plate 239) the hypostyle hall was added in Roman times to the already-completed temple.

The front of the narrower and lower temple block overlaps with the rear wall of the great hypostyle hall. On the axis of the temple, a monumental portal closed with two huge doors leads into the "hall of appearances," which is narrower than the full width of the temple; its ceiling rests on columns. When the doors were closed this hall, and indeed the whole interior of the temple proper, lay in darkness; only narrow slits in the ceiling (see Plate 239) admitted occasional dim light. In the "hall of appearances" was displayed the cult image, together with those of the lesser gods also worshiped in the temple; here the processions were organized on festival days. The hall is flanked by smaller chambers where the unguents for the cult image were prepared and the temple treasures stored. A small door led out to the well that supplied the pure water needed in the daily ritual.

The next chamber is also a transept hall, but without columns; it is the "hall of offerings" where three times each day the food offered to the god was served and consecrated. On both sides of the "hall of offerings" narrow steps lead up to the roof; one goes upward in a single straight flight, and the other, four flights of gentler steps arranged around a square, was for coming down. On the side walls are reliefs depicting processions, the gods going up or down according to the design of the stair (Plate 235).

Beyond the "hall of offerings" begins the holy of holies, which, with its accompanying chapels, occupies the entire rear part of the temple. It begins with the "middle hall," also referred to in the inscriptions as the "hall of the multiplicity of gods." This chamber forms at the same time the threshold to the

231. *Edfu. Pylon and enclosure wall of Temple of Horus, from south-west. Ptolemaic period, 237–57 B.C.*

232. *Edfu. Temple of Horus, view through "hall of appearances" toward sanctuary. Ptolemaic period, 237–57 B.C.*

233. *Edfu. Court of Temple of Horus. Ptolemaic period, 237–57 B.C.*

234. Edfu. Temple of Horus, enclosure wall (right) and temple wall (left), from north. Ptolemaic period, 237–57 B.C.

235. Edfu. Temple of Horus, western stairway on roof. Ptolemaic period, 237–57 B.C. ▷

sanctuary; the floor rises, and the shrine of the principal god turns its narrow face and closing doors to the entering worshiper. Here, before the sanctuary, appeared the other gods worshiped in the temple, to protect and defend the main god. Again two small chambers open off either side of the hall: that on the west preserved the wardrobe of the god, that on the east led to a small sanctuary with a little open court, from which steps rise to the "pure chapel" at a higher level. On the occasion of the New Year festival the cult image was anointed, clothed, and crowned in this chapel before being conveyed in solemn procession to the roof.

The sanctuary—the "holy of holies," the "throne room"—of the principal god is an elongated freestanding structure, and as such is architecturally differentiated: a narrow passage surrounds it on three sides. Opening onto this passage are the chapels of the secondary gods; only the center chapel behind the sanctuary is dedicated to a special form of the principal god.

It has already been mentioned that there were ascending and descending processions from the "hall of offerings" to the flat roof. The roof of the temple was not, however, all in one plane; the roof level from the "hall of appearances" to the sanctuary area was higher than that above the smaller rooms and chapels at the sides and rear. The lower levels of the roof were screened from view by the high outer wall of the temple (see Plate 234). During the New Year festival this particular area of the roof, accessible from the stairways, had a vital function to perform: the cult image was conveyed in solemn procession to the roof where its potency was renewed by exposing it in a special roof chapel to the rays of the rising sun. At Edfu the location and plan of this chapel can still be discerned on the roof of the temple; at Dendera, on the southwest corner of the roof, the chapel itself is preserved (see Plate 240). On the roof of Dendera there are also separate chambers for the Osiris cult.

A special feature of the great temples of the Late Period is their systems of "crypts." These are narrow chambers beneath the floor of the foundations or in the thick outside walls around the holy of holies. Their location was known only to the initiated and they could be entered only by removing a stone slab. They provided safe storage for the costly votive gifts, emblems of the gods, and ritual objects in gold and silver which are listed on the walls and depicted in relief. Sometimes the crypts were at several levels, one below the other. Their concealed locations recall the story of the treasure chambers of Rhampsinit told us by Herodotus (Histories, II, 121).

At the side before the entrance pylon to the temple of Edfu

236. *Dendera. Facade of Temple of Hathor, from northeast. Late Ptolemaic–Roman period*

237, 238. *Dendera. Exterior of Temple of Hathor, from west and south. Late Ptolemaic–Roman period*

239. *Dendera. Temple of Hathor, slits for illumination in ceiling of hypostyle hall. Late Ptolemaic–Roman period* ▷

stands the birth house (Mammisi). These small temples, always present in the great sanctuaries of the Late Period, have the form of a chapel with peripteral columns bearing a sundeck. On certain festivals they were the scene of liturgical celebrations of the god and of the birth of the king. Unknown before the fourth century B.C., they emphasize the theme of the "divine child" and the "divine mother." The walled chapel within, which is treated as an isolated building, has the entrance at the front, made lower to conform with the "baldachin temple" prototype (page 118). The stone roof-slabs of the exterior gallery rest on the architraves spanning tall columns and on the walls of the chapel inside. Screens block the spaces between the columns, extending halfway up the shafts; they are decorated with reliefs depicting the adoration of the cult of the divine mother and her child. Often above the capital is another block bearing the grotesque figure of Bes, the popular demon who watched over mother and child.

## The Temple of Hathor at Dendera

After the temple of Horus at Edfu, the next most important and best-preserved of the Ptolemaic temples is that of the goddess Hathor at Dendera (Plates 236–45), begun in 80 B.C. According to the inscriptions the founding of the historic sanctuary goes back to the period of unification of the Two Lands, and King Cheops is mentioned as one of the restorers. As with all Egyptian temples, construction began with the holy of holies and ended with the entrance and the great hypostyle hall, which at Dendera dates only from the reign of Augustus. The ceiling of the hypostyle hall rests on columns with four-sided Hathor-sistrum capitals (page 120). The succession of main rooms and subordinate chambers at Dendera corresponds almost exactly with that of the temple of Horus at Edfu. Again there are two stairways leading to the roof. The reliefs on the staircase walls depict the costumes of the members of the procession in scrupulous detail: the gods, warding off enemies, march in front; behind the emblem of the temple there follow the king and the priests with the emblems of the gods; then comes the queen with each hand swinging the sistrum, the cult symbol of Hathor; next the priests bearing Hathor's image in its shrine; closing the procession are the lesser gods of the temple.

At the southwest corner of the roof stands the goal of the procession, a kiosk with twelve Hathor columns (Plates 240–44). The roof of this small building was, as representations show, once covered with a low vault; to judge from the traces of its construction left on the walls, it must have been made of wood.

*241, 242, 243. Dendera. Pavilion on roof of Temple of Hathor. Late Ptolemaic–Roman period*

The temple precinct of Dendera is still surrounded today by a thick brick wall and entered through the ancient portal. The original birth house, dating from the Thirtieth Dynasty, was later cut through by the stone enclosure wall of the temple; the emperor Augustus therefore had a new one built near the entrance to the precinct. Close to the southwest corner of the Hathor temple lies the sacred lake (Plate 245), enclosed by walls and with steps at each corner that led down to the former water level. Alongside the south steps runs a narrow landing place, probably used in connection with the Osiris festival.

## The Temple of Mandulis at Kalabsha

The temple at Kalabsha in Nubia, on the west bank of the Nile some forty miles south of Aswan, was probably built under Cleopatra and Caesar. Well preserved, easily comprehended, and carefully composed in its relation of masses, it gives a clear idea of the latest Egyptian temple architecture (Plates 246–48). The sanctuary is dedicated to the Nubian god Mandulis. The landing place for the sacred barge is in an especially good state of preservation. The two pylon towers and the side walls of the court contain a great number of small chambers, a feature of this temple. The slight deviation of the pylons from the temple axis, necessitated by the proximity of the river, is cleverly compensated by shortening one of the towers. While the ground plan corresponds in principle to those of other temples, it has been considerably simplified. The temple proper contains only three rooms, all at right angles to the main axis, the last one forming the sanctuary. All three receive dim light from slits in the ceiling and in the upper part of the walls. The ceiling height decreases substantially in the direction of the holy of holies, and the doorways grow proportionately smaller. The remains of a well are in the narrow passage between the temple building and the enclosure wall.

The proportions of this temple are rather unusual; the ratio of length to breadth is 200 to 100 feet. The temple would have been drowned in the waters of the lake created by the new Aswan High Dam had it not been dismantled under the supervision of scholars, stone by stone, and rebuilt on higher ground. During the dismantling there came to light the outline grid of the planning and the preliminary drawing, scored in the flat surface of the rock foundation. This carved outline was probably transferred to the site from a small-scale drawing. The long sides are divided into sixteen parts, the short sides into eleven: the grid therefore did not consist of squares, as is assumed to have been the case with the older Egyptian temples. The grid also contains proportional elevations of the facades of the first hypostyle hall and the sanctuary.

## The Island of Philae

One of the most important cult and pilgrimage centers of the Ptolemaic and Roman periods was the island of Philae, just south of the first cataract (Plate 249). To judge from the extant buildings and the religious traditions, the island did not become one of Egypt's famous holy places until relatively late, in the mid-fourth century B.C. The establishing of the sanctuaries on the island brought together the religious and political ideas of the Ptolemaic and the Roman periods. Philae lay in the border zone between Egypt and Nubia. In this region the worship of Isis and Osiris, the popular universal gods of the Late Period, had taken hold, displacing the older cults on the island of Elephantine near Aswan. The Osiris tomb or "abaton" on Bige, a small rocky islet west of Philae, and Philae itself surpassed in holiness even Abydos as a center of the death ceremonies of Osiris (page 159). Here, according to late theology, the Nile with its annual fecundating flood had its source in a cave in which one of the Osiris relics was kept. The motherly Isis and her son Horus were also venerated in Nubia and by the nomads of the eastern desert, the Blemmyes. During the centuries of conflict between Egypt and the south, Philae and its sanctuaries remained an island of peace. Shrines of the Nubian divinities joined those of the Egyptian gods. Even Mandulis, the local god of Kalabsha (page 183), had a temple there. Thus the little island, only a quarter of a mile long and barely two hundred yards wide, became a temple city.

The Temple of Isis was the principal sanctuary, and still stands on the west side of the island; next to the Iseum in the Delta, it was the most important center for the worship of the goddess. The siting of the other sanctuaries, built here between the fourth century B.C. and the second century A.D., was determined by the north-south orientation of the Isis temple, the processional way of her sacred image, the cult relations with the Osiris tomb on nearby Bige, and the rocky topography of Philae itself.

The approach to the Temple of Isis lay at the southwest corner of the island where Nectanebo II, the last native ruler of Egypt, built a reception hall. The processional way leading northward to the temple was bordered on both sides by long columned halls; the western one followed the shore, the eastern one was backed by smaller shrines. Compared with the great temples of the Late Period at Edfu and Dendera the Isis temple is small, but it is unsurpassed in quality of execution. The first pylon leads into the court, closed on the north by a second pylon. The

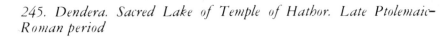
western boundary of the court is formed by the birth house, which here—like the main sanctuary—is oriented north-south and has its own entrance from the west tower of the first pylon. Opposite the birth house are the rooms for the preparation of the ritual unguents, and a library; these close off the court on the east. Directly in back of the second, smaller pylon is the great columned vestibule of the temple; to light this hall a small area near the front was left unroofed. The "hall of appearances" follows, with a stairway on the west side leading to the roof. On the east side, as in the temples at Edfu and Dendera, there is a tiny court and the "pure chapel" for the New Year festival. Beyond the "hall of appearances" lies the "middle hall," and against the rear wall of the temple stand three sanctuaries side by side. As at Dendera, the chapel for the celebration of the rebirth of Osiris is on the roof.

The emperor Hadrian's pavilion, in our picture (Plate 249) partly concealed by the big south pylon, remained unfinished; standing on the higher ground along the eastern shoreline of the island, it probably served as a way-station chapel for the festival processions. Like the pavilion on the roof of the temple of Dendera this building, surrounded by tall screened columns, once had a low rounded wooden roof.

The ancient quay walls that bordered the island are in great part preserved, especially on the southwest; they still create the impression that is compared in a contemporary inscription to a mighty "ship."

Philae was the last refuge of the pagan cults. Even in the fifth century A.D., when the Nile Valley was Christianized and the temples of the pharaonic past had long been closed, Philae's temples continued to be used by the warlike tribes of Nubia and the eastern desert. Before the first dam was constructed south of Aswan—creating a reservoir that submerged the island and its buildings for much of the year—Philae was one of the unspoilt places where the Nile, flowing through the barren rocky landscape, combined with the ancient buildings to create an atmosphere in which the presence and potency of the gods could still be felt.

## HOW TEMPLES WERE BUILT

If, after thousands of years, we can still identify the gods worshiped in the Egyptian temples and the kings who built them, and can still name the rooms and establish their cult functions in the over-all plan, it is thanks to their hieroglyphic inscriptions, reliefs, and decoration. These are essential elements of the architecture. They interpret the whole building, inside and

246. *Kalabsha. Temple of Mandulis, façade of vestibule. Roman period–beginning of Christian era*
247. *Kalabsha. Temple of Mandulis, from southwest. Roman period–beginning of Christian era*

248. *Kalabsha. Temple of Mandulis (as relocated), with pavilion of Kertassi. Roman period–beginning of Christian era*

out, as well as its portals, walls, columns, and ceilings; they also evoke with their own power the meaning and perpetuation of the daily ritual, and of the special ceremonies during the great festivals. Starting with the New Kingdom the reliefs on temple walls increasingly show the kingly role in the various phases of the liturgy. They ratify for eternity the sense of the ritual drama that symbolized the world order, and they elevate the mystery into a tangible, logical reality that is ever present. Not only the cult image in its sanctuary but the whole temple, with all its chapels, gates, pillars, reliefs, inscriptions, and emblems, was seen as having an existence which, after sleeping through the darkness of the night, had each morning to be ritually aroused from their slumber if the movement of the natural order was to continue.

Some idea of how a temple was built at Heliopolis by King Sesostris I may be gained from the text of a leather scroll. Under the aegis of the king the plans were discussed among his high officials and entrusted to the royal keeper of the seal, who directed the execution. With full pomp the king, accompanied by the high priests and the "scribe of the sacred book," betook himself to the building site to perform there the foundation-laying ceremonies.

The construction of a building with such awesome implications for the entire world order required special motives, thorough planning, and elaborate preliminary ceremonials before any real construction began. At Edfu this ceremony was based on a treatise by Imhotep, King Zoser's architect, that was written during the Third Dynasty but contained rites that were even older. The first record of the ceremony is from the Second Dynasty, in reliefs on the outer wall of a granite shrine from Hierakonpolis, and they are still found in temple reliefs of the Late Period. The king set out in festive procession, accompanied by the cult image, to the temple site. Here a ritual drama took place, in which the gods' roles were presumably taken by priests and priestesses. During the nocturnal hours the king fixed the four corner points and the correct orientation of the sanctuary as directed by the god Thoth, with the help of the stars. Then, aided by the goddess Seshat, he marked off the temple precinct by "driving in the stakes" and "stretching the cords." There followed a groundbreaking ceremony in which the king dug foundation trenches, filled them with white sand, a symbol of purity, and made the cornerstone sacrifice which, with the offerings, was buried at the four corners of the future building. Finally, in accordance with an immemorial custom that obviously goes back to the beginnings of Egyptian brick architecture, bricks

were molded of Nile mud mixed with frankincense and placed at the four corners of the foundations. In this way the foundation stone was laid.

The reasons for erecting a temple were of many kinds. They lie in the demands of theology and of the priesthood, but especially in the royal obligation to maintain, with the gods, the world order. The architect of the temple, therefore, was the Pharaoh. The royal jubilee was the principal occasion for building temples, large and small, to symbolize the eternal continuance of the dynastic succession and confirm the close relations between the king and the gods.

The planners of an Egyptian temple had to take into account the entire prevailing theological system, the nature of the principal god for whom the sanctuary was to be built and those of his co-deities, together with all their festivals and cult requirements. Accordingly the details of the plan had to be worked out by a large team of theologians, translated into drawings, and presented for the king's approval. The designs of the late temples of Edfu and Dendera went back to ancient temple plans and to the treatise written by Imhotep. There are sketch plans of smaller sanctuaries and of a royal tomb complex of the New Kingdom on papyrus and limestone tablets; the plan of the temple at Heliopolis is on the back of an inventory tablet (page 116). In translating from the sketched plans to the building site a square grid was probably used, though at Kalabsha (page 183) it was composed of rectangles.

But who were the architects and what were their tasks? We have already mentioned Imhotep, the architect of King Zoser's mortuary precinct (see Plates 146, 147) and the tomb complex of his successor. His titles and functions, preserved on a statue of his royal master, were "chief sculptor, high priest of Heliopolis, hereditary prince, the first after the king, and keeper of the seal of the king of Lower Egypt." In 470 B.C. the Persian king Darius dispatched Khenem-ib-Ra, a chief architect working under Amasis, the last great ruler of the Twenty-Sixth Dynasty, to lead an expedition to obtain stone blocks from the Wadi Hammamat. There he has left us his family tree, carved in the cliff. As proof of a long and prestigious professional tradition, he lists twenty-two generations of architects, starting with Kanofer, architect of King Khasekhemui (end of the Second Dynasty). The names of numerous architects have been handed down from all periods of Egyptian history; some tombs and statues bearing long biographical inscriptions have been preserved. The Egyptian language has no word for "architect"; each master-builder was called "director of all the king's works." They held a special position of trust in relation to the king and frequently acted as his vizier as well. In the New Kingdom, architects began their careers by entering the government service as "apprentice scribes." This reinforces the impression that their principal duties were organizational: recruiting and allocating labor, and procuring building materials, especially supervising the quarrying of stone and its transport from distant quarries to the capital. In inscriptions they boast of their outstanding technical achievements, such as the erecting of obelisks and colossal statues. Only rarely do they refer to the buildings they erected, and never to creative ideas.

*Architecture of Crete, Greece, and the Greek World* ● *Roland Martin*

   *1. Architecture of Minoan Crete and the Mycenaean World*
   *2. Architecture of the Greek City-State*
   *3. Architecture of Hellenistic Greece*

# INTRODUCTION

One hesitates to include a study of the architecture of Crete in a work devoted to Greek architecture, for one is uncertain of the bonds that can be established between two forms of monumental creation—each so different in spirit, in conception of mass and space, and in the use of decorative values. Would it not be better to combine the study of Cretan palatial architecture with that of Oriental palaces? The affinities are obvious, the plans and interiors undoubtedly similar. Nevertheless geographical connections, as well as historical ties and certain shared enduring principles, justify the present decision to treat both Greek and Cretan architecture within the covers of a single book. For the hiatus between the two is bridged by Mycenaean architecture—itself, as we now know, a Greek creation, the work of Greek-speaking peoples. In Mycenaean architecture Minoan forms and elements became integrated with structures indigenous to the mainland; and in the process of adaptation we will find a parallel, toward the close of our period, with transformations of Hellenistic architecture as it evolved toward the architecture of Rome.

Roman architecture is also an amalgam of diverse elements, some borrowed from the Greek tradition that supplied the forms, styles, and decoration, others derived from Italic structures developed by the extant civilizations of Italy. One can discern in it something of the unity that binds together the various periods and different moments of architectural creation in the Greek world during the first two millennia. Thus we begin this study with the formative stage of Minoan architecture, the period of the first palaces in the Middle Minoan era (about 2000–1900 B.C.). The different, and for our purposes largely irrelevant, forms of the Early Bronze Age, which pertain more directly to prehistory and the Neolithic epoch, have been deliberately omitted. In architecture the separation was quite abrupt, marked by the building of the early palaces which heralded a new world.

Similarly, on the mainland, our point of departure will be the Mycenaean works which, as a result of borrowings from Crete, profoundly modified the Helladic tradition in the fourteenth and thirteenth centuries. We shall be concerned only with the great moments of architectural creation that exerted a relative influence on the birth of truly Greek architecture during the Geometric period, in the course of the eighth century B.C.

It is my intention to interpret the great phases of architectural creation within their political, social, and religious context, in relation to the evolution of the human environment which conditions and explains the architectural evolution. Thus I have decided to distinguish only two great periods of Greek architecture. The first is a period of infancy and growth, of searching for plans and forms, of archaic exuberance and fecundity yielding gradually to the restraint and regulation of Classical discipline. This period lasted from the eighth to the fourth centuries B.C. The various aspects of its creative power are examined within their political or religious framework, with due allowance for the building methods and techniques peculiar to Greece.

The second period, called Hellenistic, corresponds to an architectural development encouraged and explained by profound political changes. While modifying and adapting classical forms and structures, Hellenistic architecture created a mode of expression whose evolution ends with Roman architecture and the Western world. Hellenistic architecture developed in a more restricted framework, that of the cities. The town-planning philosophy imposed upon various types of buildings—religious, civic, or private—the changes made necessary by the urban situation; this is the most characteristic element of the period, whose heritage was to be enjoyed for several centuries.

This manner of presentation seems to us to bring out more clearly the conditions and the originality of architectural creation in the Greek world than does the traditional dismemberment into chronological periods whose characteristics are largely external, less related to the actual societies as expressed in their monuments.

## ARCHITECTURE OF MINOAN CRETE AND THE MYCENAEAN WORLD

### MINOAN CRETE

With its early place in time and with the originality of its inspiration, Minoan Crete marks the historical beginning of Western architecture.

In the great palaces of the Late Minoan era, between 1600 and 1400 B.C., one recognizes both the broad principles and the many refinements and subtleties of Cretan architecture in their most explicit form; it is a royal and palatial architecture of fine shades and hierarchical distinctions, combining spatial and decorative values in a balance achieved only by a few privileged periods of architectural history.

Recent excavations and detailed studies of the ruins and ar-

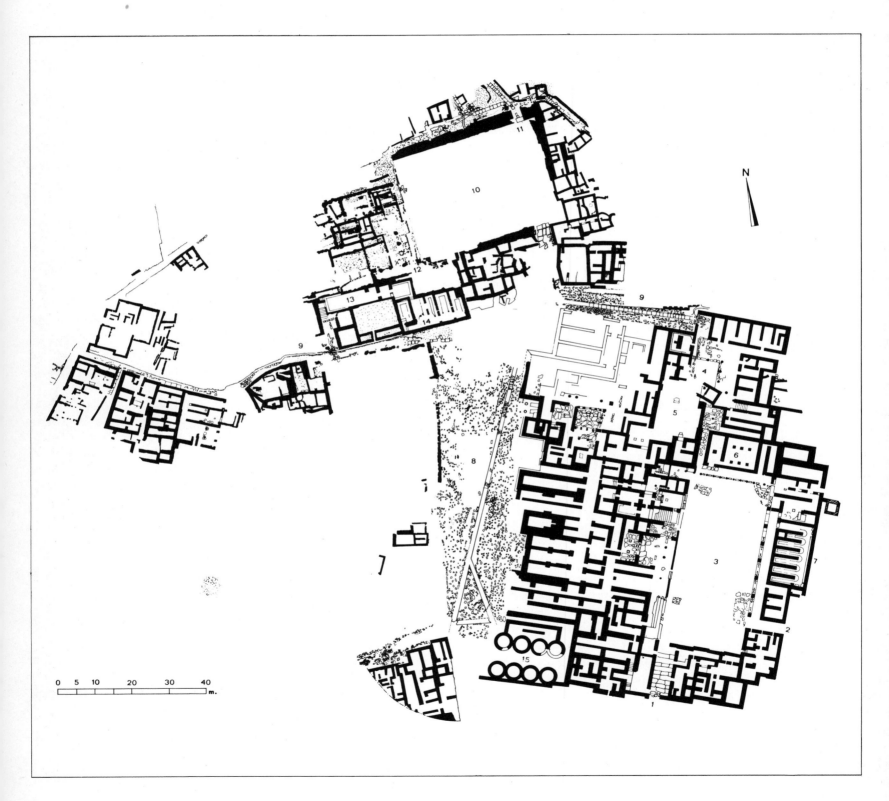

250. *Mallia. Plan of palace and northwest excavations. Middle Minoan, c. 2000-1700 B.C.*
1) *South entrance.* 2) *Southeast entrance.* 3) *Central court.* 4) *North court.* 5) *Tower court.* 6) *Hypostyle hall.* 7) *Magazines.* 8) *West court.* 9) *Street of the Sea.* 10) *Agora.* 11) *Street toward necropolis.* 12) *"Dogleg" entrance.* 13) *Crypt.* 14) *Magazines.* 15) *Cisterns*

251. *Mallia. Perspective reconstruction of palace, from northwest*
252. *Mallia. Crypt rooms. Middle Minoan, c. 2000–1700 B.C.*
253. *Mallia. Plan of House E*

tifacts of the first palaces have made it possible to trace the source of this wave of creativity to the civilization of the Middle Minoan era (2000–1700 B.C.). What were the historical circumstances that enabled Crete to pull away from the rest of the Aegean world, to seize its own style, and to create the forms of a dynamic civilization? Crete, after 1600, rescued the lands along the Aegean shore from mediocrity, as each, in its turn, emerged from the simpler and more rigid forms of the Early and Middle Helladic civilizations. The writing in hieroglyphs that appeared about this time remains undeciphered. Only archaeology, with the measure of hypothesis that it possesses, can suggest certain aspects of the evolution that transformed a fragmented society, dispersed among villages or modest territorial units, into a more centralized political entity; princes, or priest-kings, assembled in their palaces the rudiments of an urban system and established a series of city-states, of which Mallia, Knossos, Zakro, and Palaikastro are the best-known examples. These priest-kings, exercising religious as well as political functions in their territories, doubtless formed the autonomous political groups whose resources were dependent on these zones, though apparently there were no rivalries fierce enough to require defensive organizations of any great strength. The kings could not equal the power of their neighbors, with whom, however, they maintained commercial and, no doubt, artistic contacts. In Egypt, the Pharaohs of the New Kingdom had restored the authority of Thebes and resumed their policy of northward expansion into Palestine and Syria, where Egyptian products mingled with those from Cretan cities (see page 124). Through trading in these markets the Minoans became acquainted with a civilization in full renaissance whose painting offered a wealth of models and whose architecture had broken away from the severity and rigidity of the Old Kingdom by developing orders, introducing colonnades, and exploiting the majesty of the hypostyle hall. The Cretans were to feel the effects of this vigorous renaissance.

Along the eastern Mediterranean the Phoenician harbors of Byblos and Ugarit and the ports of call on Cyprus gave access to a network of interior routes that led ultimately to the great Babylonia of Hammurabi (see page 23). Mari on the Euphrates, and Tell Atchana on the Orontes where it turns southwest toward the sea, were stops along the way, and must certainly have been familiar to Minoan travelers.

Thus Cretan expansion and the first great monuments of Minoan civilization occurred, in the early second millennium, at a time of flux and dynamic creativity in the territories with which

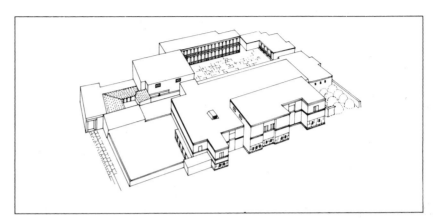

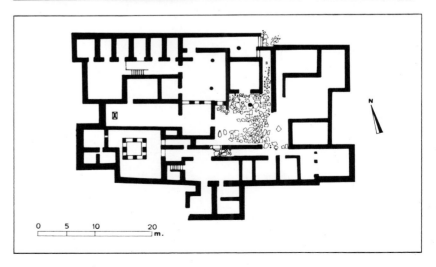

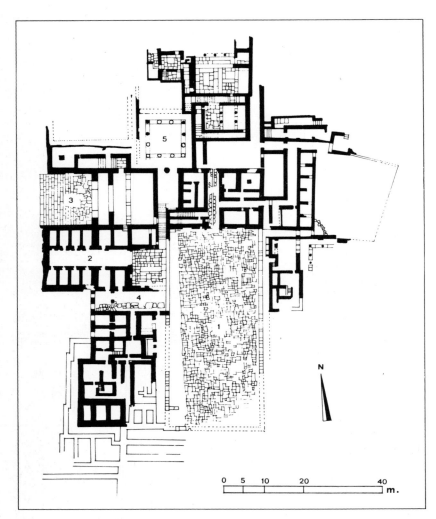

254. *Phaistos. Plan of second palace*
1) Central court. 2) Magazines. 3, 4) Principal entrances. 5) Peristyle court

255. *Phaistos. Reconstruction of propylon*

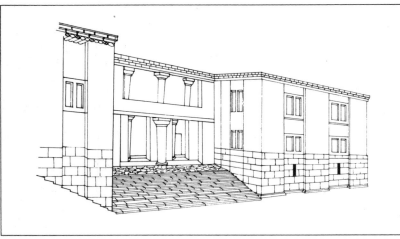

Crete had contact; the Helladic civilizations, clinging more tenaciously to pre-Bronze Age trends, were left far behind.

It was thanks to these contacts that the Cretans worked out the basic forms of their palace architecture. The full development came in the following period, under the enlightened domination of the princes of Knossos, who undoubtedly achieved the unification of Crete partly to their own advantage.

The palaces of Mallia, Zakro, and even Phaistos, if less sumptuous than Knossos, reveal more clearly the original features of this Old Palace architecture.

### The First Palaces

The rectangular court is immediately recognizable as the key element, whose unifying role was to grow steadily more important (165 by 72½ feet at Mallia; 165 by 82½ feet at Knossos, where it is equally ancient). It is not the cellular unit seen in Oriental palaces—Mari, for example—a module around which surrounding rooms are organized, its contours reflected on the exterior walls of the complex; such units, repeated as often as required, form a loosely structured whole (see Plate 39). By contrast the Minoan court has its own independent value and creates its own space; it derives its unifying influence from its role as a traffic hub and from the diversified rhythm of its facades, which reflect the diverse functions served by the "quarters" of the palace.

At Mallia the disposition of the entrances seems to have remained more or less the same (Plates 250–51). The south and southeast entrances lead directly, through a vestibule and a passageway, into the central court. The approach from the north is more devious and may have undergone some modifications: from the so-called Street of the Sea one first entered a little court bordered by an L-shaped portico, from which one emerged into the great court by way of a paved vestibule and passageway. These skirt the western wall of an impressive triple-aisled hypostyle hall with two rows of three pillars, and the hall had access to the court through a dogleg passage incorporating a pillared vestibule.

As subsequently became the rule, the sides of the court were lined with porticoes or given some monumental treatment suitable to their function: at Mallia the east facade is distinguished by a long portico of square pillars alternating with circular columns. This portico borders a string of so-called magazines, rectangular storage rooms dating from the earliest phase of the palace's history. The treatment of the south facade is less refined: a long segmented wall on a massive plinth was pierced

256. *Phaistos. West court of palace, from west. c. 1700–1400 B.C.*
257. *Phaistos. Theater and west court of palace, from northwest. c. 1700–1400 B.C.*

258. *Phaistos. Central court of palace, from south. c. 1700–1400* B.C.
259. *Phaistos. Magazines on central court of palace. c. 1700–1400* B.C.

by wide bays intended to light a series of workshops. On the west, the monumentality of the facade reflects a change of function. Service quarters took up the east and south sides of the court, but the west side contained rooms of state having religious or administrative purposes. The heart of the official life of the palace appears to have been at the center of the west side, in two communicating rooms: a triple-aisled hall entered by two side doors, which may have been a "throne room," and, through a wide opening, another pillared room beyond. This central group was flanked by two important features: to the north a monumental staircase leading to the upper floor was bordered by a platform raised a few steps above the level of the court that it dominated. On the south a broad passage gave access to the great western magazines; further south another terrace bordered by several steps was doubtless in some way connected with a slab for offerings, imbedded in the ground at the foot of the steps. Religious festivals and political life were closely associated within this architectural setting, a modest prelude to the future splendors of Knossos.

These ancient elements, scarcely modified in the course of the alterations and enlargements of the second palace at Mallia, are used to the same effect at Phaistos, on that splendid plateau that commands the Messara plain and the magnificent panoramic view of Mount Ida to the north (Plates 254–59). The access roads, the court, some of the magazines on the west, and the first few apartments to the southeast form part of the original structure. The over-all conception has crystallized. As at Mallia, the court presents a variety of facades: somewhat blank and rather less elegant toward the north, and bordered on the east by a narrow portico with squat, crowded pillars. The west side was again reserved for administrative offices and rooms of state, which were remodeled as part of the second palace when the monumental entrance on the northwest and a portion of the esplanade were built over the razed areas of the first palace.

Thus, the principles of Minoan architecture were the work of the builders of the first great palaces: the distributional and centralizing role played by the court, which was treated as an autonomous primordial element; the functional principle that controlled the siting of the various quarters—political, administrative, religious, domestic—around the sides of the court; and the juxtaposition of private accommodations, rooms of state, magazines, and workshops. Certain architectural forms have already been assimilated: the use of the column and the pillar in alternation for the porticoes that line the courts; their function of support in subdividing the interior space of the halls; their

decorative role in the loggias and baldachins of Mallia; the technique of using large slabs of *ammouda* (yellow limestone) at the base of the walls or for framing openings; the practical and monumental value of broad flights of steps.

The builders of the second palaces developed and extended these techniques and forms, eventually learning to handle them with a facility and ease that can be fully appreciated only in the palace of Knossos. It should not be forgotten, however, that these skills had been originally mastered by the Cretans of the first period, who, in turn, had borrowed them from the great neighboring civilizations of Egypt and Mesopotamia or Anatolia. The hypostyle hall at Mallia has been compared with Egyptian halls of the early New Kingdom; examples of the use of alternate columns and pillars are not unknown on the banks of the Nile. But any suggestion of a close relationship between the first Cretan palaces and the huge contemporary complexes of Mari or Mesopotamia must be treated with caution. If there seems to be a resemblance at first sight, an analysis of the construction principles and techniques reveals profound differences: the roles of the court have nothing in common; Mesopotamian facades are plainer and much more closed, and the column is used only for decoration; the plans of the halls and living quarters are very different. The true kinship is more probably toward the north, with the architectures recently discovered at Tell Atchana and Beycesultan (see Plates 65–67). Here the function of the court is the same: it articulates more flexibly the various parts of the palace, rather than being tied to a group of halls. The main court is bordered by porticoes and, as distinct from Mesopotamian practice, the column is used extensively to enlarge and animate the inside rooms. This is a more supple architecture, airier as well as more vivacious, and sharing with Minoan architecture its conception of the organization of space.

Before pursuing the development of these forms in the second palaces, we must pause to record another achievement of the Old Palace period, namely the elaboration of a genuine city system around the palace. Recent excavations over some ten years, particularly at Mallia, have revealed the broad outlines and even the precise details of a townscape with the palace as its principal feature.

A network of streets radiated from the palace in the direction of the sea and of the plain, toward the necropolises on the outskirts of the city (Plate 250). The system was not geometric but topographical and functional, reflecting the dwelling patterns of the earlier Bronze Age community. The general plan stressed the privileged situation of the palace and its approaches, but in ad-

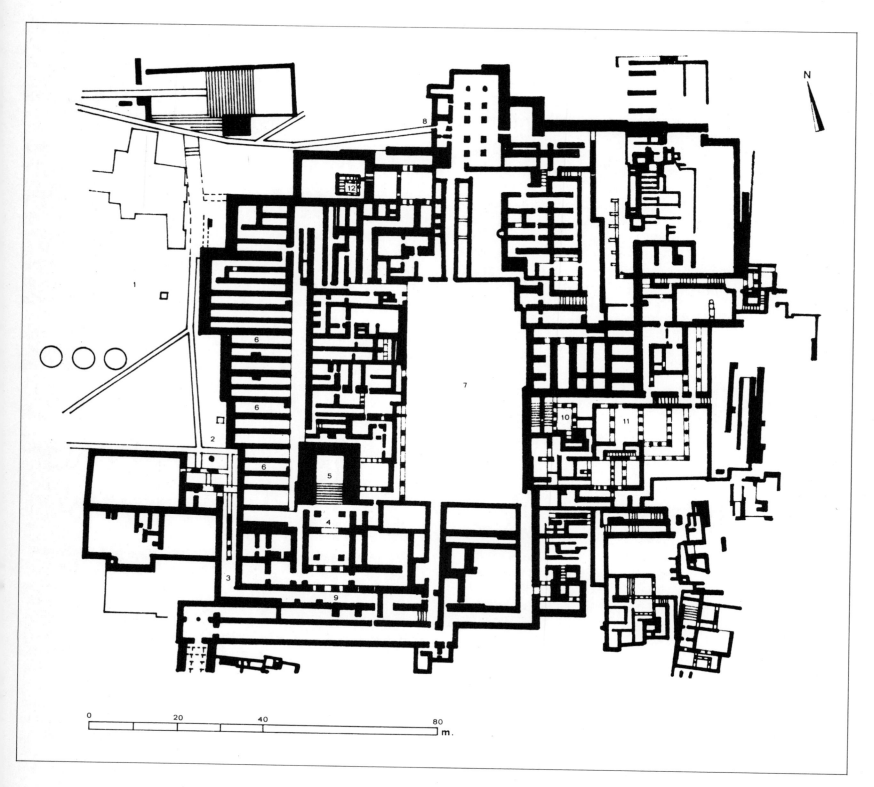

260. *Knossos. Plan of palace*
1) *West court.* 2) *West entrance.* 3) *Corridor of Processions.* 4) *Propylon.* 5) *Monumental staircase.* 6) *Magazines.* 7) *Central court.* 8) *North entrance.* 9) *Veranda.* 10) *Great staircase.* 11) *Hall of the Double Axes.* 12) *House of the Lustral Basin*

0    20    40    80
m.

dition the important role of the public square and its environs. The recent exploration and publication of this complex is a rich contribution to the urban history of Minoan Crete. The main square (96 by 132 feet), comparable in proportions to the central court of the palace, is surrounded on three sides, north, south, and east, by a high foundation wall (about three feet) of large slabs of *ammouda*. Varying in thickness from six to nearly eleven feet, this wall perhaps supported the tiers of seats for a place of assembly similar to those that existed in the cities of archaic Crete, at Lato and Dreros. On the west, buildings not yet identified ended near the southwest corner in a little L-shaped portico. Behind the south foundation wall extended a complex of rooms treated as cellars that form a crypt reached by a few steps (Plate 252). These rooms communicated toward the east with a group of rectangular magazines, very carefully built and similar to those in the palace. The stuccoed walls, several times restored, and the presence of a column in the first chamber suggest that these are the remains of a building of studied monumentality whose crypt must have counted as a floor, on the same level as the small rooms lined up behind the south foundation wall of the court. Comparable in structure to the numerous crypts known in the Minoan palaces, the crypt at Mallia does not seem, to judge from the artifacts found among the excavations, to have had the religious basis attributed to the former examples. Its relations with the adjoining square, itself treated as an agora, and with the palace justify its discoverers in assigning to it a public role.

The ensemble in any case reveals the presence in the Minoan city of a center of public life, freely accessible to the citizens and close to the palace but quite independent of it. This undoubtedly reflects a political organization less centralized and less hierarchical than originally supposed.

The pottery and the study of successive layers of stucco and of construction details, as well as the later stages of development of the site, leave no uncertainty about the chronology of this crypt-square complex. It was laid out in Middle Minoan I and used until Late Minoan I or II; it appears then to have been encroached upon by other buildings, as if a change in political power had concentrated public life around the palace.

## The Second Palaces

After 1700 the palace sites became the focus of power and authority which lasted through the sixteenth and fifteenth centuries. It led to a remarkable architectural development in the palaces and in their surroundings. Mallia dominated eastern

263. Knossos. Magazines on ground floor in western section of palace, from east

264. Knossos. Central court of palace, facade of "throne room" (restored), from east
265. Knossos. Central court of palace, west side
266. Knossos. Megaron above Hall of Double Axes, east wing of palace, from west
267. Knossos. Colonnaded landing of great staircase, east wing of palace, from southeast ▷

268, 269, 270, 271. *Knossos. Great staircase (restored), east wing of palace, interior views*

272. *Knossos. House of Lustral Basin, near northwest portico of palace, from east*

273. *Knossos. South house (restored)*
274. *Knossos. South portico of palace and "horns of consecration," from east*

Crete; Knossos and Phaistos, central Crete; Knossos may have exercised suzerainty even over the other regions. This is the time that the public square at Mallia and its adjoining structures fell into decay, whereas the palace was enlarged—a fairly obvious sign of some socio-political transformation, since the city itself continued to develop and spread, as did the city around the great palace of Knossos. The population of Knossos has been estimated at about 100,000, including those in the central quarters clustered around the palace, in the prosperous homes in the valleys bordering the paved roads, and the population of the port on the present site of Herakleion. This was an important capital, the center of a civilization whose radiance was to arouse the stagnant Aegean lands still in thrall to the civilizations of the Early and Middle Helladic eras, among which Mycenae was the most brilliant.

It would be tedious to describe in detail the great palaces of this period and the rich dwellings that surrounded them. The facts are readily available in specialized accounts. Our object is better served by concentrating upon the broad outlines and original features of New Palace architecture, illustrating our theme with examples drawn from various sites, notably Knossos, the most sumptuous (Plates 260–71). There are a few great principles that inspired the Cretan architect: a functional and organic composition, without concern for artificial bounds or symmetry; the use of the column, in isolation or to form a portico; the skillful and sometimes elaborate organization of volumes and interior spaces; a pronounced taste for linear and decorative structures, with a broad reliance on polychromy and mural painting. These buildings, palaces, and villas gave integrated expression to every aspect of public, religious, and private life.

## Functional and Organic Composition

The first impression received by a visitor to the site of a Minoan palace is one of disorder, confusion, and a jumble of multiple elements unrestrained by any formal discipline. This impression comes from the agglomerative system of construction and the absence of a unified facade. The palace of Knossos covers a rectangle measuring approximately 495 feet east to west by 330 feet north to south. The contours are uncertain and only on the west is there a regular facade. The living quarters and workshop blocks simply cluster together, forming setbacks and salients. The entrances themselves project, on the south (great staircase gallery), or are recessed, on the west (Plates 261, 262).

There are no right angles or continuous straight lines; instead

275. *Knossos. South house and, above, portion of entrance corridor to palace, from southwest*
276. *Zakro. View of excavations*
277. *Hagia Triada. General view of villa*

there is a sinuous movement of projections and recessions that is interrupted only along the western esplanade, where the great paved streets terminate, by a massive plinth composed of alabaster orthostats, large vertical slabs some three feet high. These rest on a projecting step, and above it once rose a wall of dressed stone; the second story was pierced with openings, square windows framed in wood, but the first story was perfectly blank. This bleakness was doubtless tempered by the timbers used to stiffen the masonry of rubble bedded in clay (some partitions were made of unbaked brick supported by wooden framing). This wall formed one side of a row of magazines opening on a north-south service passage, the masonry being sufficiently thick to carry the weight of the upper floors (Plate 263).

A similar sophistication is displayed at Phaistos: the Minoan architect was not insensitive to the monumental quality of an entrance facade and here exploited the remains of the first palace, which had been razed to the level of the orthostats at the base of the walls. The site was filled in and thick walls were built that enclose the magazines and enframe the propylon, set back to enlarge the esplanade which dominated, on the north, the broad steps reserved for spectators at public festivals (Plates 255, 257, 259). These steps abutted a handsome ashlar wall which formed the underpinning of another terrace. Here, as at Knossos, even the ups and downs of the site do not impose any regularity on the external contours of the palace; on the contrary, variations were cleverly exploited as terraces or platforms for the buildings annexed to the central core around the court.

In fact, the location and role of the central court provide the only unifying principle of the composition, but this unity is purely functional and makes no concessions to any demand of symmetry or axiality. It is based on the relations and lines of communication which unite the various quarters of the palace; it is physically realized in the long corridors into which the visitor to the palace is immediately plunged. At Knossos there is the famous Corridor of Processions, so named after the subject of its decorative frescoes. It starts from the innermost corner of the west porch, entered through either of two openings separated by a central column. After running for about 90 feet due south, between walls decorated by the procession of gift-bearers, it turns east and continues in that direction for another 148 feet; near the center of this stretch opens the landing and propylon of a great monumental staircase giving access to the rooms of state that occupied a large part of the upper floor of the west wing. The corridor next swings back north until it reaches the central court. This last change of direction created a sort of crossroads

where also arrived the flow of traffic coming from the south by way of the monumental stairway known as the "stepped porch." This was actually a stepped causeway or viaduct treated as a portico; starting from the bottom of the valley, it reached in terraces to a level just below the south front of the palace and ran parallel to the Corridor of Processions. Another entrance, on the north, was also developed as an ascending corridor, which, after skirting a colonnaded gallery with stucco decorations, emerged almost on the axis of the central court.

These passages and corridors separate groups of rooms having different functions. At Knossos, as at Mallia, Phaistos, and Zakro, the places of assembly and of worship, the audience chambers, and perhaps the administrative offices were ranged on two or three levels along the west side of the court. Their public character was expressed by a series of porticoes, and monumental staircases punctuated by vestibules with single or triple columns supporting in unequal rhythm the balconies and loggias of the upper floors (Plate 265). In these colorful, animated facades, developed on successive levels, motifs were freely juxtaposed with no attempt at imposing an artificial unity; their articulation reflected the diversity of the rooms within, and their functions. As we saw at Mallia and Phaistos, only the irregularities and setbacks of the domestic quarters and workshops, on the south and east, were sometimes disguised by an aligned colonnade forming a shallow portico.

One last feature of these compositions has particular appeal for the modern student of architecture: linked with movement and currents of circulation, it is never closed upon itself. At every instant it opens on the outdoors by a knowing use of porticoes and loggias disclosing neatly framed glimpses of the countryside. The best examples are found at Knossos, on the west, where the domestic apartments and the "Cretan magazines" are bordered with terraces and loggias; it is the same at Phaistos, on the north and east. The treatment of the porticoed rooms, arranging for a progressive opening from the interior light well to the unroofed terrace (Plates 267, 269), creates an agreeable rapport between the building and the surrounding landscape. Sometimes the relationship is even more subtle. Thus the so-called Caravanserai, in the valley south of the palace of Knossos, was organized around a main hall with a colonnade broadly open to the north; the view toward the terraced pile of the palace, clinging to the sides of the hill, offered a picturesque and lively prospect. The refined sense of pictorial decoration, which we will discuss shortly, leaves little doubt that these effects were consciously sought.

## Columns, Pillars, and Porticoes

Flexibility and movement make the originality of Minoan composition, and these find a particularly appropriate means of expression in columned and pillared structures. Since the early palaces the attraction of columned porticoes and facades, and of arrangements of pillars, is apparent.

The columnar motif occurs at the very entrance to the palace—the west propylon at Knossos and at Phaistos, and the entrances to the Little Palace of Knossos—and again with numerous variations inside, especially at Mallia and Knossos. Rooms of state or formal staircases to that level have a median column that divides the passageway in two. Moreover, there are many rooms with one or more columns, at basement level as well as on the various upper floors. Much more subtle and refined are the effects achieved with porticoes or by using pillars as internal partitions. These are the characteristic features of the "Cretan megaron," best exemplified in the large palace at Knossos and the Little Palace, and at Phaistos. The Hall of the Double Axes in the residential quarter of the Palace of Minos is a structure of this type. Illuminated from a light well on the west side through a triple opening formed by two columns, the principal room is divided by three rectangular pillars designed to receive a movable partition; the eastern half of the room is bordered by an L-shaped arrangement of pillars, three along the east, two along the south, pivoting on a massive corner pillar. Finally, the space beyond, similarly treated, is separated from the open terrace by an L-shaped portico with three columns along each leg and a stout corner pillar. The Little Palace offers a most appealing variation on the same theme. The megaron is at right angles to the outside walls; the two parts of the great hall, again separated by three rectangular pillars and a movable partition, are lit through columned openings by a lateral light well. Access to the hall is through a peristyle court with a small triple-column portico on all four sides, and the composition is continued on the axis by another pillared hall illuminated by a light well at the side. The agreeable charms of rhythmically filtered light combined with cunningly controlled ventilation can be readily appreciated.

The use of the interior peristyle court, admitting light and air into otherwise somewhat crowded spaces, was common in Cretan houses and villas. The architects of Phaistos made frequent use of it (Plate 254), especially on the north side, where porticoes continue the rhythm of the central court and smooth the transition to the north megaron with its view of the majestic slopes of Mount Ida.

Columns and pillars were also combined within single porticoes. At Mallia and Phaistos they border certain parts of the central court; in both palaces they are associated with the northern approaches. At Knossos, the portico along the north entrance had a more monumental function; with its double aisle, it became a veritable picture gallery sheltering a relief fresco of a charging bull (Plate 278).

In the villa of Hagia Triada, not far from Phaistos, the portico became an independent building opening onto an esplanade and concealing a row of small rooms (Plate 277), a sort of prototype of the chambered porticoes variously utilized by Greek cities in later centuries.

Finally must be mentioned the pleasing effect of the short columns placed on the substructure accompanying the flights of the stairwells. Two splendid examples are to be found at Knossos. To the east of the central court the residential quarter spreads over the face of the hill on five different levels, two of them no doubt higher than the court, one at the same level, and two lower. A great staircase, with two flights per floor, extended between landings around a light well pierced by columned openings (Plates 268–71). Traditional wooden columns, thinner at the bottom than at the top and crowned by thick cushion capitals, were found in place, heavily charred; plaster casts were promptly made and the restoration carried out in painted cement. The south "stepped porch" at Knossos, discussed above (page 210), was treated in exactly the same way—as a covered stairway whose roof was supported by a double row of columns resting on the low side walls; thus, along the entire stretch of nearly 300 feet it was possible to enjoy a broad view of the countryside and the successive projections of the south front of the palace.

## Organization of Volumes and Interior Spaces

A corollary of the agglomerative plan was the diversified treatment of the different parts of the palace. The result was a rather sharp disparity between masses and levels, tending to create a first impression of somewhat anarchical congestion. No doubt this impression has some measure of validity for the peripheral areas of the palace. But to the extent that the excavations make possible a reliable reconstruction of the elevations, one can now glimpse some of the means employed to avoid an effect of harsh disparity.

The Minoan architect did not hesitate to use on occasion solid masses and blank surfaces: among such examples are the west facade of the palace of Knossos, the south side of the court at

278. "Bull's Head," painted relief from north portico, Palace of Knossos. Herakleion, Museum
279. "Blue Girls," fresco from Palace of Knossos. Herakleion, Museum

278. "Bull's Head," painted relief from north portico, Palace of Knossos. Herakleion, Museum
279. "Blue Girls," fresco from Palace of Knossos. Herakleion, Museum

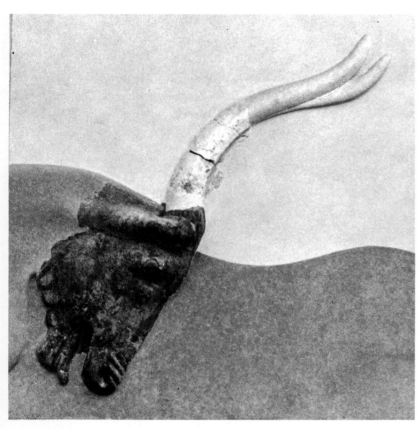

Mallia, and the north side of the court at Phaistos. These are massive structures on base courses of orthostats, enlivened only by a few jogs in the line of the wall and, no doubt, the wood-framed openings.

The play of diversified and animated facades is to be seen in full refinement in the monumental structures that lined the west sides of the great courts at Phaistos, Mallia, and Knossos. The rhythm in this case is very different, and the composition depends on the alternation of solids and voids at the various levels created by terraces and loggias, arranged above the ramps of formal staircases. At Phaistos the northern part of the west wall is developed in a series of alternating pillars and columns that opens on a wide room divided in two by a pair of central columns; beyond this an opening with pillars and columns gives access to a long corridor leading to the dimly lit magazines. This dynamic stretch of facade was followed, it seems, by flat surfaces whose details are still obscure. The same arrangement is found at Mallia, but there the levels make a further diversity. The central section of the facade was plain, edged by a long wall setting apart the great "throne room." At either end, however, there were voids: on the north were two series of steps, one defining a platform with a single central pillar, the other forming a staircase, doubtless leading to the upper floor; on the south, terracing aligned with the flat wall occupied the space left free by the setback of the rooms in the southwest corner.

At Knossos the skill of the architects found its boldest expression. Along the straight front a double rhythm of pillars is developed on each side of the principal element giving access to the throne room and the small sanctuaries: facades with a single pillar contained between two massive antae. To the south, the pillars form a regular border to conceal various projections and ill-related passages; to the north, the rhythm is enlivened by incorporating them in staircases, first a single pillar, then a group of three, all resting on intermediate steps. Moreover, the idiosyncrasies now discernible at the ground-floor level were accentuated in the second story by a succession of balconies, simple windows, and loggias. This was a true pictorial architecture, whose attraction lay in the skillful manipulation of solids and voids that created contrasts of light and shade, and in the correspondence of horizontal and vertical planes.

The planning of the interior spaces indicates equal skill. We have already cited the plan of the "Cretan megaron" and the subtly graded transitions from the outdoor light to the diffused luminosity of the light well (page 211). The great staircase on the east side of the court can justly claim to be the finest example

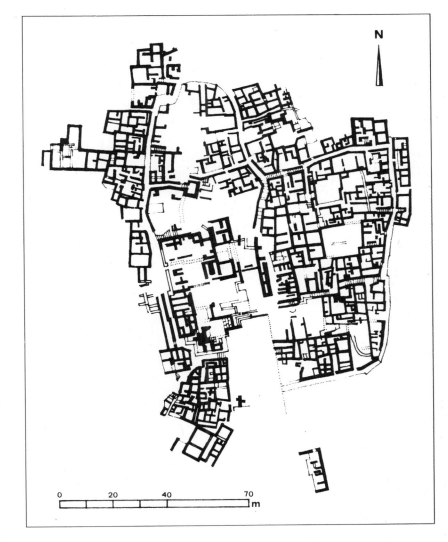

of this art. Its successive flights, adorned with columns, unfold around a light well, the sides opposite the flights bordered by loggias from which run corridors serving the dwelling apartments on each floor (Plates 268-70). An astonishing impression of balance, freedom, even subtlety and boldness results from a rhythm artfully mastered, wholly inspired by the movement that animates the composition, whose charm comes not so much from the ampleness of the volumes as from the elegance of the design.

## Decorative Values, Polychromy, Murals

Although the Minoan architect did not overlook the arrangement of volumes and the subtle art of treating interior spaces harmoniously, his special domain was for linear and pictorial composition. The very technique of building and the nature of the materials favored the development of a taste for polychromy. The timbering that stiffened the stone and clay construction; the foundation walls of big well-mortared limestone slabs; the geometric wooden framing of the doors and windows; the play of pillars and columns, likewise in wood; the angular contours of the facades and terrace roofs, at various levels because of the juxtaposition of blocks of different height—all these suggest a feeling for contrast, polychromy, and pictorial effects. Since the period of the first palaces, perhaps under the influence of Egyptian painting, colors applied to plaster had enlivened the interiors, but the great frescoes were not made before 1600 B.C.

The frescoes at Knossos, like the architecture they complement, are vivacious and rich in movement. Columns, pillars, beams, lintels and jambs, all made of wood picked out with paint, formed the framework of the pictorial decoration. Brown or red backgrounds, as in the stairway and the corridor of the Hall of the Double Axes, brought out the ornamental motifs, in particular the great figure-eight shields. A characteristic feature of this decoration, so well adapted to the architectural lines, is the absence of corner limitations. The corners are, in fact, obliterated so as not to interrupt the movement, which appears to keep pace with the observer as he advances. An example is the great Procession Fresco in the long corridor leading from the west porch. As usual, the figured scenes are treated as a frieze, here a double frieze; the procession of gift-bearers keeps step with the visitor's progress from the door to the great south staircase. The forward motion is sustained, as it were, by a central undulating band of blue, drawn at mid-height just above or below the top of the men's loincloths; these are colored yellow, to contrast with the reddish tints of the flesh. These undulating

281. *Tiryns. Plan of palace*
1, 2) *Casemates.* 3) *Entrance.* 4, 5) *Posterns.* 6) *Outer court.* 7) *Propylon.* 8) *Inner court.* 9) *Megaron.* 10) *Small megaron*

283. *Tiryns. South casemates, from east* ▷

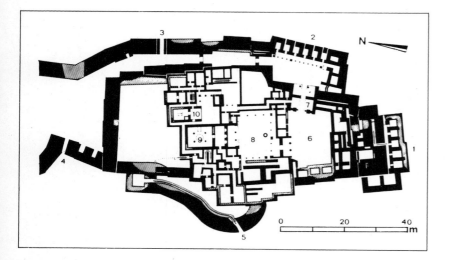

lines turn the corners without interruption, thus creating unity of movement among the figures in the frieze. The frieze itself unfolds together with the interior space.

Other frescoes, such as those portraying crowds of men and women gathered on steps framed by architectural decoration to witness a religious ceremony or public games, carry into the palace eddies from a gay and colorful life (Plate 279); the rustling of skirts, the echo of shouts, and the hum of conversation are almost audible in these scenes, where unity and continuity of movement are suggested by the diversity of the attitudes, the heads and bodies turned in all directions, and the typically Mediterranean gesticulations. The general admiration aroused by the fresco called "La Parisienne" when it was first discovered about 1900, is well known.

Architectural composition was preoccupied with the problem of integrating the interior with the landscape outside. The same preoccupation is reflected in the frescoes at Amnisos and the landscape scenes at Knossos, with a blue bird swooping among the flowers of a rock garden, blue monkeys in a charmingly whimsical landscape, or evocations of a marine world. These paintings open up and brighten the inside rooms. Many centuries later, in the villas of Pompeii, landscapes were to supplement the gardens and peristyles by dissolving their walls and leading the eye beyond, toward broader horizons.

Of course, one should not overlook the hieratic and more restrictive scenes that decorate the so-called throne room at Knossos; more probably this room was a place of worship, with a chair for the priest tucked away in the dimness of the pillared vestibules behind the sanctuary—whose facade has been convincingly restored as the central motif of the west side of the great court. Even these scenes, slower paced but still far from static, are well adapted to the function and structure of the room. More sharply delimited than the friezes, the paintings are also inseparable from the architecture.

Both are closely united in the same conception of space. They divide and animate space, release it from all restrictions, free it to respond to the dynamism of life, modulate it, soften and sharpen it to provide a setting for a society in which both men and women appear to have led full and joyous lives.

## MYCENAEAN ARCHITECTURE

Toward 1400 B.C. the Cretan mode of life seems to have come to an end, or at least to have grown increasingly somber and muted. The Minoan heritage had already been partly assimilated by the

284. *Mycenae. Lion Gate*
285. *Mycenae. Cyclopean walls and approach to Lion Gate*
286. *Mycenae. Stairs leading to "Secret Cistern"*
287, 288. *Mycenae. Stairs leading to and from "Secret Cistern"* ▷

289. *Pylos. Main hall of palace*
290. *Pylos. Bathroom of palace*
291. *Mycenae. Entrance and facade of "Treasury of Atreus"*
292. *Mycenae. Dome of "Treasury of Atreus"* ▷

mainland population; these mainland people were Greeks, as their recently deciphered language plainly shows. Their civilization flourished in the Peloponnese and, more especially, in the Argolid, where Mycenae became the center of the civilization and gave it its name.

For the visitor fresh from Crete who arrives before the Lion Gate at Mycenae, or threads his way through the fortified passages that guard the entrance to the palace of Tiryns, the impression of a new world is immediate and acute (Plates 281–88). This architecture is of a very different order, even though, once inside the walls, he discovers forms and elements that recall the Cretan palaces. But Minoan fluidity and dispersion have given way to concentration; spaces are tightly circumscribed by mighty perimeter walls with their bastions, curtains, constructed approaches, and heavily fortified gates protecting against any surprise attack. This is an architecture of conquering soldier kings, feudal overlords occupying dominant positions that have contours filled not with the ingeniously terraced, invitingly open apartments of Knossos, but by thick walls built of cyclopean blocks, barely hewn yet cunningly assembled. These walls are pierced by occasional posterns at the foot of fortified stairs or "casemates," like those at Tiryns, whose vaults of corbeled arches, closed at the top by two blocks leaning one against the other, have withstood the passage of the centuries (Plate 283). The gates are set back within these walls, and defensive works jut out to dominate the approaches and outflank the besieger. The doorway is framed by monolithic pillars; at Mycenae, the lintel of the Lion Gate is still in place and supports the famous ten-foot-high relief that fills the triangle of the relieving arch required by so great a span (Plates 284, 285). The two lions, confronting from either side a column with capital and crown, assured the religious protection of the citadel.

Inside the citadel the buildings were grouped around the palace, itself reduced to a few rooms surrounding the megaron. At Mycenae the palace clung to a crumbling terrace; it is Tiryns, on its platform only eighty-six feet above the plain of Nauplia and Argos, that offers the best example of Mycenaean palace construction (Plates 281, 282).

This is not to overlook the importance of the palace at Pylos (Plates 289, 290), the remains of the fortification of Athens, the still uncertain traces of the palace at Thebes, the fortifications of Gla in Boeotia, or the ruins of Malthi. Nonetheless, one always returns to Tiryns, whose plan, developed in the thirteenth century B.C. with remarkable unity of conception, reads like a working drawing. From the east entrance (the only one, except for a few posterns) leads a long ramp, twice interrupted by intermediate gates, toward the southern tip of the knoll; there, through a gate flanked by guardhouses, one enters the first court. This esplanade was surrounded by defense works on several levels, including casemates commanding the approach to the foot of the wall on the east and south. On the north side of the court opens a columnar propylon, already more Greek than Minoan with its two double-columned porticoes back-to-back on the central wall; the visitor then enters the main court porticoed on the east, west, and south sides, the north side being occupied by the facade of the megaron, the principal element of the palace around which the suites of domestic apartments were clustered. Very different from the Cretan megaron, the rectangular Mycenaean hall is entirely enclosed and preceded by a double vestibule; the first is an outer vestibule with two columns in antis, the inner one gives access through a single central door to the principal area. This span, in accordance with tradition, was occupied by a central hearth and four columns arranged in a square supporting the clerestory lantern that rose above the terrace roof. The wall frescoes here, with their essentially military themes, and the floors and stuccowork recall Minoan decoration and techniques. Although, compared to the Minoans, the Mycenaeans knew much more about large-scale stone work, both in polygonal blocks with rough-hewn faces and rectangular blocks laid in regular courses (as we will see in the tholos tombs), they also used the Minoan masonry of rubble bedded in clay, stiffened by horizontal and vertical timbers. This method involved plaster and stucco, and the Mycenaeans had quickly acquired the Cretan art of fresco. The porticoes, columned propylons, vestibules, and decorative techniques may have been derived from the Cretan repertory, but the principles of construction remained firmly within the mainland tradition. The centralizing role of the megaron is particularly conspicuous at Pylos; the mass of the megaron is detached by the lateral corridors that link it with the smaller rooms on either side. The court itself is an annex of the megaron, intended merely to free the approaches and display the facade; unlike the Cretan court, it has no structural function. The result is a progressive, hierarchic composition organized around the megaron, with a concern for monumentality and privileged areas that is foreign to Minoan architecture.

The taste for the monumental is expressed with special force in the tholos tombs of Mycenae, the most successful example of which is the so-called Treasury of Atreus (Plates 291–93). A long open-air passage or "dromos," carved out of the hillside, forms

294. *Dreros (Crete). Diagrammatic reconstruction of a temple*
1) *East facade.* 2) *North facade.* 3) *Plan.* 4) *Longitudinal section.* 5) *Transverse section*

295. *Argos. Terra cotta model of temple, from Sanctuary of Hera. Athens, National Museum*

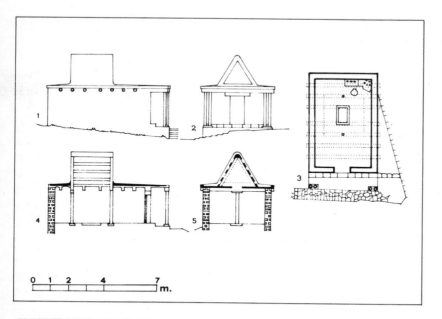

an entranceway 116 feet long and 20 feet wide between walls built of uniform blocks perfectly dressed and carefully laid. At the end of this passage rises the facade of the tholos, flanked by half columns of green stone more than thirty-three feet high and decorated with spiral and chevron motifs. The door is monumental—nearly eighteen feet high and nine feet wide—and crowned by a monolithic lintel that occupies the entire width and depth of the opening. The relieving triangle above repeats the spiral motif on the columns around the door. The interior of the chamber is profoundly impressive. Circular in plan with a diameter of nearly fifty feet, the corbeled vault rises forty-five feet in thirty-three annular courses of regular blocks, cut to a smooth curve of perfect elegance. Rarely have art, technique, and proportions been combined in such complete harmony.

During the fourteenth and thirteenth centuries many regions of the Mediterranean world received the impress of Mycenaean culture. But violent upheavals, touched off either by new waves of Hellenic migration—the Dorian invasion—or, as now seems more likely, by a series of revolts, were soon to bring about the downfall of Mycenae and obliterate its name from the map of the civilized world. The power and vigor of its architecture and the dynamism of its expansion, faint echoes of which still linger in Homeric poetry, must have had their effect on the birth of Greek art. This point is still debated, and it is not easy to determine the precise contribution of the Mycenaean heritage in the progressive inventions of early Greek architecture, to which we now must turn, passing over several centuries, notably the eleventh and tenth, that remain shrouded in obscurity.

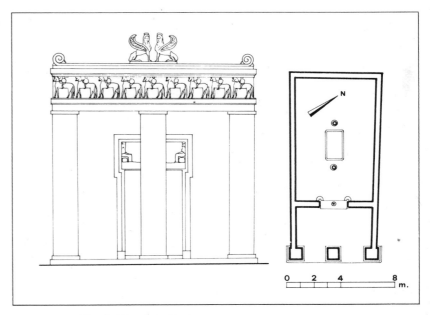

## ARCHITECTURE OF THE GREEK CITY-STATE: BIRTH AND DEVELOPMENT

From one end to the other of the Mediterranean regions that later formed the "Greek world," the collapse of Mycenaean civilization provoked migratory movements of people who were either simply drawn into the vacuum or driven by difficulties, external and internal, from one shore of the Aegean to the other. Dorian invasions from the north, Achaean movements, and Ionian migrations allowed few areas to escape these upheavals, and were hardly favorable to artistic and, in particular, architectural creation. Only the useful arts, especially ceramics, enable us to trace the threads that run through this Dark Age during which, from the eleventh to the eighth centuries B.C., the Greek peoples sought a new equilibrium and tested the political and social structures that were to result in the formation of the *polis*, the Greek city-state, an original and fruitful institution that fostered the most expressive forms of Greek art and architecture.

As evoked in the last books of the *Odyssey* and the poems of Hesiod, this social and political community was precariously based on an often uneasy partnership between clan structures and embryonic social groupings founded on common interests, between the landed aristocracy and the little men, tenant farmers, or smallholders. In this society political rights depended on property and family connections.

## ORIGINS

The architecture first generated by these communities was merely practical and utilitarian, with no pretensions to monumentality; the abode of the gods was cast in the image of the abode of men.

This architecture retained nothing of the Mycenaean palatial tradition. A few isolated examples or more extensive sites such as ancient Smyrna account for our knowledge of the early forms of this renaissance. Each structure was separate and independent. Typically a house had only one room; this was first elliptical, then rectangular, later apsidal in plan. At Old Smyrna, the first two types are the oldest (eleventh to ninth century), the third was contemporary with the last Geometric period (end of ninth to first half of eighth century). Eighteen to twenty-three feet in length, in width eleven and one-half to thirteen feet at the most, these houses were made of sun-dried brick or rammed clay on a foundation of stones or rubble. Very soon these foundations became more important and were built of hewn blocks, then of orthostats, the large slabs set on edge that continue to be used

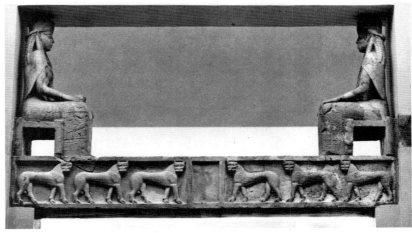

298. *Thermon. Plan of successive buildings of Temple of Apollo*
A) *First epoch (9th century B.C.)* B) *Second epoch (8th century B.C.)* C) *Third epoch*
*(end of 7th century B.C.)*
299. *Samos. Plan of Sanctuary of Hera*
1) *South stoa.* 2) *Second hekatompedon.* 3) *Processional corridor.* 4) *Altar*

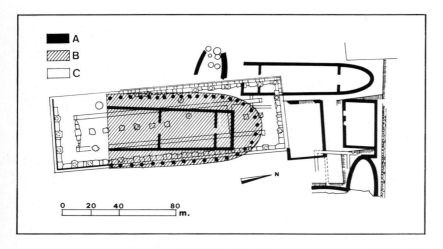

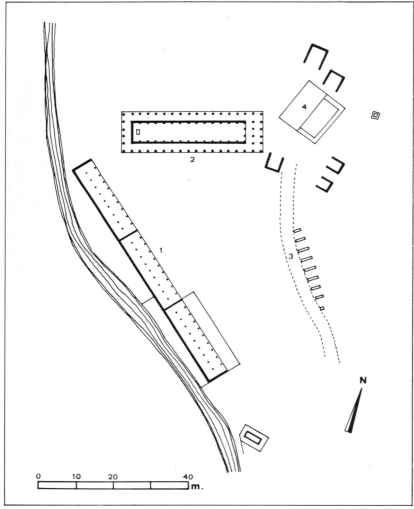

throughout Greek architectural history. Wood posts on the in-side, aligned on the principal axis, supported a rudimentary structure of ridge pole and branching lateral elements.

The roof was double-hipped, translated into stone in the manner of the little votive building on Samos. At Smyrna, as in the little Temple of Apollo Daphnephoros recently discovered at Eretria, the interior posts are asymmetrically distributed. There is a single post at one end, a double post at the other; it may be assumed that this double post supported a beam that received a heavier load because it carried the radial framing that reinforced the hip, whereas at the other end, corresponding to the facade, the pitched roof ended in a gable with a triangular pediment. Here again temple models in terra cotta from Perachora and Argos suggest and justify this reconstruction (Plate 295). Traces of the same system are to be found as late as the sixth century in the treasury of the Heraion at the mouth of the Sele River near Paestum (Greek Poseidonia).

The origin of the triangular pediment, often associated with an opening that lit and made habitable the attic space, is linked with the introduction of apsidal or elliptical plans having a straight facade; the long sides being barely curved, it was only the apse at the back that remained rounded and the plan as a whole was horseshoe-shaped. There is quite a long list of these buildings, which in the seventh and sixth centuries had a dual function, profane and religious. Within the great sanctuaries at Delphi and Delos, and on the Athenian acropolis, there were numerous chapels with an apsidal plan. The latest to be discovered and structurally the most interesting is that of Apollo Daphnephoros at Eretria. About thirty-eight feet long by twenty-five wide, the horseshoe plan has an entrance opening about six and one-half feet wide in the straight facade. Two pillars stood in front of this facade, almost in line with the side walls that supported a broad overhang of the roof, in the manner of the terra cotta model from the Argive Heraion. Inside, one post in line with the door and two others further back formed a triangle that served to support the roof framing; this consisted of a triangular truss at the facade end, and radial poles supporting the hip above the apse. The most original feature is in the two rows of bases, made of rammed clay and gravel; these bases are arranged in pairs on either side of the walls, and there are eleven groups of pairs, about ten feet apart. Thus the temple, inside and out, had a total of twenty-seven wood posts defining an unusual but very distinctive structure, of particular interest in relation to the history of the Greek house and temple at the beginning of the first millennium.

300. *Samos. Plan of Temple of Hera III, by Rhoikos and Theodoros*
1) North stoa. 2) Dipteros of Rhoikos. 3) Altar. 4) Altar of offerings. 5) Processional
corridor
301. *Samos. Plan of Temple of Hera IV, by Polycrates of Samos*
302. *Eretria. Plan of first Temple of Apollo Daphnephoros*

From these known elements in connection with the apsidal plan, there emerged the first examples of the columned porch intended to protect and enlarge the initial cell. In company with the Daphnephoreion of Eretria one should mention the megaron B of Apollo at Thermon, which is contemporary or a little later (Plate 298). Around the apsidal megaron, whose long sides are slightly curved, a series of slabs attests to the existence of a surrounding portico that supported either the overhang of the main roof or a lean-to. The posts were not continued across the front. The general lines were similar to those of the primitive temple at Eretria. These constitute the best examples of a still rudimentary architecture employing the "base" materials of wood, brick, rammed clay, rough stones—and perhaps even simple branches, as in the hut of laurel dedicated to Apollo, evoked by the texts in the Delphic sanctuary and illustrated by the finds at Eretria.

In the course of the sixth century Greek architecture succeeded in mastering the "noble" materials: limestone first, and then marble. Walls of rubble and brick were slowly transformed into a regular masonry of carefully hewn blocks—at that time called *plinthoi,* the same term used for bricks. The wood post became a trim stone column, at first fine and slender beneath an entablature that remained light; then that, too, was transformed from wood to stone.

During this process the architecture diversified its forms, specializing its shapes and plans as functions became ever more precisely defined. The city, itself more structured and organized, translated these trends into a varied and vigorous architecture whose subdivisions we must now examine in more detail.

## RELIGIOUS ARCHITECTURE: MASTERPIECES OF THE IONIC ORDER

The most ancient remains of religious architecture, in which coexist the new forms and the older Aegean tradition, are found in two different parts of the Greek world.

First, in Crete, the primitive temples of Prinias and Dreros stand apart from the apsidal structures of mainland Greece (Plates 294, 296, 297). Their plans recall the Minoan chapels; squarish or oblong, the buildings incorporate sacrificial altars, libation tables, and benches for offerings and divine effigies. The enlarged interior required intermediate posts to support the terrace roof. The shape of the pillars, the predominance of uneven rhythms, and the taste for painted and sculptured borders around the openings and at the eaves reveal the bond between these archaic structures (eighth to seventh centuries) and the Minoan heritage.

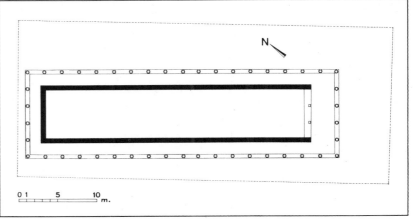

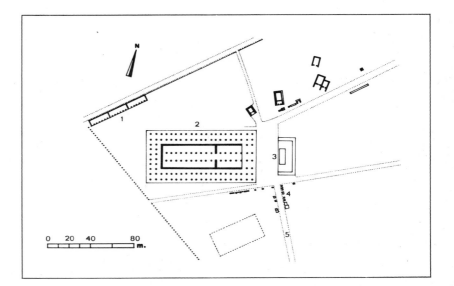

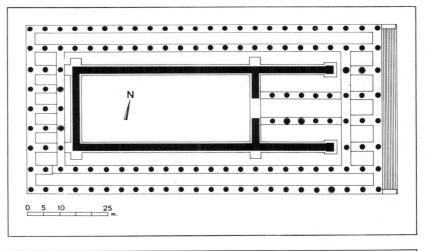

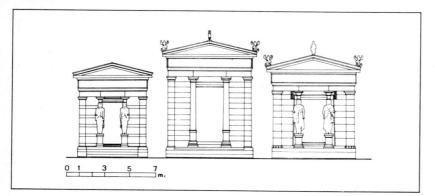

303. *Larissa. Aeolic capital. Istanbul, Archaeological Museum*
304. *Neandria. Aeolic capital. Istanbul, Archaeological Museum*
305. *Delphi, Sanctuary of Apollo. Reconstruction of front elevations of treasuries of Cnidos, Marseilles, and Siphnos*

Further east, on Delos and Samos in particular, these features, still recognizable in the Delian sanctuaries of Apollo and Artemis and of Leto, evolved rapidly into a broader, more monumental conception unmistakably influenced by the luxuriant Egyptian colonnade.

The requirements of ritual and worship had led to the creation of new forms adapted to a specific religious function. On the banks of the Imbrasos River, not far from the town of Samos, the effigy of Hera brought by the Argonauts was venerated beneath a baldachin among open-air altars and clumps of sacred willow. These were permanent elements of the cult that never disappeared, despite the multiple architectural transformations that the sanctuary underwent in the course of the centuries. The first Hecatompedon ("hundred-footer"; 100 by 20 feet) was built at the beginning of the eighth century; it was a large, very elongated hall whose roof was supported by an axial row of interior pillars. Soon there came to the fore the same preoccupation as at Thermon: by the end of the century the volume and monumentality were augmented by a peristyle of wood pillars, seven by seventeen, the first manifestation of the peripteral plan.

During the first half of the seventh century, around 660 B.C., this building was replaced by a new temple, differently conceived and better adapted to the cult (Plate 299). A cella 101 feet long and over 21 feet wide, preceded by a tetrastyle vestibule, was surrounded by an eighteen-by-six-column peristyle (124 by 29 feet). The interior was largely unobstructed, the better to display the cult statue. The axial row of columns was eliminated and the weight of the roof was distributed among square pillars attached to the inside faces of the walls; these pillars stood on a light stylobate in exact correspondence with the columns of the exterior peristyle. These elements were now harmonized and coordinated, a notable advance in the composition of the building.

Further progress was made in the decade about 570–560 B.C. by the architects Rhoikos and Theodoros, who built the great Temple of Hera at Samos (Plate 300); and Theodoros, at least, in collaboration with Chersiphron the Cretan and his son Metagenes, also contributed to the building of the Artemision of Ephesus. These men belonged to that first generation of great Greek builders whose vigorous powers of creation and exceptional technical mastery enabled them to purge their art of groping primitivism. They were sculptors and engineers as well as architects, and filled with curiosity about the outside world—the two Samian architects traveled to Egypt—and, in the image of their times, they were preoccupied by technique and inclined

228

306. *Delphi, Sanctuary of Apollo. Caryatid from Treasury of the Siphnians. Delphi, Museum*

307. *Delphi, Sanctuary of Apollo. Pediment and frieze from Treasury of the Siphnians. Delphi, Museum*

308. *Delphi, Sanctuary of Apollo. Frieze from Treasury of the Siphnians. Delphi, Museum*

309. *Delphi, Sanctuary of Apollo. Decorated foundation wall, Treasury of Marseilles*

310. Delphi, Sanctuary of Apollo. Frieze (detail) from Treasury of the Siphnians. Delphi, Museum

311. Delphi, Sanctuary of Apollo. Trabeation from Treasury of the Siphnians. Delphi, Museum

312. Athens, Acropolis. Olive-tree Pediment, of painted poros. Athens, Acropolis Museum

toward ingenious research: "Theodoros," Pliny the Elder tells us, "who built the labyrinth of Samos [the great dipteral temple], made a statue of himself in bronze. This brought him fame not only because of the astonishing likeness of the portrait but also because of the great cunning of his art." Among themselves, moreover, they established the tradition of commentaries written by great artists on their works. The rare echoes of these writings that one finds in Vitruvius and Pliny make one regret the loss of a technical and theoretical literature that would have enlightened us on many aspects of Greek architectural creation.

The remains of the great Temple of Hera at Samos are all we have left from which to judge the work of Rhoikos and Theodoros. The scale is now vastly greater (347 by 173 feet); the peristyle is doubled to form a near "labyrinth" of 104 columns, their rhythm being established by the spacing of the interior columns of the temple; the intervals between the center facade columns, reflecting the interior columns and walls of the cella, were much greater (27 feet) than the side intervals (17 feet).

The Artemision at Ephesus, a contemporary work and equally huge (380 by 182 feet), surpassed its rival in richness of decoration. Likewise dipteral in plan, it had an octastyle facade (the rear facade had nine columns) and similar variations in the widths of the bays. The sculptural decoration, which the Classical epoch would confine to certain specific zones, here curiously spread over the outer columns of the facades: the lowest drum of each column, resting on an elaborately molded base with a double scotia surmounted by a torus, was decorated in low relief—unless, according to a more recent hypothesis, the decoration was indeed located at the top, beneath the capital. Croesus, the wealthy king of Lydia, evidently intended to offer some of these sumptuous columns to the great goddess of Ephesus; several of them are inscribed with his name.

For hundreds of years the forms and motifs of Ionic architecture in Asia continued to be modeled on these two buildings; when the temples at Ephesus and at Sardis were rebuilt in the fourth century only the details were changed. The novel proportions, and new ideas of Hellenistic architects were necessary to bring fresh decoration to Magnesia on the Meander, and to Didyma.

From its domain in Asia Minor certain echoes of the Ionic style, at first timid and discreet, reached both inland Greece and the west (Plates 303, 304), where the Doric order still reigned supreme. One receives the impression of a few variations grafted onto the basic theme.

In mainland Greece, the sanctuary of Apollo at Delphi and

the Athenian acropolis have preserved the finest examples of Ionic architecture applied to buildings of modest proportions. These are refined, conceived as jewels, and intended to introduce into the sober Doric a bit of brightness and fantasy, to add decorative grace and charm to the more monumental displays in these sanctuaries. The treasuries of Delphi, the Temple of Athena Nike at the entrance to the Athenian acropolis, and the Erechtheion across from the Parthenon relieve the relative severity of the great Doric structures.

In this miniature architecture the taste for sculptural decoration is most freely expressed in the Ionic treasuries of Delphi, dating from the period 550 to 525 B.C. (Plate 305). In the treasuries of Clazomenae and of Marseilles the voluted capital of Asia Minor was replaced by a palm capital, doubtless based on an Egyptian model; the elongated leaves, their ends curled over, form a basket or *calathos*. The Cnidians, then the Siphnians, substituted for columns the figures of caryatids, closely related in style to the Archaic *korai* (Plate 306). The walls themselves bear molded and sculptured decorations: at the base is a strip of ornament, a grooved torus in the treasuries of Cnidus and Marseilles (Plate 309), a luxuriant bead-and-reel molding in that of Siphnos. At the top a sculptured frieze crowns the alternate courses of stretchers and headers (Plates 307, 308, 310, 311). The architrave itself has a decoration of rosettes; it is separated from the frieze by a row of egg-and-dart ornaments. The frieze of warriors based on Homeric themes, beautifully carved in high relief of island marble, has touches of paint highlighting the sculptural effects. Finally, the soffit of the cornice that crowns the entablature is ornamented with a garland of palmettes and lotus flowers in a plump, expressive style.

Somewhat ostentatious efforts still accentuate the Ionian taste for decorative values, already perceptible in the great works of Rhoikos and Chersiphron. It ultimately modified the Asian scheme of the Ionic entablature by introducing a sculptured frieze to replace the dentils, those toothlike blocks projecting above the architrave in a decorative transformation of the beam-ends used in primitive construction to support the terrace roof. This was an insular feature of the Ionic order that only took hold in Asia Minor in the Hellenistic epoch.

On the Athenian acropolis, the Attic architects did not discount the decorative value of the Ionic style. They adopted it for small structures (Plates 312, 313) and introduced it into the interiors of Doric compositions, in both the Parthenon and the Propylaea. Callicrates, an architect in the service of Cimon who began to rebuild the acropolis between 460 and 451, designed

315. *Athens, Acropolis. East portico, Temple of Athena Nike*
316. *Athens, Acropolis. Corner of east portico, Temple of Athena Nike*
317. *Athens, Acropolis. Ceiling of portico, Temple of Athena Nike*

the Temple of Athena Nike that projects like a figurehead at the entrance to the acropolis (Plate 314). A first version, built about 450, was the Temple of Demeter and Kore on the banks of the Ilissus River; it has since disappeared, but is known from the eighteenth-century accounts of Stuart and Revett. The Temple of Athena Nike was not built until about 420, at the end of the great Periclean phase. It is a successful Attic adaptation of island and Asian traditions. Almost square in plan—the cella is slightly wider than deep (13 feet 9 inches by 12 feet 5 inches)—it has the prostyle facade dear to the Athenians, the entrance portico in front of the vestibule (Plates 315–17). A columned order replaces the two columns in antis, a theme recalled at the corners of the rear wall; this has also a prostyle portico. The decorative value of the two facades—their deep-fluted monolithic columns resting on tall bases with grooved torus, and crowned with vigorous, amply voluted capitals—contrasts sharply with the deliberately bare walls of fine blocks of Pentelic marble, hewn and laid in accordance with the perfect regularity of the isodomic bond. At the same time, unity is established by the recurring grooved torus around the foot of the wall, and by the sculptured frieze that surrounds the walls as well as the facades. The same movement associating architecture and decoration was continued in the panels of the balustrade along the edge of the bastion; reliefs of winged Victories evoked the various moments of the procession and sacrifices celebrated in honor of Athena Nike.

Toward the center of the acropolis, north of the Parthenon, rises the Erechtheion (Plates 318–24); the complexity of this temple, imposed by cult requirements and religious functions, finds resolution in the freedom and imaginativeness of the Ionic style. It is a veritable repertory of late fifth-century decorative forms assembled in a building that does not quite succeed in assimilating them all into a genuine architectural unity. The Erechtheion, begun about 421 and completed in the final years of the century, is the first work to introduce rococo into Classical harmony and simplicity.

The building consists of a rectangular core (38 by 75 feet) to which various elements are annexed. On the east, the facade is composed of a prostyle hexastyle Ionic portico of six columns. Opposite, on the west side, were four supports in a mixed order—Ionic half columns associated with half pilasters; a low balustrade originally ran between the supports, replaced in Roman times by a windowed wall. The west facade rests on a solid wall that forms a plinth to compensate for the ten-foot difference in grade between east and west. The interior is divided into four rooms, one open to the east, the others communicating

319. *Athens, Acropolis. Northeast corner of north porch, Erechtheion, showing upper portion of Ionic order*
320. *Athens, Acropolis. Erechtheion and Parthenon, from northwest*
321. *Athens, Acropolis. Northeast corner of north porch, Erechtheion, showing lower portion of Ionic order*

325. *Xanthos. New restoration of Monument of the Nereids. London, British Museum*
326. *Xanthos. Structural diagram of Monument of the Nereids*

327. *Xanthos. Perspective reconstruction of Monument of the Nereids*

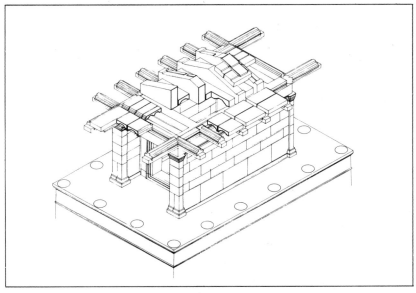

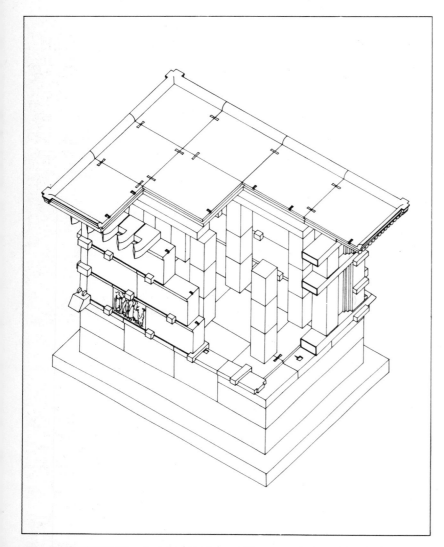

with the north porch; these divide the space among the several deities to whom the shrine is dedicated.

The north portico, a gem of the Ionic style with four columns across the front and one behind at either side, extends straight out from the wall. Independently beautiful, it destroys the total unity. The columns combine lightness of proportion with vigorous flutings and graceful decoration: the upper torus of the Attic bases are decorated with interlaces; broad neckings are carved with anthemion ornament; the capitals have wide volutes whose spirals are underlaid by fillets. The portico shelters a monumental doorway whose jambs and lintels are richly framed with carved moldings and bands of egg-and-tongue and leaf-and-dart ornament. The opening is crowned by a cornice profiled with honeysuckle, where palmettes and lotus flowers nestle in the curve of the cyma; acanthus cups and elegant convolvulus spill from the spiral consoles at either side. The entablature frieze echoes the frieze on the outer walls and is treated in the same manner: figures carved in the round from white marble are set against slabs of blue Eleusinian marble.

On the south, another baldachin conceals the steps in the southwest corner of the building that gave access to the tomb of Cecrops, legendary king of Athens. This is the famous Caryatid portico. Sturdy maidens, the napes of their necks reinforced by wavy locks, support a dentiled Ionic entablature that contrasts with the ornamental frieze above it on the wall against which it rests.

Such, in broad outline, is the Erechtheion, in which are gathered all the innovations that the architects of fifth-century Athens tried to introduce into the decorative repertory of their art. Certain forms and details were later borrowed from the building, but it was too complicated, the cleavage between its architectural functions and decorative values too deep, to have ever served as a model. It remains a witness to the experiments at the end of the Classical epoch, a prelude to the great creative movement in the fourth century and Hellenistic period.

The Attic tendency to confine the use of the Ionic order to buildings of modest proportions set a fashion in the fourth century, particularly in funerary architecture. Two monuments of exceptional importance belong to this tradition, which persisted into Hellenistic and Roman times: the Nereid monument at Xanthos and the Mausoleum at Halicarnassus. They are alike both in their funerary character and in their structure, a curious blend of "barbarian" elements—Lycian and Anatolian—with Greek forms superficially applied.

The idea of a monument raised upon a terrace, and comprising a tall massive podium supporting an Ionic chapel—further developed at Halicarnassus by a huge stepped pyramidal base that supports a crowning marble quadriga with statues of Mausolos and his wife – had already become a reality in Lycian heroic monuments of the sixth and fifth centuries. These stone copies of primitive wooden structures, in technique purely Lycian and Anatolian, had nothing in common with Greek architecture (Plates 325–29). The use of figured friezes at the top of terrace walls, or to crown a plinth, is more Oriental than Greek. The transformation of these indigenous monuments was a consequence of the penetration of Greek influence and of the Hellenizing policies practiced by the native princes or Persian satraps; local and traditional structures were simply clothed in Greek forms.

The terrace, supported by a handsome, regularly bonded stone wall, was ornamented with sculptured figures (Nereids on the acropolis of Xanthos, lions on Halicarnassus); the podium was itself decorated with one or two friezes whose subjects were sometimes drawn from Greek mythology but often borrowed from the triumphal themes of the Oriental repertory (processions of chariots, combat, the hunt, etc.); finally, the chapel forsook the geometric forms of Oriental tradition and assumed the guise of a small Greek temple: an Ionic building either in antis or peripteral; Ionic columns with bases and capitals in the Asian style; entablature with sculptured decoration, doors embellished with egg-and-tongue ornament, volutes, and palmettes. The very fame of these monuments and their success as funerary architecture bear witness to the remarkable decorative value of the Ionic style as developed by the first Ionian architects of the sixth century, modified and perfected by fifth-century Athenians. This was the heritage that artists of the Hellenistic epoch were to exploit.

## THE DORIC ORDER: INFANCY AND YOUTH

In the second half of the seventh century B.C. religious architecture, in mainland Greece and the west, found in the Doric style the forms and features that enabled the Doric order, within a few decades, to achieve its most balanced expression.

The Peloponnesus was the birthplace of the Doric column with its fluted shaft, planted directly on the stylobate with no base or transitional molding, and its flattened capital, whose broadly projecting echinus is separated from the shaft by vigorous annulets with a sculptured necking of curling leaves fringing a necking groove of variable depth. The square abacus above is never omitted. Was the Doric an adaptation of the

333. *Olympia. Terrace of the treasuries and entrance to stadium, from west*
334. *Paestum, Sele River. Plan of Treasury, Sanctuary of Hera*
335. *Paestum, Sele River. Reconstruction of facade of Treasury, Sanctuary of Hera*

Mycenaean capital, which also had a necking groove and a very thick torus? or an independent Dorian invention?

The evidence suggests that the form may have been derived from an ancient prototype, versions of which are to be found forming part of the facade of the "Treasury of Atreus" and the relief of the Lion Gate at Mycenae (see Plates 284, 292). It is hardly surprising therefore that the earliest Doric capitals come from Tiryns, Mycenae, and Argos, or from the older Dorian colonies at Syracuse, Megara Hyblaea, and Selinus. Was this the order of the first peristyle temple, erected on the highest terrace of the Heraion of Argos in the mid-seventh century? In any event, the broad lines of the order were established in the temples of Apollo, Artemis, and Hera, at Thermon (c. 620–610), Corfu (c. 600), and Olympia (c. 600) respectively, even before the transformation from wood to stone was completed. The columns were still of wood; they sometimes rested on stone plinths that protected the foot of the post; they were crowned by stone capitals (Plates 330, 332, 333). Architraves of wood and friezes of brick and terra cotta added to this strange mixture, whose polychromy was particularly lively. The metopes and cymas at Thermon, of terra cotta in the Geometric Corinthian style, attest to the importance of the northeast Peloponnesus in creating and developing the Doric order (Plate 331). The plan is elongated (5 by 15 columns at Thermon, 8 by 17 at Corfu); the cella already has interior supports (two rows of columns at Corfu) or spur walls and intermediate columns in the Heraion at Olympia (where the peristyle of 6 by 16 columns is more regular); there is always a pronaos, less systematically a rear vestibule or opisthodomos. The rhythms of the Olympian Heraion, with its division into five small chapels on each side wall, are complex; they betray the perplexity of the architects, confronted with the extended scale demanded by the triumphal monumentality of the period, and by the transition from simple linear construction to the new subtlety of internal volumes and external masses. The porticoes reflect this process in their greater thickness and heaviness of proportion, which at first had retained the lightness and slimness of wood construction. More than a century was needed to recover the slenderness of the *poros* limestone column of the first Temple of Athena at Delphi (c. 600 B.C.).

The technique seems to hesitate in substituting one material for another. There was still uncertainty about the strength of stone when used in these varied places: proportions were strengthened, spans diminished, and points of stress were modified. A fine example of this cautious experimentation is provided by the Treasury in the sanctuary of Hera at the mouth

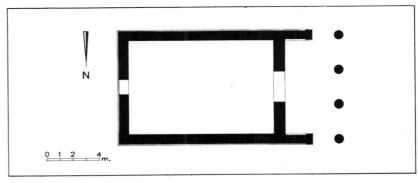

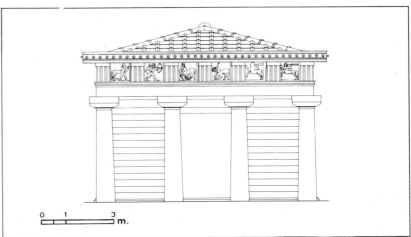

336. *Paestum, Sele River. Reconstructed frieze of Treasury, Sanctuary of Hera. Paestum, Museum*

337. *Paestum, Sele River. Transverse section of Treasury, Sanctuary of Hera*

338, 339. *Paestum, Sele River. Two metopes from Treasury, Sanctuary of Hera*

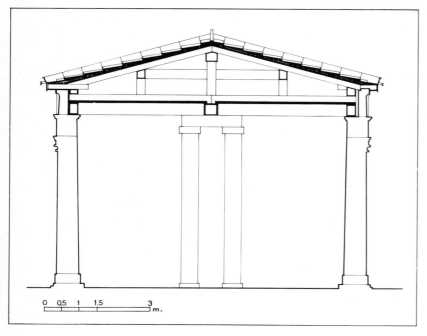

of the Sele River, five miles north of Paestum. Though constructed as late as 560 to 540 B.C. (Plates 334, 335), it clearly illustrates the ingenuity of the Archaic builders, still relatively unfamiliar with the qualities of the new material. The Treasury was a rectangular building, without a peristyle. The east porch had two columns with Doric capitals firmly profiled and vigorously set off by fillets carved at the base of the echinus; these contrast with the delicacy of the anta capitals decorated with palmettes and lotus flowers which are not integrated with, but applied to, the ends of the walls. The antae are not load-bearing; they are merely decorative, like the primitive boards that held up, in brick construction, the somewhat fluctuating projection of walls.

The builder was equally mistrustful of the entablature, despite the vigor of its frieze of sculptured metopes framed by emphatic triglyphs, carved separately and projecting strongly (Plates 336, 338, 339). It is, in fact, merely a screen erected in front of the timber framing that supported the roof; this structure has left marks on the inside faces of the frieze blocks. The sculptured metopes of the frieze were slid in between the triglyphs, and notches in the back face show that they were installed when the timber framing was already in place. This framing was composed of vertical and horizontal members pegged together to form a rigid structure capable of carrying the horizontal ceiling beams; these beams rested in between, on three interior supports—one, as in the Daphnephoreion of Eretria, nearer to the doubtless pedimented facade and the other two paired at the back to carry the radial hip rafters (Plate 337). The main rafters were stiffened by posts that rested on the horizontal beams. Altogether a remarkable survival of Archaic building methods in a part of the Greek world already well acquainted with a variety of extremely vigorous, though still immature, works in the Doric style. Powerful and severe, its lines sober yet capable of flowering into massive, well-balanced compositions, this style expressed the raw energy of the young Greek colonies in the west. They had been formed in a hard school but they quickly prospered and were eager to express their new character and magnificence. The grand buildings at Syracuse, Selinus, Acragas, and Paestum were the outcome of this fortunate conjunction of ample material resources and a politico-religious spirit anxious to assert itself through an architecture of extraordinary promise.

The earliest and crudest of these temples was the Apolloneion built about 570–560 B.C. on Ortygia, the island just off Syracuse (Plates 340–42). Already regular in plan, peripteral and hex-

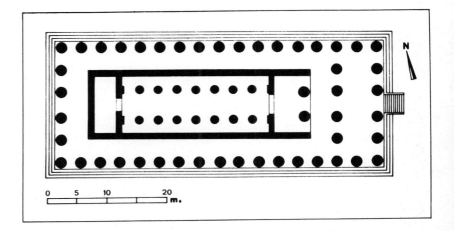

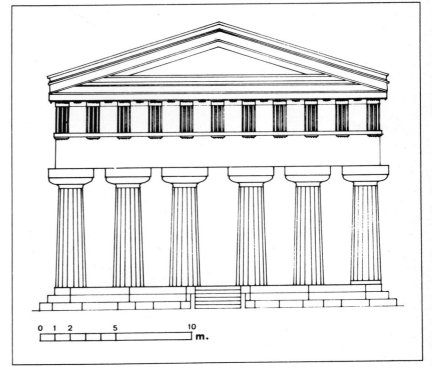

astyle (6 by 17 columns) and measuring 71 feet wide and 183 feet long, it simultaneously expresses both the clumsiness and the pride of the architects and stone carvers, Kleomenes and Epikles, who incised their names on one step of the crepidoma cut in enormous monolithic blocks. The columns are cramped and heavy (diameter 6 feet 7 inches; interaxial dimension 13 feet 7 inches; height 26 feet 2 inches); the entablature is crushing (nearly 22 feet high), worthy of the impressive consumption of materials represented by this early example of Syracusan architecture, which was never to lose its taste for strength and power.

The architects of Magna Graecia very rapidly mastered the materials and principles of the Doric order. In the middle of the sixth century (550–540) Temple C, the first of the great temples at Selinus, was erected within the already ancient sanctuary that occupied the southeast portion of the acropolis (Plates 343–46). Everything here is light and airy, an expression of the creative freedom of the Sicilian architects. The elongated plan is in the tradition of the early cult megarons of Selinus; the long narrow cella, with an adyton (sacristy) at the back, appears to stand independently inside the colonnade (6 by 15 columns), from which it is separated by a wide gallery (nearly 21 feet); in front, a double row of columns accentuated the disengagement of the principal spaces, the handsome mass being thrown into relief by a flight of eight steps stretching the full width of the facade. The rhythm of the colonnade is perfectly free, not governed by the internal divisions of the cella; the interaxial dimension of the facade columns is 14 feet 6 inches; those on the sides are closer (12 feet 9 inches), and the diameters fluctuate between 60 and 72 inches. Here the Doric style is animated by a precise sense of plasticity and a refined exploitation of the contrast between light and shade. The entablature, thanks to the energy of its forms, is full of movement. The frieze and the cornice are very strongly modeled, the triglyphs projecting forward from the plane of the metopes, and the mutules and guttae having imposing volume. The same concern also accentuates the ten sculptured metopes. The subjects, detached from the background by their high relief, were framed by flat slabs that made the figures stand out as if on a stage: Apollo driving a quadriga, seen in front view; Perseus beheading Medusa; Heracles striding along with two Cercopes slung over his shoulders (Plate 345). Finally, the edge of the roof had a splendid revetment of painted terra cottas, the facing of the beams that crowned the entablature as well as the cyma proper, all ornamented with clear-cut palmette and lotus motifs. This was the first big project of the Sicilian workshops, which for more than a century continued to produce these original works

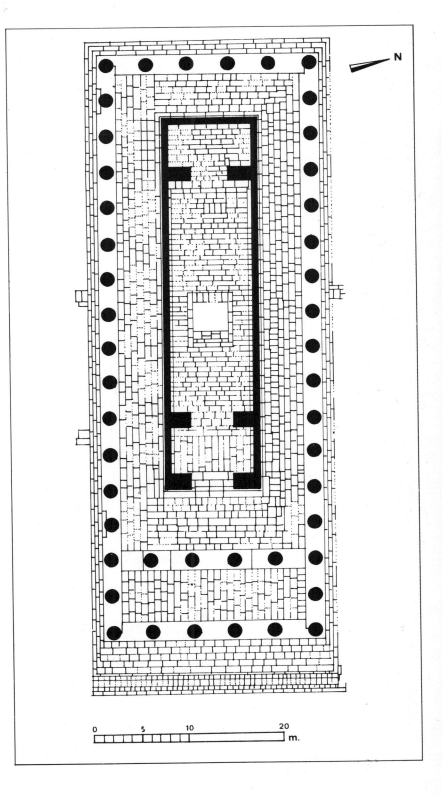

344. *Selinus, Acropolis. North gallery of Temple C, from west*
345. *Selinus, Acropolis. Portion of frieze, Temple C. Palermo, Archaeological Museum*
346. *Selinus, Acropolis. North side of Temple C, from northeast* ▷

347. Selinus (Marinella). Temple E (Hera), from northeast
348. Selinus (Marinella). Metope of Artemis and Actaeon, from Temple E (Hera). Palermo, Archaeological Museum
349. Selinus (Marinella). Portion of frieze, Temple E (Hera). Palermo, Archaeological Museum

257

350. Selinus (Marinella). Cella of Temple E (Hera), from east
351. Acragas. Interior of Temple of Juno Lacinia (Temple D), from southeast
352. Acragas. Air view of Temple of Juno Lacinia (Temple D)
353. Metapontum. Temple of Hera (Tavoline Paladine), from southeast

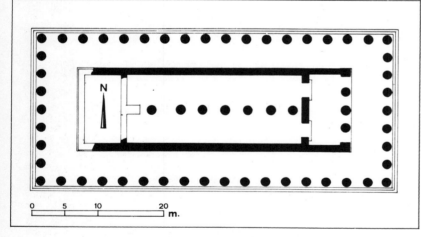

that were used throughout southern Italy: Selinus, Syracuse, Gela, Locri, Metapontum, and Paestum all showed rich ensembles of architectural terra cottas. These have such pictorial and monumental value that some were exported to Greece itself; the Treasury of Gela at Olympia is a good example of this.

The architects of Western Greece, i.e., Sicily and South Italy, throughout the sixth century and the first half of the fifth remained faithful to the Doric style, with such exceptions as Syracuse and Locri. They employed it flexibly, however, with more liberty than the builders of mainland Greece, who were quickly trapped in the rigid rules of the order; the western architects had a more developed taste for the monumental, a keener appreciation of the relations between masses and volumes, and a refined sense of architectural plasticity.

In proof of these statements, a few examples may be cited. First, there is the tendency to proceed by juxtaposition, by playing off one building against another; this concerns architectural composition and the organization of space, questions to which we shall return later on. The acropolis of Selinus with its four great temples; the sacred hill of Marinella nearby with all the variants represented by its three temples, E, F, and G; the string of temples that fringed the southern edge of the city of Acragas (Plates 351, 352); the sacred area of Paestum whose temenos wall borders the great north-south axis; the massive remains of the temples erected within the temenos of the Lycian Apollo in the very heart of the city of Metapontum—all of these reflect a systematically developed concept of monumentality doubtless linked with the expression of material power and the manifestation of an effective political ascendancy, but also with the more or less conscious desire to ensure the good will and protection of the traditional gods for these colonial cities in a land that was not always favorable or even friendly.

The details of each building reveal the spirit of independence and the originality of western Doric by numerous innovations. Since there can be no question of studying each temple individually, a few pertinent examples will suffice to illustrate this point. At Selinus, on the hill of Marinella, each temple had its own distinct physiognomy; the imposing mass of Temple G was offset by the lighter, more graceful, and yet more mysterious silhouette of Temple F, of which the pteron was sealed off, doubtless for some ritual purpose, by a wall extending halfway up the slender columns. Temple E, to the south, with its poised, more classical lines, is the only one so far restored and thus sets the scale for this grandiose landscape (Plates 347–50).

Temple G, dedicated to Apollo or Zeus, was one of the finest

357. *Paestum. Doric capital of Temple of Hera I (Basilica)*
358. *Paestum. Columns of Temple of Hera I (Basilica)*
359. *Paestum. Temple of Hera I (Basilica) and Temple of Hera II (Poseidon), from northeast* ▷

360. *Paestum, Sele River. Elevation of Temple of Hera, Sanctuary of Hera*
361. *Paestum, Sele River. Plan of Temple of Hera, Sanctuary of Hera*

362. *Paestum, Sele River. Construction of trabeation of Temple of Hera, Sanctuary of Hera*

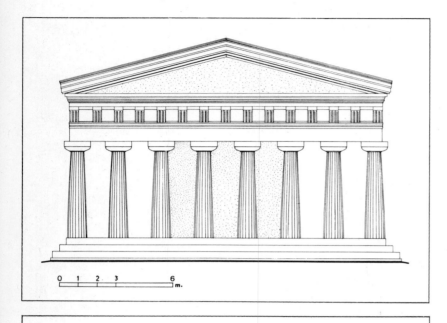

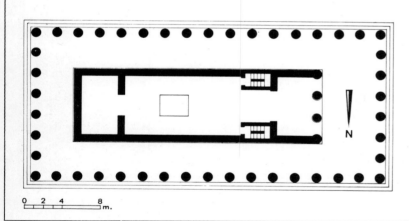

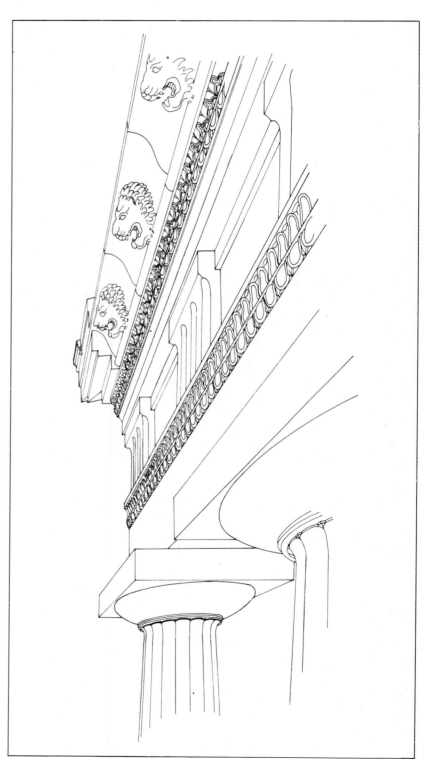

363. *Paestum. Ionic capital from Temple of Athena. Paestum, Museum*
364. *Locri. Capital from Ionic temple. Reggio Calabria, National Museum*
365. *Paestum. Plan of Temple of Hera II (Poseidon)*

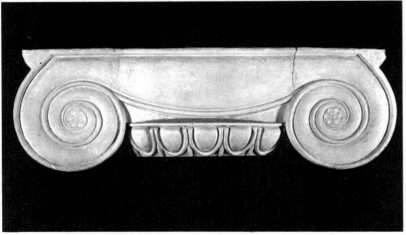

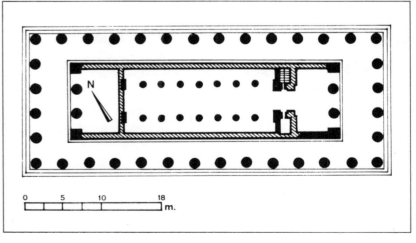

and most ambitious realizations of the Doric order in Western Greece. Temple F still retains the Archaic features of temples C and D on the Selinus acropolis in its elongated proportions (132 by 30 feet) and tripartite cella, and the spirit of Temple C is further reflected in the treatment of the intercolumnial voids (intervals of 14 feet 9 inches in the facade and 15 feet 2 inches along the sides, with a diameter of 5 feet 11 inches at the foot of the columns) and in the lightness of the colonnade. The Apolloneion, Temple G, has another object in view. The tyrant Peithagoras, who presided over the groundbreaking ceremonies about 520 and doubtless commissioned the enterprise, was certainly bent on rivaling the great temples of Ionia, but the architect succeeded in adapting to this project the possibilities of the Doric order.

The proportions of Temple G (363 by 165 feet) are those of the colossal sanctuaries of Ephesus and Samos, but volume and space are handled in a totally different spirit. Accumulations of columns, sometimes loaded with sculpture, have given place to broad spaces; the external colonnade (8 by 17 columns) is not doubled as in the dipteral plan, but the pteron itself is wide enough to include a double row (almost 40 feet), and is a nave in itself. The cella departed from the traditional Sicilian plan: the adyton, it is true, was preserved, but transformed into an independent chapel at the end of the cella; this was a vast hall 60 feet wide, divided into three equal aisles by a double row of columns; it was, no doubt, only partially roofed over, but it was intended to be entirely enclosed and the temple was not meant to be hypaethral. Possibly during construction some influence was exerted by the example of the Didymaion and its interior chapel. The treatment of the cella entrance is also conservative: a prostyle porch consisting of four columns in advance of two aligned with the ends of the walls, it is no longer independent of the peristyle; the supports, columns as well as antae, are all aligned with exterior columns. Thus, the plan as a whole is perfectly unified and all the traditional elements are interpreted harmoniously and flexibly in terms of space and volumes. This temple, in our opinion, is the finest achievement of Doric architecture in Sicily and Magna Graecia.

At about the same time an attempt was made at Syracuse to introduce the Ionic order. About 525 B.C., in the sanctuary where the Temple of Athena was to be built at the beginning of the fifth century, the close relations between Sicily and Ionia, discernible in commerce and the other arts, resulted in the choice of the Aegean Ionic style for this temple, whose dimensions were the same as those of the later Athenaion (about 195

267

367, 368. *Paestum. Interior of Temple of Hera II (Poseidon), from west*
369. *Segesta. Interior of Doric temple, from west* ▷

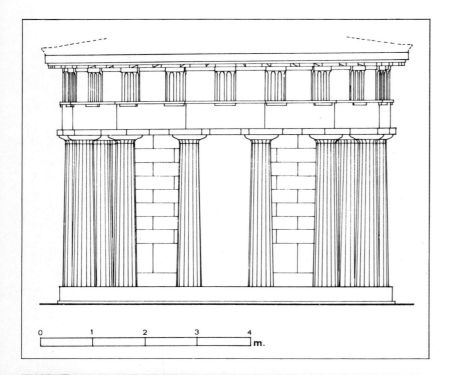

by 83 feet), but the plan and the proportions remained Doric. The style of the column bases and capitals was influenced by the architecture of the coast of Asia Minor. Though it remained an isolated attempt, it is evidence of a penetration of which traces are to be found at Megara Hyblaea, at Gela, even at Selinus, and still more distinctly in the Achaean colonies of Magna Graecia, where the Doric tradition was less deeply rooted. The architecture at Paestum is quite typical of the suppleness introduced by the Ionian trend into the details of an order that had never become fixed in solid structures.

The older (c. 530 B.C.) of the two temples of Hera at Paestum, that known as the Basilica, has a number of noteworthy features (Plates 355–59). To begin with the plan, there is an odd number of columns in the facade (9 by 18 columns; 81 by 179 feet). The disruptive effects of this are also apparent in the interior of the building: the cella is divided into two equal aisles by one axial colonnade; the pronaos has two doors into the nave, one for each aisle, and in front three columns in antis. The architect has struggled to bind the elements of the plan together: the long pterons correspond in width to exactly two intercolumniations, and the cella walls and the three columns of the vestibule are aligned with the five central columns of both east and west facades. The cross walls correspond with peristyle columns, so that the entire area enclosed by the peristyle is geometrically divided into four equal parts, though for practical reasons the principle could not be applied to the building in detail. In order to free sufficient space at the end of the cella for the cult statue, the interior columns were spaced wider toward the west; consequently, they are unrelated with the peristyle columns. The Ionian taste of the decoration is displayed in the treatment of the capitals, foliated grooves underscoring the heavily flattened echinus, and in the details of the entablature, where the flat band of the architrave has been replaced by a cyma with Lesbian leaves.

A similar molding enriched with egg-and-tongue ornament was doubtless introduced in the nearby Temple of Athena and in the great Heraion on the Sele River, both built around 500 B.C. (Plates 360–63). These two temples went even further in seeking plastic effects, multiplying the decorative courses and transforming the mutuled taenia. In the sanctuary on the Sele the taenia was replaced by an only slightly projecting molded course, which accentuated the height of the entablature; the raking cornice of the Temple of Athena projected far enough to have coffers beneath, decorated with gilded bronze rosettes. Here, the Ionic order has crept even into the interior of the

372. *Corinth. Temple of Apollo, from north*

374. *Corinth. Temple of Apollo, from northeast*

Doric shell. The architect has preserved the monumental character of the cella; as in certain temples at Selinus, it has a prostyle portico (4 by 2 columns) with half columns at the ends of the walls, but the order is Ionic and the capital belongs to a series familiar in Asia Minor and different from the Samian Ionic types (Plates 363, 364); the proportions are less elongated, the central mass is plumper, the ample volutes are compressed against the shaft.

None of these innovations is to be found in the last temple at Paestum, the Temple of Hera II (Poseidon) erected in the middle of the fifth century near the Basilica. Here, all the rules of the Classical Doric order are respected (Plates 365–68): regular plan of cella with pronaos and opisthodomos; principal chamber divided into three aisles by two Doric colonnades, each with a superimposed order; design and proportions of the entablature comparable to the temples of mainland Greece, such as those of Zeus at Olympia and of Athena Aphaia on Aegina.

Thus at the beginning of the fifth century the rules of the Doric order were imposed in both Magna Graecia and Sicily, but their application preserves a freedom and flexibility from the Archaic heritage and from innovative traditions proper to Western Greece. This originality will become confirmed as we pursue our study of Doric religious architecture on mainland Greece and in the west.

## DORIC RELIGIOUS ARCHITECTURE: MATURITY

On mainland Greece, the birthplace of the Doric order, the early Doric monuments lack the flavor of those in the west; the age of masterpieces begins only with the period around 500 B.C.

Of course, there are numerous and varied buildings whose Archaic features and other particularities permit us to follow the progress of the order. One of the oldest and most significant is the Temple of Artemis on Corfu; erected at the beginning of the sixth century during Corfu's flourishing years as a staging point for colonists on their way to Italy and Sicily, the temple reveals the innate potential of the Doric style. The long cella (116 by 31 feet) with pronaos and opisthodomos, divided into three aisles by two rows of ten columns, is surrounded by an impressive peristyle of 8 by 17 columns (depth of pteron 21 feet 6 inches), whose capitals are among the best balanced of the Archaic series. The proportions of the order are robust but not at all massive; the entablature is also lightened by the mixture of materials, stone and terra cotta, and animated by the lively polychromy that accents the geometric and plant motifs of the decoration; the pediment already begins its sculptural role with the imposing

376. *Aegina. Temple of Aphaia, from north*
377. *Aegina. Interior of cella, Temple of Aphaia, from west*

378. *Aegina. Interior colonnade of Temple of Aphaia, from northeast*

Gorgon who assures the protection of the edifice.

At this point, a more technical and more detailed account would have to introduce the aediculae and treasuries of the great sanctuaries, in particular Delphi's ancient tholos (Plate 370) and the Sicyonian peristyle decorated with a series of metopes of thoroughly Peloponnesian inspiration. Numerous fragments of the *poros* treasuries preserve curious formal peculiarities which mark the progressive elaboration of the Classical style. Corinth certainly played an important part in the development of this architecture and still, in addition to numerous ruins, retains the mighty Temple of Apollo, not to mention that of Poseidon in its sanctuary at the Isthmus. A few heavy columns of the Apolloneion, which dominated the agora at Corinth, still stand out against the somber background of Acrocorinth (Plates 372–74). It influenced the builders of the Old Temple of Athena on the Athenian acropolis and of the Temple of Apollo at Delphi, which replaced and eclipsed the structure dating from the beginning of the century. The peristyle of the unfinished Old Temple of Athena was modeled on that of the temple at Corinth, with its slightly squatter columns, irregular rhythm of the bays (13 feet 4 inches in the front facade, 12 feet 8 inches along the sides), and shortened corner interaxials; even the cella had the same two-chamber plan.

Nor did the two sons of Pisistratus show much originality when they started in the mid-sixth century to build the Temple of Zeus, south of the Athenian acropolis on the banks of the Ilissus; drawing inspiration from the works of the tyrant Polycrates of Samos (see Plate 301), they adopted a dipteral Ionian plan of ample proportions (356 by 135 feet; 108 columns distributed in two rows down the long sides and three rows of eight columns at front and rear). The plan scarcely reflects the usual style of the tyrants' architects, of whom Vitruvius mentions four: Antistates, Callaischros, Antimachides, and Porinos. The irregularity of the bays in the facade, copied from Ephesian and Samian temples, is not compatible with the strict requirements imposed by a Doric frieze, with its regular alternation of triglyphs and metopes; moreover, the heaviness of the columns (diameter at the base almost eight feet) and the shortening of the side spans contrast oddly with a light Ionic entablature. Work was interrupted by the fall of the tyrants in 510 B.C., not to be resumed for three centuries.

In truth, it was only with the early fifth-century temples at Aegina and Olympia, and finally with the Parthenon, that the Doric order came into its own, before undergoing the transformations in the following century that led to its decline.

380. *Aegina. Cella wall, Temple of Aphaia, from northwest*

381. *Aegina. Trabeation of Temple of Aphaia, from northwest*
382. *Olympia. Capital of Temple of Zeus*
383. *Delphi. Treasury of the Athenians (in background, portion of polygonal wall)* ▷

384. Olympia. Sculpture of west pediment, Battle of Lapiths and Centaurs, from Temple of Zeus. Olympia, Museum
385. Olympia. Sculpture of east pediment, Contest between Pelops and
Oenamaus, from Temple of Zeus Olympia, Museum

The Temple of Aphaia on the eastern tip of the island of Aegina combines the energy and life of Archaism with the elegance and poise of the Classical style (Plates 375–81). Quite small in size (95 by 45 feet) and hexastyle in plan (6 by 12 columns), it is built of local limestone that blends in perfectly with the surrounding landscape, from which it seems to draw the harmony and exquisite balance of its forms and volumes. The columns, many still coated with the pale stucco that concealed the pores and irregularities of the bluish-gray stone, are light and slender; the ratio of the diameter at the base of the column to its height is in this case 1:5.32, whereas at Corinth it was 1:4.15. The delicate, almost immaterial lines of the flutings lead the eye upward to the supple profile of the capital, in which the strength of the Archaic echinus has not yet been displaced by the purely functional stiffness of its Classical counterpart. There is here no compromise with foreign influences nor distortion of Doric geometry in the interests of any decorative concern; the cool, pure play of simple lines and harmonious volumes constitutes the charm of this architecture, so perfectly at home in the island landscape.

The cella is thoroughly Classical, with pronaos and opisthodomos, each opening on a portico with two columns in antis. Despite its narrowness (21 feet) it is divided into three aisles by two double-storied Doric colonnades; the role of these is more decorative than structural, and a fifth-century architect would have had no compunction about bridging so modest a span without the upper colonnades. But they formed the setting, required by the Classical plan, within which were displayed the cult statue and its baldachin, elements associated with the play of columns—not without difficulty in a center aisle only ten feet wide.

Slightly later another building, the Treasury of the Athenians at Delphi, achieved the same high level in the harmony of its Doric forms (Plate 383). Its youthful vigor and flexibility are characteristic of the brief moment of balance between the sometimes overpowering weight of Archaic structures and the cold severity of the Classical style. Architecture and plastic art flow effortlessly together.

The Temple of Zeus at Olympia, perhaps because of the personality of its Peloponnesian architect, Libon, was built along heavier lines than the Temple of Aphaia at Aegina, though the latter is older; the principal edifice of the sanctuary of the Olympian Zeus certainly dates from the period 470–460 B.C. (Plate 382). The extreme coarseness of the building material, shell limestone, was overcome by a coating of white marble stucco

386. *Athens. Plan of Acropolis*
*1) Temple of Athena Nike. 2) Propylaea. 3) Erechtheion. 4) Temple of Athena.*
*5) Parthenon*

387. *Athens, Acropolis. Plan of Parthenon*
388. *Athens, Acropolis. Sectional reconstruction of front portico of*
*Parthenon*

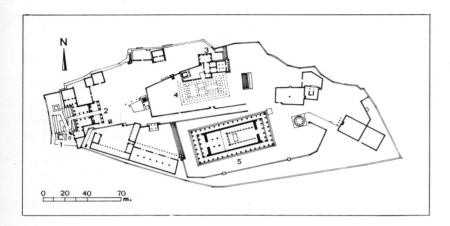

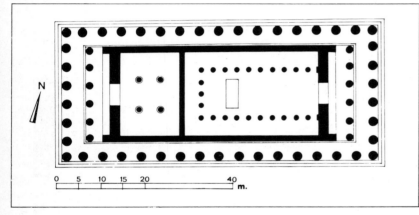

enlivened by vigorous polychromy; the blues and reds of the triglyphs contrasted with the milky whiteness of columns and walls. The sculptures in the east pediment glorified Zeus, the lord of these precincts, shown presiding over the chariot race in which Oenomaus died and Pelops triumphed; in the western pediment Apollo extends a protective arm over the Lapiths in their bitter combat with the Centaurs (Plates 384, 385). In the half-light of the interior porticoes, high on the pronaos and opisthodomos walls, were twelve metopes portraying the labors of Heracles, in homage to the victories of the benevolent hero.

The massive temple rose above an artificial embankment that gave it a dominant position in the sacred wood. Its construction marked the beginning of an increasingly rigid application of the modular system which later architects would make into a rule that became often sterile. The rhythm of the colonnade was based on the standard interaxial dimension of sixteen Doric feet, and multiples or submultiples of this module are repeated in the cella (3 by 9 modules, or 48 by 144 feet) and in various parts of the entablature: one triglyph and metope together equal one-half module (8 feet); in the cornice, one mutule and via make one-quarter module (4 feet); while the tiles are one-eighth module (2 feet) wide.

In the three-aisled cella the gold-and-ivory statue of Zeus sat enthroned, a masterpiece by Phidias; the sculptor's workshop has recently been excavated and described, and the unusual finds include many of the artist's tools and other traces of his activities. The double two-story Doric colonnade, as usual dividing the cella into three parts, formed the setting for the cult statue; its severity was moderated by the coloring of the floor, composed of a mosaic of white pebbles, and by the decorative accessories grouped around the statue that Pausanias listed in the second century A.D. To judge from the literary testimony, Phidias' work was far from harmoniously adapted to the architectural setting; the seated figure of Zeus was too large to fit comfortably between the rows of columns. The architects of the next generation were to have the task of creating, within the traditional plan, a free and uncramped space capable of accommodating cult groups whose scale and grandeur continually increased.

The true character of this architecture cannot be fully appreciated without an effort to visualize the decoration. Moreover, one should never forget the close ties that existed between architects and sculptors, and especially between Ictinus and Phidias, the creators of the Parthenon. That great temple of Athena Parthenos, the gem of Pericles' program for the Athenian acropolis, occupies a privileged place in the history of Doric ar-

chitecture. Tied to the past by the need to conform to previous programs, it heralded the profound transformations that were to mark the end of the predominance of the traditional Doric style and its gradual ousting by the Ionic and Corinthian.

In 447 B.C., when work on the Parthenon entered a particularly active phase, the site was far from being unencumbered and numerous constraints imposed their limitations on the new architect. Without wanting to enter into matters that are still under discussion, let us try and visualize the approximate condition of the site handed over to Phidias and Ictinus (Plate 386).

The desolation that must have followed the agony of the Persian wars and the occupation of the sacred rock by the Persians is chillingly conveyed by Thucydides' restrained account. "As for the Athenians..., they began to bring back their wives and children and what property they had left from the places where they had hidden them away. They also started to rebuild their city and their fortifications. For of their walls, little was left standing, and as for their houses, most were in ruins; only the few that had been occupied by high officers of the Persian army remained intact" (I, 89, 3). Themistocles, faithful to his politics of grandeur, at first left aside the city and its monuments to concentrate on rebuilding the city walls and equipping the port of Piraeus, which was necessary to the economic independence of Athens and the success of its expansionist foreign policy. The fortification walls of the acropolis still confirm visually Thucydides' words, as he continues: "It was thus that the Athenians fortified their city in a very short time. Even today it is apparent that the building was done in haste. Indeed, the lower courses consist of different sorts of stones, in some cases not shaped to fit, but laid just as they were brought up at the time. Columns taken from tombs and fragments of sculpture were mixed in freely with the rest."

The rebuilt ramparts of the acropolis (Plate 390) consumed the columns and pieces of entablature intended for the first Parthenon. Only after the fortifications had been rebuilt and the city had erased the traces of invasion did the Athenians think anew of the gods and the acropolis. Cimon, with his well-known religious scruples, initiated the programs. It was first necessary to prepare the site and replace the ancient ramparts on the south. A vast filling and leveling operation made possible a southward extension of the platform on which the new temple was to be erected. A handsome wall, still well preserved (Plate 389), served both to protect the sanctuary and to retain the new terraces. This part of the program, accurately dated from the objects found among the fill, was certainly the work of Cimon. However

393. *Athens, Acropolis. View upward into west portico of Parthenon, showing frieze above pronaos*
394. *Athens, Acropolis. South ambulatory of Parthenon*
395. *Athens, Acropolis. View across east portico of Parthenon* ▷

it is not so certain, as recently suggested, that it was he and his architect, Callicrates, who resumed construction of the temple and carried it, on its south side at least, as far up as the entablature. There are both technical and chronological reasons for hesitating to follow the author of this suggestion in all his conclusions: it is hard to see how, after the death of Cimon and the disgrace of Callicrates, the entire southern colonnade could have been dismantled and rearranged to conform with the new plan of Phidias and Ictinus.

Cimon's share in the construction of the temple itself cannot be determined with precision; but however far the work had advanced, Phidias and Ictinus took over a site already containing construction. They were charged with the execution of a state commission, conceived and interpreted at Pericles' instigation as a design at once national and Panhellenic. A massive foundation originally laid of Piraeus limestone had by now become partly buried beneath Cimon's terracing. The crepidoma and certain elements of the colonnade, if not entire sections of the colonnade and entablature (as Rhys Carpenter maintains), were already in place. These imposed constraints from which there was no escape except by razing everything; this was impossible, because the siting of the structure was predetermined by the existing foundations and the nature of the terrain; the most that could be done was to lengthen it a little on the west and widen it on the north (Plates 387, 388).

Actually the temple already begun corresponded to traditional structures at Aegina and Olympia. The plan was hexastyle (6 by 16 columns), the proportions elongated (221 by 78 feet); and, like the Temple of Apollo at Corinth and the Old Temple of Athena, its neighbor to the north, it had a two-chambered cella. The main hall was divided quite conventionally into three aisles by a double two-story row of ten columns; the second hall, more square in plan, had four columns, a formula repeated in the rear hall, or Parthenon, of the later Periclean structure. This traditional plan, however, failed to provide the space that Phidias needed for his gold-and-ivory statue; moreover, it was probably unsatisfactory to Pericles, who wished to make the new temple a symbol of Athenian greatness, perhaps even a reflection of his Panhellenic ambitions. A more imposing external volume called for a more vast and empty interior space.

No doubt for reasons of economy, the architect also found himself compelled to use the Pentelic marble drums already hewn and placed in position on the site; from the outset he was saddled with proportional consequences imposed by the diameter of the columns.

The Parthenon was thus the result of a series of compromises between sometimes contradictory requirements; in this way it becomes easier to understand the anomalies and innovations, some of which were to have far-reaching repercussions (Plates 391–98). The architect could not increase the interaxial spans without upsetting the proportions established by the given diameter of the columns; in order to enlarge the interior he introduced additional columns in the peristyle, adopting the unorthodox rhythm of eight columns in the facade instead of six, and seventeen along the sides instead of sixteen. The width of the pteron was reduced, which made it possible to widen the cella to 62 feet 6 inches; the resulting building was only slightly longer than before (229 feet, instead of 221), but considerably wider (102 feet, instead of 78 feet). To support the enlarged superstructure the foundations were extended to the north, onto the rocky plateau where no terracing was needed. The pronaos and opisthodomos were reduced to the minimum, their facades accentuated by a second row of columns in conformity with the prostyle arrangement adopted in the original plan.

These changes, as archaeological observations have confirmed, were so cleverly calculated as to enable the architect to establish within the new structures a close modular relationship that was based on the very dimension he had been forced to accept—namely, the diameter of the base of the columns. The ratio of this diameter (75 inches) to the typical interaxial dimension (170 inches) is 4:9. The same ratio is repeated in the dimensions of the stylobate (length 228 feet, width 102 feet), and in the corresponding dimensions of the cella; it also appears in the elevations: the width of the facade to its height (up to the horizontal cornice beneath the pediment). These proportions are inscribed within the pyramiding movement involving all the external lines: the curvature of the stylobate is reflected in the entablature; the columns incline inward and toward the diagonals. The architect found in this system of simple ratios and geometric relations a sort of guaranty against effects of dispersion that might have resulted from so difficult and complex a project.

Having established the exterior contours and volumes, Ictinus was free to provide the liberal interior spaces required by the sculptor. He retained the two halls from the previous structure. The smaller, opening to the west beneath the opisthodomos, had the same square arrangement of four columns springing straight to the roof. Ictinus chose the Ionic style as more appropriate to such tall proportions, a notable decision that introduced the Ionic order into an otherwise wholly Doric building. This in-

400. *Sunium. Temple of Poseidon, from north*
401. *Sunium. South side of Temple of Poseidon*
402. *Sunium. Trabeation, southeast corner of Temple of Poseidon*

403. *Sunium. Inner side of south colonnade, Temple of Poseidon*

404. *Rhamnus. View of fortress walls and acropolis*
405. *Bassae. Plan of Temple of Apollo*
406, 407. *Tegea. Plan and longitudinal section of Temple of Athena Alea*

novation opened the way to a mixing of styles in an architecture previously much concerned about homogeneity; thenceforth the advance of the Ionic style was not to be restrained.

In the great hall, the convention of a two-story Doric colonnade was maintained, but its use marked an important departure in creating interior space. The colonnade arranged in two rows no longer formed three more or less equal aisles; instead the columns were pushed nearer to the walls and were carried around the central area to create a U-shaped portico, ten columns along the sides and five across the back of the hall. Thus was formed a background for the cult statue, a more monumental and appropriate plastic setting. The success of the formula can be judged from the changes promptly made in the plan of the Temple of Hephaestus then being built on the Kolonos Agoraios, dominating the western edge of the Athenian agora (see Plate 520). The foundations of this building show clearly that the arrangement of the interior colonnade was revised in the very process of construction.

The architectural value of the Parthenon is further enhanced by its all-important sculptural decoration. In accordance with the Classical tradition, the pediments and metopes bore sculptures whose themes were taken from the legendary history of Athens and evoke the critical moments of Athena's intervention. The main pediment on the east represented the birth of the goddess, an event quite Parthenonian since she sprang fully armed from the head of Zeus. The other Olympians looked on the scene within their calm, serene world conquered from the giants, whose violent and brutal gestures were to be seen in the metopes beneath the pediment. In these reciprocal scenes were celebrated the victory of intelligence, beauty, and light over the maleficent powers of darkness; the chariot of the sun, in the angle of the pediment, emerged from the sea to displace the chariot of Selene, the moon goddess, whose eclipse at the opposite angle was part of the same symbolism.

The meaning of the great building was already clear to the pilgrim from his inspection of the scene in the west pediment, the contest between Athena and Poseidon for Attica; the two gods finally combined their powers in the alliance of the olive tree and the sea, the two sources of Athenian wealth. The onlookers were the legendary families of Cecrops and Erechtheus, whose very tombs lay close at hand on the sacred rock, here enthroned amid their descendants. The geographical limits were set by the waters that made Athens fruitful: the Cephisus and Eridanus rivers on the north, the Ilissus River and the Callirrhoe fountain on the south.

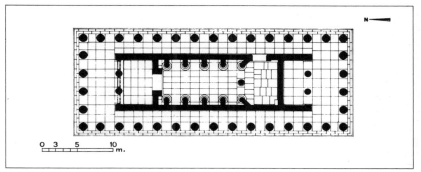

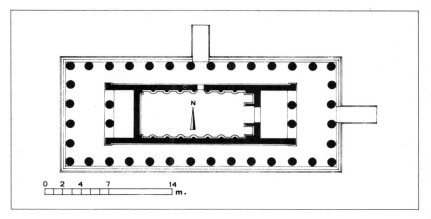

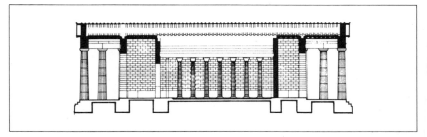

408. *Bassae. Southwest corner, Temple of Apollo*

409. *Bassae. Interior of cella, Temple of Apollo, from south*
410. *Bassae. Pronaos, Temple of Apollo, from north*
411. *Bassae. Interior of cella, east wall, Temple of Apollo* ▷

412. *Delphi, Marmaria. Sanctuary of Athena, from northwest*
413. *Delphi, Marmaria. Tholos, Sanctuary of Athena, from northeast*

414. *Delphi, Marmaria. Tholos, Sanctuary of Athena, from north*

415. *Delphi, Marmaria. Crepidoma of Tholos, Sanctuary of Athena, from south*

In the subdued light of the ambulatory Phidias unrolled a frieze around the upper wall, the greatest paean ever sung by the Athenian people in honor of its patron goddess. Phidias himself contributed to the homage of the great procession of the Panathenaic maidens that honored her every four years. Caught in the youthful agitation of departure, the procession started off from the west portico (Plate 393), a natural focus of attention for the pilgrim, and proceeded along the north and south sides of the cella. In spite of the conspicuous presence of city magistrates and the citizenry in general, the accent is on the Athenian youth: the ephebes on horseback, the arrephores carrying the peplos, the maidens, the youths bearing amphoras. At the southeast and northwest corners the divided stream converged on the east portico where the gods were gathered to welcome the Athenian people, whose privileged destiny was thus made manifest to all. Architecture and sculpture, symbolism and realism here find their perfect balance.

After the Parthenon, it was difficult to make innovations. The lessons of the two great masters were not misunderstood, however, and the alliance of styles, like that of disciplines, was still to produce a number of original works that successfully combined the two characteristic aspects of the second period of Classical architecture: the organization of interior space, and the development of decorative structures. Both aspects favored the extension of the Ionic style within exterior colonnades that remained faithful to the strict rules of the Doric order.

Attic architects continued to use Ionic forms with discretion. The Temple of Poseidon on the rocky promontory of Sunium (Plates 399–403) and the Temple of Nemesis at Rhamnus (Plate 404) were more slender in proportion, had moldings in the entablature or at the base of the walls and more luxuriant painted decoration, but these minor changes left the Doric structures essentially intact. A different situation developed in the Peloponnesus, where the intrusion of the Ionic style produced a distinct clash between the exterior Doric colonnades and the treatment of the interior; the interiors became completely autonomous and independent. The Temple of Apollo at Bassae illustrates this new conception (Plates 405, 408–11). Ought we to believe Pausanias when he attributes it to Ictinus? The novel form may indeed have been conceived by the Athenian architect, but the execution was certainly left to local teams whose technique remained traditional and rather clumsy. The plan bears traces of a certain archaism expressed in its elongated proportions (48 by 126 feet, 6 by 15 columns), in the depth of its pronaos, and in the rather spare style of the exterior order. But the interior stems

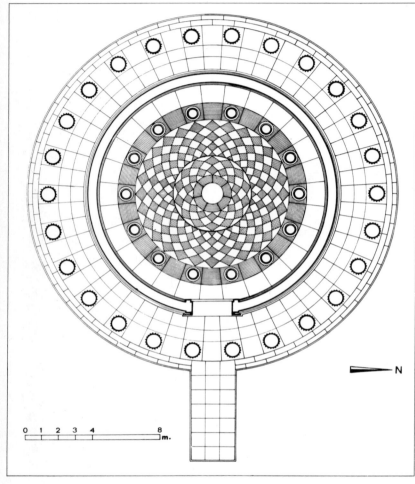

N

0 1 2 3 4     8
m.

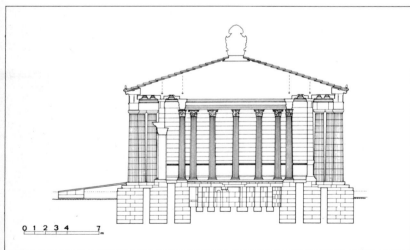

0 1 2 3 4     7
m.

from a totally new approach; the columns, Ionic and Corinthian, bore an entablature with a sculptured marble frieze and a limestone cornice. This was architectonically unrelated with the exterior structure, since the ceiling and the roof framing rested on the walls of the cella; the Ionic system below was merely applied as independent ornament. Thus, the main hall was fringed with Ionic half columns attached to the ends of spur walls, but the back was closed off by flanking Ionic half columns and a single Corinthian column, the earliest known example of that order in all of Greek architecture. The Ionic capitals with their broad volutes were modified to suit their unusual situation; the channel that links the volutes was given a quite strong curvature to accentuate the supporting function. The limestone architrave was embellished with sleek moldings (cyma reversa and cavetto); these merged into the sculptured marble frieze, the whole being crowned by a limestone cornice. Beyond the Corinthian column lay a second smaller hall of uncertain function, its independence emphasized by the unusual presence of a door that opened on the north. Was this a survival of the primitive adyton? or perhaps the mark of a cella, transformed in the course of construction?

Again in Arcadia, Scopas of Paros, an architect and sculptor, clothed the same idea a few years later in a more elaborate and harmonious form in the Temple of Athena Alea at Tegea (Plates 406, 407), having been commissioned to design both the temple and its sculptured decoration. For the exterior Scopas followed tradition by adopting an elongated plan (6 by 14 columns), with the normal distance between cella and peristyle and a wider spacing of the columns in the facade; in the proportions he respected the fourth-century preference for subtler lines, more continuous voids, slimmer columns, and a lighter entablature. The marble afforded greater possibilities than limestone, and it was in the interior that Scopas' creativeness found full expression. He deliberately suppressed the cella colonnades and cross walls, transforming them into an engaged order attached to the wall so as to liberate the entire volume of the cella. Moreover, to accentuate the decorative values he used throughout the Corinthian order, an extremely luxuriant capital composed of a basket of acanthus leaves with vigorously modeled stems and folioles, all in high relief. The Corinthian half columns stood on a plinth decorated with a strong Lesbian molding to set off the Classical profiles of the bases; they supported a slightly projecting band forming the architrave on which, according to the most probable reconstruction, rested another small engaged order, doubtless Ionic, consisting of pilasters or half columns.

418. *Epidaurus. Reconstructed section, including wall and trabeation of Tholos. Epidaurus, Museum*
419. *Epidaurus. Corinthian capital from interior of Tholos. Epidaurus, Museum*

420. *Epidaurus. Interior corridors in foundations of Tholos*

421. *Eleusis. Plans showing evolution of Telesterion*
1) *Mycenaean temple, before 1200 B.C. 2) Megaron, period of Solon, before 560 B.C. 3) Telesterion, period of Pisistratids, c. 525 B.C. 4) Telesterion, beginning 5th century B.C. 5) Telesterion, Ictinus, mid 5th century B.C. 6) Telesterion, final solution, 4th century B.C.*

422, 423. *Eleusis. Views of Telesterion*
424. *Priene. View of agora*

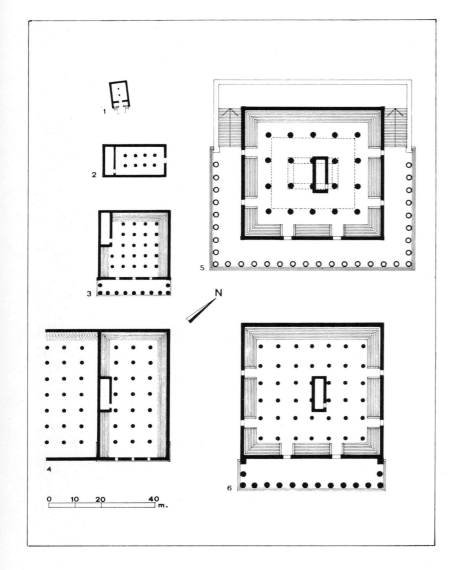

425. Priene. Ekklesiasterion

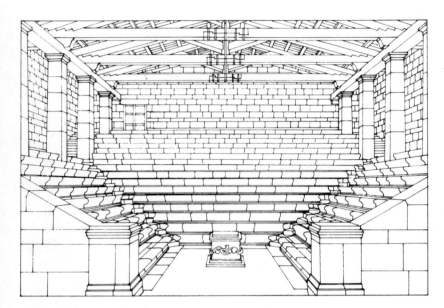

426. *Priene. Reconstruction of Ekklesiasterion*
427. *Piraeus. Reconstruction of Arsenal*
428. *Piraeus. Section of Arsenal*

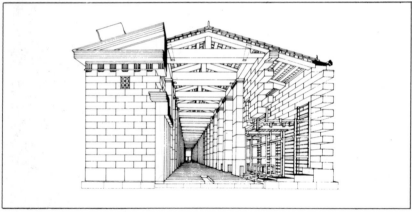

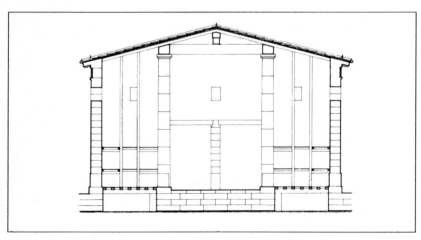

The religious architecture of the fourth century was thus crystallized in its definitive form.

These characteristics reappear with a few variations in most of the temples and sanctuaries of the period. The mixing of styles became the rule, the development of the decoration a primary concern. The famous and mysterious Tholos of Epidaurus, called Thymele in the building accounts found nearby, bears splendid witness to the new taste—due in large part to the collaboration of architects and sculptors, unless the same artist performed both functions, as Scopas had done (Plates 416–20). The circular monument was built during the last third of the fourth century to the glory of Asclepius, the healing god; it is a masterpiece of decorative architecture, of the period preceding the excesses of the Hellenistic age. Erected on an artificial mound about ten feet high, the tholos was ringed by twenty-six Doric columns, surely very slim, since the ratio of height (22 feet 6 inches) to the diameter at the base (3 feet 3 inches) was 6:82, close to Hellenistic values. The architrave and frieze, like the columns, were in limestone; the metopes were decorated with large rosettes in a refined style; upon a center in the form of an omphalos unfolded two calyxes of twelve petals each, and among them entwined twelve lotus flowers borne on a long bulbous stem. The conical roof, tiled with marble and bordered by a gutter enriched with foliated scrolls, was topped by an extraordinary finial formed of palmettes and twisted scrolls that emerged from a basket of acanthus leaves; the whole must have been ten feet tall. All this heralded the floral repertory displayed in the other parts of the building and associated with the natural polychromy of the materials and with the Corinthian order employed for the interior colonnade. The ceiling of the peristyle, of Pentelic marble, and the cella door are models of architectural elements enhanced even functionally by traditional motifs intelligently adapted. In the cella the fourteen Corinthian columns, also of Pentelic marble, stand out from a stylobate of black stone. The capitals became the first of a long line: the bell is composed of two tiers of eight acanthus leaves each, from which spring the volutes with deeply hollowed stalks that supported the angles of the abacus; in the intervening space is a central volute terminated by a flower with wide-open petals.

The Tholos of Epidaurus comes at the end of a long process of evolution that permitted the combining, in an unstable equilibrium, of decorative elements and architectural structures. It marks the beginning of a swing toward an architecture in which the functional elements are increasingly submerged beneath a flood of decoration.

## CIVIC ARCHITECTURE

The brilliance and splendor of Greek temples tend to over-shadow the originality of parallel achievements in civic architecture. This is unfortunate, for the civic buildings reflect the development of the political community, the most original feature of ancient Greece.

The early city structures are scarcely distinguishable from the elementary forms of domestic architecture and have no special historical importance. The first buildings intended specifically to house the political and administrative agencies of the *polis* appeared in the sixth century.

The origins of the agora are dealt with in greater detail in the following chapter, on the organization of space; here, we shall consider only the building types that illustrate the particular aspect of this architecture for meetings and assemblies: the prytaneum or town hall, the council hall or Bouleuterion, and the theater.

The prytaneum was at the very heart of the city, the home of the inner council. Its structure was dictated by its function. It sheltered the hearth of the city and the cult of the goddess Hestia; it was a repository for the most precious archives; and it provided for communal living imposed on the magistrates, or prytaneis, during their term of office. As so often in the life of the citizen of ancient Greece, the religious and the secular were closely associated. The best examples of this building type are preserved at Priene, Megara Hyblaea, and Delos. Rectangular in plan, it consisted of a sequence of three rooms: the chapel of Hestia; the dining room where the prytaneis or foreign ambassadors and privileged guests of the city ate their meals; and the archives. These rooms opened on a court bordered by one or two porticoes, and by the facade itself; this was more or less monumental in character, with a light colonnade or propylon, and was closely connected with the agora.

A citizen assembly met in the open air, before it obtained facilities such as the Athenian Pnyx, or was admitted to the theater; but the Boule, or advisory council, had had buildings of its own since the sixth century. The evolution of the Bouleuterion illustrates the progressive conquest of interior space, from which the temples gradually profited. The early examples of a Bouleuterion remained captive to the rectangular plan, ill-adapted to a semicircular seating arrangement; at Delphi and Olympia the ruins show simple, workaday rooms with the councillors' benches ranged along the walls on either side of a central aisle—a system adopted by the Roman Curia

432. Epidaurus. Theater, from north
433. Segesta. Theater, from southwest
434. Aegosthena. Fortified tower

315

435, 436. *Eleutherai. Fortification walls with towers*
437. *Acragas. Temple of Castor and Pollux, Sanctuary of Chthonic Deities, from east* ▷

and revived centuries later in the British House of Commons. In sixth-century Athens, on the west side of the agora an Athenian architect attempted to reconcile a semicircular seating arrangement with a rectangular plan; the porticoed facade, flanked by a fountain, was eclipsed by neighboring structures. The experiment was not followed up, and the square plan was used in subsequent efforts.

It is important to mention here the influence exerted by the Telesterion, the great hall of mysteries at Eleusis (Plates 421–23) and scene of the initiation ceremonies in the sanctuary of Demeter, especially because the name of Ictinus, the architect of the Parthenon, marks a decisive phase of its evolution. At the beginning of the sixth century the primitive holy place, a rectangular megaron of the Mycenaean type, was incorporated into a great hall with a double interior colonnade, still elongated in plan and little different from contemporary temples. It was about 525 B.C., following the intervention of the Pisistratids, that the critical transition took place, from a rectangular to a square plan. A large square hall (89 by 89 feet) was lined on three sides with tiers of benches (interrupted only in the southeast corner, where part of the original megaron was respected); the east facade had three entrances emphasized by a long portico; the interior space was divided into several aisles by five rows of five columns each, the outer ones abutting the bottom row of benches. This solution was awkward, for the closeness of the columns and their contact with the benches interfered with the sight lines and prevented the spectators from following the ceremonies taking place in the middle of the floor. After Cimon's architects had tried, around 470 B.C., to enlarge the hall and create a central focus out of the primitive sanctuary, it remained for Ictinus to devise the optimal solution. Ictinus took up the same principle but he concentrated, as in the Parthenon, upon freeing the interior space. In the new enlarged hall (170 by 163 feet) the convergence on the center was better defined by the tiers of benches, arranged around all four sides and enclosing the space; passages in three sides, north, south, and east, permit easier circulation. The seven rows of seven columns that featured in Cimon's plan were replaced by twenty columns arranged in two concentric squares; these reinforced the centripetal effect of the composition, freed the sight lines, and gave all the spectators a better view, since the interval between columns measured more than thirty-three feet, a distance equivalent to the widest interior span of the Parthenon.

This was the first great hall in Greek architecture, and it would be interesting to know more about the design of the structure that covered it; surely it was calculated to enhance the artistic value of the ensemble. In addition, the traditional concerns of an architecture that remained highly sensitive to the balance of volumes, and to the relationship of the building to its environment, are reflected in the exterior porticoes that were to be added to Ictinus' monument on three sides, though this colonnade was never realized. The present state of the Eleusinian hall still retains the broad principles established by Ictinus, but during the fourth century the number of interior columns was again increased and the Archaic portico was simply resumed on the east facade.

Not until the Hellenistic epoch did Ictinus' solution find its full application in vast structures such as the hypostyle hall of Delos. But ruins as well as written records preserve the memory of other square structures, public halls built for political assemblies or spectacles and designed with Classical restraint on a scale appropriate to contemporary cities. Several are preserved in Asia Minor, at Notium, Nysa, and Priene. The Ekklesiasterion, for the Assembly of citizens at Priene (late fourth century), is the most accomplished and best-balanced example (Plates 424–26). Square in plan, on the north it was built into the hillside and opened on the south through the long portico with a double colonnade that formed the border of the agora; there was access to the assembly hall through two doors that had an exedra between. In the center of the floor, which was free of columns, stood an altar. Tiers of benches surrounded the three sides of the hall opposite the doors. Between each topmost tier and the wall there was space for a narrow gallery, and these contained the pillars that supported the roof (five on the east and west, six on the north). The original span across the hall was about forty-nine feet; subsequently, this had to be reduced at the expense of the central space. Four flights of steps, at the north and south ends of each lateral bank of benches, enabled the Assemblymen to reach their seats.

Another utilitarian building whose layout was closely adapted to its function was the Arsenal of the Piraeus, built by Philo and known from an inscription (Plates 427, 428). Over 100 yards long, it was conceived as a monumental gallery linking the naval dockyard and the agora; the central hall was thus a public thoroughfare, open to the citizens, who could glimpse on either side, beyond the rows of pillars, the sails and tackle of the fleet entrusted to the care of the magistrates; this equipment was stored against the walls and in small lofts, and bore witness to Athenian sea power. A very handsome roof, with strong but simple lines, enhanced the monumentality of the Arsenal, whose

438. *Acragas. Temple of Concord (Temple F), from west*
440. *Paestum. Temple of Hera II (Poseidon), from southwest* ▷
439. *Paestum. Temple of Hera I (Basilica), from north*

external appearance was rather severe despite the Doric frieze that crowned the bare walls. It is a fine example of Classical architecture whose beauty derives from the strict composition dictated by its function.

Though these Greek buildings are not as famous as the temples, they show better their architects' skill in organizing interior space. This mastery is found before or at the same date as the great complexes of the Orient, Egypt, and Rome, all expressing a different spirit and permitting technical developments to which the Greeks did not resort.

The Greek theater never lost its intimate relationship with the terrain and did not become an autonomous building, despite its antiquity as an institution. Religious in origin, political and social in function, the literary works of Aeschylus, Sophocles, and Euripides could not be separated from the role they played within the city nor confined within walls; they were too closely associated with open-air festivals and popular assemblies. At first no more than a level space reserved for dances and ceremonial choruses, the theatral area had no architectural pretensions; spectators clustered on the surrounding slopes or possibly occupied some sort of temporary wooden grandstands.

The theater did not assume a definitive architectural form until the fourth century, when stone tiers of seats, arranged in a semicircle, partially enclosed the orchestra, where the chorus evolved the action of the drama (Plates 429–33). The actors performed on a low platform in front of the facade for the scenic structure; scenery was strictly schematic, a matter of wings and coulisses. The theater achieved architectural monumentality only in the Hellenistic age.

## THE ORGANIZATION OF SPACE AND ARCHITECTURAL COMPOSITION

The evolution of the peripteral temple with its steadily unfolding external colonnade is direct evidence of the sense for volumes and plasticity naturally possessed by the Greek architect, whose situation and aesthetic concerns were no different from those of the sculptor. It is hardly surprising, therefore, that architects very quickly sensed the value of the rapport between architecture and landscape, and among the buildings themselves in the space surrounding them; thus they sought to organize the space within which they placed their structures. But the trends that can be discerned throughout Archaic and Classical times never became strict rules or laws; and although such trends sometimes reflected certain mathematical, even geometric preoccupations, neither were they a matter of pure

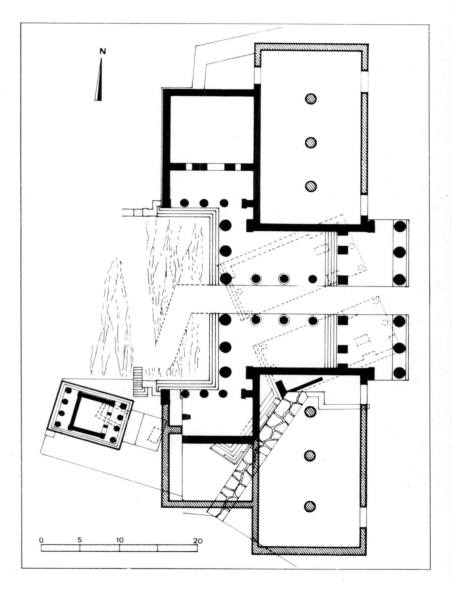

*444. Athens, Acropolis. Ionic capital, interior of Propylaea*

aesthetics. Social and economic conditions, the political structure of the city, and the evolution of philosophical speculation—all these at one time or another exerted influence on the organization of space within the urban setting where the great works of architecture were erected. The outcome was a considerable degree of diversity. Each region of the Greek world and, indeed, each city developed its own variants according to its particular social or political circumstances. Our aim here is to be aware of nuances, and not to formulate the precepts of a code but to pursue the great trends that express the various aspects of the life and history of the Greek city.

The first and oldest concern was to individualize the abode of the god. The Greek countryside offered its own resources, but it was also necessary to integrate and adapt the temple with the lines of the landscape. In this task came the first success. Whether the temple stood on the summit of a hill (as at Aegina) or on a terrace carefully differentiated from its rolling surroundings (Bassae, Rhamnus, Segesta, the Argive Heraion, Delphi), whether it terminated a promontory (Sunium, Croton, Panionion, Notium), dominated or enframed a cityscape (Athens, Acragas, Paestum), or was spread over the back of a valley or on a seashore (Samos, Didyma, Claros, Caulonia, the Heraion of Paestum), the temple always preserved its individuality, stole into the landscape while developing or complementing the natural lines. There is no need to elaborate on a rule so consistently respected (Plates 437–41).

There were problems, however, variously solved by resorting to diverse architectural elements, and having implications that extend far beyond the boundaries of the sanctuary. We will examine them in turn, studying the relations between the principal building and associated structures in the same complex; the organization of space and its utilization in architectural ensembles, sanctuaries, or public places; and finally the links between architectural groupings and the urban setting whose tendencies or deep-seated characteristics they express.

### Relations Among Individual Buildings

Whether it is a sanctuary comprising several buildings or a public place collecting the elements necessary to the public life of the city, functional considerations are the key to composition.

In the Archaic sanctuaries the temple, the house of the deity, is isolated and sharply individualized, but nonetheless closely related with the altar, the place of sacrifice, which was outside but not far away. Ritual necessities led to the erection of the altar in an arrangement that quickly became standardized, opposite to

446. *Olympia. Southeast corner of palaestra*
447. *Olympia. Vaulted entrance to stadium*

◁ 448. Delphi, Sanctuary of Apollo. Sacred Way and Treasury of the Athenians
449. Olympia. Terrace of the treasuries, from east

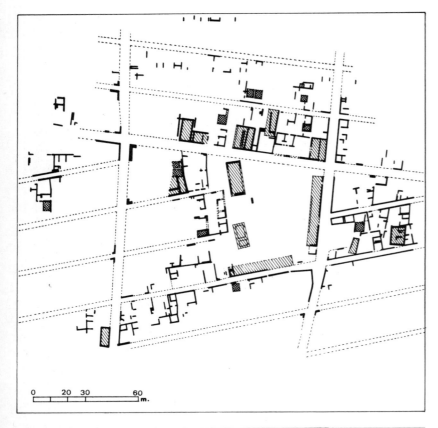

0 20 30 60 m.

the facade of the temple and often linked with it by a paved path. There were numerous variants, more often attributable to the ritual forms of a cult rather than to purely aesthetic considerations. It should not be forgotten that the faithful had to be able to follow the sacrificial ceremonies, to participate in the processions that wound through the sanctuary, and to accompany the cult statue when, on festive occasions, it left the temple to be shown publicly—sometimes, after certain purification rites, to be exposed to the gaze of the faithful.

The first attempts at composition were associated with the development of the separate monumental entrance, the propylon. Whatever its location with respect to the temple, it disclosed the latter from an angle chosen with the more or less explicit intention of displaying it to best effect. It is worth noting that, from the outset, the architects avoided a frontal or axial disclosure; the building is progressively revealed, and along oblique or diagonal lines. The sanctuaries of Athena on Aegina, the early structures on Delos, the path that had to be followed by pilgrims to the Heraion of Samos or the Altis at Olympia, the first sanctuary on the acropolis of Selinus—all offer excellent illustrations of this concern, expressed with ultimate refinement by Attic architects on the Athenian acropolis.

In the Propylaea Mnesicles acknowledged the subtleties introduced by Callicrates and Ictinus in designing the Parthenon. While duly respecting the individuality of the two buildings separated by an interval of some ten years' time, the architect closely coordinated their relative positions in space and their mathematical proportions. One feels a growing admiration for the skill of Mnesicles, placing his building in the most difficult topographical site and inventing handsome architectural forms to accommodate the various functions of the edifice. Forbidden to infringe on the sanctuary of Athena Nike to the southwest, confined on the south by the sacred precincts of Artemis, and obliged to incorporate a portion of the sixth-century propylaea and to accommodate on the west the twists and turns of the Sacred Way (the route followed by the procession with its chariots and sacrificial animals), Mnesicles succeeded in designing a building that accepts these multiple constraints yet still achieves a profound and genuine unity (Plates 442–44; see Plates 314, 386, 389). He respected the fundamental rhythm of the Archaic propylaea, which gave access to the sacred plateau through five gates pierced through a cross wall that cut off the corridor between two lateral ramparts. However, a slight difference in orientation brought the axis of the new building into relation with the point of arrival of the Sacred Way and with the east-west axis of the plateau separating the Parthenon from the Erechtheion. To acknowledge and emphasize the ascending motion of the procession, the central block of the new Propylaea with its five doors was sited where the break in the western slope was most abrupt, on a five-step substructure that compensates for the difference in level between the front and back thresholds. The continuity of movement was underscored by the superior proportions of the central western gate (13 feet 8 inches wide, 24 feet 4 inches tall), and the smooth ramp that replaced the steps to facilitate the passage of the chariot of the goddess; the central bay of the portico in front of it is correspondingly enlarged (nearly 18 feet wide, as opposed to 12 feet for the lateral bays). An approaching procession was greeted by a facade of six Doric columns springing from a four-step crepidoma, which projected at a right angle on either side to support the colonnades of the lateral facades that framed the broad platform of the entrance.

The problem, however, was how to arrange the way of access into the vestibule behind the portico. It was here that a correspondence was established with the Parthenon, the main building of the sanctuary; the width of the vestibule (60 feet) approximates that of the principal cella of the Parthenon, and the depth (42 feet) that of the Parthenon's western cella. Moreover, the Ionic order supporting the ceiling of the cella was adopted by Mnesicles for the vestibule, which thus became a sort of prelude to the composition of Ictinus. Bordering the axial corridor that ascended toward the great central opening, Mnesicles placed two rows of three Ionic columns each, whose slenderness surpasses all Classical and Hellenistic norms. The aisles were covered by coffered marble ceilings whose marble beams were almost twenty feet long. Here, Mnesicles had to resort to an unusual technique in order to reinforce the Ionic architraves that held up the ceiling—he inserted metal bars. As the pilgrim finally emerged into the east portico, he was confronted with the two unequal and asymmetrical masses—the Parthenon to the south and the Erechtheion to the north (see Plates 322, 391)—on either side of the median axis marked by votive shrines and isolated statues or groups of statuary. The details of the composition and decoration of each monument were only progressively revealed to him. The first glimpse of the mighty volume of the Parthenon was from an oblique angle, encompassing the Propylaea's sharply defined east facade and the Parthenon's receding north colonnade. One can only conclude that the concept of axiality was systematically spurned and the possibilities of symmetry deliberately rejected.

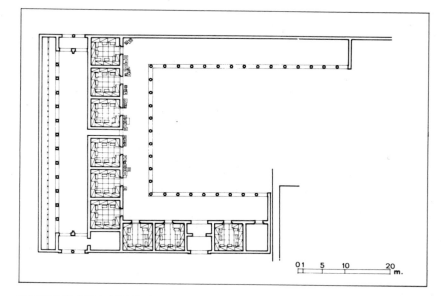

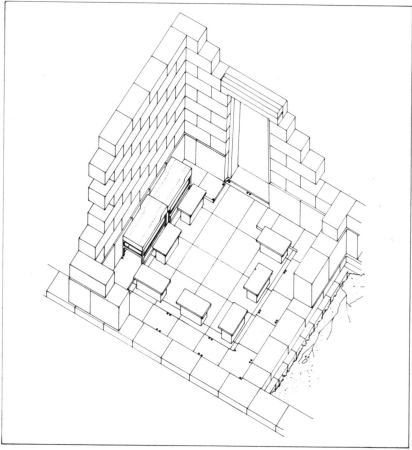

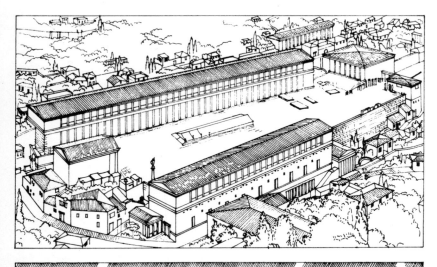

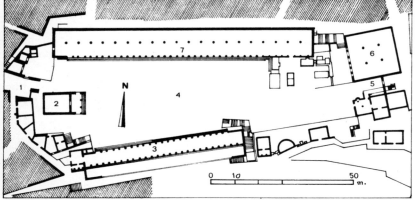

454, 455. *Assos. Reconstruction and plan of stoa*
1) *West gate.* 2) *Temple.* 3) *Upper floor or baths.* 4) *Agora.* 5) *East gate.*
6) *Bouleuterion.* 7) *Stoa*

With variations dictated by landscape and site, the same concerns are equally apparent in complexes as different as Delos and Olympia. And at Delphi the pilgrim who mounted the Sacred Way at the foot of the Phaedriades discovered progressively from one level to the next the ex-votos dedicated to Apollo, all placed at different angles. Leaving behind the groups of sculpture that adorned the approaches, he skirted the Treasury of the Sicyonians, noting the back of the Treasury of the Siphnians (its sumptuous facade, with its caryatids, revealing itself only at the turning of the path), at which point the Treasury of the Athenians was already in full view (Plate 448; see Plate 383). As he continued upward he saw, beyond the Athenian Stoa and over the polygonal terrace-wall, the top of the colonnades of the main Temple of Apollo; its facade as well as the long north flank would come into view only as he emerged at the northeast corner of the esplanade, after rounding the back of the great blue limestone Apollo Altar of Chios. He was then in the heart of the sanctuary, which had revealed itself to him gradually, from a variety of angles.

Without occupying the geometric center or playing the part of a controlling element, the Temple of Zeus at Olympia dominated the lines of colonnades that accompanied the steps of the pilgrim entering the compound at the northwest corner. From this point the temple can be instantly apprehended, first the west facade and the long north flank, which one had to skirt before contemplating the pediment of the main facade, where Zeus presided over the historic race in which Pelops won both the hand of Hippodamia and power over Elis (see Plate 385). Even the processions of the competitors in the Olympic Games followed a winding path among various colonnades until, at the foot of the Terrace of the Treasuries, they reached the gateway of the stadium, flanked by embankments where the spectators gathered (Plates 445–47, 449; see Plates 330, 382).

In all these instances one can discern the same principles linking the buildings in indefinite and fluid relationships. One volume is played off against the other, but not in the strict lines of geometric composition. Only in the following epoch did Hellenistic architects, under other influences, fall back upon axiality and symmetry for organizing their vast building projects.

## THE ORGANIZATION OF SPACE WITHIN ARCHITECTURAL COMPLEXES

The functional relationships among buildings associated in the same complex, whether sanctuary or public square, came to

456. *Athens, Agora, Plan of west side, end of 6th century* B.C.
1) *Cemetery.* 2) *Old Bouleuterion.* 3) *Temple of Demeter.* 4) *Temple of Apollo.*
5) *Sanctuary.* 6) *Altar of Zeus.* 7) *Eponymous Heroes.* 8) *Altar of the Twelve Gods*
457. *Athens. View of agora, from southeast*

determine the principles that controlled their grouping in space.

First we notice the definite contours that delimited the reserved area; these grew from the sacredness of such zones. The sanctuary constituted a temenos, a word whose etymology implies a particular sector dedicated to a divinity. An enclosure, materialized in the form of a wall or merely indicated by boundary markers, limited the extent of construction. The same was true of the marketplace or agora, which belonged to the public domain and formed a zone protected by religious sanctions. These sacred bounds required a definite architectural composition that could not dissolve into an indetermined area. As early as the eighth and seventh centuries one can discern these characteristics in sites as far apart as, for example, the sanctuary of Hera on Samos (see Plate 299) and the agora of Megara Hyblaea in Sicily (Plate 450). One can follow the formation of the main sanctuary on the acropolis of Selinus a century later, for the procedures are the same: to give the contours of the sacred zone a more definite structure, the simple boundary wall was gradually replaced by the portico, its colonnade originally in wood.

The first known stoa at Samos, the south stoa, ran behind the temple and along the edge of the sanctuary; its wooden posts have disappeared, but the stone bases remain. About the middle of the seventh century the agora of Megara Hyblaea recalls the same arrangement; the marketplace was separated from the surrounding streets and quarters toward north and east by two simple stoas opening on the square. In the next century the stoa on the acropolis of Selinus, as at Samos, had two wings joined at a right angle, accentuating the function of the porticoes.

Not only did stoas enclose and accurately delimit space, they also provided a decorative motif; they formed a background that set off the principal structures—the temple and its altar, or the main buildings of the agora—while providing refuge and shelter for pilgrims and citizens. The usefulness of these porticoes led to their rapid proliferation. The large covered areas at the Athenian agora and in the sanctuary of Artemis Brauronia in Attica had been converted by the end of the fifth century into rooms or shops for administrative or religious functions (Plates 452, 453).

There was no stopping the development of this major architectural theme as it adapted itself to new sites and purposes. A further advance was registered in the fifth century when the L-shaped stoa was given one more wing so that it now enclosed space on three sides. The first example was apparently the stoa of the sanctuary of Artemis at Brauron on the northeast coast of Attica. In this sanctuary, a sort of monastery where young Athenian girls lived as acolytes of Artemis, a little temple with a

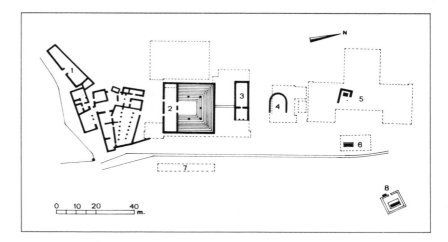

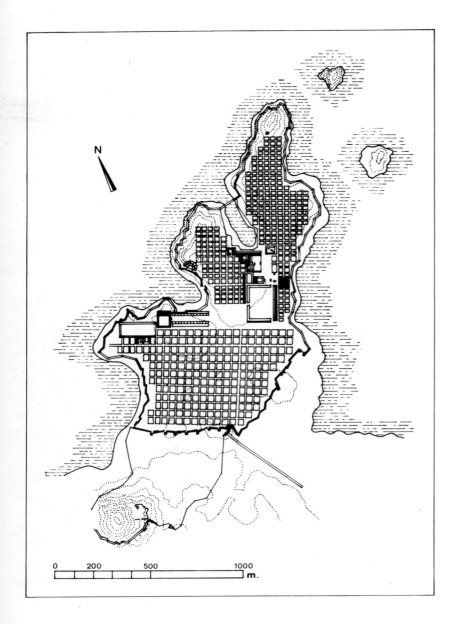

N

| 0 | 200 | 500 | 1000 |
| | | | m. |

sacred spring was built on the south, against the rocky cliff. The sanctuary extended to the north, and consisted of a U-shaped portico whose central building communicated with an interior court and another parallel structure where the offerings were stored. Beyond the north and west colonnades there were rooms whose furnishings indicate their purpose: here the servants of the goddess took their communal meals. The temple, offset in relation to the axis of the porticoes, closed a composition organized around a carefully delimited space.

Within zones thus defined the buildings could be arranged with considerable freedom. In the sanctuaries the temple served as a center of attraction for the ex-votos which customarily lined the sacred way, or were placed in a circle around the temple esplanade when the nature of the site permitted. At Delos the treasuries built in the sixth and fifth centuries were distributed in a semicircle around the sacred enclave occupied by the three temples of Apollo; whereas the offerings connected with the Temple of Artemis in the area more exactly defined by the L-shaped stoa of the Naxians, were arranged around that esplanade and along the sacred way leading from the harbor. This dual principle is equally evident at Samos. The temple, associated with the altar and the enclosure around the sacred tree of Hera, formed the principal mass, and was freely surrounded by small shrines dedicated to the deity. Other chapels and pedestals bordered the sacred way. These progressive and rather random groupings reflected the living evolution of the sanctuaries, and also the complexity and disparity of the secondary cults that were often associated with the worship of the principal deity.

Agora buildings were also grouped according to a functional principle. The first clear example, as we have seen, is afforded by Megara Hyblaea in the mid-seventh century, when the city became organized on a definite plan. Stoas formed the boundaries of the trapezoidal marketplace at north and east. On the south two rectangular temples, without peristyles, were laid out along one line; the connections with the quarters adjacent to the square remained ill-defined. The west side lay along one of the great arteries of the city, beyond which stood a row of public buildings of a civic or religious character. Passing from north to south, one encounters sanctuaries where the finds (*bothroi*, tablets with cupules) suggest heroic cults, then an anonymous building, and then a complex within which the plan of a prytaneum is clearly discernible.

At the beginning of the sixth century the reforms of Solon had given positive direction toward a democratic regime in the city of Athens, where the architectural framework was created that symbolized its form of government and welcomed the first organizations needed for its functioning. The agora was detached from the acropolis. Along its western edge, at the foot of the Kolonos Agoraios, there arose as at Megara a row of religious and political buildings: the first sanctuary of Zeus Agoraios, the temples of Apollo and Demeter, the Bouleuterion, and the first Prytaneum that preceded the Tholos (Plates 456, 457). This was a disorderly succession of buildings with dissimilar plans, which later caused a great deal of trouble when Hellenistic taste insisted upon the regularization of the colonnaded facades. The limits of public land reserved for the agora were fixed by boundary markers, several of which have been found in their original positions. During the fifth and fourth centuries the contours of the square were regularized, and girded with the succession of civic and religious buildings. On the northeast, on the north, and to the south, utilitarian stoas were erected to house the offices, meeting places, tribunals, and picture galleries where mythical and historical achievements of the city were celebrated. The ruins, as excavated by the American School of Classical Studies, confirm that the Athenian agora was not organized on any systematic principle, but simply performed the multiple functions of a public square and a symbol of Athenian democracy. The testimony of Demosthenes, in the second half of the fourth century, graphically evokes its teeming life and colorful complexity (Oration XVIII, 169): "It was evening, and one had come to the Prytanes with the news that Elateia had been taken [by Philip of Macedon]. Upon this they rose up from supper without delay; some of them drove the occupants out of the booths in the market place and set fire to the wicker-work; others sent for the generals and summoned the trumpeter; and the city was full of commotion."

## THE RELATIONS BETWEEN ARCHITECTURAL COMPLEXES AND THE URBAN FRAMEWORK: THE BIRTH OF GREEK CITY-PLANNING

Closely linked with the political and social structure of the Greek city, the architectural complexes of sanctuaries, agoras, and gymnasia could not be detached from the urban framework that formed the core of the political community; in particular the Hellenic conception of the *polis,* the city-state, required autonomy and independence for all the institutions that made it unique. Thus the city left its mark on the shaping of the principles of architectural composition.

These principles and interrelationships depended, however, upon the historical conditions that had kept alive the evolution of the city-state. In the ancient cities progressive transformations brought about the traditional succession of regimes as defined by Plato: monarchy rooted in Mycenaean traditions, then the oligarchy or aristocracy of the great landowners, and finally democracy, which initiated the redistribution of wealth and the importance of expanded trade. The acropolis, site of the royal palace, was associated with the temple of the protective god; together they dominated the city and formed its monumental crown. The agora, endowed with public buildings and serving commercial functions, was a later development, situated in the new city and oriented outward, toward the ports.

Athens is a good example of the ancient type of urban growth, Miletus of the later (Plate 458). In this planned type the urban land is divided to conform with the social and economic functions of the city, and then into lots determined by a more or less regular grid; within this system the most important architectural features are allocated the privileged sites. It is important to realize that Athens and Miletus reacted in quite different ways at about the same time and under more or less comparable historical conditions. In 494 B.C. the Persians razed Miletus and drove out its inhabitants; in 480 they invaded Athens, burned the buildings on the acropolis, and set fire to part of the town: when the two cities began the work of reconstruction, Athens remained faithful to the ancient system, but Miletus opted unreservedly for geometrism, for the rectangular system.

Athens clung to its acropolis, once the site of the royal palace and of the legendary family of the Cecropes but now entirely reserved for the worship of the gods. We know from the records that the agora was situated in Archaic times on the low western slopes of the acropolis, almost at the foot of the Mycenaean fortifications that are still preserved at several points. The city itself developed along the adjacent valley between the Areopagus and the Pnyx, and to the south, the area to the north being occupied by necropolises; it was a narrow, cramped city with winding streets, clinging to the skirts of the isolated sacred rock with its own buildings on top. The break came at the beginning of the sixth century, with Solon and his social reforms; the agora was transferred to the site of the ancient necropolises, between the fortified zone of the acropolis and the new quarters of the artisans and merchants. The old roads formed the axes along which the various buildings were distributed: the north-south thoroughfare, defined toward the close of the sixth century by boundary markers reading "I am where the agora ends," fronted

the administrative and religious side (Prytaneum, Bouleuterion, and cults of Demeter, Apollo Patroos, Zeus Phratrios, Zeus Agoraios); the square was crossed diagonally, from northwest to southeast, by the Panathenaic Way, whose path remained unchanged through the centuries. The new square received an articulating and communicating role in the city with the Altar of the Twelve Gods, the zero milestone from which distances from Athens were reckoned. In connection with other streets, stoas and buildings were irregularly sited around the edges of the square, with the established traffic patterns scrupulously respected. The Athenian agora exercised no real influence on the city's architecture, and did not become an object of systematic planning until the advent of the Hellenistic age.

It is significant that about the same time, in the years following the victories over the Persians (480–479 B.C.), the Athenians concentrated their first efforts on refortifying the acropolis, then restored the lower city to its traditional appearance. But they rebuilt the Piraeus along entirely new lines, calling in as planner the theoretician Hippodamus. He was then supervising the reconstruction of Miletus, and his name, Hippodamus of Miletus, was to become the symbol of Greek city-planning; more philosopher than architect, he formulated rules derived from his reflections on what would be optimal living conditions for city dwellers, and on the realizations already to be found in the cities of Archaic Greece, particularly in Magna Graecia. Applying these rules to the Piraeus, the space within the city was allocated to various urban functions; administrative, religious, and business zones intercommunicated, and served political, religious, social, and economic interests with buildings adapted to their functions. Each zone considered the property of the state (the *demosion)* was delimited by boundary markers, several of which have been found, some still on the very spots where the ancient surveyors placed them. Thus it has been possible to identify the commercial port zone, the mooring zone, and the boundaries of the agora in relation to the naval dockyard. The agora was connected with the dockyard by the long gallery already mentioned (page 318), built in the fourth century by the architect Philo, where the sails and tackle of the Greek navy were stored. The commercial zone, surrounded by great porticoes used as warehouses, was linked by a monumental route with the temples and sanctuaries, as well as with the agora. This monumental complex occupied the center of the site, around which extended the residential quarters, in three principal zones.

The growth of modern Piraeus has obscured the architectural lines of the ancient city, though it is well defined in plan by the

boundary markers and other sporadic finds. But the excavations at Miletus illustrate the precise architectural forms generated by the Hippodamian planning principles. Within the rectangular grid laid out by the surveyors, a certain number of lots were reserved for public buildings; these were distributed along the two branches of an L-shaped route connecting the two main harbors, separated by the theater promontory. At the meeting point of the two branches was located the principal agora, whose boundaries were sharply defined by great porticoes with rooms; links with the street system were provided at either end of the colonnades. The succession of buildings along the north branch included the Bouleuterion, gymnasia, the sanctuary of Apollo Delphinios, and finally the markets and big warehouses of the large Lion Harbor; to the east lay other markets and the principal sanctuary of the city, that of Athena. The three distinct residential quarters were regularly laid out in blocks.

Stoas and colonnades formed the bony structure of these compositions, defining the boundaries and establishing the orientation of the main axes; they impressed a certain unity on otherwise unrelated structures by combining them in groups behind formally composed facades. Thus the architecture was closely linked with the city plan, an expression of its principles and functions. This plan was realized gradually, and not fully implemented until the end of the Hellenistic epoch, but it had been so firmly conceived that the empty areas were steadily filled in the course of the centuries, with little incentive to depart from it. Moreover, the city fathers were steadfast in imposing the rules, even on princely benefactors, as may be seen from the proscriptions in a decree that required the architects of Antiochus III to conform to the city law when the king offered to build a great stoa for Miletus.

Several centuries before Hippodamus, the origin of the principles can be discovered that the philosophers were later to analyze and impose as rules on their ideal city. Plato drew liberally on the examples offered by the Greek colonies in the west. The excavations at Megara Hyblaea in eastern Sicily, and studies pursued at Camarina, Selinus, Monte Casale, and Metapontum, permit us to reconstruct with some precision the evolution of this urban architecture. Its first manifestations can be found in the seventh century, in the urbanizing trend that followed the establishment of Greek colonies in Sicily and southern Italy. The plan of Megara Hyblaea shows that in the middle of the seventh century several main axes created a division of the site of the city with the secondary streets, and defined a space composed of more or less regular blocks, though the layout was not strictly geometric. A public zone was bounded by two east-west axes (though not strictly parallel), by a cross street on the north, and, less definitely, by the siting of two temples on the south. Trapezoidal in plan, the marketplace was separated from the streets that bounded it by stoas designed not to cut the flow of traffic. The north stoa, in particular, had a wide gateway in the middle communicating with the secondary street to the north, which was interrupted by the agora. On the west side the street was incorporated in the square; along its outer edge, beyond the roadway, the buildings were inlaid, as it were, in an otherwise residential block. It is noteworthy that no earlier foundations were uncovered beneath the lowest level of the agora; the agora was part of the original plan, and no structures had to be cleared away to make room for it.

Wherever our study of the Archaic cities of Sicily has revealed the existence of a rational plan, it has proved to be based on the same block principle. At Camarina the primitive nucleus controlled the direction of subsequent growth; at Monte Casale a large part of the plateau was divided by parallel streets branching off the principal axis, which originated on a platform constituting a sort of acropolis. The regular plan of Metapontum goes back in large part to the seventh or early sixth century, and in it one can see the primacy of the sanctuary of the Lycian Apollo and of the agora that doubtless formed its continuation on the east. Inscriptions, recently published, bear witness to the importance of the *horoi,* boundary markers that fixed the limits of the sacred domain, the religious domain, and the zones allocated to the citizens. The acropolis is conspicuously absent from these sites; for the emigrants it stood for a regime from which they had fled. Plans based on a regular partitioning of the land into blocks, permitting space to be reserved immediately for the religious organizations that symbolized both the reality and the aspirations of the new community, were well suited to their political and social requirements. There was no need to defer to ancient eastern traditions; the plan evolved from the conditions themselves and from the exigencies that prevailed at each settlement. This form of urbanization and the principles of architectural composition that followed from it explain the specific characteristics of Greek colonial cities.

Monumental composition was at first subjected to the city plan, but did not long submit to that condition; it was particularly stimulated by the political and economic development of the colonies. The ambitions of the tyrants and their desire for ostentation, combined with the financial resources at their dis-

posal, led to an architectural expansion that burst apart the original frame. The evolution of the first sanctuary on the acropolis of Selinus is a good example of this process. The temenos, which enclosed altars and shrines whose earliest remains are from the seventh century, was laid out at the intersection of two roads, one linking the acropolis with the city spread out over the hills to the north, and the other the two ports flanking the plateau on east and west. Its irregular contours were first recognized by E. Gabrici and fixed more precisely by M. di Vita. The initial extension of the terrace toward the east came as early as 570–560 B.C., when the first great temple, Temple C, was built. During the last quarter of the sixth century the development of the sanctuary was included in a scheme for the regularization of the great axes, as part of a vast public works program. A second temple, Temple D, was added to the complex. On the west and the south the temenos walls were aligned with the streets; a great terrace was constructed on the east, stabilized with a massive stepped retaining wall; an L-shaped stoa was erected to define the boundaries of the esplanade, following the principles already seen on Samos. By a sort of reduplication of masses, the temples were to succeed one another to the south, on the acropolis, and still more superbly to the east, where each temple was parallel to the next.

About the same time, toward the end of the sixth century, an almost identical program was initiated at Paestum (Plates 459, 460). A great north-south thoroughfare formed the backbone of the plan; a uniform succession of residential blocks stretched between this axis and the western limits of the site, toward the sea. The main thoroughfare was bordered on the east by the wall of an immense temenos that received the temples of Hera, then the sanctuaries of the agora, and at the north the Temple of Athena. At Acragas the monumental zone was located south of the city, where it could take excellent advantage of a stretch of terrain that dominated the plain on which the city lay. The whole was subtended by a great thoroughfare, which formed the base of the triangle whose apex was to be the acropolis, itself crowned by a sanctuary. Along the road that led westward, to the sanctuary of the chthonian deities, lay the agora, the great Temple of Zeus, and, at some distance, adjacent to the walls, the temples of Heracles, Concord, and Juno Lacinia, erected during the fifth century but following a plan doubtless prepared a century earlier.

Such, then, is the meaning and importance of the great monumental ensembles of Sicily and southern Italy. Today they appear to be isolated, cut off from the cities of which they are the most brilliant ornament. But they should not be seen detached from the urban setting; on the contrary, they are closely linked

465. *Epidaurus. Restoration of Corinthian capital and trabeation from Tholos. Epidaurus, Museum*

466, 467. *Sarcophagus of the Mourning Women, end reliefs. Istanbul, Archaeological Museum*

468. *Acragas. Restored telamones from Temple of Zeus. Agrigento,*      471. *Thasos. Relief on Gate of Silenus* ▷
*Museum*
469. *Acragas. Plan of Temple of Zeus*
470. *Epidaurus. Isometric reconstruction of Temple L*

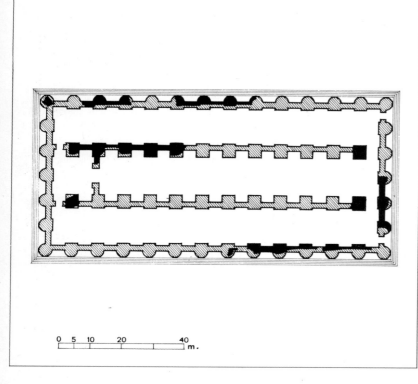

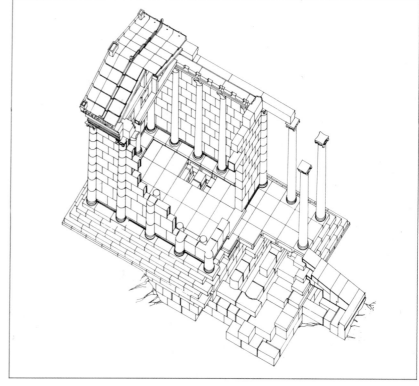

to it by their function and their architectural prominence. Too important to be squeezed into the compartments of a sometimes constricting rectangular grid, they form, as it were, a backdrop that occasionally has truly theatrical effect, but always they express a sense of proportions and a flare for the art of siting that are rooted in the fundamental traditions of Greek architecture.

# ARCHITECTURE OF HELLENISTIC GREECE

Greek architecture of the Hellenistic age gives rise to varied judgments, not all of them favorable. What sometimes deceives us is the degradation of the Classical forms and motifs; these tend to become dry and impoverished and lose their strength and vigor, but in this period one should not overlook the luxuriance and diversity of their many themes. And at the same time the development of the vault and the arcade, the knowing use of engaged orders in decorative compositions, and the variety demanded of sculpture and painting constitute a repertory that is new, or at least much enriched by all the Classical forms. But the originality of Hellenistic architecture is not confined to its formal aspects; these could not compensate for inferior workmanship. The strength of the architects lies in the creative vigor of their monumentality and the amplification of their structures. They adapted the Classical tradition to the new conditions of the Greek world, its geography now vastly extended.

The civic style of architecture yielded to a princely and monarchical architecture; ostentation, political prestige, and a desire to enlist the arts on the side of economic or financial power drastically upset the proportions and balances that the structure of Classical cities had imposed. Let us pause to consider the methods of this architecture before examining its finest achievements, those that furnished later ages with a repertory of forms and structures that were used for several centuries.

The Hellenistic architects, who first built for Alexander and then lavished their skill on the kingdoms of his successors in Asia Minor, Syria, and Egypt (before nurturing the infant architecture of Rome), were not revolutionaries; on the contrary, they were decidedly conservative in their use of forms and motifs.

The traditional orders, Doric and Ionic, continued to live on, but the difficulties inherent in the Doric frieze, as well as the taste for decorative expression, favored the spread of the Ionic style. The most Classical of these architects, Pythius of Priene in the late fourth century and Hermogenes a century later, held forth on the superiority of the Ionic order. Vitruvius preserves an echo of their arguments (*De architectura*, IV, iii, 1): "Some ancient architects have said that temples should not be constructed in the Doric style, because faulty and unsuitable correspondence arose in them; for example Arcesius, Pythius and especially Hermogenes. For the last named after preparing a supply of marble for a temple in the Doric style, changed over, using the same marble, and built an Ionic temple to Father Bacchus [Temple of Dionysus at Teos] not because the form or style or dignity of the

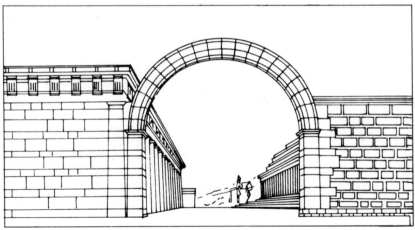

plan is displeasing, but because the distribution of the triglyphs and soffits is confused and inconvenient."

The rhythm of the Doric frieze had indeed to satisfy two contradictory requirements (Plates 462–64). First, the center of each triglyph should coincide with the axis of the column below; this presented no difficulty along a colonnade, but at the corner of the portico two triglyphs were supposed to abut so as to form a neat articulation. This meant the metope must be offset from above the corner column, and consequently the last metope must be wider than the others. This problem had been evaded since the end of the Archaic period by reducing the width of the last bay of the facade, or, to make the interruption less obtrusive, by dividing this reduction between the last two bays. But this brought necessary changes into proportions at all levels, from the slabs of the crepidoma on which the columns stood, to the blocks of the entablature and the cornices; the consequences became more disturbing when geometric procedures were developed to define the interrelationships among all the elements of the colonnade. In a system where the discipline of geometry tended to impose rather rigid formulas, the shortening of the corner spans meant a disrespect for symmetry and a want of rhythm that was alien to the very nature of the Doric order. And if to this is added the evolution of forms that made the columns increasingly slender and the lines in general more dry and rigid, and reduced the proportions of the entablature and accentuated its narrowness, then the progressive disappearance of the Doric order from the temples is easy to understand; it continued to be used in the great stoas and long colonnades, where, reduced to aligned facades between the antae of lateral walls, it posed no architectural problem. During the Hellenistic age the Doric order was essentially the order of stoas.

At the same time the Ionic order, whose entablature was free of these shortcomings, was being developed and enriched; moreover, its easy acceptance of decorative motifs commended it to the prevailing taste. With the invention of the angle capital that is square in plan with its four volutes placed on the diagonals, the first known example coming from the Nereid Monument at Xanthos (see Plates 325, 327), was solved one of the difficulties associated with the use of the order in the peristyle. Formerly the volutes had been confined to the two principal faces; as the ends displayed only the cushion connecting the spirals, the capital did not meet the requirements of an angle location, to be viewed from both sides, nor did it provide the extra volume that an exposed support needed at the point of intersection of two colonnades. Bases and capitals were given a

more vigorous and elaborate ornamentation. In the Temple of Artemis Cybele at Sardis, a fleuron appeared in the center of the channel, above a more vigorous ovolo that is half-concealed by broad palmettes (see Plate 486). In the Temple of Apollo at Didyma, figures of gods were applied to the volutes of certain capitals. The two motifs, on the channel and between the volutes, became developed, and the popularity of the historiated capital in the Hellenistic and Roman epochs is well known.

Hellenistic architecture did not invent the Corinthian capital but welcomed it very warmly—at the expense of the Ionic order, retaining only its base and shaft. The origins of the Corinthian style, hidden from the eyes of the ancient historians, remain something of a mystery. According to Pliny, the capital was invented by the Athenian sculptor Callimachus, Phidias' pupil, who is supposed to have been seduced by the sight of an offering basket left on a tomb and enveloped naturally by the leaves of an acanthus plant that chanced to take root there. The legend, as so often, contains a degree of truth. The origin of the Corinthian capital is doubtless associated with the motif of acanthus leaves so freely used on fifth-century funerary steles, either forming a basket at the base, or replacing the earlier palmette at the top. Representations of the same motif on white-ground funerary lekythoi illustrate the same affiliation.

Furthermore, the motif satisfied the taste for architectural decoration that emerged during the fourth century, and the Corinthian colonnade reflected new developments in organizing interior space where the pillars and columns had architectonic functions as well as decorative ones. The bell covered with acanthus provided a flexible means of adorning a cylindrical capital that was easily adaptable, either in its complete form or as crowning a half column or square pillar, to the various purposes it might serve in the architectural and decorative design of a hall. This is why a Corinthian column occurs in curious association with the Ionic order in the cella of the Temple of Apollo at Bassae. Subsequently in the Tholos at Delphi it was employed on the columns attached inside the cella wall supporting the roof framing; it flourished vigorously in the hands of the sculptor-architect Scopas at the temple of Tegea, becoming the principal theme of the interior order of half columns of the handsome cella; and it assumed final form in the interior columns of the Tholos of Epidaurus, rising unsuspected behind the severity of the Doric peristyle outside.

The acanthus leaf was treated timidly at first, a simple applied motif, the leaves arranged in a single row of modest height around the central calathus that formed the body of the capital;

485. *Sardis. Column bases of east portico, Temple of Artemis Cybele*
486. *Sardis. Ionic capital of Temple of Artemis Cybele*
487. *Sardis. Column base of east portico, Temple of Artemis Cybele*

*488. Didyma. Plan of Temple of Apollo*

*489. Didyma. Columns on north side of Temple of Apollo* ▷

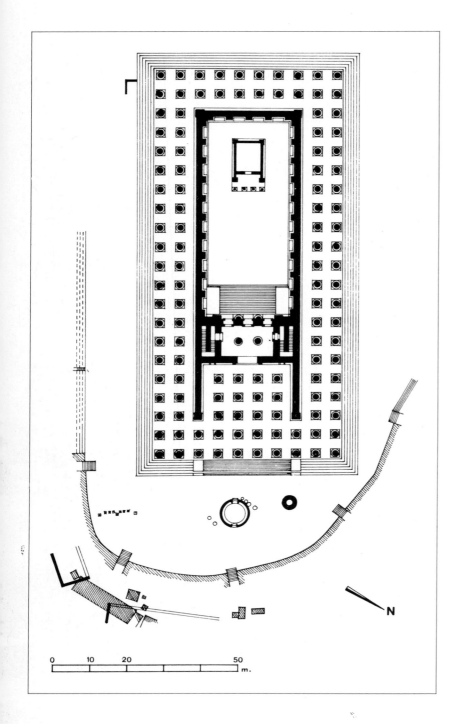

0   10   20              50
                            m.

in the hands of Scopas and the artists at Epidaurus it sprouted luxuriantly, arranged in two superimposed tiers from which escape twisted stalks that are surmounted by a curled leaf or calyx continuing into the volutes that supported the four projecting angles of the abacus. Early in the Hellenistic period the Corinthian capital assumed its definitive form on the Olympieion of Athens, for the last void of the capital was filled by decorative volutes on the axes, and these were crowned by a convolvulus flower nestled in the central depression of the abacus.

Hellenistic architecture had at its disposal a rich repertory of forms, much more varied than those it had inherited. But its inventiveness did not stop there; to satisfy the new requirements of architectural composition it perfected two other elements which the Classical age had known but deliberately left unstressed, namely, the engaged orders and the vault.

Since the end of the sixth century architects had used the half column engaged with the end of a wall (Temple of Athena, Paestum) or the column associated with a wall (especially where closures or interior balustrades were required: Temple of Athena Aphaia at Aegina, Temple of Zeus at Olympia), but the motif remained discreet, restricted to interior use. During the fifth century there were isolated attempts to develop special orders, such as the half columns and telamones of the great Temple of Zeus at Acragas (Plates 468, 469), but in style and proportions it could not exert much influence. The engaged order, more decorative than structural, first entered upon an independent existence with the transformation of the interior hall; eventually it became an exterior element as well, and the principal theme of certain facades. Behind the Classical peristyles of the temples at Bassae and Tegea we have seen the role of engaged columns and pillars in the interior decoration: against cella walls displaying the Classical bond, with its strict regularity of alternate staggered and carefully centered joints, independent decoration of half columns was applied with no true architectonic function, though they supported sculptured friezes — with figures at Bassae, and with plant motifs at Tegea, where Corinthian half columns were surmounted by Ionic pilasters.

This theme of an applied order, distinct from the structural elements (Plates 466, 467, 470), marked a break with the great Classical tradition of form inseparable from function, but it belonged to a new trend that was assured of quick success and a tremendous future, for it became fundamental to Hellenistic and Roman architecture.

First seen in the scene structures associated with the Hellenistic theater, the engaged style spread rapidly to the facades of fu-

*493. Didyma. Interior pilaster capital from Temple of Apollo*

nerary monuments and then to the great decorative gateways within city walls. The style suited the rather theatrical taste in architecture of the Hellenistic princes. Often arranged in two stories, one Ionic or Doric, the other Ionic or Corinthian, the half columns or pillars projected from the walls that filled the bays on either side of arches and passageways. A gate in the walls of Thasos was built in this style at the end of the fourth century (Plates 471–73), and heralds the richer and more dynamic forms of the great Roman gate to the south agora at Miletus, abutting one of the back walls of one of the stoas.

The Macedonian tombs, such as the fine facade of that at Leucadia, exploit the same theme, often enhanced by painted decoration. This introduces one of the most important aspects of Hellenistic architecture: its pictorial effects and its close connections with painting. If the decorative mural painting of later periods was able to make such free use of huge architectural compositions, it was because architecture itself had called upon painting to accentuate the decorative values of its facades and interiors. The resulting experiments in effects of light and shade exerted a reciprocal influence on proportions: the spans of colonnades were widened, the supports heightened. Hermogenes adopted the so-called eustyle rhythm, the space between the columns equaling two and one-quarter column diameters, the height of the column being nine and one-half diameters; even more open was the diastyle rhythm, the column spacing equaling three diameters; as for the araeostyle (spacing at three and one-half diameters), according to Vitruvius it was unusable unless the entablature were of wood, since the span was too great for stone.

Effects of shadow and relief were enhanced on the engaged orders by applications of stucco and paint. On the facade of the tomb at Leucadia (early third century) the Ionic upper order was picked out with lines of dark red paint which defined the shafts and put them into relief. There were also false windows in paint, and the decorative frieze, between the two levels, was of painted stucco. The refinements of perspective are better understood; the play of shadow and the opposition of lighted zones have been systematically exploited in the mural decoration, which opened onto an imaginary architectural composition.

Finally, the arch and the vault were accepted definitively into the Hellenistic repertory (Plates 478–80). Mediterranean architecture had always employed the corbeled vault, as splendidly exemplified in the great Mycenaean tholoi. The tradition was not lost by the architects of Archaic Greece, who used it for tombs and aqueducts. But the bonded keystone arch does not

495. Priene. Plan of Temple of Athena Polias
496. Magnesia. Plan of Temple of Artemis

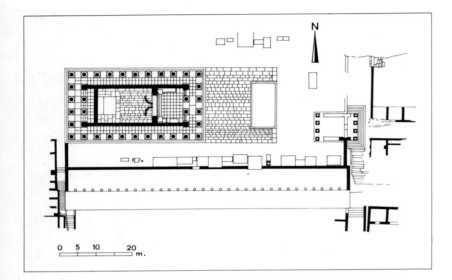

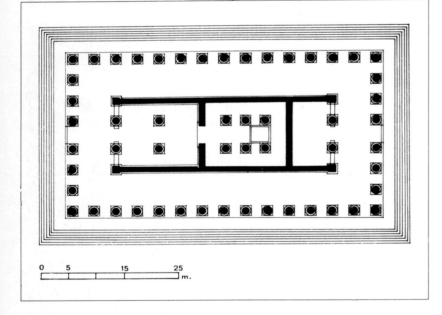

appear until the fourth century, when it is superbly handled in the gateways of certain city walls; for examples, there are the Porta Rosa of the city of Velia, the ancient Phocian colony south of Paestum; the gates of Oeniadae in Acarnania; the subterranean passages of the theater at Alinda; and the vaulted tomb of Labranda in Caria. The Macedonian tombs of the late fourth and early third centuries offer fine illustrations of hemispherical vaults. The painted facade of the great tomb at Leucadia conceals a spacious hall covered by a vault, which is separate from the lower vault of the funerary chamber.

The Greeks had limited their use of the vault to subterranean buildings, where the structure had to resist powerful external thrusts (Plates 475–77). Its full significance stands revealed in the Nekyomanteion (oracle sanctuary) of Epirus, recently discovered in western Acarnania. The outer rooms of the sanctuary, built of rustic polygonal blocks whose deep joints vigorously set off the roughness of the picked faces, have linteled doors and the ceilings are flat-arched. The inner room was reserved for oracular consultation in the necromantic rites, and covered by a hemispherical vault reinforced by a series of overlapping arches in the walls.

Hellenistic architecture quickly took advantage of the possibilities of the arch, particularly in the construction of monumental gateways. At Priene, the eastern gate of the agora was enlarged this way in the second century (Plate 481). Thasos followed suit a century later. The theater of the Letoön at Xanthos offers one of the first examples of the vaulted opening with exterior decoration of pilasters and a pediment. The vault and vaulted stairways and exedrae are known to have been used by the architects of Pergamum (Plates 482, 483).

### The Buildings

A few examples of major buildings will suffice to illustrate the architectural forms at the disposal of the Hellenistic architect. Two great Ionic temples at Sardis and Didyma best expressed the broad trends in religious architecture of the period without breaking totally with the permanent elements of the Ionic order; the new Artemision of Ephesus, so often cited, adhered too closely to the Archaic model.

The remains of the Temple of Artemis Cybele at Sardis, including the walls of the opisthodomos and a few of the east peristyle columns near it (Plates 484–87), still sprout from the wild Lydian landscape on the banks of the Pactolus River, where once was the famous capital of Croesus, whose very name has become a symbol of wealth. Several phases of construction have

497. *Sarcophagus of the Mourning Women. Istanbul, Archaeological Museum*
498. *Pergamum. Restoration of Great Altar of Zeus. Berlin, Pergamum Museum*

499. *Magnesia. Plan of Altar of Artemis*
500. *Magnesia. Front elevation of Altar of Artemis*

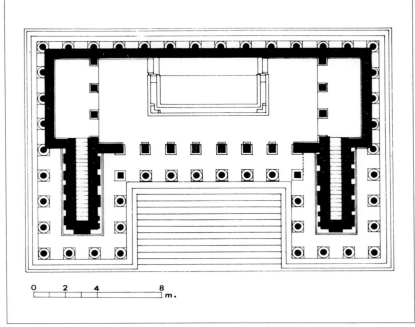

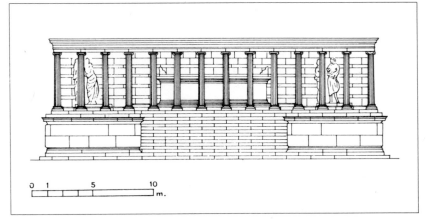

501. *Argos. Plan of Sanctuary of Hera*
1) *Temple of Hera I, before 600 B.C. 2, 3, 8) Doric stoa, Archaic period. 4) Hypostyle*
*hall, similar to telesterion. 5) Temple of Hera II, end of 5th century B.C. 6) Stoa.*
*7) Ancient banquet house. 9) Roman baths. 10) Gymnasium*

502. *Labranda. Plan of Sanctuary of Zeus*
1) *West terrace of temple. 2) Temple of Zeus. 3) North stoa. 4) East house. 5) East ter-*
*race of temple. 6) Palace (?). 7) West stoa. 8) South propylon. 9) Doric house. 10) East*
*propylon*

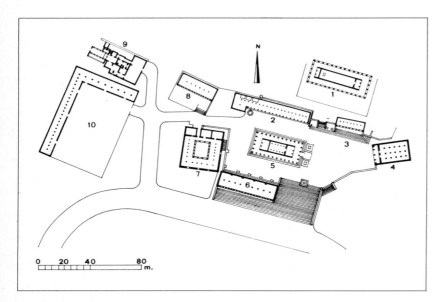

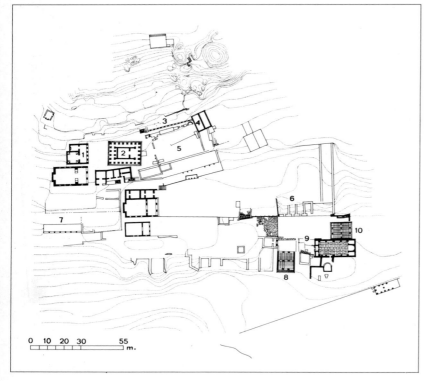

been distinguished, linked with different uses of the temple: in Roman times the west cella was reserved for Artemis, whereas the east hall was devoted to the cult of Faustina.

The sanctuary at Sardis originated with an altar erected at the edge of a level area. In the third century it was decided to build a huge peripteral edifice that would enclose this area within its dipteral plan. At that time only the naos was completed, consisting of a long cella divided into three aisles by two rows of six Ionic columns; the pronaos, deep like those of the Archaic temples at Ephesus and Samos, was originally adorned by two rows of three columns. A handsome capital from the interior order reveals the drift of the Ionic style away from the sober lines of the capitals inside the Propylaea at Athens. The Ionic peristyle was erected only a century later, but the design is transformed by the example of the Temple of Artemis at Magnesia on the Maeander, then being built by Hermogenes. The inner row of peristyle columns was suppressed to form a wide gallery (28 feet 9 inches) which set off the volume of the inner building.

The Temple of Apollo at Didyma remains the most grandiose example of religious architecture of this period and it also provides a virtual repertory for the forms devised and exploited by later centuries (Plates 488–94). It replaced an Archaic temple, a few traces of which have been found, but the architects Paeonius of Ephesus and Daphnis of Miletus, who supervised the reconstruction about 300 B.C., produced a most original design. Outwardly it appeared to be a large conventional dipteral Ionic temple, the tall cella surrounded by a double row of columns; the ten columns of the facade rose above a high crepidoma of seven steps, doubled to fourteen steps in the center along the width of the entrance stair. Columns sixty feet high were spaced apart 18 Ionian feet (17 feet 6 inches); the nine-foot square based on half of that column spacing was used as a module throughout the structure.

This sumptuous facade gave access to a deep twelve-column vestibule, the dodecastyle, four columns wide and three deep, and famous for their rich decoration. The bases present great variety: some have the Classical Attic profile of torus-scotia-torus; others remained in the Asian tradition derived from the bases of the Heraion at Samos, with layers of concave moldings, or smooth convex astragals crowning or crowned by a single torus. The square plinths with nine-foot sides are ever-present reminders of the underlying module, but the base moldings are sometimes replaced by an octagonal set of panels, framed by flat moldings and bearing motifs in low relief: rinceaux variously unrolled, marine animals or dragons, palmettes unfurled, spiral

503. Lindos (Rhodes). View of cliff and temple, from west

504. *Lindos (Rhodes). Cella of Temple of Athena, on upper terrace*
505. *Lindos (Rhodes). Great portico at foot of grand staircase, lower terrace of acropolis*
506. *Lindos (Rhodes). Grand staircase to upper terrace of acropolis* ▷

scrolls; the toruses are sometimes grooved, sometimes decorated with interlace or overlapping leaves. The decorative motifs on the toruses pass over to the comparable moldings along the base of the Ionic wall. The capitals express the same resourceful spirit of decoration: on the capitals of the angle columns, the volutes are capped by griffins' heads; beneath the gallery, some capitals bear the heads of Zeus, Apollo, Artemis, or Leto. Finally, the smooth architrave was crowned by a sculptured frieze of rinceaux and pilasters.

From this lavishly decorated pronaos were three openings with different uses. In the center, where one would expect the cella doors, there was a huge opening (18 feet wide, 46 feet high) made inaccessible by a sill over five feet higher than the pavement of the dodecastyle. No one could enter by this door: rather it was the "sacred doorway," having a special function emphasized by the enormous monoliths of its jambs and lintel, and from it were probably delivered the answers to the oracular consultations performed inside. The two openings on either side of this tribunal gave access to sloping barrel-vaulted passages whose construction displays remarkable technical skill (see Plate 479); these passages led down to the interior court that replaced the traditional cella. Huge (177 by 72 feet), and boldly structured by the high surrounding walls (height over 80 feet), the cella enclosed the primitive natural attributes of the oracle: the site of the spring, the laurel bush, and the adyton. The latter, in the form of an Ionic shrine or *naiskos,* sheltered the cult statue, and was situated at the west end of the court; from the east end a majestic flight of twenty-four steps, between the mouths of the two subterranean passages, led to the so-called labyrinth hall, on a level with the great "doorway" that dominated the twelve-columned pronaos.

The architects and sculptors of Didyma, the details of whose work is preserved in numerous inscriptions recording the costs of construction, displayed flexibility and skill in adapting every decorative resource to a project broadly conceived on a scale that far surpassed the Greek norm. In the second and first centuries B.C., and even later during Imperial times, decorators dipped into the repertory at Didyma and drew from its riches numerous motifs considered characteristic of later architectures; whether these systems originated in the western or the eastern Mediterranean world, many details were modeled upon the decoration of the temple of Didyma, such as carved rinceaux, decorative friezes with vegetable motifs, historiated capitals, the pilasters of the interior court, and decorated panels used on column bases.

There is another aspect of Hellenistic architecture that we

must consider, namely, its new aesthetic approach based on a system of mathematical relations and proportions. This bears the imprint of Hermogenes from Priene or Alabanda, the great theoretician of the period, whose work exerted a strong influence on Vitruvius. His theories and aesthetic concerns are embodied in the buildings that he designed at Magnesia on the Meander River.

To lighten the complex plans of Archaic and Classical Ionia, Hermogenes suppressed the inner row of columns in the peristyle of dipteral temple plans, while preserving the volumes and exterior proportions (Plates 495, 496). Vitruvius has given Hermogenes' definition of this pseudo-dipteral design (*De architectura*, III, ii, 6): "The *pseudodipteros* is so planned that there are eight columns both in front and at the back, and fifteen on each side, including the angle columns. But the walls of the cella are to face the four middle columns in front and at the back. Thus there will be a space all around, from the walls to the outside rows of the columns, of two intercolumniations and the thickness of one column. There is no example of this at Rome; but there is at Magnesia the temple of Diana built by Hermogenes of Alabanda..." In elevations Hermogenes intended to apply the same principles, with the object of freeing the interior volumes and enlarging the voids and open spaces, and thus he classified the different kinds of colonnades by their ratio of intercolumniation to column diameter (see page 358), from the pycnostyle colonnade, the most crowded, to the araeostyle, with too few columns to support a stone entablature.

In buildings at Magnesia we can see the application of Hermogenes' principles, and the facade of the Temple of Zeus Sosipolis, which he built on the agora of Magnesia, exactly reproduces his scheme. The deep pronaos, as large as the cella, is preceded by a tetrastyle porch; the opisthodomos, half the size of the pronaos, has two columns in antis; the ratio of these three spaces is 2:2:1, and the square of the pronaos (21 by 21 feet) reappears in the facade (column height and distance between lateral axes, 21 feet each); the proportions of the order are eustyle, the height of the columns corresponding to nine and one-half times the diameter (26 inches) and the intercolumniation to two and one-quarter diameters.

Shortly after the temple was built, the agora was enclosed by a system of stoas associated with the neighboring sanctuary of Artemis Leukophryne, located on that site before the order of a regular city plan was imposed. As Vitruvius points out, the Temple of Artemis is also a strict example of the pseudo-dipteral plan. The column spacing constitutes the module on which the design of the temple was based. The width of the pteron is equal to two modules. The naos, like the cella, is four modules deep, whereas the opisthodomos has only half that depth; this gives the same ratio (2:2:1) as in the Temple of Zeus. The entablatures of both temples include all the traditional Ionic elements: architrave, and frieze with dentils. In the tympanum of the pediment there is a large opening above the middle bay, which is slightly wider than the others, and two smaller openings are symmetrically disposed on the axes of the second and sixth bays. The insistence on slender proportions and lightened columns made it necessary to lighten the entablature and pediment; moreover the interior layout, with two rows of very close-set columns, required illumination appropriate to the nature of the rites and ceremonies of the cult.

Thus Hermogenes emerges as the great theoretician of Hellenistic architecture, whose principles and completed buildings exerted a distant influence on the proportions of the Ionic order into Imperial Roman times.

Let us bring to a close these observations on buildings of the Hellenistic period with a group of works that illustrate one of its most important attributes, its relationship with sculpture.

Of course, temples and funerary monuments since Archaic times had had sculptured decorations, first in relief, later in the round. It was placed in favored positions and associated with particular parts of the structure. There were precise rules controlling the use and development of monumental sculpture. The korai and caryatids in the Ionic treasuries at Delphi and the Erechtheion on the Athenian acropolis supported an entablature, and were closely linked with the architecture because of their structural functions (see Plates 305, 306, 324); in the Olympieion at Acragas, the telamones attached to the walls rhythmically punctuated each bay formed by the Doric half columns, themselves integral with the masonry (see Plate 468).

The integration of sculptural groups and architecture began early in the fourth century with the Nereid Monument at Xanthos (see Plate 325), and, a little later, the Mausoleum at Halicarnassus. Friezes proliferated, and tall podiums supported not only the tomb chamber, but statues of gods or heroes; these sometimes stood between the columns, as at Xanthos, introducing a movement and rhythm that seemed to break the strict architectural composition. The origins of these characteristics can be found in monuments on the Lycian acropolis; in the fifth century they belonged to the eastern traditions which, as in Egypt, had since the second millennium more readily associated

509. *Pergamum. Plan of acropolis*
1) *Theater.* 2) *Temple of Dionysus.* 3) *Temple of Trajan.* 4) *Arsenals.* 5) *Barracks.*
6) *Palaces.* 7) *Citadel gate.* 8) *Heroon of the kings.* 9) *Agora.* 10) *Great Altar of Zeus.* 11) *Temple of Athena.* 12) *Sanctuary of Athena*

510. *Pergamum. Model of acropolis. Berlin, Pergamum Museum*

511. *Pergamum, Acropolis. Foundations of Palace of Eumenes II, from northwest*

512. *Pergamum, Acropolis. Theater, from north* ▷

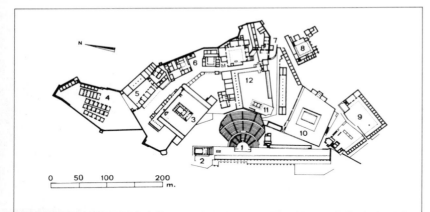

divine or royal effigies with the interior or exterior colonnades of
religious buildings. The Lycian princes, like the satraps of Caria,
were sympathetic to the eastern and the indigenous traditions,
while adapting them to the Hellenic decorations that they commissioned from Greek artists.

It is important to think of the silhouette of the Lycian and
Carian monuments, rising on massive podia crowned by one or
two friezes and an Ionic-type cornice enriched with two or three
rows of superimposed egg-and-tongue ornament. The effigies,
divine or heroic, were distributed at both Halicarnassus and
Xanthos along the top of the podium, either isolated or in association with the colonnades of the tomb chambers (Plate 497).
The same principle was later applied in the great monumental
altars of Pergamum, Priene, and Magnesia during the third and
second centuries (Plates 498–500).

The most famous of these altars is the one dedicated by the
Attalids to Zeus and Athena, perhaps even to all the gods of the
city, on one of the terraces of the acropolis at Pergamum. The
plan was in the tradition of Ionian altars, the sacrificial slab
placed on a tall stepped base with lateral salients. Eumenes II, at
the beginning of the second century, transformed this traditional scheme into a sumptuous monumental ensemble whose
architectural forms and sculptural motifs were closely associated. The whole rested on a five-step crepidoma inscribed in a
square (120 by 113 feet); from this a majestic flight of steps led
up to the central platform, framed by two projecting wings; the
podium consisted of a lower course of smooth orthostats whose
crowning molding formed the base of a mighty frieze celebrat-
ing the legendary struggles of the gods and giants. This frieze,
seven and one-half feet tall and unfolding over a length of four
hundred feet, was one of the finest achievements of the sculptors
of Pergamum, indeed of the entire Hellenistic period. Above the
frieze ran a decorated cornice, completing the podium as well.
On the podium, walls fronted by an Ionic colonnade enclosed
the altar slab on north, south, and east, the west side being occupied by the monumental stairway. Along the inner face of this
wall ran another smaller frieze illustrating the story of Telephus.
Finally, in the bays overlooking the stairway stood statues of the
gods or of allegorical figures.

The same plan and the same decorative themes were used for
the altars at Priene and Magnesia, though less lavishly and on a
smaller scale. In each case the platform bearing the altar slab was
on top of a crepidoma with several steps and there were two projecting wings, the whole surrounded by an Ionic colonnade. The
podium did not have a frieze, but a series of figures carved in

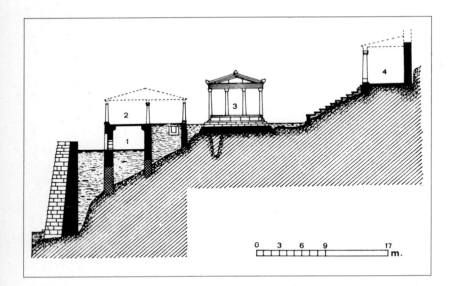

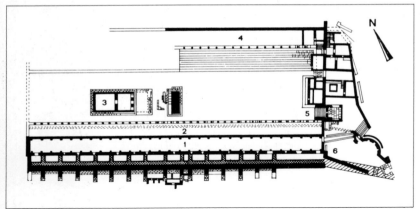

516, 517. *Pergamum, middle city. Sanctuary of Demeter: section of south stoa, temple, steps, and north stoa*
1) Basement. 2) South stoa. 3) Temple and altar of Demeter. 4) South stoa. 5) Gate.
6) Fountain of Demeter

518. *Athens, Agora. Colonnade of Stoa of Attalus (in background, Temple of Hephaestus)*

high relief occupied the bays of the colonnade on the facade and along the short sides.

In these compositions one can discern the origins of the theme which in later centuries took the form of niches integrated with the architectural design framed by columns and pediments; these niches decorated the tall facades of theater buildings, nymphaea, and palaces in Roman architecture.

519. *Athens, Agora. View from northwest, toward Stoa of Attalus*
520. *Athens, Agora. East facade of Temple of Hephaestus (Theseum)*
521. *Athens, Agora. Restoration of Stoa of Attalus*

## THE ORGANIZATION OF SPACE AND HELLENISTIC CITY-PLANNING

The design of monumental ensembles and their relationship to the surrounding space underwent a fundamental change at the beginning of the Hellenistic period. In the history of Greek architecture this transformation was perhaps the greatest Hellenistic innovation. For the buildings of the Archaic and Classical sanctuaries and agoras had been designed according to their specific function and individual character; space was organized around them freely, and it accommodated, without much regularity, the secondary structures. Whenever urban policy required a more rigid frame, architectural space was still treated openly, in direct relation to the surrounding zones.

Many factors combined to create a new conception of the architectural ensemble: the political evolution, that substituted the centralizing tendencies and ostentation of the Hellenistic princes for the diverse and sometimes divergent forms of monumental expression preferred by the Greek cities; the transformation of aesthetic interests toward plastic and pictorial effects, as well as monumentality; and the corresponding influence of the arts of painting and sculpture. Buildings lost their autonomy, becoming integrated with the surrounding structures that enclosed and unified them; the monumental masses thus became dependent, one and all, upon a space sharply defined and rigorously delimited; esplanades and squares were surrounded by porticoes, cutting off an area in which the interior was treated as a single uniform design. Out of this was created an architectural landscape, all of the elements interdependent and organized according to their plastic or pictorial effects; thus the door was opened to the great laws of axial planning and symmetrical ponderation which entered discreetly at first, later to be asserted with ever-increasing boldness.

This evolution was facilitated by two methods that seem to be contradictory, but in reality acted in the same direction. One was the development of city plans based on a rectangular grid, the space blocked out in well-defined zones contained by long colonnades; the other was the success of terrace composition, a type of planning that proceeds with precise, compact groupings unrelated to one another.

The latter trend, the more innovative of the two, deserves particular attention. The sanctuary of Apollo at Delphi, that of Hera on the edge of the plain of Argos (Plate 501), and other less well-known sites in the Peloponnesus prove that Greek architects since Archaic times had taken advantage of the different levels of the terrain to enhance their buildings. Each was treated independently, however, with no attempt to establish a relationship between masses or volumes.

In the course of the fourth century a new element was introduced by the architects who worked for the satraps of Caria—for Mausolus at Halicarnassus, for his brother Idrieus in the sanctuaries at Labranda and Amyzon, and for his sister Adda in her capital of Alinda. Vitruvius' description of the city of Halicarnassus; the excavations at Labranda (Plate 502) and Amyzon; and the remains at Alinda—each of these points to a system of great terraces, boldly defined by handsome retaining walls and linked by flights of stairs crowned by propylaea. On these terraces the buildings are placed and grouped with the clear intention to treat them as parts of an ensemble; though relatively small, they occupy privileged positions that integrate the buildings with the lines of the artificial landscape. The Greek architects were here inspired more by Achaemenid than by Hellenic tradition, and more by royal architecture than by that of the democratic cities (page 65).

The terraces also made use of great porticoes, the lower level acting as a retaining wall and housing basement service quarters, the upper story enlarging the terrace while limiting it. The large portico of the agora at Alinda was one of the splendid models that herald the Pergamenian porticoes.

The development of this terrace architecture is illustrated by two great sanctuaries, that of Athena at Lindos, on Rhodes, and the Asclepieion of Kos. Lindos (Plates 503–6) is especially instructive because the modeling of the successive terraces with the aid of porticoes, colonnades, and interlocking stairways was carried out in successive stages, so that one can recognize the processes used by the architects to impose a unity that is sometimes artificial. The holy place dedicated to Athena Lindia goes back to Archaic times, and the first temple was built on the highest terrace at the edge of the cliff, to be associated, it seems, with the sacred grotto hollowed out beneath. This ritual siting remained unaffected by later quests for symmetry.

The first plan for developing the upper terrace was prepared early in the third century, according to the new concepts of that epoch: a huge propylon marks the entrance to the sanctuary, with five doorways pierced in the central wall; to these corresponds a portico with a ten-column facade having at each end, following the example of Mnesicles' Propylaea, a prostyle bastion with four columns enclosing the passageway. The altar is aligned with the entrance and the court is bordered by porticoes on the north, east, and west sides. At the end of the same century or the beginning of the second, the lower terrace was integrated

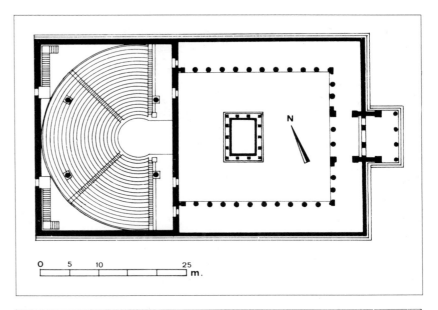

0  5  10        25
                m.

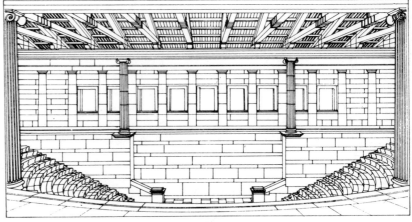

with the sanctuary and to it was assigned the role of monumental gateway: a grand staircase was broadly laid out in front of the propylon, and the foot of the terrace was developed as a large colonnade 225 feet wide, also having projecting wings. Where it met the grand staircase the portico had to be interrupted, and only the colonnade continued; across the opening was drawn the long curtain of Doric columns with no serious attempt at solving the problem of continuity. Thus the same themes were repeated at each level, at the price of certain anomalies but with the result that the contours and elevations of the successive terraces were perfectly modeled within an all-encompassing architectural structure.

A comparable and no less grandiose evolution may be traced in the development of the sanctuary of Asclepius on Kos. It was located on the slopes of the hills forming the southern boundary of the plain where stood the city and port of Kos; this spot, like all the Asclepieia, was made holy by the presence of natural springs welling from the hillside. The first modest Ionic temple (Temple C) was built on an intermediate terrace, where an altar had been erected at the beginning of the fourth century; the surviving portions of the temple were part of a rebuilding program carried out in the second century in accordance with Hermogenes' recommendations. At the beginning of the second century a small portico and what may have been a square abaton (reclining house) were added to complete the still rudimentary installation; the buildings were arranged in the old manner, placed without thought for anything but cult practices, and there is no evidence of conscious architectural grouping.

The main monumental building program appears to have been started about the middle of the second century. A relatively level stretch at the foot of the hill was treated as a huge entrance court; the uppermost terrace became the site of a new sanctuary, associated with the old intermediate terrace but designed according to quite different principles, with axial symmetry an overriding concern. The forecourt, which measured 307 by 155 feet, was surrounded on the north, east, and west sides by a Doric colonnade. A massive retaining wall closed off the south side and incorporated the two springs that were the object of the primitive cult; the upper level of the wall regularized the extent of the original terrace. The dispersion of the early buildings and the irregularity of the terrace prevented the use of axial symmetry, but where possible the principle was observed. Thus, the forecourt at the bottom of the hill was entered through a propylon on the axis of the central portico, dividing it into two symmetrical parts with projecting wings. On the same

525. *Miletus. Theater, from east*

axis was placed the first monumental stair leading to the middle terrace.

The organization of the uppermost terrace was also ruled by the concept of axial symmetry. A U-shaped portico, corresponding to the forecourt portico but open to the north, enclosed the terrace on three sides. On the axis was the stairway linking the two upper terraces and the great Doric peripteral Temple of Asclepius, a larger replica of the god's temple at Epidaurus.

These two examples illustrate the dual preoccupation of Hellenistic architecture, that of composing a monumental ensemble of columns and masses interrelated with one another and mutually reinforced by the terrace system, and of arranging these ensembles along axial or symmetrical lines. Both intentions were completely alien to Classical Greek architecture, but their lesson was not lost, and the effect that these experiments had on early Roman architecture is well known. The sanctuary of Fortuna at Praeneste was a direct descendant of Hellenistic terrace architecture, adapted to an Italic tradition that was itself predisposed in favor of axial symmetry.

The great movement of urbanism in the Hellenistic age adapted and transformed the principles evolved during the preceding period in accordance with the rules of the new aesthetics. The more effective disposition of monumental masses, the concern for space much more strictly delimited and organized, the imposition of architectural unity and closed contours, and the systematic use of long colonnades to accentuate the monumentality of dispersed urban architecture—all these were primary concerns in Hellenistic urbanism and found expression in the many new cities created by the expansionary policies of Hellenistic princes. Their wealth and ambition assured the best use of the techniques and forms that the architects had at their disposal—indeed, architecture was one part of their propaganda.

Among these masterworks, Pergamum and its acropolis offer an excellent example of a terraced urban architecture, the very irregularities of the terrain displaying the monumental masses to best advantage (Plates 509–14). Halfway up the acropolis, whose highest level is more than a thousand feet above sea level, the gymnasia received first attention, laid out on three terraces in a great curve formed by the city's main thoroughfare which hugs the twisting contours of the steep hillside. From the rising street, a porticoed fountain at its side, a staircase leads to the first terrace through a vaulted passage with two flights, their barrel vaults at right angles to one another and at different levels (see Plates 482, 483). From the first triangular esplanade, which

formed the tip of the composition, one ascended stairs leading to the second terrace, whose longest side was bordered by a covered track one stadium in length (100 Greek feet; about 600 feet), its roof at the same height as the level of the upper terrace. This ensured the optimal aesthetic and functional relationship with the great gymnasia, which extended around a broad esplanade 600 by 150 feet. The view, as always at Pergamum, was toward the south, and the principal halls of the gymnasia backed into the north cliff. The ephebeion, with its odeum, or music theater, was linked with the facade portico by a group of four columns, and followed by several exercise rooms covered in Roman times with semidomes. The Hellenistic buildings were made of local stone, a dark volcanic andesite that blended with the countryside; all the porticoes were Doric. Rebuilding programs carried out during the Roman period made greater use of marble and introduced the more decorative Corinthian column.

To the northwest lay the sanctuary of Demeter, linked with the gymnasia by a small terrace that ran along both sides of the main street (Plates 515–17). Perched on a terrace oriented east and west, the sanctuary was especially dear to the Attalid rulers. When inaugurated by Philetairos, the founder of the dynasty, it consisted of a small temple and its altar, opposite the entrance. Against the north slope, along the eastern esplanade, was the altar, where tiers of steps were arranged for the faithful; these terminated toward the west in a simple portico accompanying the temple.

At the end of the third century Apollonia, wife of Attalus I, was responsible for certain drastic changes that express with unusual clarity the extraordinary technical skill of the Pergamene architects. On the south, where the ground fell sharply toward the plain, the terrace was extended by building a monumental portico 280 feet long; its foundations were beyond and below the edge of the esplanade, in direct relationship with the steep terrain; an underground gallery was then constructed at the lower level, reached by a narrow path leading from the entrance to the sanctuary. At terrace level the south stoa, double-aisled and with two colonnades, provided a splendid open gallery for the view over the plain; on the west it turned to close off the sanctuary and join the north portico; this portico continued toward the east, above the tiers of steps, creating another gallery overlooking the south portico, to the plain and shore beyond.

We must mention that the lowest level, beneath the underground gallery, was reserved for basement service quarters. Here, in the third century, is the prototype of a long series of buildings combining porticoes and underground rooms which the architects of the Attalids were to export to the subject territories of the Pergamene dynasty, or its friends and allies—to Aegaea, Assos, and Pamphylia; their successors would later adopt it and, as the cryptoporticus system, make it an essential element of private and civic architecture in Roman cities. The Imperial age is rich in examples in all provinces, from the agora at Smyrna to the fora at Arles and at Conimbriga in Portugal.

One can only remark again, before leaving the subject of Pergamum, on the success of the Attalid architects in designing the acropolis. The theater (Plate 512) was placed like the pivot of a fan of terraces at different levels, limited at the top by the arsenal and at the south extremity by the agora. Between these utilitarian installations the area to the east held the princely palaces (Plate 511), protected by walls and rocky cliffs, and the west was reserved for the gods with Athena at the center, her sanctuary dominated by the Temple of Trajan above it and the Great Altar of Zeus and Athena below it (see Plate 498). To Attalus I and Eumenes II goes the glory for this splendid architectural composition, realized mainly during the last third of the third century and the first quarter of the fourth; what followed were continuations or finishing touches.

The influence of Pergamene architecture is linked with the political and historical conditions that marked the evolution of the Attalid kingdom. The Attalids were proud of their achievements, ambitious and desirous of being the true representatives of Hellenism in Asia Minor; with considerable resources at their disposal, they sent architects along with their ambassadors. The cities allied with Pergamum, and the venerable cities of Greece, such as Athens, as well as great sanctuaries such as those at Delphi and Delos, welcomed the teams of architects and masons dispatched by the Attalids (Plates 518, 519, 521). Later, their close understanding and cordial relations with Rome favored the spread of Pergamene art to the west, where the extent of its influence is well known. Imperial Rome learned much about composition from the architects and sculptors of Pergamum and borrowed extensively from their repertory of forms and motifs.

But no account of architecture in the Hellenized and Romanized countries east and south of the Mediterranean would be complete without the monumental architecture of Miletus (Plates 522–25). Within a geometric framework more rigorously defined than the terraces of Pergamum, a taste for en-sembles and for unified, organized monumental masses accompanied the expansion of the rectangular grid system. At Miletus, within the network laid out in the fifth century B.C., one follows the formation of enclosed structures. Colonnades were progressively substituted for the simple walls bounding the north agora, the Bouleuterion and its precincts, the adjoining sanctuary, and the gymnasia, and, finally, for the monumental street that formed the common axis along which these complexes were grouped. Porticoes gave better definition to the sides of the grid, and colonnades enclosed the main buildings according to the principles of axial symmetry.

It would be well to mention here, however sketchily, the architectural splendors at Alexandria, where Hellenistic techniques were combined with the sense of spaciousness and grandiosity inherent in the local tradition. The monumental zones were grouped together in the north, where they were dominated by Alexander's Pharos. The palaces, museums, and great sanctuaries such as the Serapeum appear to have made extensive use of long colonnades and porticoes to form broad squares within which the principal buildings were subsequently erected. Museum collections in Cairo and Alexandria show the taste for vigorous decoration, and the particular popularity of the Corinthian style. The great features of ancient Alexandria must be evoked in large Hellenistic and Roman cities of Cyrenaica and Libya. Certain details are also supplied by the Alexandrian landscape paintings at Pompeii, in which piers, column-decorated waterfronts, monumental arches, long porticoed streets, and formal facades recall the ruined cities of Asia Minor and Syria. How pleasant to stroll for a moment along the great avenue of Cyrene, past the gymnasia, the Caesareum, and the sanctuary of Zeus, and before the porticoes of the agora! One would find there, as at Perge and Side on the Mediterranean shore of Anatolia, or at Gerasa in the Syrian interior, long porticoed streets lined with shops, colorful and bustling with life; the closed symmetrical contours of great buildings would be now concealed, now splendidly revealed; beyond a propylon with its four or six columns the visitor would glimpse a monumental Ionic or Corinthian temple facade; broad colonnades unfolded to right and left in subtle harmonies of light and shade. This lavish repertory was available to the architects from east and west, and later to the architects who served the Roman emperors.

SYNOPTIC TABLES / SELECTED BIBLIOGRAPHY / LIST OF PLATES
INDEX / LIST OF PHOTOGRAPHIC CREDITS

| NEAR EAST | | EGYPT | |
|---|---|---|---|
| VIII millennium | first architectural forms at Jericho (Jordan) | | |
| Neolithic pre-pottery B (VII millennium) | building complex of Catal Huyuk | | |
| | circular stone tower and fortified wall at Jericho | | |
| | building complex of Khirokitia (Cyprus) | | |
| End of Neolithic | building complex of Hacilar, near Burdur (S. Anatolia) | | |
| Beginning of Chalcolithic (mid VI millennium) | building complex of Djarmo | | |
| | Mersin (Cilicia): small military fortress | | |
| | building complex of Hassuna | | |
| | building complex of Arpachiyah, near Nineveh | | |
| Proto-Sumerian period (from c. 5000 B.C.) | Eridu: temples (reconstruction from end of V millennium to beginning of IV millennium) | | |
| | Tepe Gawra: temples | | |
| Protoliterary period (last centuries, IV millennium) | Uruk: "White Temple" | | |
| | temples of the Eanna area | | |
| | Tell Brak: temple | | |
| | Al 'Uqair: temple | *Archaic (Thinite) period* | |
| *Protodynastic period (c. 3000–2340 B.C.)* | | 3000 B.C. | first unification of Kingdom of Two Lands. Founding of Memphis |
| | Khafaje: "high" temple | I and II Dynasty (2955–2665) | tumulus tombs at Abydos |
| | Al 'Ubaid: "high" temple | | palace tombs near Memphis |
| | Khafaje: "low" temple of Sin | | Abydos (environs): temple of the "Foremost among the Westerners" |
| | Tell Agrab: "low" temple | | Hierakonpolis: granite chapel |
| | Tell Asmar (Eshnunna): architectural complex, civic buildings | *Old Kingdom: III–VI Dynasty (2665–2155)* | |
| | Kish: Palace A | III Dynasty (2665–2570) | |
| | Eridu: palaces, city walls, temple | Zoser | Saqqara (environs of Memphis): funerary enclosure |
| | Ur: royal cemetery | | IMHOTEP |
| | | Huni (?) | Medum: pyramid with large steps |
| | | IV Dynasty (2570–2450) | |
| | | Cheops (2545–2520) | Giza: funerary complex with pyramid |
| | | Radedef (2520–2510) | Abu Roash: funerary temple |
| | | Chephren (2510–2485) | Giza: funerary complex with pyramid |
| | | | Harmakhis temple of the Sphinx |
| | | | Qasr el Sagha: temple |
| | | Mycerinus (2485–2457) | Giza: funerary complex with pyramid |

| NEAR EAST | | EGYPT | |
|---|---|---|---|
| | | Queen Khent-kaw-s | Giza, necropolis: "Buto tomb" |
| | | V Dynasty (2450–2290) | |
| | | Userkaf (2450–2442) | Saqqara: funerary complex with pyramid |
| | | | Abusir: sun temple |
| | | | SENNEDJEM |
| | | Sahura (2442–2430) | Abusir: funerary complex |
| *Akkadian period (c. 2340–2180)* | | Ne-user-ra (2390–2360) | Abusir: funerary complex with pyramid and sun temple |
| XXIV century | Sumerian city-states united under dynasty of Sargon I of Akkad | | |
| | Tell Asmar: palace, alterations | Unas (2310–2290) | Saqqara: funerary complex with pyramid |
| | Tell Brak: palace of Naramsin | VI Dynasty (2290–2155) | funerary complexes with pyramids |
| c. 2230 | fall of the Akkadian Empire | | |
| | | *First intermediary period: VII–X Dynasty (2155–2040)* | |
| *Neo-Sumerian period (2125–2025) and Isin-Larsa and Babylonian period* | | *Middle Kingdom: XI–XII Dynasty (c. 2040–1785)* | |
| | invasion by the Gutae | XI Dynasty (2061–2010) | |
| | Lagash: temple of god Ningirsu | | |
| III Dynasty of Ur (2050–1950) | Ur: restructuring of city (fortifications, palaces, temples) | Neb-hepet-ra Mentuhotep | Deir el Bahari: funerary complex |
| | | | VIZIER AMENEMHAT |
| | Great Ziggurat | XII Dynasty (1991–1775) | |
| | Great Mausoleum | | |
| | | Amenemhat I (1991–1971) | Lisht: funerary complex with pyramid |
| | | | Karnak: development of the temple |
| End of III millennium, beginning of II millennium | Tell Asmar: Temple of Shusin and Palace of the Governors | Sesostris I (1971–1929) | Heliopolis: sanctuary |
| | Elamites invade Mesopotamia | | Karnak: "White Chapel" |
| | fall of Ur; Isin-Larsa Dynasties | | SENUSRETANH and MERI |
| II millennium, first two centuries | Ischali: temple of goddess Ishtar-Kititum | Sesostris II (1897–1878) | Lahun: funerary complex with pyramid |
| | | | SIMONTU |
| | Mari: Palace of Zimrilim | | |
| | | Sesostris III (1872–1842) | Bubastis: palace |
| | | | VIZIER MENTUHOTEP? |
| | | Amenemhat III (1842–1798) | Hawara: sepulchral monument ("Labyrinth") |
| | | | Medinet Madi: temple |

| NEAR EAST | | EGYPT | |
|---|---|---|---|
| c. 1800 | Anitta, king of Hittites, conquers Hattusas and Kanesh | XII Dynasty | Dahshur: funerary complex |
| | Elamite kingdom subdued by Babylonia | | Beni Hasan: rock tombs |
| | | | Aswan: rock tomb of Prince Sirenpowet II |
| | | | Qaw el Kebir: rock tombs |
| Hammurabi (1792–1750) | Byblos: princely tombs | | Medamud: temple |
| | | | Tod: temple (of Mentu) |
| XVIII century | Tell Atchana: Palace of Yarimlim | | Hermopolis: first pylon with two towers |
| | | *Second intermediary period: XIII–XVII Dynasty (1786–1554)* | |
| *Kassite Dynasty (c. 1600–1100)* | | | Hyksos domination (XV–XVI Dynasty) |
| | | | rebirth of Thebes and expulsion of Hyksos |
| c. 1600 | Tlabarna, Hittite king, extends kingdom to the sea | *New Kingdom: XVIII–XX Dynasty (1554–1080)* | |
| | southern Mesopotamia falls under rule of Kassites | XVIII Dynasty (1554–1305) | |
| | Ur: reconstruction and restoration of existing temples | Amenhotep I (1529–1508) | Karnak: temple complex of Amon-Ra |
| | Dur Kurigalzu (Aqar Quf): Ziggurat, temples, palaces | Tuthmosis I (1508–1493) | Karnak: completion of temple (pylons IV and V) |
| | Uruk: Kassite temple dedicated to goddess Inanna | Tuthmosis III (1490–1439) | large works begun throughout country and in Nubia<br>SENMUT and VIZIER HAPUSENEB |
| XV–XIV century | Tell Atchana: Palace of Niqmepa | | |
| | Ras Shamra (Ugarit): palace | | |
| XIV–XII century | Hattusas becomes capital of Hittite kingdom | Regency of Queen Hatshepsut (1488–1470) | Deir el Bahari: funerary temple of queen<br>SENMUT |
| | Hattusas: city walls, five temples | | Medinet Habu: temple of primitive origin |
| | Kultepe: temple, merchant houses | | |
| | Arzawa (near Beycesultan): palace | Tuthmosis III, absolute ruler after 1470 | Karnak: "Hall of Annals" |
| | Yasilikaya: rock temple | | Karnak: jubilee temple<br>REKHMIRA |
| | Alaca Huyuk: city walls | | |
| | | Tuthmosis IV (1413–1403) | Giza: excavation of Sphinx |
| | | Amenhotep III (1403–1365) | Western Thebes: "Colossi of Memnon" |
| | | | Karnak: Pylon III of temple |
| | | | Luxor: temple |
| | | | Malkata: palace<br>SUTI and HORI |
| | | Amenhotep IV-Akhenaten (1365–1349) | Karnak: Temple of Aten<br>RAMOSE |

| NEAR EAST | | EGYPT | |
|---|---|---|---|
| | | 1360 | monotheistic religious reform and transfer of capital to Amarna |
| | | | Amarna: Temple of Aten and laying out of city |
| | | | Amarna: Palace of Amenhotep IV-Akhenaten |
| | | 1349 | Semenkhkara and Tutankhamen restore old religion and transfer capital to Thebes |
| | | Horemheb (1332–1305) | Karnak: Pylons IX and XI of temple |
| *Beginnings of Assyrian art (c. 1350–1000)* | | | |
| XIV–XIII century | Assur: walls and fortifications | XIX Dynasty (1305–1196) | capital on Delta at Qantir |
| | ziggurat of god Assur | | |
| | ziggurat of Anu and Adad | Ramesses I (1305–1303) | Karnak: Pylon II |
| Tukulti-Ninurta I (c. 1250–1210) | conquest of kingdoms of Carchemish and Babylonia | Sety I (1303–1290) | Western Thebes: funerary temple |
| | Assur: Temple of Ishtar | | Karnak: large hypostyle hall |
| | ziggurat of Assur (outside city) | | Abydos: temple and cenotaph |
| | Kar Tukulti-Ninurta: palace, temple of Assur | Ramesses II (1290–1224) | Western Thebes: funerary temple (Ramesseum) with palace |
| | | | Luxor: large temple courtyard |
| *Middle Assyrian period* | | | Abu Simbel: rock temple |
| | | | Karnak: completion of large hypostyle hall |
| | Assur: Temple of Ishtar (refacing and additions) | Merenptah (1224–1214) | Memphis: coronation palace |
| | Tell Rimah: temple | | Temple of Ptah |
| | Nuzi (near Kirkuk): Palace of Hurrian | | |
| | Minet el Beida (port of Ugarit): tombs | | |
| | Ras Shamra (Ugarit): sepulchers | | |
| | Tell Atchana: refacing of temples | XX Dynasty (1196–1080) | |
| Tiglath-Pileser I (1112–1074) | expansion of Assyrian power | Ramesses III (1193–1156) | Medinet Habu: funerary complex with fortified walls and palace |
| | formation of Syro-Hittite states in northern Syria: Phrygia, Lydia, Urartu | | Karnak: temple of moon god Khonsu |
| | Aramaean invasion and end of old Assyrian kingdom | | temple of sun god, east of Karnak |
| | | *Third intermediary period: XXI–XXIV Dynasty (1080–712)* | |

| NEAR EAST | | EGYPT | |
|---|---|---|---|
| *Neo-Assyrian period (c. 1000–612)* | | | |
| Shalmaneser III (859–827) | Nimrud: Fort of Shalmaneser | | |
| | Balawat (Nimrud): Bronze Gates | | |
| Tiglath-Pileser III (745–727) | Arslan Tash: temple-palace of Tiglath-Pileser | | |
| | Tell Halaf: Palace of Kaparu | | |
| | Sinjirli: citadel Upper Palace | | |
| | Tell Tayanat: palace, temple | | |
| Sargon II (721–705) | Khorsabad: ziggurat, Temple of Nabu, Palace of Sargon II | *Late period* | |
| | | XXV Dynasty (713–665) | |
| c. 709–675 | Persia: reign of Achaemenes, first king of dynasty | Ethiopian kings | Napata: funerary complexes |
| | end of Neo-Hittite kingdoms | | Karnak: pylon I of temple |
| Esarhaddon (from c. 680) | conquest of Egypt | 664 | Assyrian invasion; sack of Thebes |
| | pressure at frontiers by Cimmerians and Scythians | XXVI Dynasty (664–525) | |
| 625–585 | Cyaxares defeats Scythians and rules over Medes | Saitic kingdom in Delta | Sais: royal tombs in temple (not preserved) |
| | | | beginning of construction of Ibis Temple, oasis of El Kharga |
| 612 | Medes and Babylonians storm Nineveh | | |
| *Neo-Babylonian period (c. 615–539)* | | | |
| 612 | beginning of Babylonian period | | |
| | Babylon: Processional Way, Ishtar Gate, Etemenanki (giant ziggurat), Esagila (low temple), Temple of Marduk, Palace of Nebuchadnezzar | | |
| *Achaemenian art* | | | |
| 559–529 | Persia: reign of Cyrus II the Great | | |
| 539 | Cyrus II conquers Babylonia. Mesopotamia becomes province of Persian Empire | | |
| | Pasargadae: Tomb of Cyrus, Palace of Cyrus the Great, reception and residential palaces | | |
| | Masjid-i-Suleiman: terracing | | |

## NEAR EAST

| | |
|---|---|
| 528–522 B.C. | Cambyses II, king of Persia, conquers Egypt |
| c. 518–460 B.C. | Persepolis: palace<br>Naksh-i-Rustam: royal tombs |
| 331 B.C. | Battle of Arbela: fall of Persian Empire |

## EGYPT

| | |
|---|---|
| XXVII Dynasty (525–404 B.C.) | Egypt becomes satrapy of Persian Empire |
| 521–486 B.C. | Darius I finishes construction of Ibis Temple, El Kharga |
| XXVIII-XXIX Dynasty (404–380 B.C.) | |
| XXX Dynasty (380–342 B.C.) | large works throughout the country, at Thebes, Memphis, and in the Delta; Dendera, Edfu, and Philae; hypostyle vestibule of Ibis Temple |
| XXXI Dynasty (342–332 B.C.) | second Persian domination |
| 332 B.C. | Alexander the Great annexes Egypt to his empire. Founding of Alexandria<br>reconstruction of sanctuary opposite Luxor<br>Karnak: Philip Arrhidaeus renovates sanctuary |
| *Ptolemaic Dynasty (305–30 B.C.)* | |
| Ptolemy II Philadelphus (283–247 B.C.) | Philae: Temple of Isis |
| Ptolemy III (246–231 B.C.) | Hermopolis: sanctuary dedicated to Ptolemy III |
| 237 B.C. | Edfu: construction of Temple of Horus (completed 57 B.C.) |
| Ptolemy VI Philometor (180–145 B.C.) | beginning of construction of temple at Kom Ombo |
| Ptolemy VIII Euergetes II (145–116 B.C.) | Kom Ombo: Birth House<br>Dendera: beginning of construction of temple |
| Ptolemy XII Neos Dionysus (85–81 B.C.) | Kom Ombo: beginning of construction of pronaos of temple |
| 30 B.C. | Egypt becomes province of Roman Empire |
| Augustus (30 B.C.–14 A.D.) | Kalabsha: temple<br>Dendera: vestibule of temple<br>Kom Ombo: temple completed |
| Claudius (41–54 A.D.) | Esneh: beginning of construction of temple vestibule |

| ATHENS AND ATTICA | CONTINENTAL GREECE | ISLANDS AND COLONIES |
|---|---|---|
| | | Beginning of II millennium first Middle Minoan palaces (Mallia, Phaistos) |
| | | 1600–1400 large Late Minoan palaces |
| | | 1600 Knossos: palace |
| c. 1400 Athens: fortifications | c. 1400 Mycenae: palaces and fortifications Tiryns: palaces and fortifications Pylos: palaces and tombs Thebes: palace | XI–IX century Smyrna Eretria: Temple of Apollo Daphnephoros |
| | | Beginning of VIII century Samos: first Hekatompedon |
| | IX–VIII century Thermon: Temple B (Apollo) | 757 founding of Naxos |
| | | 750 founding of Megara Hyblaea (Sicily) |
| | | 733 founding of Syracuse (Sicily) |
| | | VII century Megara Hyblaea: Agora |
| | | c. 660 Samos: second Hekatompedon |
| | | 650 founding of Selinus (Sicily) |
| 630 Athens: Draconian Laws | 620–610 Thermon: Temple C (Apollo) | c. 630 Prinias (Crete): Temple A Dreros (Crete): temple Delos: Temple of Hera |
| | c. 600 Olympia: Temple of Hera Delphi: Temple of Athena | c. 600 founding of Marseilles (France) |
| 594 Athens: reforms of Solon | | 600–590 Corfu: Temple of Artemis |

| ATHENS AND ATTICA | CONTINENTAL GREECE | ISLANDS AND COLONIES |
|---|---|---|
| | | VI century<br>Selinus (Sicily): Acropolis |
| | | 580<br>founding of Acragas (Sicily) |
| 570<br>Athens: First Temple of Athena, first buildings of Agora | c. 570<br>Delphi: old tholos, Treasury of Sicyon<br>570<br>Delphi: Temple of Apollo | c. 570–560<br>Syracuse (Sicily): Temple of Apollo<br>CLEOMENES and EPIDUS<br>Samos: Temple of Hera<br>RHOIKOS and THEODOROS |
| 561–560<br>beginning of tyranny of Pisistratus | | c. 550<br>Selinus: Temples C and D<br>Ephesus (Ionia): Temple of Artemis<br>THEODOROS, CHERSIPHRON, METAGENES<br>Syracuse: Temple of Zeus |
| | 550–540<br>Olympia: Treasury of Gela<br>Argos: Sanctuary of Hera (central and western structure) | 550–540<br>Paestum (S. Italy): Treasury, Sanctuary of Hera at Sele River<br>Selinus: Megaron of Demeter |
| | 550–525<br>Delphi: Ionian treasuries | |
| | 540<br>Corinth: Temple of Apollo, Temple of Poseidon<br>Argos: porticoes, Sanctuary of Hera | c. 540<br>defeat of the Phocaeans at Alalia |
| 530<br>Athens: Peristyle temple of Athena | | c. 540–523<br>Samos: tyranny of Polycrates |
| 528<br>death of Pisistratus | | c. 530–520<br>Paestum: Temple of Hera I (Basilica)<br>Selinus: Temple F<br>Didyma (Ionia): First Temple<br>Marseilles (France): Temple of Artemis |
| 520<br>Athens: beginning of Temple of Olympian Zeus<br>Eleusis: Telesterion of the Pisistratids | | c. 525<br>Syracuse: First Temple of Athena |
| 508–507<br>Athens: reforms of Cleisthenes | | c. 520 and later<br>Selinus: Temple G (Apollo) |
| 506<br>Athenians defeat Boeotians and Chalcidians | | end of VI century<br>Metapontum (S. Italy): "Palatine Tables" |

## ATHENS AND ATTICA

V century
Athens: Agora

c. 500
Sunium: Old Temple of Poseidon

489
Athens: archonship of Aristides

480
Persian War, destruction of Athens

460–451
Athens: first programs for Acropolis
CALLICRATES

460–450
Eleusis: Telesterion (begun in VI century, alterations and additions until IV century)

c. 450
Athens: Temple of Demeter and Kore on bank of Ilissos River

449
Peace of Callias

447–430
Athens: Parthenon
ICTINUS

446
Pericles concludes Thirty Year Peace with Sparta

c. 440
Athens: Temple of Hephaestus (Theseum)

440–430
Sunium: Temple of Poseidon
Rhamnus: Temple of Nemesis

437–431
Athens: Propylaea
MNESICLES

## CONTINENTAL GREECE

c. 490
Delphi: Treasury of Athenians

470–460
Olympia: Temple of Zeus
LIBON
Delphi: Portico of Athenians

440
Delos: Temple of Apollo

## ISLANDS AND COLONIES

500
Paestum (S. Italy): Temple of Athena

c. 500–450
Aegina: Temple of Aphaia
Syracuse (Sicily): Second Temple of Athena
Acragas (Sicily): Temple of Herakles

from c. 485
Syracuse: tyranny of Gelon

c. 480
Acragas: beginning of Temple of Zeus

470
Selinus (Sicily): Temple E
Delos: Treasuries
Miletus (Ionia): Temple of Athena

c. 450
Paestum (S. Italy): Temple of Hera II (Poseidon)
Acragas: Temple of Juno Lacinia

| ATHENS AND ATTICA | CONTINENTAL GREECE | ISLANDS AND COLONIES |
|---|---|---|
| 431<br>beginning of Peloponnesian War | | |
| 430–428<br>plague in Athens.<br>death of Pericles<br>Athens: Stoa of Zeus in Agora | | 430<br>Delos: Prytaneum<br>Acragas (Sicily): Temple of Concord |
| 421<br>Peace of Nicias | | c. 400<br>Segesta (Sicily): Doric temple |
| 420–last years of century<br>Athens: Erechtheion | 420–410<br>Bassae: Temple of Apollo<br>ICTINUS?<br>Argos: New temple of Hera | 400–390<br>Xanthos (Ionia): Monument of Nereids<br>Selinus (Sicily): new design of acropolis<br>Acragas: Temple of Asclepius |
| 420<br>Athens: Temple of Athena Nike<br>Brauron: Stoa | | IV century<br>Lindos (Rhodes): Temple of Athena |
| 415–413<br>Sicilian expeditions | | |
| 411<br>Athens: oligarchic revolution | | |
| 404–403<br>Athens: Tyranny of the Thirty | | |
| | 400<br>Olynthus: town development | |
| 399<br>trial and death of Socrates | | |
| | 390–380<br>Epidaurus: Temple of Asclepius | |
| 378–377<br>Athenian League | | |
| | 369–380<br>founding of Messena and Megalopolis | 367<br>Syracuse (Sicily): death of Dionysius |
| | 362<br>Battle of Mantinea | |
| | 360<br>Tegea: Temple of Athena Alea<br>SCOPAS | 359<br>Philip II becomes king of Macedon |

| ATHENS AND ATTICA | CONTINENTAL GREECE | ISLANDS AND COLONIES |
|---|---|---|
| 350<br>Athens: Temple of Asclepius | | 350<br>Halicarnassus (Ionia): Mausoleum<br>PYTHIUS and SATYRUS<br>founding of new Priene (Ionia) |
| 338<br>Battle of Chaeronaea | | 334<br>Priene: Temple of Athena |
| | 337<br>Panhellenic League of Corinth | 333<br>Battle of Issus |
| 330<br>Athens: Theater of Dionysus | c. 330<br>Epidaurus: Tholos, theater<br>Olympia: Philippeion<br>Pella: town development<br>Stratos: Temple of Zeus | 331<br>Battle of Arbela<br>founding of Alexandria (Egypt)<br>DEINOKRATES |
| 323<br>death of Alexander | | 330<br>Ephesus (Ionia): work begun on new Temple of Artemis<br>Sardis (Lydia): beginning of Temple of Artemis Cybele |
| | | c. 325–beginning of Hellenistic era<br>Didyma (Ionia): Temple of Apollo<br>PAEONIUS and DAPHNIS |
| | | 323–285<br>Alexandria: Library |
| | | end of IV century<br>Priene: Bouleuterion<br>Thasos: Bastion gate<br>Claro: Temple of Apollo |
| | | beginning of III century<br>Lindos (Rhodes): Sanctuary of Athena<br>Olbia (S. Russia): Temple of Zeus Olbios<br>Alexandria: Pharos of port<br>SOSTRATOS<br>Leucas: tomb |
| | III century<br>Megalopolis: Portico of Philip V | III century, 1st half<br>Kos: Sanctuary of Asclepius, initial plan<br>Theaters of Priene, Delos, Ephesus, Segesta, Tyndaris<br>Priene: Ekklesiasterion<br>Delos: Portico of Antigonus Gonatas, Portico of Philip V<br>Delos: "Portico of Bulls" in Sanctuary of Apollo |

393

| ATHENS AND ATTICA | CONTINENTAL GREECE | ISLANDS AND COLONIES |
|---|---|---|
| | | c. 285–250<br>Samothrace: propylon of sanctuary |
| | | c. 270<br>Samothrace: temple |
| | | 260–250<br>Miletus (Ionia): fountain dedicated to Queen Laodicaea |
| | 240–230<br>Delphi: Stoa of Attalus I | 250–220<br>Syracuse (Sicily): Altar of Gelon II |
| | c. 237<br>Corinth: Upper Pirene | c. 210<br>Delos: Hypostyle Hall |
| | end of III century<br>Olympia: Palaestra | end of III century–beginning of II century<br>Pergamum (Mysia): Acropolis |
| | | III–II century<br>Paestum (S. Italy): Temple of Peace<br>Sardis (Lydia): Temple of Artemis |
| | | end of III century–II century<br>Magnesia (Ionia): Temple of Artemis Leucophryene<br>HERMOGENES<br>Teos (Ionia): Temple of Dionysus<br>HERMOGENES<br>Mesa (Lesbos): Temple of Aphrodite<br>Pergamum: Stoa of Athena |
| | | II century<br>Alabanda (Ionia): Temple of Apollo<br>MENESTHES<br>Pergamum: small temple of upper market<br>Theaters of Delphi, Pergamum, and Teos |
| | | 200–150<br>Kos: Doric temple in Sanctuary of Asclepius |
| 196<br>freedom of Greeks proclaimed during Isthmian Games | | 197–160<br>Pergamum: Altar of Zeus |
| c. 180 and later<br>Athens: Stoas of Eumenes II and Attalus II | | II century, 1st half<br>Miletus: Bouleuterion<br>Antioch (Syria): Bouleuterion |

| ATHENS AND ATTICA | CONTINENTAL GREECE | ISLANDS AND COLONIES |
|---|---|---|
| c. 170<br>Athens: Temple of Olympian Zeus (continued under Augustus and completed under Hadrian)<br>COSSUTIUS | | |
| | 146<br>Romans take Corinth, submission of Greece to the Romans | |
| | | c. 130<br>Delos: Agora "of the Italians" |
| | | c. 110<br>Delos: House of Poseidoniastes of Berytos |
| | | II century<br>Pergamum: Gymnasium |
| | | II–I century<br>Lagina (Ionia): Temple of Hecate |
| 50<br>Eleusis: small propylaea of Appius Claudius | | 50–40<br>Alexandria (Egypt): Caesareum<br>Antioch (Syria): Caesareum |
| | 46<br>Aegae: Temple of Apollo Chresterios | |
| 14<br>Athens: Odeon of Agrippa in the Agora | | |

# SELECTED BIBLIOGRAPHY

## ANCIENT NEAR EAST

### GENERAL WORKS

FRANKFORT, H. *Art and Architecture of the Ancient Orient.* London, 1954.

LLOYD, S. *Art of the Ancient Near East.* London, 1961.

PIGGOTT, E. S., ed. *The Dawn of Civilization.* London, 1961.

PORTOGHESI, P., ed. *Dizionario enciclopedico di architettura e urbanistica.* Rome, 1968–69.

### PREHISTORY

GARSTANG, J. *Prehistoric Mersin.* Oxford, 1953.

LLOYD, S., and SAFAR, F. "Tell Hassuna," in *Journal of Near Eastern Studies,* vol. IV, no. 4, 1945.

MELLAART, J. *Catal Höyük: A Neolithic Town in Anatolia.* London, 1967.

———. *Earliest Civilizations of the Near East.* London, 1965.

THESIGER, W. *The Marsh Arabs.* London, 1964.

### MESOPOTAMIA

General works:

BEEK, M. A. *Atlas of Mesopotamia.* London, 1962.

STROMMENGER, E., and HIRMER, M. *5000 Years of the Art of Mesopotamia.* New York, 1964.

Sumerians and Akkadians:

DELOUGAZ, P. *The Oval Temple at Khafaje.* Chicago, 1940.

———, and LLOYD, S. *Pre-Sargonid Temples in the Diyala Region.* Chicago, 1942

———, HILL, H. D., and LLOYD, S. *Private Houses and Graves in the Diyala Region.* Chicago, 1967.

FRANKFORT, H., LLOYD, S., and JACOBSEN, T. H. *The Gimil-Sin Temple and the Palace of the Rulers at Tell Asmar.* Chicago, 1940.

LLOYD S., and SAFAR, F. "Tell 'Uqair," in *Journal of Near Eastern Studies,* vol. II, no. 2, 1943.

PARROT, A. *Sumer.* London, 1960.

WOOLLEY, C. L. *The Development of Sumerian Art.* London, 1935.

———. *Ur Excavations,* vol. V: *The Ziggurat and Its Surroundings.* London, 1939.

Second millennium:

ANDRAE, W. *Das Wiedererstandene Assur.* Leipzig, 1938.

BAQIR, T. "Dur Kurigalzu," in *Iraq,* supplement 1944–45, and *Iraq,* vol. VIII, 1946.

PARROT, A. *Mission Archéologique de Mari,* vol. II: *Le Palais.* Paris, 1958.

Assyrian and Neo-Babylonian period:

JACOBSEN, T., and LLOYD, S. *Sennacherib's Aqueduct at Jerwan.* Chicago, 1935.

LOUD, G. *Khorsabad,* vol. II. Chicago, 1938.

MACQUEEN, J. G. *Babylon.* London, 1964.

MALLOWAN, M. E. L. *Nimrud and Its Remains.* London, 1966.

PARROT, A. *Nineveh and Babylon.* London, 1961.

———. *Assur.* Paris, 1961.

### IRAN AND THE LEVANT

GODARD, A. *The Art of Iran.* London, 1962.

HARDEN, D. *The Phoenicians.* London, 1962.

POPE, A. UPHAM. *Survey of Persian Art.* London, New York, 1938.

SCHMIDT, E. *Persepolis,* vol. I. Chicago, 1953.

YADIN, Y. *The Art of Warfare in Biblical Lands.* London, 1963.

### ANATOLIA

General works:

AKURGAL, E. *The Art of the Hittites.* New York, 1962.

LLOYD, S. *Early Highland Peoples of Anatolia.* London, 1967.

NAUMANN, R. *Architectur Kleinasiens.* Tübingen, 1955.

Bronze and Iron Ages:

AKURGAL, E. *Phrygische Kunst.* Ankara, 1955.

BLEGEN, C. W. *Troy and the Trojans.* London, 1963.

LLOYD, S., and MELLAART, J. *Beycesultan,* 3 vols. London, 1962–72.

ÖZGÜÇ, T. *Altintepe.* Ankara, 1966.

PIETROVSKI, B. B. *The Kingdom of Van and Its Art.* London, 1967.

PIGGOTT, E. S. *Vanished Civilizations.* London, 1963.

This bibliography is limited to modern works containing plans, reconstructions, and photographs, with brief descriptions and comments. The primary sources can be found in numerous archaeological reports listed in the bibliographical appendixes of the general works indicated above.

## EGYPT

Landscape and monuments of Egypt and Nubia:

BAEDEKER, K. *Ägypten und der Sudan, Handbuch für Reisende.* Leipzig, 1928.

*Egypte, Encyclopédie de voyage.* Nagel Editions. Geneva, Paris, Munich, 1969.

KEES, H. *Das Alte Ägypten, eine kleine Landeskunde.* Berlin, 1955.

PORTER, B., and MOSS, R. L. B. *Topographical Bibliography of Ancient Egyptian Hieroglyphic Texts, Reliefs, and Paintings,* vols. I–VII. Oxford, 1927–51.

SCHLOTT, A. *Die Ausmasse Ägyptens nach altägyptischen Texten.* Darmstadt, 1969.

History of ancient Egypt:

DERCHAIN, P. "Le Rôle du roi d'Egypte dans le maintien de l'ordre cosmique," in *Le Pouvoir et le Sacré: Annales du Centre d'Etudes des Religions,* I, Brussels, 1962, pp. 61–73.

FRANKFORT, H. *Kingship and the Gods: A Study of Ancient Near Eastern Religion as the Integration of Society and Nature.* Chicago, 1958.

JACOBSOHN, J. H. "Die dogmatische Stellung des Königs in der Theologie der Alten Ägypter," in *Ägyptologischen Forschungen,* vol. 8, Glückstadt, 1939.

MORET, A. *Du caractère religieux de la royauté pharaonique.* Paris, 1902.

POSENER, G. *De la divinité des pharaons.* Paris, 1960.

WILDUNG, D. "Die Rolle ägyptischer Könige im Bewusstsein ihrer Nachwelt, I," in *Münchner Ägyptologische Studien,* 17, Berlin 1969.

Egyptian culture of the archaic period:

BADAWY, A. "La Première architecture en Egypte," in *Annales du Service des Antiquités d'Egypte,* no. 51, Cairo, 1951, pp. 1–28.

COTTEVIEILLE-GIRAUDET, R. "Rapport sur les fouilles de Médamond (1931): Les Monuments du Moyen Empire," in *Bulletin de l'Institut Français d'Archéologie Orientale,* IX, Cairo, 1933.

JÉQUIER, G. "Les Temples primitifs et la persistance des types archaïques dans l'architecture religieuse," in *Bulletin de l'Institut Français d'Archéologie Orientale,* VI, Cairo, 1908, pp. 25–41.

REYMOND, E. A. E. *The Mythical Origin of the Egyptian Temple.* Manchester, 1969.


History of Egyptian art in general:

DONADONI, S. *Arte egizia.* Turin 1955.

HAMANN, R. *Ägyptische Kunst, Wesen und Geschichte.* Berlin, 1944.

LANGE, K., and HIRMER, M. *Ägypten; Architektur, Plastik, und Malerei in drei Jahrtausenden.* Introduction by E. Otto and C. Desroches-Noblecourt. Munich, 1957.

MÜLLER, H. W. *Ägyptische Kunst: Monumente alter Kulturen.* Frankfurt, 1970.

SMITH, W. S. *The Art and Architecture of Ancient Egypt.* Baltimore, 1958.

STEINDORFF, G. *Die Kunst der Ägypter.* Leipzig, 1928.

WOLF, W. *Die Kunst Ägyptens, Gestalt und Geschichte.* Stuttgart, 1957.

——. *Il mondo degli Egizi.* Rome, 1958.

YOYOTTE, J. "Egypte ancienne," in *Encyclopédie de la Pléiade.*


Egyptian architecture:

BADAWY, A. *A History of Egyptian Architecture,* vols. I–III. Cairo, 1954; Berkeley and Los Angeles. 1966 and 1968.

——. *Architecture in Ancient Egypt and the Near East.* London, 1966.

BORCHARDT, L. "Zur Geschichte des Luqsortempels," in *Zeitschrift für ägyptische Sprache und Altertumskunde,* XXXIV, Berlin – Leipzig, 1896.

——. "Ägyptische Tempel mit Umgang," with drawings by Herbert Ricke, in *Beiträge zur Ägyptischen Bauforschung und Altertumskunde,* vol. 2, Cairo, 1938.

CAPART, J. *L'Art égyptien,* vol. I: *L'Architecture.* Brussels, Paris, 1922.

DAVIES N. DE GARIS. *The Mastaba of Ptahhetep and Akkethetep at Saqqarah* (Archaeological Survey of Egypt, 8/9), 2 vols. London, 1900–1901.

DE CÉNIVAL, J. L. *Egypte, Epoque pharaonique.* Freiburg, 1964.

——. *Ägypten, Das Zeitalter der Pharaonen.* Munich, 1966.

GIEDION, S. *The Beginnings of Architecture.* New York, 1963.

HAENY, G. "Basikale Anlagen," in *Beiträge zur Ägyptischen Bauforschung and Altertumskunde,* vol. 9, Wiesbaden, 1970.

HÖLSCHER, U. "Medinet Habu. Ausgrabungen des Oriental Institutes des Universität Chicago. Ein Vorbericht," in *Morgenland: Darstellung aus Geschichte und Kultur des Ostens,* 2, Leipzig, 1933.

JÉQUIER, G. *L'Architecture et la décoration dans l'ancienne Egypte,* vols. I–III. Paris, 1920-24.

LAUER, J. P. *La Pyramide à degrés: L'Architecture,* 3 vols. Cairo, 1936–39.

OTTO, E., and HIRMER, M. *Ancient Egyptian Art: the Cults of Osiris and Amon.* New York, 1967

PETRIE, W. M. FLINDERS. "The Royal Tombs of the First Dynasty," with a chapter by F. L. Griffith, in *Eighteenth Memoir of the Egypt Exploration Fund,* part I. London, 1901.

PORTOGHESI, P., ed. *Dizionario enciclopedico di architettura e urbanistica.* Rome, 1968–69.

SMITH, E. BALDWIN. *Egyptian Architecture as Cultural Expression.* New York, London, 1938.

VANDIER, J. *Manuel d'Archéologie Egyptienne,* vol. II, 1 and 2: *L'Architecture funéraire, religieuse et civile.* Paris, 1954–55.


# CRETE AND MYCENAE

BOSSERT, H. *Altkreta,* 3rd ed. Berlin, 1937.

CHARPOUTHIER, F., CHARBONNEAUX, J., JOLY, R., DEMARGNE, P. *Etudes Crétoises. Fouilles de Mallia,* vols. I and II. Paris, 1928–.

DEMARGNE, P. *Naissance de l'art grec.* Paris, 1964.

EVANS, A. J. *The Palace of Minos at Knossos,* vols. I–VII. London, 1921–36.

GRAHAM, J. W. *The Palaces of Crete.* Princeton, 1962.

MARINATOS, S., and HIRMER, M. *Crete and Mycenae.* New York, 1960.

MATZ, F. *Creta e la Grecia preistorica.* Milan, 1963.

MYLONAS, G. E. *Ancient Mycenae.* Princeton, 1957.

PERNIER, L., and BANTI, L. *Guida degli scavi italiani in Creta.* Rome, 1967.

PLATON, N. *La Crète et la Grèce primitive.* Geneva, 1968.

TAYLOUR, W. *I Micenei.* Milan, 1966.

WACE, A. J. B. *Mycenae.* Princeton, 1949.


# GREECE

General works:

BERVÉ, H., GRUBEN, G., and HIRMER, M. *Greek Temples, Theatres, and Shrines,* New York, 1962.

CHARBONNEAUX, J., MARTIN, R., and VILLARD, F. *Grèce archaïque.* Paris, 1968.

——. *Grèce classique.* Paris, 1969.

CHOISY, A. *Histoire de l'architecture,* 2 vols. Paris, 1929.

DINSMOOR, W. B. *The Architecture of Ancient Greece,* 3rd ed. London, 1950.

ESPONY, H. *Fragments d'architecture d'après les relevées et restaurations des anciens pensionnaires de l'Académie de France à Rome,* 2 vols. Paris, 1905.

GRUBEN, G. *Die Tempel der Griechen.* Munich, 1966.

LAWRENCE, A. W. *Greek Architecture.* Baltimore, 1957.

MARTIENSSEN, R. D. *The Idea of Space in Greek Architecture,* 2nd ed. Johannesburg, 1964.

MARTIN, R. *Monde grec,* in series *Architecture Universelle.* Freiburg, 1966.

——. *Manuel d'architecture grecque,* I: *Materiaux et techniques.* Paris, 1965.

ORLANDOS, A. *Les Matériaux de construction et la technique architecturale des Anciens Grecs.* Paris, 1966.

PORTOGHESI, P., ed. *Dizionario enciclopedico di architettura e urbanistica.* Rome, 1968–69.

WEICKERT, C. *Typen der archaischen Architektur in Griechenland und Kleinasien.* Augsburg, 1929.


City planning:

CASTAGNOLI, F. *Ippodamo di Mileto e l'urbanistica a pianta ortogonale.* Rome, 1956.

DI VITA, A. "La stoà nel temenos del tempio C e lo sviluppo programmato di Selinunte," in *Palladio,* 1967, pp. 1–60.

GIULIANO, A. *Urbanistica delle città greche.* Milan, 1966.

MARTIN, R. *L'Urbanisme dans la Grèce antique.* Paris, 1956.

WYCHERLEY, R. E. *How the Greeks Built Cities,* 2nd ed. London, 1962.

Special studies:

ADRIANI, A., BONACASA, N., et al. *Himera I.* Rome, 1970.

AKERSTRÖM, A. *Die Architektonischen Terrakotten Kleinasien.* Lund, 1966.

ANTI, C. *Teatri greci arcaici.* Padua, 1967.

AUBERSON, P. *Eretria, I: Temple d'Apollon Daph-néphoros.* Bern, 1968.

BERGVIST, B. *The Archaic Greek Temenos.* Lund, 1967.

BOERSMA, J. S. *Athenian Building Policy from 561/560 to 405/404 B.C.* Groningen, 1970.

BOURAS, C. *The Restoration of the Stoa of Brauron: Architectural Problems.* Athens, 1967 (in Greek).

BÜSING, H. *Die Griechische Halbsaüle.* Wiesbaden, 1970.

BUTLER, H. C. *Sardis II, Architecture, I: The Temple of Artemis.* Leyden, 1925.

DEMARGNE, P., and COUPEL, P. *Fouilles de Xanthos, III: Le Monument des Néréides, l'Architecture.* Paris, 1969.

GABRICI, E. "Per la storia dell'architettura dorica in Sicilia," in *Estratto dai Monumenti Antichi, R. Acc. dei Lincei,* Rome, 1935 and 1936.

GERKAN, A. VON, *Der Altar des Artemistempels in Magnesia am Mäander.* Berlin, 1929.

——. MÜLLER-WIENER, M. *Das Theater von Epidauros.* Stuttgart, 1961.

GINOUVÈS, R. *Balaneutikè: Recherches sur le bain dans l'antiquité grecque.* Paris, 1962.

HILL, B. H., and KAUFMANN, C. H. *The Temple of Zeus at Nemea.* Princeton, 1966.

KLEINER, G. *Die Ruinen von Milet.* Berlin, 1968.

KOLDEWEY, R., and PUCHSTEIN, O. *Die griechische Tempel in Unteritalien und Sizilien.* Berlin, 1899.

LEHMANN, K. *Samothrace, 4–1: The Hall of Votive Gifts.* New York, 1962; *4–2: The Altar Court.* New York, 1964. *4–3: The Hieron.* New York, 1969.

MAIER, F. G. *Griechische Mauerbauinschriften.* Heidelberg, 1959.

MANSEL, A. M. *Die Ruinen von Side.* Berlin, 1963.

MANSUELLI, G. A. *Architettura e città.* Bologna, 1970.

MILTNER, F. *Ephesos: Stadt der Artemis und des Johannes.* Vienna, 1958.

NOVICKA, M. *La Maison privée dans l'Egypte Ptolemaïque.* Warsaw, 1969.

RIDER, B. C. *Ancient Greek Houses,* rev. ed. Chicago, 1964.

ROUX, G. *L'Architecture de l'Argolide au IVe et IIIe siècles avant J. C.* Paris, 1961.

——. *Delphi.* Munich, 1972.

SCHEDE, M. *Die Ruinen von Priene,* 2nd ed. Berlin, 1964.

SHOE, L. T. *Profiles of Greek Mouldings,* 2 vols. Cambridge, Mass., 1936.

——. *Profiles of Western Greek Mouldings.* Rome, 1952.

VALLET, G., and VILLARD, F. *Megara Hyblaea, IV: Le Temple du IVe siècle.* Paris, 1966.

VALLOIS, R. *L'Architecture héllenique et héllenistique à Délos,* 2 vols. Paris, 1964 and 1966.

WESENBERG, B. *Kapitelle und Basen.* Dusseldorf, 1971.

WESTHOLM, A. "Labranda, Swedish Excavations and Researches, I, 2: The Architecture of the Hieron," in *Acta instituti Atheniensis regni Sueciae,* vol. no. 2, Lund, 1963.

WINTER, F. *Greek Fortifications.* London, 1971.

YAVIS, C. G. *Greek Altars: Origins and Typology.* St. Louis, Mo., 1949.

ZANCANI-MONTUORO, P., and ZANOTTI-BLANCO, U. *Heraion alla foce del Sele.* Rome, 1951.

For individual buildings and their characteristics consult the collections and periodical publications devoted to particular localities: Athens, Corinth, Delos, Delphi, Labranda, Miletus, Olympia, Pergamum, Sardis, Thasos.

# LIST OF PLATES

|  | Plate |
|---|---|
| Jericho. Projected plan of Neolithic shrine (from Piggott, 1961). | 1 |
| Catal Huyuk. Portion of town plan, Level VI B (from Mellaart, 1967). | 2 |
| Catal Huyuk. Perspective reconstruction of one section of town, Level VI B (from Mellaart, 1967). | 3 |
| Catal Huyuk. Reconstruction of interior of typical shrine-chamber (from Mellaart, 1967). | 4 |
| Catal Huyuk. Reconstruction of interior of typical house (from Mellaart, 1967). | 5 |
| Jericho. Remains of Neolithic tower. | 6 |
| Khirokitia (Cyprus). Reconstruction of Neolithic village (from Piggott, 1961). | 7 |
| Hacilar. Isometric diagram of Fortress II A (from Mellaart, 1965). | 8 |
| Hacilar. Isometric diagram of Neolithic house (from Mellaart, 1965). | 9 |
| Mersin. Isometric diagram of military fortress (from Garstang, 1953). | 10 |
| Hassuna. Isometric reconstruction of farmhouse (from Lloyd, 1961). | 11 |
| Southern Mesopotamia. Modern Arabian reed-built structure. | 12 |
| Proto-Sumerian alabaster trough, with traditional representation of Sumerian temple. London, British Museum. | 13 |
| Eridu. Plan of temple, Level VII (from Strommenger, 1963). | 14 |
| Tepe Gawra. Perspective reconstruction of group of temples (from Lloyd, 1961). | 15 |
| Uruk. "White Temple." | 16 |
| Uruk. Perspective reconstruction of "White Temple" (from Piggott, 1961). | 17 |
| Uruk. Integrated plan of ziggurat and "White Temple" (from Strommenger, 1963). | 18 |
| Uruk. Temple plans, Level IV A, Eanna precinct (from Strommenger, 1963). | 19 |
| Uruk. Temple plans, Levels V–VI, Eanna precinct (from Strommenger, 1963). | 20 |
| Tell Brak. Plan of "Eye Temple" (from Piggott, 1961). | 21 |
| Uruk. Cone mosaic courtyard, Eanna precinct. | 22 |
| Eridu. Perspective reconstruction of Temple I (from Lloyd, 1961). | 23 |
| Khafaje. Perspective reconstruction of Oval Temple (from Delougaz, 1940). | 24 |
| Al 'Uqair. Model of Protoliterate temple. Baghdad, Iraq Museum. | 25 |
| Al 'Ubaid. Frieze of Milkers, from facade of Minkhursag Temple. Baghdad, Iraq Museum. | 26, 27, 28 |
| Khafaje. Plans of Sin temples (from Strommenger, 1963). | 29 |
| Tell Agrab. Plan of Shara Temple (from Delougaz and Lloyd, 1942). | 30 |
| Tell Asmar. Plan of Akkadian palace and contemporary buildings (from Delougaz, Hill, and Lloyd, 1967). | 31 |
| Kish. Plan of "Palace A" (from Strommenger, 1963). | 32 |
| Tell Brak. Plan of Palace of Naramsin (from Strommenger, 1963). | 33 |
| Ur. Plan of city at the time of Abraham (from Woolley, 1939). | 34 |
| Ur. Ziggurat, Third Dynasty; northeast facade with flight of steps, as presently restored. | 35 |
| Ur. Royal Mausoleum, Third Dynasty. | 36 |
| Tell Asmar. Plan and reconstruction of Temple of Gimilsin and Palace of the Governors (from Frankfort and Lloyd, 1940). | 37 |
| ...hali. Perspective reconstruction of Temple of Ishtar-Kititum (from ...rold D. Hill). | 38 |
| ...ari. Plan of Palace of Zimrilim (from Portoghesi, 1968–69). | 39 |
| ...ari. Mural paintings from Palace of Zimrilim. Paris, Louvre. | 40 |
| ...ur Kurigalzu (Aqar Quf). Ziggurat. | 41 |

|  | Plate |
|---|---|
| Uruk. Plan of Temple of Kara-indash (from Strommenger, 1963). | 42 |
| Uruk. Molded brick ornament from facade of Temple of Kara-indash. Berlin, Vorderasiatisches Museum. | 43 |
| Assur. Perspective reconstruction of city, north sector (from Lloyd, 1961). | 44 |
| Assur. Plan of city (from Strommenger, 1963). | 45 |
| Assur. Plans (from Frankfort, 1954; and Strommenger, 1963). | 46 |
| Assur. Reconstruction of mural paintings, Palace of Kar Tukulti-Ninurta I. | 47 |
| Nuzi. Fragment of mural paintings, Palace of Hurrian. | 48 |
| Troy. Plans of city, Levels I and II (from Anatolian Studies, 1959). | 49, 50 |
| Troy. Reconstruction of surviving walls, Level VI (from Naumann, 1955). | 51 |
| Beycesultan. Reconstructions of Bronze Age shrines (from Lloyd, 1967). | 52, 53 |
| Kultepe. Reconstruction of megaron in Bronze Age palace (from Lloyd, 1967). | 54 |
| Bogazkoy. Plan of citadel of Buyukkale (from Akurgal, 1962). | 55 |
| Bogazkoy. Reconstruction and section of walls and gate (from Akurgal, 1962). | 56 |
| Bogazkoy. Lion Gate. | 57 |
| Bogazkoy. Lion Gate (detail). | 58 |
| Alaca Huyuk. Sphinx Gate. | 59 |
| Bogazkoy. Plan of Temple I and surrounding storerooms (from Akurgal, 1962). | 60 |
| Bogazkoy. Relief of war god from King's Gate. Ankara, Museum. | 61 |
| Bogazkoy. Plan of rock shrine at Yasilikaya (from Akurgal, 1962). | 62 |
| Kultepe. Reconstruction of Assyrian merchants' quarter (from Piggott, 1961). | 63 |
| Kultepe. Examples of wall construction (from Naumann, 1955). | 64 |
| Tell Atchana. Plan of Palace of Yarimlin (from Frankfort, 1954). | 65 |
| Tell Atchana. Plan of Palace of Niqmepa (from Frankfort, 1954). | 66 |
| Beycesultan. Perspective reconstruction of Bronze Age palace (from Lloyd and Mellaart, 1965). | 67 |
| Nimrud. Plan of palace platform (from Mallowan, 1966). | 68 |
| Khorsabad. Plan of city (from Strommenger, 1963). | 69 |
| Nineveh. Plan of site (from Strommenger, 1963). | 70 |
| Khorsabad. Plan of Royal Palace of Sargon II, including Temple complex (right); plan of temples in Royal Palace (left) (from Strommenger, 1963). | 71 |
| Khorsabad. Perspective reconstruction of citadel with Palace of Sargon II (from Strommenger, 1963). | 72 |
| Nimrud. Plan of Fort Shalmaneser (from Mallowan, 1966). | 73 |
| Khorsabad. Perspective reconstruction of city, south from Ziggurat (from Strommenger, 1963). | 74 |
| Khorsabad. Portal A of citadel, with guardian human-headed winged bulls. | 75 |
| Khorsabad. Guardian human-headed winged bull (detail), from entrance to throne room, Palace of Sargon II. Paris, Louvre. | 76 |
| Nimrud. Relief from palace, showing fugitives swimming with inflated skins. London, British Museum. | 77 |
| Nineveh. Relief from palace, showing the sack of the city of Hamanu. London, British Museum. | 78 |
| Khorsabad. Reconstruction of temple facade, Portal Z (from Parrot, 1961). | 79 |
| Khorsabad. Reconstruction of mural paintings, Palace K. | 80 |
| Til Barsip. Mural painting from Assyrian palace. Paris, Louvre. | 81 |
| Balawat. Bronze Gates (details). London, British Museum. | 82, 83 |
| Balawat. Drawings of fortifications, in Bronze Gates (from Naumann, 1955). | 84 |

| | Plate |
|---|---|
| *Nineveh. Relief from Palace of Sennacherib, showing Sennacherib at the capitulation of Lakish. London, British Museum.* | 85 |
| *Balawat. Bronze Gates (detail): Assyrian warriors; prisoners brought from Sugunia. London, British Museum.* | 86 |
| *Balawat. Bronze Gates (detail): Assyrian warriors; massacre of prisoners. London, British Museum.* | 87 |
| *Balawat. Bronze Gates (detail): Assyrian warriors; procession of women prisoners and animals. London, British Museum* | 88 |
| *Gordion. Reconstruction of interior of a megaron (from Lloyd, 1967).* | 89 |
| *Pazarli (Phrygia). Terra cotta relief, showing ibexes. Ankara, Museum.* | 90 |
| *Yasilikaya (Phrygia). "Midas Monument."* | 91 |
| *Pazarli (Phrygia). Terra cotta relief, showing warriors. Ankara, Museum.* | 92 |
| *Karmir Blur. Plan of Urartian citadel (from Lloyd, 1967).* | 93 |
| *Toprakkale. Bronze model of a building. London, British Museum.* | 94 |
| *Toprakkale. Bronze model of a building. London, British Museum.* | 95 |
| *Altintepe. Plan of Urartian temple (from Özguc, 1966).* | 96 |
| *Altintepe. Reconstruction of a mural painting.* | 97 |
| *Carchemish. Wall relief with funeral cortege (details). London, British Museum.* | 98, 99 |
| *Khorsabad. Reconstruction of relief, showing the sack of the Temple of Musasir by Sargon II (from Strommenger, 1963).* | 100 |
| *Carchemish. Seated statue on base of paired lions. London, British Museum.* | 101 |
| *Sinjirli. Plan of city (from Akurgal, 1962).* | 102 |
| *Sinjirli. Plan of citadel (from Akurgal, 1962).* | 103 |
| *Carchemish. Relief on orthostat, showing King Katuwas. London, British Museum.* | 104 |
| *Sinjirli. Wall construction, showing interior "paneling" (from Naumann, 1955).* | 105 |
| *Tell Tayanat. Carved column base of palace.* | 106 |
| *Tell Tayanat. Isometric diagram of palace and temple (from Frankfort, 1954).* | 107 |
| *Carchemish. Plan of city (from Akurgal, 1962).* | 108 |
| *Tell Halaf. Plan of Kapara Palace (from Parrot, 1961).* | 109 |
| *Tell Halaf. Wall construction of Kapara Palace, showing armature of wood (from Naumann, 1955).* | 110 |
| *Tell Halaf. Reconstruction of portico, Kapara Palace. Berlin, Museum.* | 111 |
| *Hazor. Plan of Israelite fortifications (from Yadin, 1963).* | 112 |
| *Jerusalem. Reconstructed plan, elevation, and sections of Solomon's Temple (from Harden, 1962).* | 113 |
| *Babylon. Plan of city (from Strommenger, 1963).* | 114 |
| *Babylon. Perspective reconstruction of city (from Parrot, 1961).* | 115 |
| *Babylon. Perspective reconstruction of Ishtar Gate and Processional Way (from Parrot, 1961).* | 116 |
| *Babylon. Line reconstruction of Ishtar Gate (from Strommenger, 1963).* | 117 |
| *Babylon. Reconstruction of Ishtar Gate. Berlin, Museum.* | 118 |
| *Babylon. Plan of Nin-Makh Temple (from Strommenger, 1963).* | 119 |
| *Babylon. Plan of the Great Palace (from Strommenger, 1963).* | 120 |
| *Babylon. Plan of largest private house (from Macqueen, 1964).* | 121 |
| *Babylon. Glazed brick facade of throne room from Palace of Nebuchadnezzar. Berlin, Museum.* | 122 |
| *Pasargadae. Tomb of Cyrus II.* | 123 |
| *Pasargadae. Plans, elevations, and sections of Tomb of Cyrus II (from Iran, 1964).* | 124, 125 |
| *Pasargadae. Residential Palace, from southwest.* | 126 |
| *Choga Zambil. Perspective reconstruction of ziggurat (from Strommenger, 1963).* | 127 |
| *Persepolis. General view, from east: foreground, Hall of One Hundred Columns (throne hall of Xerxes); behind, audience hall of Darius I (apadana); left, tripylon.* | 128 |
| *Persepolis. North staircase of audience hall of Darius (apadana), front view of outer ramps.* | 129 |
| *Persepolis. Palace of Xerxes, from northeast.* | 130 |
| *Persepolis. Reconstruction of Hall of One Hundred Columns (throne hall of Xerxes) (from Frankfort, 1954).* | 131 |
| *Persepolis. Audience hall of Darius (apadana), ramps of north staircase.* | 132 |
| *Persepolis. Reliefs showing bearers of gifts, on north staircase to audience hall of Darius (apadana).* | 133 |
| *Persepolis. Relief showing lion attacking a bull, on staircase to tripylon.* | 134 |
| *Susa. Glazed brick reliefs: archer of royal guard. Paris, Louvre.* | 135 |
| *Persepolis. Bull capital (detail).* | 136 |
| *Persepolis. Plan of site (from Frankfort, 1954).* | 137 |
| *Hieroglyphs representing primitive forms of Egyptian temples [a, b) from Petrie, 1901; c) from Lauer, 1935; d, e) from Davies, 1900–1901].* | 138 |
| *Walled Lower Egyptian city, from Palette of Menes (Narmer). Unification period, c. 3000 B.C. Cairo, Egyptian Museum.* | 139 |
| *Abydos. Funerary stele with the "Horus name" of King Zet; below, representation of palace facade. First Dynasty, c. 2900 B.C. Paris, Louvre.* | 140 |
| *Abydos. Reconstruction of royal tumulus tomb with steles. First Dynasty (from Lauer, 1955).* | 141 |
| *Abydos. Plan of Temple of Khentiamentiu. First Dynasty (from Smith, 1958).* | 142 |
| *North Saqqara. Reconstruction of Tomb of Queen Herneith (from Lauer, 1955).* | 143 |
| *North Saqqara. "Buto tomb" with elaborate niche articulation. First Dynasty, c. 2900 B.C.* | 144 |
| *North Saqqara. "Buto tomb" of Queen Herneith, with simple niche articulation. First Dynasty, c. 2850 B.C.* | 145 |
| *Saqqara. Mortuary precinct of King Zoser, re-erected enclosure wall with niche articulation and step pyramid. Third Dynasty, c. 2650 B.C.* | 146 |
| *Saqqara. Plan of Mortuary precinct of King Zoser (from Lange-Hirmer, 1957).* | 147 |
| *Saqqara. Mortuary precinct of King Zoser, reconstruction of Upper Egyptian tent building for the government of Lower Egypt (from Lauer, 1955).* | 148 |
| *Saqqara. Mortuary precinct of King Zoser, remains of Upper Egyptian tent building for the government of Lower Egypt.* | 149 |
| *Saqqara. Mortuary precinct of King Zoser, detail of building for government of Lower Egypt: fluted masts, stretched matting in lower section, entrance with rolled-up mats. Third Dynasty, c. 2650 B.C.* | 150 |
| *Saqqara. Mortuary precinct of King Zoser, east side of building for government of Lower Egypt: papyrus stalks as half-column supports. Third Dynasty, c. 2650 B.C.* | 151 |
| *Saqqara. Mortuary precinct of King Zoser, Jubilee Court with re-erected chapel of Upper Egyptian tent-building type. Third Dynasty, c. 2650 B.C.* | 152 |
| *Saqqara. Mortuary precinct of King Zoser, chapel of Lower Egyptian type: in foreground, podium for royal baldachin (on side, steps leading to statue niche of older chapel). Third Dynasty, c. 2650 B.C.* | 153 |
| *Saqqara. Mortuary precinct of King Zoser, great court on south of step pyramid and "sacristy." Third Dynasty, c. 2650 B.C.* | 154 |
| *Saqqara. Mortuary precinct of King Zoser, "sacristy," half-open wooden door simulated in stone. Third Dynasty, c. 2650 B.C.* | 155 |

| | Plate |
|---|---|
| *Medum. Offering temple and two steles on east side of step pyramid; remains of enclosure wall and upper portion of causeway. Third-Fourth Dynasty, c. 2600 B.C.* | 156 |
| *Medum. Step pyramid, from east; in foreground, site of former valley temple and causeway. Third–Fourth Dynasty, c. 2600 B.C.* | 157 |
| *Giza. Pyramids, from east; right to left, Cheops, Chephren, Mycerinus. Fourth Dynasty, 2550–2480 B.C.* | 158 |
| *Giza. Valley temple of Chephren's pyramid complex; passage leading from antechamber to T-shaped hypostyle hall. Fourth Dynasty, c. 2520 B.C.* | 159 |
| *Giza. Plan of temples in Chephren's pyramid complex: above, veneration temple adjoining pyramid; below, valley temple (from Smith, 1958).* | 160 |
| *Giza. Valley temple of Chephren's pyramid complex; transversal area of T-shaped hypostyle hall.* | 161 |
| *Giza. Valley temple of Chephren's pyramid complex; longitudinal area of T-shaped hypostyle hall (statues of the king once stood against the walls).* | 162 |
| *Giza. Pyramid of Chephren, Great Sphinx of Chephren, and pyramid of Cheops, from southeast.* | 163 |
| *Giza. Pyramid complex of Chephren: plan of Harmakhis temple, valley temple, and Sphinx (from Ricke, 1970).* | 164 |
| *Giza. Great Sphinx of Chephren and remains of Harmakhis temple, from east (behind, left and right: pyramids of Mycerinus and Chephren).* | 165 |
| *Giza. Pyramid complex of Chephren. Great Sphinx, from northeast.* | 166 |
| *Giza. "Buto type" tomb complex of Queen Khent-kaw-s. End of Fourth Dynasty, c. 2450 B.C.* | 167 |
| *Abusir. Pyramid complex of Sahura, valley temple in foreground. Fifth Dynasty, c. 2440 B.C.* | 168 |
| *Abusir. Plan of pyramid complex of Sahura (from Smith, 1958).* | 169 |
| *Abusir. Reconstruction of sun sanctuary of Ne-user-ra. Fifth Dynasty, c. 2370 B.C. (from Smith, 1958).* | 170 |
| *Aswan, west bank of Nile. Tomb complexes, including causeways and double tomb of nomarchs Sabni and Mekhu. Sixth Dynasty, c. 2250 B.C.* | 171 |
| *West Thebes. Tomb complex of Djar, broad court and pillared vestibule in manner of older princely tombs. Eleventh Dynasty, c. 2050 B.C.* | 172 |
| *Deir el Bahari (West Thebes). View from east: left, mortuary temple of Neb-hepet-ra Mentuhotep (Eleventh Dynasty, c. 2050 B.C.); right, funerary temple of Hatshepsut (Eighteenth Dynasty, c. 1480 B.C..)* | 173 |
| *Deir el Bahari (West Thebes). View from southeast: foreground, mortuary temple of Neb-hepet-ra Mentuhotep (Eleventh Dynasty, c. 2050 B.C.); beyond, newly excavated mortuary temple of Tuthmosis III (Eighteenth Dynasty, c. 1470 B.C.); toward right, funerary temple of Hatshepsut (Eighteenth Dynasty, c. 1480 B.C.).* | 174 |
| *Deir el Bahari (West Thebes). Reconstruction of mortuary temple of Neb-hepet-ra Mentuhotep (from Arnold, unpublished).* | 175 |
| *Deir el Bahari (West Thebes). Mortuary temple of Neb-hepet-ra Mentuhotep, from northwest.* | 176 |
| *Beni Hasan. Cult chamber of rock tomb of Prince Kheti (detail). Eleventh Dynasty, c. 2000 B.C.* | 177 |
| *Beni Hasan. Cult chamber of rock tomb of Prince Kheti. Eleventh Dynasty, c. 2000 B.C.* | 178 |
| *Aswan, west bank of Nile. Rock tomb of Prince Sirenpowet II. Twelfth Dynasty, c. 1870 B.C.* | 179 |
| *Beni Hasan. Triple-aisled cult chamber, rock tomb of Prince Amenemhat; from statue niche toward entrance. Twelfth Dynasty, c. 1950 B.C.* | 180 |
| *Heliopolis. Obelisk of Sesostris I. Twelfth Dynasty, c. 1950 B.C.* | 181 |
| *Karnak. "White Chapel" of Sesostris I. Twelfth Dynasty, c. 1950 B.C.* | 182 |
| *Principal forms of Egyptian columns (drawings by Gehrke).* | 183 |
| *Deir el Bahari (West Thebes). Funerary temple of Queen Hatshepsut, from east. Eighteenth Dynasty, c. 1470 B.C.* | 184 |

| | Plate |
|---|---|
| *Deir el Bahari (West Thebes). Funerary temple of Queen Hatshepsut, first terrace: right, entrance hall to Anubis chapel; left, north portico of facade ("birth room"). Eighteenth Dynasty, c. 1470 B.C.* | 185 |
| *Deir el Bahari (West Thebes). Funerary temple of Queen Hatshepsut, first terrace: left, "birth room"; center, Anubis chapel; right, north colonnade. Eighteenth Dynasty, c. 1470 B.C.* | 186, 187 |
| *Deir el Bahari (West Thebes). Funerary temple of Queen Hatshepsut, south end of first terrace: Hathor chapel, interior of rock-cut sanctuary. Eighteenth Dynasty, c. 1470 B.C.* | 188 |
| *Deir el Bahari (West Thebes). Funerary temple of Queen Hatshepsut, north wall of second terrace: interior of Chapel of Tuthmosis I. Eighteenth Dynasty, c. 1470 B.C.* | 189 |
| *Medinet Habu (West Thebes). Reconstruction of Queen Hatshepsut's baldachin temple, in original state (from Holscher, 1933).* | 190 |
| *Medinet Habu (West Thebes). Section and plan of Queen Hatshepsut's baldachin temple (from Borchardt, 1938).* | 191 |
| *Medinet Habu (West Thebes). Remains of Queen Hatshepsut's baldachin chapel, from south. Eighteenth Dynasty, c. 1460 B.C.* | 192 |
| *Karnak. Temple of Amon-Ra, sacred lake, from south. Left to right in background: pylon VII, pylon I, great hypostyle hall, obelisk of Hatshepsut.* | 193 |
| *Karnak. Temple of Amon-Ra, view toward south from pylon I: great court with kiosk of Taharqa; facade of temple of Ramesses III; pylons VIII and IX on south axis.* | 194 |
| *Karnak. Temple of Amon-Ra, landing place and avenue of sphinxes toward pylon I.* | 195 |
| *Karnak. Temple of Amon-Ra, heraldic pillars in hall of annals of Tuthmosis III. Eighteenth Dynasty, c. 1450 B.C.* | 196 |
| *Karnak. Plan of Temple of Amon-Ra (from Lange-Hirmer, 1957).* | 197 |
| *Karnak. Temple of Amon-Ra, great festival hall of Tuthmosis III, from west. Eighteenth Dynasty, c. 1460 B.C.* | 198 |
| *Karnak. Temple of Amon-Ra, longitudinal section of great festival hall of Tuthmosis III (from Haeny, 1970).* | 199 |
| *Karnak. Temple of Amon-Ra, great festival hall of Tuthmosis III, with tent pole columns, from south. Eighteenth Dynasty, c. 1460 B.C.* | 200, 201 |
| *Karnak. Temple of Amon-Ra, great hypostyle hall from north, and obelisks of Tuthmosis I (left) and Hatshepsut (right).* | 202 |
| *Karnak. Temple of Amon-Ra, transverse section of great hypostyle hall (from Haeny, 1970).* | 203 |
| *Karnak. Temple of Amon-Ra, south side of great hypostyle hall. Nineteenth Dynasty, c. 1290 B.C.* | 204 |
| *Karnak. Temple of Amon-Ra, view toward south, through aisle of great hypostyle hall with ancient grille preserved. Nineteenth Dynasty, c. 1290 B.C.* | 205 |
| *Karnak. Temple of Amon-Ra, view toward central aisle of great hypostyle hall. Nineteenth Dynasty, c. 1290 B.C.* | 206 |
| *Karnak. Temple of Amon-Ra, obelisk of Tuthmosis I and central aisle of great hypostyle hall, from east.* | 207 |
| *Karnak. Temple of Khonsu, porticoed court, from south. Ramesses III, Twentieth Dynasty, c. 1150 B.C.* | 208 |
| *Karnak. Temple of Khonsu, inner face of access portal. Ptolemaic period, c. 220 B.C.* | 209 |
| *Karnak. Temple of Khonsu, outer face of access portal. Ptolemaic period, c. 220 B.C.* | 210 |
| *Karnak. Temple of Khonsu, reliefs in access portal. Ptolemaic period, c. 220 B.C.* | 211 |
| *Luxor. Temple of Amenhotep III, from north; colonnaded passage and great court. Eighteenth Dynasty, c. 1370 B.C.* | 212 |
| *Luxor. Plan of temple of Amenhotep III (from Borchardt, 1896).* | 213 |

Plate

Luxor. Temple of Amenhotep III, papyrus-bundle columns at northeast corner of great court. Eighteenth Dynasty, c. 1370 B.C.  214

Luxor. Temple of Amenhotep III, pylon and exterior wall of north court (colonnaded passage beyond). Ramesses II, Eighteenth Dynasty, c. 1250 B.C.  215

Luxor. Temple of Amenhotep III, entrance pylon with obelisk and colossi of Ramesses II. Nineteenth Dynasty, c. 1250 B.C.  216

Luxor. Temple of Amenhotep III, view from court of Ramesses II to colonnaded passage of Amenhotep III. Eighteenth–Nineteenth Dynasties, c. 1370–c. 1250 B.C.  217

Medinet Habu (West Thebes). Reconstruction of High Gate, southeast precinct gate of mortuary temple of Ramesses III. Twentieth Dynasty, c. 1150 B.C. (from Holscher, 1933).  218

Medinet Habu (West Thebes). Interior face of High Gate, southeast precinct gate of mortuary temple of Ramesses III. Twentieth Dynasty, c. 1150 B.C.  219

Abu Simbel. Great rock temples of Ramesses II, from north (as relocated). Nineteenth Dynasty, c. 1250 B.C.  220

Abu Simbel. Facade of great rock temple and four colossi of Ramesses II (as relocated). Nineteenth Dynasty, c. 1250 B.C.  221, 222

Abu Simbel. Interior of great rock temple of Ramesses II, longitudinal and lateral views of royal statues before pillars. Nineteenth Dynasty, c. 1250 B.C.  223, 224

Abu Simbel. View toward entrance of great rock temple of Ramesses II. Nineteenth Dynasty, c. 1250 B.C.  225

Abydos. Plan of temple and cenotaph of Sety I (from Hirmer-Otto, 1967).  226

Abydos. Cenotaph of Sety I, from northeast. Nineteenth Dynasty, c. 1290 B.C.  227

Edfu. Birth house in front of Temple of Horus. Ptolemaic period, 237–57 B.C.  228

Edfu. Plan of Temple of Horus (from Baedeker, 1928).  229

Edfu. Pylon of Temple of Horus. Ptolemaic period, 237–57 B.C.  230

Edfu. Pylon and enclosure wall of Temple of Horus, from southwest. Ptolemaic period, 237–57 B.C.  231

Edfu. Temple of Horus, view through "hall of appearances" toward sanctuary. Ptolemaic period, 237–57 B.C.  232

Edfu. Court of Temple of Horus. Ptolemaic period, 237–57 B.C.  233

Edfu. Temple of Horus, enclosure wall (right) and temple wall (left), from north. Ptolemaic period, 237–57 B.C.  234

Edfu. Temple of Horus, western stairway on roof. Ptolemaic period, 237–57 B.C.  235

Dendera. Facade of Temple of Hathor, from northeast. Late Ptolemaic–Roman period.  236

Dendera. Exterior of Temple of Hathor, from west and south. Late Ptolemaic–Roman period.  237, 238

Dendera. Temple of Hathor, slits for illumination in ceiling of hypostyle hall. Late Ptolemaic–Roman period.  239

Dendera. Pavilion and enclosure wall of Temple of Hathor, and sacred lake, from northeast. Late Ptolemaic–Roman period.  240

Dendera. Pavilion on roof of Temple of Hathor. Late Ptolemaic–Roman period.  241–43

Dendera. Hathoric columns of pavilion, Temple of Hathor. Late Ptolemaic–Roman period.  244

Dendera. Sacred lake of Temple of Hathor. Late Ptolemaic–Roman period.  245

Kalabsha. Temple of Mandulis, facade of vestibule. Roman period–beginning of Christian era.  246

Kalabsha. Temple of Mandulis, from southwest. Roman period–beginning of Christian era.  247

Kalabsha. Temple of Mandulis (as relocated), with pavilion of Kertassi. Roman period–beginning of Christian era.  248

Plate

Island of Philae with temples, from west. Thirtieth Dynasty to Roman period, c. 380 B.C.–2nd century A.D.  249

Mallia. Plan of palace and northwest excavations. Middle Minoan, 2000–1700 B.C. (after Graham, 1962).  250

Mallia. Perspective reconstruction of palace, from northwest (from Graham, 1962).  251

Mallia. Crypt rooms. Middle Minoan, c. 2000–1700 B.C.  252

Mallia. Plan of House E (from Graham, 1962).  253

Phaistos. Plan of second palace (from Graham, 1962).  254

Phaistos. Reconstruction of propylon (from Graham, 1962).  255

Phaistos. West court of palace, from west. c. 1700–1400 B.C.  256

Phaistos. Theater and west court of palace, from northwest. c. 1700–1400 B.C.  257

Phaistos. Central court of palace, from south. c. 1700–1400 B.C.  258

Phaistos. Magazines on central court of palace. c. 1700–1400 B.C.  259

Knossos. Plan of palace (from Graham, 1962).  260

Knossos. South portico and monumental staircase of palace.  261

Knossos. Western section of palace, from north.  262

Knossos. Magazines on ground floor in western section of palace, from east.  263

Knossos. Central court of palace, facade of "throne room" (restored), from east.  264

Knossos. Central court of palace, west side.  265

Knossos. Megaron above Hall of Double Axes, east wing of palace, from west.  266

Knossos. Colonnaded landing of great staircase, east wing of palace, from southeast.  267

Knossos. Great staircase (restored), east wing of palace, interior views.  268–71

Knossos. House of Lustral Basin, near northwest portico of palace, from east.  272

Knossos. South house (restored).  273

Knossos. South portico of palace and "horns of consecration," from east.  274

Knossos. South house and, above, portion of entrance corridor to palace, from southwest.  275

Zakros. View of excavations.  276

Hagia Triada. General view of villa.  277

"Bull's Head," painted relief from north portico, Palace of Knossos. Herakleion, Museum.  278

"Blue Girls," fresco from Palace of Knossos. Herakleion, Museum.  279

Gournia. Plan of city (from Graham, 1962).  280

Tiryns. Plan of palace (from Mylonas, 1957).  281

Tiryns. Fortification walls on west.  282

Tiryns. South casemates, from east.  283

Mycenae. Lion Gate.  284

Mycenae. Cyclopean walls and approach to Lion Gate.  285

Mycenae. Stairs leading to "Secret Cistern."  286

Mycenae. Stairs leading to and from "Secret Cistern."  287, 288

Pylos. Main hall of palace.  289

Pylos. Bathroom of palace.  290

Mycenae. Entrance and facade of "Treasury of Atreus."  291

Mycenae. Dome of "Treasury of Atreus."  292

Mycenae. Interior of "Treasury of Atreus."  293

Dreros (Crete). Diagrammatic reconstruction of a temple (from Demargne, 1964).  294

Argos. Terra cotta model of temple, from Sanctuary of Hera. Athens, National Museum.  295

Plate

Prinias. Reconstruction of front elevation and plan, Temple A (from Charbonneaux-Martin-Villard, 1968). 296

Prinias. Lintel of Temple A. Herakleion, Museum. 297

Thermon. Plan of successive buildings of Temple of Apollo (from Charbonneaux-Martin-Villard, 1968). 298

Samos. Plan of Sanctuary of Hera (from Bervé-Gruben, 1962). 299

Samos. Plan of Temple of Hera III, by Rhoikos and Theodoros (from Bervé-Gruben, 1962). 300

Samos. Plan of Temple of Hera IV, by Polycrates of Samos (from Bervé-Gruben, 1962). 301

Eretria. Plan of first Temple of Apollo Daphnephoros (from Auberson, 1968). 302

Larissa. Aeolic capital. Istanbul, Archaeological Museum. 303

Neandria. Aeolic capital. Istanbul, Archaeological Museum. 304

Delphi, Sanctuary of Apollo. Reconstruction of front elevations of treasuries of Cnidos, Marseilles, and Siphnos (from Charbonneaux-Martin-Villard, 1968). 305

Delphi, Sanctuary of Apollo. Caryatid from Treasury of the Siphnians. Delphi, Museum. 306

Delphi, Sanctuary of Apollo. Pediment and frieze from Treasury of the Siphnians. Delphi, Museum. 307

Delphi, Sanctuary of Apollo. Frieze from Treasury of the Siphnians. Delphi, Museum. 308

Delphi, Sanctuary of Apollo. Decorated foundation wall, Treasury of Marseilles. 309

Delphi, Sanctuary of Apollo. Frieze (detail) from Treasury of the Siphnians. Delphi, Museum. 310

Delphi, Sanctuary of Apollo. Trabeation from Treasury of the Siphnians. Delphi, Museum. 311

Athens, Acropolis. Olive-tree Pediment, of painted poros. Athens, Acropolis Museum. 312

Athens, Acropolis. Apotheosis of Heracles Pediment, of painted poros. Athens, Acropolis Museum. 313

Athens, Acropolis. Temple of Athena Nike, from Propylaea. 314

Athens, Acropolis. East portico, Temple of Athena Nike. 315

Athens, Acropolis. Corner of east portico, Temple of Athena Nike. 316

Athens, Acropolis. Ceiling of portico, Temple of Athena Nike. 317

Athens, Acropolis. North porch, Erechtheion, from northwest. 318

Athens, Acropolis. Northeast corner of north porch, Erechtheion, showing upper portion of Ionic order. 319

Athens, Acropolis. Erechtheion and Parthenon, from northwest. 320

Athens, Acropolis. Northeast corner of north porch, Erechtheion, showing lower portion of Ionic order. 321

Athens, Acropolis. West side of Erechtheion, seen from Propylaea. 322

Athens, Acropolis. South side of Erechtheion. 323

Athens, Acropolis. South porch, with caryatids, Erechtheion. 324

Xanthos. New restoration of Monument of the Nereids. London, British Museum. 325

Xanthos. Structural diagram of Monument of the Nereids (from Demargne-Coupel, 1969). 326

Xanthos. Perspective reconstruction of Monument of the Nereids (from Demargne-Coupel, 1969). 327

Xanthos. Isometric diagram including interior, Monument of the Nereids (from Demargne-Coupel, 1969). 328

Halicarnassus. Amazon frieze from Mausoleum, by Scopas. London, British Museum. 329

Olympia. View toward palaestra, from south. 330

Plate

Thermon. Painted terra cotta metope from Temple of Apollo. Athens, National Museum. 331

Olympia. Temple of Hera, from southwest. 332

Olympia. Terrace of the treasuries and entrance to stadium, from west. 333

Paestum, Sele River. Plan of Treasury, Sanctuary of Hera (from Zancani-Montuoro and Zanetti-Bianco, 1951). 334

Paestum, Sele River. Reconstruction of facade of Treasury, Sanctuary of Hera (from Zancani-Montuoro and Zanetti-Bianco, 1951). 335

Paestum, Sele River. Reconstructed frieze of Treasury, Sanctuary of Hera. Paestum, Museum. 336

Paestum, Sele River. Transverse section of Treasury, Sanctuary of Hera (from Zancani-Montuoro and Zanetti-Bianco, 1951). 337

Paestum, Sele River. Two metopes from Treasury, Sanctuary of Hera. 338, 339

Syracuse (Ortygia). Plan of Temple of Apollo (from Bervé-Gruben, 1962). 340

Syracuse (Ortygia). Reconstruction of facade of Temple of Apollo (from Bervé-Gruben, 1962). 341

Syracuse (Ortygia). South side of Temple of Apollo. 342

Selinus. Plan of Temple C (from Bervé-Gruben, 1962). 343

Selinus, Acropolis. North gallery of Temple C, from west. 344

Selinus, Acropolis. Portion of frieze, Temple C. Palermo, Archaeological Museum. 345

Selinus, Acropolis. North side of Temple C, from northeast. 346

Selinus (Marinella). Temple E (Hera), from northeast. 347

Selinus (Marinella). Metope of Artemis and Actaeon, from Temple E (Hera). Palermo, Archaeological Museum. 348

Selinus (Marinella). Portion of frieze, Temple E (Hera). Palermo, Archaeological Museum. 349

Selinus (Marinella). Cella of Temple E (Hera), from east. 350

Acragas. Interior of Temple of Juno Lacinia (Temple D), from southeast. 351

Acragas. Air view of Temple of Juno Lacinia (Temple D). 352

Metapontum. Temple of Hera (Tavoline Paladine), from southeast. 353

Acragas. Temple of Castor and Pollux, in Sanctuary of Chthonic Deities, from south. 354

Paestum. Plan of Temple of Hera I (Basilica) (from Bervé-Gruben, 1962). 355

Paestum. North-south axis, with temples of Hera I and II (Basilica and Temple of Poseidon). 356

Paestum. Doric capital of Temple of Hera I (Basilica). 357

Paestum. Columns of Temple of Hera I (Basilica). 358

Paestum. Temple of Hera I (Basilica) and Temple of Hera II (Poseidon), from northeast. 359

Paestum, Sele River. Elevation of Temple of Hera, Sanctuary of Hera (from Bervé-Gruben, 1962). 360

Paestum, Sele River. Plan of Temple of Hera, Sanctuary of Hera (from Zancani-Montuoro and Zanetti-Bianco, 1951). 361

Paestum, Sele River. Reconstruction of trabeation of Temple of Hera, Sanctuary of Hera (from Zancani-Montuoro and Zanetti-Bianco, 1951). 362

Paestum. Ionic capital from Temple of Athena. Paestum, Museum. 363

Locri. Capital from Ionic temple. Reggio Calabria, National Museum. 364

Paestum. Plan of Temple of Hera II (Poseidon) (from Bervé-Gruben, 1962). 365

Paestum. Temple of Hera II (Poseidon), from northeast. 366

Paestum. Interior of Temple of Hera II (Poseidon), from west. 367, 368

Segesta. Interior of Doric temple, from west. 369

Delphi, Sanctuary of Apollo. Reconstruction of ancient Tholos (from Charbonneaux-Martin-Villard, 1968). 370

| | Plate |
|---|---|
| *Delphi, Sanctuary of Apollo. Capitals of Sicyonian Treasury (on foundations).* | 371 |
| *Corinth. Temple of Apollo, from north.* | 372 |
| *Corinth. Capitals of Temple of Apollo.* | 373 |
| *Corinth. Temple of Apollo, from northeast.* | 374 |
| *Aegina. Temple of Aphaia, from southwest.* | 375 |
| *Aegina. Temple of Aphaia, from north.* | 376 |
| *Aegina. Interior of cella, Temple of Aphaia, from west.* | 377 |
| *Aegina. Interior colonnade of Temple of Aphaia, from northeast.* | 378 |
| *Aegina. Foundations of Temple of Aphaia, from northwest.* | 379 |
| *Aegina. Cella wall, Temple of Aphaia, from northwest.* | 380 |
| *Aegina. Trabeation of Temple of Aphaia, from northwest.* | 381 |
| *Olympia. Capital of Temple of Zeus.* | 382 |
| *Delphi. Treasury of the Athenians (in background, portion of polygonal wall).* | 383 |
| *Olympia. Sculpture of west pediment, Battle of Lapiths and Centaurs, from Temple of Zeus. Olympia, Museum.* | 384 |
| *Olympia. Sculpture of east pediment, Contest between Pelops and Oenamaus, from Temple of Zeus. Olympia. Museum.* | 385 |
| *Athens. Plan of Acropolis (from Charbonneaux-Martin-Villard, 1969).* | 386 |
| *Athens, Acropolis. Plan of Parthenon (from Charbonneaux-Martin-Villard, 1969).* | 387 |
| *Athens, Acropolis. Sectional reconstruction of front portico of Parthenon (from Lawrence, 1957).* | 388 |
| *Athens, Acropolis. Sacred Way, Propylaea, and south wall, from southwest.* | 389 |
| *Athens, Acropolis. View from northwest.* | 390 |
| *Athens, Acropolis. West facade of Parthenon, seen from Propylaea.* | 391 |
| *Athens, Acropolis. North side of Parthenon.* | 392 |
| *Athens, Acropolis. View upward into west portico of Parthenon, showing frieze above pronaos.* | 393 |
| *Athens, Acropolis. South ambulatory of Parthenon.* | 394 |
| *Athens, Acropolis. View across east portico of Parthenon.* | 395 |
| *Athens, Acropolis. South colonnade and cella wall, Parthenon.* | 396 |
| *Athens, Acropolis. Trabeation, west facade, Parthenon.* | 397, 398 |
| *Sunium. Promontory and Temple of Poseidon.* | 399 |
| *Sunium. Temple of Poseidon, from north.* | 400 |
| *Sunium. South side of Temple of Poseidon.* | 401 |
| *Sunium. Trabeation, southeast corner of Temple of Poseidon.* | 402 |
| *Sunium. Inner side of south colonnade, Temple of Poseidon.* | 403 |
| *Rhamnus. View of fortress walls and acropolis.* | 404 |
| *Bassae. Plan of Temple of Apollo (from Roux, 1961).* | 405 |
| *Tegea. Plan and longitudinal section of Temple of Athena Alea (from Bervé-Gruben, 1962).* | 406, 407 |
| *Bassae. Southwest corner, Temple of Apollo.* | 408 |
| *Bassae. Interior of cella, Temple of Apollo, from south.* | 409 |
| *Bassae. Pronaos, Temple of Apollo, from north.* | 410 |
| *Bassae. Interior of cella, east wall, Temple of Apollo.* | 411 |
| *Delphi, Marmaria. Sanctuary of Athena, from northwest.* | 412 |
| *Delphi, Marmaria. Tholos, Sanctuary of Athena, from northeast.* | 413 |
| *Delphi, Marmaria. Tholos, Sanctuary of Athena, from north.* | 414 |
| *Delphi, Marmaria. Crepidoma of Tholos, Sanctuary of Athena, from south.* | 415 |
| *Epidaurus. Plan of Tholos (from Roux, 1961).* | 416 |
| *Epidaurus. Section of Tholos (from Roux, 1961).* | 417 |

| | Plate |
|---|---|
| *Epidaurus. Reconstructed section, including wall and trabeation of Tholos. Epidaurus, Museum.* | 418 |
| *Epidaurus. Corinthian capital from interior of Tholos. Epidaurus, Museum.* | 419 |
| *Epidaurus. Interior corridors in foundations of Tholos.* | 420 |
| *Eleusis. Plans showing evolution of Telesterion (from Charbonneaux-Martin-Villard, 1969).* | 421 |
| *Eleusis. Views of Telesterion.* | 422, 423 |
| *Priene. View of agora.* | 424 |
| *Priene. Ekklesiasterion.* | 425 |
| *Priene. Reconstruction of Ekklesiasterion (from Schede, 1964).* | 426 |
| *Piraeus. Reconstruction of Arsenal (from Lawrence, 1957).* | 427 |
| *Piraeus. Section of Arsenal (from Lawrence, 1957).* | 428 |
| *Dodona. Theater, from north.* | 429 |
| *Dodona. Theater, from east.* | 430 |
| *Priene. Theater, from north.* | 431 |
| *Epidaurus. Theater, from north.* | 432 |
| *Segesta. Theater, from southwest.* | 433 |
| *Aegosthena. Fortified tower.* | 434 |
| *Eleutherai. Fortification walls with towers.* | 435, 436 |
| *Acragas. Temple of Castor and Pollux, Sanctuary of Chthonic Deities, from east.* | 437 |
| *Acragas. Temple of Concord (Temple F), from west.* | 438 |
| *Paestum. Temple of Hera I (Basilica), from north.* | 439 |
| *Paestum. Temple of Hera II (Poseidon), from southwest.* | 440 |
| *Segesta. Doric temple seen from theater hill, on southeast.* | 441 |
| *Athens, Acropolis. Plan of Propylaea (from Bervé-Gruben, 1962).* | 442 |
| *Athens, Acropolis. East portico of Propylaea.* | 443 |
| *Athens, Acropolis. Ionic capital, interior of Propylaea.* | 444 |
| *Olympia. East side of palaestra.* | 445 |
| *Olympia. Southeast corner of palaestra.* | 446 |
| *Olympia. Vaulted entrance to stadium.* | 447 |
| *Delphi, Sanctuary of Apollo. Sacred Way and Treasury of the Athenians.* | 448 |
| *Olympia. Terrace of the treasuries, from east.* | 449 |
| *Megara Hyblaea. Plan of agora.* | 450 |
| *Morgantina. View of agora.* | 451 |
| *Brauron. Plan of stoa, Sanctuary of Artemis Brauronia (from Bouras, 1967).* | 452 |
| *Brauron. Isometric reconstruction of stoa room, Sanctuary of Artemis Brauronia (from Bouras, 1967).* | 453 |
| *Assos. Reconstruction and plan of stoa (from Lawrence, 1957).* | 454, 455 |
| *Athens, Agora. Plan of west side, end of 6th century B.C. (from Lawrence, 1957).* | 456 |
| *Athens. View of agora, from southeast.* | 457 |
| *Miletus. Plan of city (from Kleiner, 1968).* | 458 |
| *Paestum. Air view of city and temples, from east.* | 459 |
| *Paestum. View of forum.* | 460 |
| *Marseilles. Ancient port, as recently excavated.* | 461 |
| *Segesta. Doric temple, from southeast.* | 462 |
| *Segesta. Trabeation of west facade, Doric temple.* | 463 |
| *Athens, Agora. Trabeation of southeast corner, Temple of Hephaestus (Theseum).* | 464 |
| *Epidaurus. Restoration of Corinthian capital and trabeation from Tholos. Epidaurus, Museum.* | 465 |

| | Plate |
|---|---|
| Sarcophagus of the Mourning Women, end reliefs. Istanbul, Archaeological Museum. | 466, 467 |
| Acragas. Restored telamones from Temple of Zeus. Agrigento, Museum. | 468 |
| Acragas. Plan of Temple of Zeus (from Bervé-Gruben, 1962). | 469 |
| Epidaurus. Isometric reconstruction of Temple L (from Roux, 1961). | 470 |
| Thasos. Relief on Gate of Selinus. | 471 |
| Thasos. Views of Gate of Zeus. | 472, 473 |
| Athens. Monument of Lysicrates. | 474 |
| Syracuse. Moats and subterranean passages in fortifications of Euryale Castle. | 475-77 |
| Corinth. Facade and court of Pirene Fountain. | 478 |
| Didyma. Vaulted passage to interior court of Temple of Apollo. | 479 |
| Locri. Terra cotta model of fountain-sanctuary. Reggio Calabria, National Museum. | 480 |
| Priene. Reconstruction of gate to agora (from Schede, 1964). | 481 |
| Pergamum, lower city. Vaulted stairway to first terrace. | 482, 483 |
| Sardis. Interior view toward east facade, Temple of Artemis Cybele. | 484 |
| Sardis. Column bases of east portico, Temple of Artemis Cybele. | 485 |
| Sardis. Ionic capital of Temple of Artemis Cybele. | 486 |
| Sardis. Column base of east portico, Temple of Artemis Cybele. | 487 |
| Didyma. Plan of Temple of Apollo (from Bervé-Gruben, 1962). | 488 |
| Didyma. Columns on north side of Temple of Apollo. | 489 |
| Didyma. Temple of Apollo, from north. | 490 |
| Didyma. Interior court of Temple of Apollo, toward entrance. | 491 |
| Didyma. Column bases of east portico, Temple of Apollo. | 492 |
| Didyma. Interior pilaster capital from Temple of Apollo. | 493 |
| Didyma. Column base of east portico, Temple of Apollo. | 494 |
| Priene. Plan of Temple of Athena Polias (from Bervé-Gruben, 1962). | 495 |
| Magnesia. Plan of Temple of Artemis (from Lawrence, 1957). | 496 |
| Sarcophagus of the Mourning Women. Istanbul, Archaeological Museum. | 497 |
| Pergamum. Restoration of Great Altar of Zeus. Berlin, Pergamum Museum. | 498 |

| | Plate |
|---|---|
| Magnesia. Plan of Altar of Artemis (from Gerkan, 1929). | 499 |
| Magnesia. Front elevation of Altar of Artemis (from Gerkan, 1929). | 500 |
| Argos. Plan of Sanctuary of Hera (from Bervé-Gruben, 1962). | 501 |
| Labranda. Plan of Sanctuary of Zeus (from Westholm, 1963). | 502 |
| Lindos (Rhodes). View of cliff and temple, from west. | 503 |
| Lindos (Rhodes). Cella of Temple of Athena, on upper terrace. | 504 |
| Lindos (Rhodes). Great portico at foot of grand staircase, lower terrace of acropolis. | 505 |
| Lindos (Rhodes). Grand staircase to upper terrace of acropolis. | 506 |
| Camirus (Rhodes). View of upper city. | 507 |
| Camirus (Rhodes). Sanctuary and square, lower city. | 508 |
| Pergamum. Plan of acropolis (from Bervé-Gruben, 1962). | 509 |
| Pergamum. Model of acropolis. Berlin, Pergamum Museum. | 510 |
| Pergamum, Acropolis. Foundations of Palace of Eumenes II, from northwest. | 511 |
| Pergamum, Acropolis. Theater, from north. | 512 |
| Pergamum, Acropolis. Temple of Dionysus and north end of theater terrace, from northwest and south. | 513, 514 |
| Pergamum, middle city. East end of Sanctuary of Demeter. | 515 |
| Pergamum, middle city. Sanctuary of Demeter: section of south stoa, temple, steps, and north stoa (from Bervé-Gruben, 1962). | 516, 517 |
| Athens, Agora. Colonnade of Stoa of Attalus (in background, Temple of Hephaestus). | 518 |
| Athens, Agora. View from northwest, toward Stoa of Attalus. | 519 |
| Athens, Agora. East facade of Temple of Hephaestus (Theseum). | 520 |
| Athens, Agora. Restoration of Stoa of Attalus. | 521 |
| Miletus. Plan of Bouleuterion (from Kleiner, 1968). | 522 |
| Miletus. Reconstruction drawing of Bouleuterion (from Kleiner, 1968). | 523 |
| Miletus. Theater, from north. | 524 |
| Miletus. Theater, from east. | 525 |

Abu Simbel, Ramesses II, rock temple of, 159, *Plates 220-25*

Abusir, Ne-user-ra, sun sanctuary of, 102, 115, *Plate 170;* Sahura, pyramid complex of, *Plates 168-69*

Abydos, 80-81, 84, 90, 93, 104, 159, 183; Khentiamentiu, temple of, 80-81, *Plate 142;* Sety I, cenotaph of, 159-60, 167, *Plates 226-27;* Sety I, temple of, 159-60, *Plate 226;* tumulus tomb, 80-81, *Plate 141;* Zet, King, stele of, 79-80, *Plate 140*

Acarnania, Epirus, Nekyomanteion of, 360; Oeniadae, gates of, 358, 360

Achaemenids, architecture of, 60, 65, 68, 72

Acragas, 251; Castor and Pollux, temple of (sanctuary of Chthonic Deities), 342, *Plates 354, 437;* Concord, temple of (Temple F), 326, 342, *Plate 438;* Juno Lacinia, temple of, 260, 342, *Plates 351-52;* Zeus Olympus, temple of, 342, 354, 367, *Plates 468-69*

Acropolis, Athens, *see* Athens

Aegina, Athena Aphaia, temple of, 275, 277, 281, 292, 332, 354, *Plates 375-81*

Aegosthena, fortified tower, *Plate 434*

Agora: Alinda, 375; Assos, *Plates 454-55;* Athens, 312, 318, 335-38, *Plates 456-57, 518-21;* Megara Hyblaea, 335-37, 339-40, *Plate 450;* Morgantina, *Plate 451;* Priene, 318, 360, *Plates 424-26, 481*

Akhenaten (Amenhotep IV), 116, 122, 158; *see also* Amarna period

Akhetaten (Tell el Amarna), 116, 158

Alabanda, 367

Alaca Huyuk, Sphinx Gate, *Plate 59*

Alexander the Great, 167, 348, 380

Alexandria, 167, 380

Alinda, Adda, sanctuary of, 375; agora, 375; theater, 360

Alishar, 43

Altintepe, Urartian temple, 51, *Plate 96;* mural painting, *Plate 97;*

Al 'Ubaid, Minkhursag temple, decorations of, 16, *Plates 26-28*

Al 'Uqair, protoliterate temple (model), 15, *Plate 25*

Amarna, Akhenaten, temple complex of, 104, 121

Amarna period, 121-22, 158

Amasis, 190

Amenemhat I, 112

Amenemhat III and IV, temple of, Medinet Madi, 114-15

Amenemhat, Prince, rock-cut tomb of, Beni Hasan, 114, 120-21, *Plate 180*

Amenhotep III, 135, 156, 158; palace complex of, West Thebes, 122; temple of, Luxor, *see* Luxor

Amenhotep IV, *see* Akhenaten

Amenhotep, son of Hapu, 156, 158

Amnisos, 214

Amon-Ra, 110, 116, 121, 124, 127, 130, 132, 135, 147, 150, 155-56, 159-60; temple of, Karnak, *see* Karnak

Amyzon, Idrieus, sanctuary of, 375

Antimachides, 277

Antiochus III, 339

Antistates, 277

Anu and Adad, temple of, Assur, 25, *Plate 46*

Apollonia, wife of Attalus I, 379; influence at Pergamum, 379

Aqar Quf, *see* Dur Kurigalzu

Arcesius, 348

Argos, Hera, sanctuary of, 249, 326, 374-75, *Plate 501;* model of temple from, *Plate 295*

Arin Berd, fortifications, 48-51

Arpachiya, 12

Arsenal, Piraeus, 318, 323, *Plates 427-28*

Arslan Tash, 40

Artaxerxes I, 72

Assos, agora, *Plates 454-55*

Assur, 23, 37, *Plates 44-45;* Anu and Adad, temple of, 25, *Plate 46;* Ishtar, temple of, 27, *Plate 46;* Tukulti-Ninurta I, ziggurat of, 25, *Plate 46*

Assurbanipal, 37

Assurnasirpal II, 37

Assyria, civilization of, 23, 25, 48, 58; building techniques of, 27, 38, 40, 65; arts of, 68

Aswan, Sabni and Mekhu, rock-cut tomb of, 104, 110, 150, *Plate 171;* Sirenpowet II, Prince, rock-cut tomb of, 114, *Plate 179*

Athens, 283, 318, 337, 380
  Acropolis: 235, 238, 283, 332, 337-38, *Plates 312-24, 386-98;* Athena Nike, temple of, 235, 238, *Plates 314-17;* Erechtheion, 235, 238, 246, 333, 367, *Plates 318-24;* Old Temple of Athena, 277, 292; Parthenon, 235, 277, 283, 292, 297, 303, 318, 332-33, *Plates 320, 387-88, 391-98;* pedimental sculpture from, 235, *Plates 312-13;* Propylaea, 235, 332-33, 362, 375, *Plates 314, 322, 389, 442-44;* Sacred Way, *Plate 389*
  Agora: 312, 318, 335-38, *Plates 456-57, 518-21;* Altar of the Twelve Gods, 338; Apollo, temple of, 337-38; Attalus I, stoa of, 380, *Plates 518-19, 521;* Bouleuterion, 337-38; Demeter, temple of, 337-38; Hephaestus, temple of, 297, 349, *Plates 464, 518, 520;* Panathenaic Way, 338; Prytaneum, 337-38; theater, 312; tholos, 337; Zeus Agoraios, sanctuary of, 337-38
  Lysicrates, monument of, *Plate 474*
  Olympieion (Temple of Zeus), 277, 354

Atreus, Treasury of, Mycenae, 233-24, 249, *Plates 291-93*

Attalid dynasty, 370, 379-80

Attalus I, 380; stoa of, Agora, Athens, 380, *Plates 518-19, 521*

Augustus, 178, 183

Bab el Hosan, 110-12

Babylon, 12, 58-60, *Plates 114-15, 120;* Esagila, 59; Etemenaki, 59; Ishtar Gate, 59, *Plates 116-18;* Merkez, 59; Nebuchadnezzar, palace of, *Plate 122;* Nin-Makh Temple, 59, *Plate 119;* Processional Way, 59-60, *Plate 116*

Balawat, Bronze Gates, 40-43, *Plates 82-84, 86-88*

Bassae, Apollo, temple of, 303-4, 326, 350, 354, *Plates 405, 408-11*

Beni Hasan, Amenemhat, Prince, rock-cut tomb of, 114, 120-21, *Plate 180;* Kheti, Prince, rock-cut tomb of, 114, *Plates 177-78*

Beycesultan, Arzawan palace, 32, 37, 199, *Plate 67;* Bronze Age shrines, 29, *Plates 52-53*

*bît-hilani,* 32, 52

Blemmyes, 183

Bogazkoy, 31, 43
  Buyukkale, citadel of, 31, *Plates 55-56;* King's Gate, 31, *Plate 61;* Lion Gate, 31, *Plates 57-58;* Temple I, 31, *Plate 60;*
  Yasilikaya, rock shrine of, 32, *Plate 62*

Brauron, Artemis Brauronia, sanctuary of, 335-36, *Plates 452-53;* Naxians, stoa of, 335-36

Bronze Gates, *see* Balawat

Buto, 78, 81, 84, 93, 119

Buyukkale, citadel of, *see* Bogazkoy

Caesar, Julius, 183

Callaischros, 277

Callicrates, 235-38, 283, 292, 332

Callimachus, 350

Camarina (Sicily), 340

Camirus, lower city, *Plate 508;* upper city, *Plate 507*

capitals: Aeolic, 233, *Plates 303-4;* Corinthian, 304, 350, 354, *Plates 419, 465;* Doric, 247, 249; Ionic, 270, 275, *Plates 363-64; see also* Orders

Carchemish, 52, *Plate 108;* relief sculpture from, 51-52, *Plates 98-99, 104;* statue from, 52, *Plate 101*

Caria, 370, 375; *see* Labranda

Catal Huyuk, house, 9, 11, *Plate 5;* shrine chamber, 9, *Plate 4;* plan, Level VIB, 9, 11, *Plates 2-3*

Chalcolithic period, 11

Cheops, 178; pyramid of, Giza, 89, *Plates 158, 163*

Chephren, pyramid complex of, Giza: pyramid, 89, *Plates 158, 163-66;* pyramid temple, 89-90, *Plate 160;* Great Sphinx, 94, 102, *Plates 163-66;* valley temple, 89-90, 94, 167, *Plates 159-62, 164;* veneration temple, 89-90, *Plate 160*

Chersiphron, 228, 235

Choga Zambil, ziggurat of, 65, *Plate 127*

Cimon, 235, 283, 292, 318

Clazomenae, treasury of, Delphi, 235

Cleopatra, 183

Cnidos, treasury of, Delphi, 235, 367, *Plate 305*

colonnade rhythms, *see* Hermogenes

columns: Cretan, 211; Egyptian, 119-21, *Plate 183;* Greek, *see* Orders

Corfu, 275; Artemis, temple of, 249, 275-77

Corinth, 277; Apollo, temple of, 277, 281, 292, *Plates 372-74;* Pirene fountain, 358, *Plate 478*

Croesus, 233, 360

cryptoporticus system, 379-80

Cyrene, 380

Cyrus II (the Great), 60; tomb of, Pasargadae, 51, *Plates 123-25*

Daphnis of Miletus, 362

Darius I, 65, 190; audience hall of, Persepolis, 68, 72, *Plates 128-29, 132-33*

Deir el Bahari:
  Hatshepsut, funerary temple of: 112, 116, 150, 155-56, 158, *Plates 173-74, 184-89;* Anubis chapel, 120-21, 155-56, *Plates 185-87;* "birth

room," *Plates 185-87;* Hathor chapel, 155, *Plate 188;* Tuthmosis I, chapel of, 156, *Plate 189*
Neb-hepet-ra Mentuhotep, mortuary temple of, 110, 112, 150, *Plates 173-76*
Tuthmosis III, mortuary temple of, 158, *Plate 174*
Delos, 228, 312, 318, 332, 336, 380
Delphi: Apollo, sanctuary of, 233-35, 277, 334, 374-75, *Plates 305, 370-71, 448;* Apollo Altar of Chios, 334; Athena, temple of, 249; Athenians, treasury of, 281, 334, *Plates 383, 448;* Bouleuterion, 312; Clazomenae, treasury of, 235; Cnidos, treasury of, 235, 367, *Plate 305;* Marseilles, treasury of, 235, 367, *Plate 305;* Sacred Way, 334, *Plate 448;* Sicyonians, treasury of, 334, *Plate 371;* Siphnians, treasury of, 235, 334, 367, *Plates 305-8, 310-11*
Delphi (Marmaria), Athena, sanctuary of (tholos), 350, *Plates 412-15*
Dendera, Hathor, temple of: 79, 168, 174, 178, 183, 185, 190, *Plates 236-45;* Hathoric columns, 120, 178, *Plate 244;* roof pavilion, 178, *Plates 240-43;* sacred lake, 183, *Plate 245*
Didyma, Apollo, temple of, 267, 326, 350, 360, 362, 366, *Plates 479, 488-94*
Djar, tomb complex of, Thebes, 110, *Plate 172*
Dodona, theater, *Plates 429-30*
Dreros, temple, 227, *Plate 294*
Dur Kurigalzu, 25; ziggurat, 25, *Plate 41*

Eanna precinct, Uruk, 15, *Plates 19-20, 22*
Edfu, Horus, temple of: 118, 168-70, 174, 178, 185, 188, 190, *Plates 228-35;* birth house, 79, 169, 174, 178, *Plate 228;* "hall of appearances," *Plate 232;* pylon, 115, *Plate 230*
*ekal mashati*, 38
Elam, architecture of, 65
Eleusis, Demeter, sanctuary of, 318; Telesterion, 318, *Plates 421-23*
Eleutherai, fortifications, *Plates 435-36*
Ephesus, Artemision, 228, 233, 267, 360, 362
Epidaurus: Temple L, 354, *Plate 470;* theater, *Plate 432;* tholos, 350, 354, *Plates 416-20, 465*
Epikles, 253
Epirus, Nekyomanteion of, Acarnania, 360
Erechtheion, Acropolis, Athens: 235, 238, 246, 333, 367, *Plates 318-24;* caryatid porch, 246, *Plates 322-24*
Eretria, Apollo Daphnephoros, temple of, 226, 227, 251, *Plate 302*
Eridu, 12, 19; Temple, Level VII, 12-13, *Plate 14;* Temple I, 15, *Plate 23*
Eshnunna, 23
Eumenes II, 370, 380
"Eye Temple," Tell Brak, 15, *Plate 21*

Fortification towers: Aegosthena, *Plate 434;* Arin Berd, 48-51; Bogazkoy, 31, *Plates 55-56;* Eleutherai, *Plates 435-36;* Hacilar, 11, *Plate 8;* Hazor, 52, 58, *Plate 112;* Jericho, 11, *Plate 6;* Karmir Blur, 48-51, *Plate 93;* Mersin, 11, *Plate 10;* Syracuse (Euryale), 360, *Plates 475-77*
Fortuna, sanctuary of, Praeneste, 379

Gela, 253-60, 270
Gimilsin, temple of, Tell Asmar, 22-23, *Plate 37*
Giza: Cheops, pyramid of, 89, *Plates 158, 163;* Chephren, Great Sphinx of, 94, 102, *Plates 163-66;* Chephren, pyramid of, 89, *Plates 158, 160, 163-66;* Chephren, pyramid temple of, 89-90; Chephren, valley temple of, 89-90, 94, 167, *Plates 159-62, 164;* Chephren, veneration temple of, 89-90, *Plate 160;* Harmakhis, temple of, 94, 102, *Plates 164-165;* Khent-kaw-s, buto tomb of, 81, 90, *Plate 167;* Mycerinus, pyramid of, *Plates 158, 165*
Gordion, 43, 48; megaron, 43, *Plate 89*
Gournia, *Plate 280*
Governors, palace of, Tell Asmar, 22-23, *Plate 37*

Hacilar, Fortress IIA, 11, *Plate 8;* Neolithic house, 11, *Plate 9*
Hadrian, pavilion of, Philae, 185, *Plate 249*
Hagia Triada, villa, 211, *Plate 277*
Halicarnassus, Mausoleum: 246-47, 367, 370; frieze from, 247, *Plate 329*
Hall of One Hundred Columns, Persepolis, 72, *Plates 128, 131*
Halys River, 31
Hammurabi, 23, 25, 32
Hapu, son of, Amenhotep, *see* Amenhotep, son of Hapu
Harmakhis, temple of, Giza, 94, 102, *Plates 164-65*
Hassuna, 12; farmhouse, 12, *Plate 11*
Hathor, 110, 150, 155; temple of, Dendera: 79, 120, 168, 174, 178, 183, 185, 190, *Plates 236-45*
Hatshepsut, 112, 116, 135, 147, 150, 156; baldachin temple of, Medinet Habu, 79, 147, *Plates 190-92;* obelisk of, Temple of Amon-Ra, Karnak, 130, *Plates 193, 202;* funerary temple of, Deir el Bahari: 112, 116, 150, 155-56, 158, *Plates 173-74, 184-89;* Anubis chapel, 120, 121, 155-56, *Plates 185-87;* "birth room," *Plates 185-87;* Hathor chapel, 155, *Plate 188;* Tuthmosis I, chapel of, 156, *Plate 189*
Hattusas, *see* Bogazkoy
Hazor, fortifications, 52, 58, *Plate 112*
Heliopolis, 84, 90, 102, 104, 115-16, 158, 188, 190; Sesostris I, obelisk of, 104, 115-16, *Plate 181*
Hermogenes, 348, 358, 362, 367, 376
Hermopolis, excavations at, 115
Herneith, tomb of, Saqqara, 80-81, *Plates 143, 145*
Herodotus, 58, 60, 114, 167, 174
Hierakonpolis, 188
Hieroglyphs, early Egyptian building types, *see* Predynastic period
Hill, Harold, 23
Hippodamus, 338-39
Hittites, civilization of, 31-32; Syro-Hittites, 51-52
*horoi*, 340
Horus, 79, 94, 102, 155, 159-60, 183; temple of, Edfu, *see* Edfu; *see also* Harmakhis, temple of
Hurrian, palace of, Nuzi, 27, *Plate 48*
Hyksos, 124

Ictinus, 283, 292, 303, 318, 332-33
Imhotep, 84, 156, 188, 190

Ischali, Ishtar-Kititum, temple of, 23, *Plate 38*
Ishtar, Gate, Babylon, 59, *Plate 116-18;* temple of, Assur, 27, *Plate 46*
Ishtar-Kititum, temple of, Ischali, 23, *Plate 38*
Isis, 115, 160, 183; temple of, Philae, 183, 185, *Plate 249*
*iwan*, 23

Jericho, 9, 11; Neolithic shrine, 9, *Plate 1;* Neolithic tower, 11, *Plate 6*
Jerusalem, Solomon's Temple, 58, *Plate 113*
Jordan, and Neolithic period, 9

Kalabsha: Mandulis, temple of, 168, 183, 190, *Plates 246-48;* Kertassi, pavilion of, *Plate 248*
Kanofer, 190
Kantir, Sety I, residence of, 159
Kapara Palace, Tell Halaf, 52, *Plates 109-11*
Kara-indash, temple of, Uruk, 25, *Plates 42-43*
Karmir Blur, Urartian citadel, 48-51, *Plate 93*
Karnak, 110, 124, 127, 132, 135
Amon-Ra, temple of: 116, 127, 130, 132, 158, 169, *Plates 193-207;* Aten, sanctuary of, 116; great hypostyle hall, 130, 132, 135, *Plates 193, 202-7;* Hatshepsut, obelisk of, 130, *Plates 193, 202;* Mut, temple of, 130; pylons, 116, 130, *Plates 193-95;* Ramesses III, temple of, *Plate 194;* sacred lake, 130, 169, *Plate 193;* Sesostris I, "White Chapel" of, 79, 116, 118, *Plate 182;* Taharqa, kiosk of, *Plate 194;* Tuthmosis I, obelisk of, 130, *Plates 202, 207;* Tuthmosis III, hall of annals of, 119, 130, *Plate 196;* Tuthmosis III, great festival hall of, 120, 130, *Plates 198-201*
Khonsu, temple of: 124, 132, 135, *Plates 208-11;* Ramesses III, court of, *Plate 208*
Kar Tukulti-Ninurta, Tukulti-Ninurta I, palace of, 27, *Plate 47*
Kassites, 23, 27
Kertassi, pavilion of, Kalabsha, *Plate 248*
Khafaje, Oval temple, 16, *Plate 24;* Sin temples, 16-19, *Plate 29*
Khasekhemui, 190
Khenem-ib-Ra, 190
Khentiamentiu, temple of, Abydos, 80-81, *Plate 142*
Khent-kaw-s, buto tomb of, Giza, 81, 90, *Plate 167*
Kheti, Prince, rock-cut tomb of, Beni Hasan, 114, *Plates 177-78*
Khirokitia (Cyprus), Neolithic village, 11, *Plate 7*
Khonsu, 124, 132, 135; temple of, Karnak, 124, 132, 135, *Plates 208-11*
Khorsabad, 37, *Plates 69, 74*
Sargon II, royal palace of: 37-38, 40, 51, 60, *Plates 71-72, 76, 100;* citadel, 38, 60, *Plates 72, 75;* Nabu, temple of, 38, 40, *Plate 69;* Palace F, 38; Palace K, 40, *Plate 80;* Portal Z, 40, *Plate 79;* ziggurat, 40
King's Gate, Bogazkoy, 31, *Plate 61*
Kish, 16; "Palace A," 19, *Plate 32*
Kleomenes, 253
Knossos, 193, 195, 196, 207; Palace at: 32, 37, 196, 199, 207, 210-14, 223; *Plates 260-75, 278;*

Caravanserai, 210; Corridor of Processions, 210; central court, *Plates 264-65;* decorations from, 211, 213-14, *Plates 278-79;* Hall of Double Axes, 211, 213; "horns of consecration," *Plate 274;* House of Lustral Basin, *Plate 272;* south house, *Plates 273, 275;* Little Palace, 211; magazines, 210, *Plate 263;* megaron, *Plate 266;* south portico, 207, *Plates 261, 274;* great staircase, 211, *Plates 267-71*
Kos, 376; Asclepius, sanctuary of, 375-76, 379; Temple C, 376
Kultepe, Assyrian merchants' quarter, 32, *Plate 63;* Bronze Age palace (megaron), 31, *Plate 54*
Kuyunjik, *see* Nineveh

Labranda, Idrieus, sanctuary of, 375; tomb, 360; Zeus, sanctuary of, 375, *Plate 502*
Larissa, Aeolic capital from, 233, *Plate 303*
Letoön, theater of the, Xanthos, 360
Leucadia, tomb, 358, 360
Libon, 281
Lindos, Athena, temple of, 375-76, *Plates 503-6*
Lion Gate: Bogazkoy, 31, *Plates 57-58;* Mycenae, 223, 249, *Plates 284-85*
Lisht, Sesostris I, mortuary temple of, 112, 118
Locri, 253-60; Ionic capital from, 275, *Plate 364;* fountain-sanctuary, *Plate 480*
Luxor, Amenhotep III, temple of: 119-20, 127, 132, 135, 147, *Plates 212-17;* colonnaded passage, 135, *Plates 212, 215, 217;* "hall of offerings," 135; Ramesses II, pylon of, 115, 135, 158, *Plate 216;* Ramesses II, court of, 135, *Plate 217*
Lycia, acropolis, 367-70
Lysicrates, monument of, Athens, *Plate 474*

Magnesia, Artemis, Altar of, 370, 372, *Plates 499-500;* Artemis Leukophryene, temple of, 233, 362, 367; Zeus Sosipolis, temple of, 367
Mallia, 195, 199, 201, 207; House E, *Plate 253;* palaces: 196, 199, 210-12, *Plates 250-52;* crypt rooms, 201, *Plate 252*
Mandulis, 183; temple of, Kalabsha, 168, 183, 190, *Plates 246-48*
Mari, 23, 195; Zimrilim, palace of, 23, 40, 196, 199, *Plates 39-40*
Marseilles, treasury of, Delphi, 235, 367, *Plate 305*
Marseilles, excavation of, *Plate 461*
mastaba, origin of, 104
Mausoleum, Halicarnassus, 246-47, 367, 370; frieze from, 247, *Plate 329*
Medamud, Monthu-Ra, temple of (near Thebes), 110, 114
Medinet Habu, 147; Hatshepsut, baldachin temple of, 79, 147, *Plates 190-92;* Ramesses III, mortuary temple of, 121, 147, 158-59, *Plates 218-19*
Medinet Madi, Amenemhat III and IV, temple of, 114-15
Medum, step pyramid, 84-89, *Plate 157;* offering temple, 89, *Plate 156*
Megara Hyblaea, 249, 270, 339-40; agora, 312, 335-37, 339-40, *Plate 450*
Memphis, 79-81, 84, 89-90, 93, 104, 110, 112, 118, 124, 167; Ptah, temple of, 132; Qasr el Sagha,

temple of (near the Faiyum), 93-94; *see also* Saqqara
Mendes, 167
Menes (Narmer), 79, 160; palette of, 79, *Plate 139*
Mersin, military fortress, 11, *Plate 10*
Metagenes, 228
Metapontum, 253-60, 340; agora, 340; Apollo, sanctuary of, 340; Hera, temple of, *Plate 353*
Midas, 48; monument of, Yasilikaya, 48, *Plate 91*
Miletus, 337-39, 354, 380, *Plates 458, 522-25*
Minkhursag Temple, Al 'Ubaid, facade reliefs, 16, *Plates 26-28*
Min of Coptos, 116, 124
Mnesicles, 332-33, 375
Monte Casale (Sicily), 340
Monthu-Ra, temple of, Medamud, 110, 114
Morgantina, agora, *Plate 451*
Mourning Women, Sarcophagus of the, *see* Sarcophagus of the Mourning Women
Mut, 124; temple of, Karnak, 130
Mycenae, 12, 223, 249; Atreus, treasury of, 223-24, 249, *Plates 291-93;* Lion Gate, 223, 249, *Plates 284-85;* "Secret Cistern," *Plates 286-88*
Mycerinus, pyramid of, Giza, *Plates 158, 165*

Nabu, temple of, Khorsabad, 38, 40, *Plate 69*
*naiskos,* 366
Napata, 167
Naramsin, palace of, Tell Brak, 19, *Plate 33*
Narmer, *see* Menes (Narmer)
Neandria, Aeolic capital from, *Plate 304*
Neb-hepet-ra Mentuhotep, mortuary temple of, 110, 112, 150, *Plates 173-76*
Nebi Yunus, *see* Nineveh
Nebuchadnezzar, 59; palace of, Babylon; *see* Babylon
Nectanebo II, 168, 183
Nephthys, 115
Nereids, monument of, Xanthos: 246-47, 349-50, 367, 370, *Plates 325-28*
Ne-user-ra, sun sanctuary of, Abusir, 102, 115, *Plate 170*
Nimrud, 37-38, 60; Fort Shalmaneser, 38, *Plate 73;* palace: platform, 37, 60, *Plate 68;* relief from, 38, *Plate 77*
Nineveh, 37, 58, *Plate 70;* Kuyunjik, 37; Nebi Yunus, 37; reliefs from, 38, 43, *Plates 78, 85*
Nin-Makh Temple, Babylon, 59, *Plate 119*
Niqmepa, palace of, Tell Atchana, 32, *Plate 66*
Nubia, 183
Nuzi, Hurrian, palace of, 27, *Plate 48*

Oeniadae, gates of, Acarnania, 358, 360
Olympia, Bouleuterion, 312; Gela, treasury of, 260; Hera, temple of, 249, *Plate 332;* palaestra, 249, 334, *Plates 330, 445-46;* stadium, *Plates 333, 447;* Terrace of the Treasuries, 249, 334, *Plates 333, 449;* Zeus, temple of, 275, 277, 281-82, 334, 354, *Plates 382, 384-85*
Orders: Corinthian, 304, 350, 354, 380; Doric, 303, 348-49; Ionic, 292, 297, 303, 348-49, 360, 362, 367

Osiris, 84, 118, 130, 155-56, 159-60, 167, 183, 185; temple precinct of, Abydos, 118; cult practices of (near Philae), 183, 185

Paeonius of Ephesus, 362
Paestum, 251, 253-60, 270, 326, 342, *Plate 459;* Athena, temple of, 270, 275, 342, 354, *Plate 363;* forum, *Plate 460;* Hera I, temple of (Basilica), 270, 342, *Plates 356-59, 439, 459;* Hera II, temple of (Poseidon), 275, 342, *Plates 356, 359, 365-68, 440, 459*
Paestum (Sele River), Hera, sanctuary of: 249-51, 270, 326; temple, *Plates 360-62;* treasury, 226, 249-51, *Plates 334-39*
Palaikastro, 195
Parthenon, Acropolis, Athens, 235, 277, 283, 292, 297, 303, 318, 332-33, *Plates 320, 387-88, 391-98*
Pasargadae, 65; Cyrus II, tomb of, 51, *Plates 123-25;* Residential Palace, 65, *Plate 126*
Pausanias, 303
Pazarli (Phrygia), reliefs from, 48, *Plates 90, 92*
Peithagoras, 267
Pergamum, 360, 370, 375, 379-80; acropolis: 379-80, *Plates 509-14;* Dionysus, temple of, *Plate 513;* theater, 380, *Plates 512-14;* lower city, 360, 379, *Plates 482-83;* Demeter, sanctuary of, 379, *Plates 515-17;* Zeus, Great Altar of, 370, 380, *Plate 498*
Pericles, 292
Persepolis, *Plate 137;* Xerxes, palace of: 65, 68, 72, *Plates 128-34;* Darius I, audience hall of, 68, 72, *Plates 128-29, 132-33;* Hall of One Hundred Columns, 72, *Plates 128, 131;* sculpture from, 65, 68, 72, *Plates 133-34, 136;* tripylon, *Plates 128, 134*
Phaistos, palace, 199, 201-7, 210-12, *Plates 254-59*
Phidias, 282-83, 292, 303
Philae, 183, 185; Hadrian, pavilion of, 185, *Plate 249;* Isis, temple of, 183, 185, *Plate 249*
Philetairos, 379
Philo, 318, 338
Phrygia, civilization of, 43, 48, 51
Piraeus, 283, 338-39; agora, 339; Arsenal, 318, 323, *Plates 427-28;* Athena, sanctuary of, 339; Lion Harbor, 339
Pirene fountain, Corinth, 358, *Plate 478*
Pisistratus, 277; Pisistratids, 277, 318
plano-convex, 19
*polis,* formation of, 225, 312, 337
Polycrates of Samos, 277
Pompeii, paintings from, 214, 380
Porinos, 277
Porta Rosa, Velia, 358-60
Praeneste, Fortuna, sanctuary of, 379
Predynastic period, Egypt, heiroglyphs depicting early building types, 78-79, *Plates 138-40*
Priene, agora: 318, 360, 370, 372, *Plates 424, 481;* Bouleuterion, *Plate 426;* Ekklesiasterion, 318, *Plate 425;* prytaneum, 312; theater, *Plate 431;* Athena Polias, temple of, *Plate 495*
Prinias, Temple A, 227, *Plates 296-97*
Propylaea, Acropolis, Athens, 235, 332-33, 362, 375, *Plates 314, 322, 389, 442-44*

Protodynastic period, Mesopotamia, 9, 11-13, 15-16, 19
Protoliterate period, Mesopotamia, 13, 16
Ptah, 124, 132, 159-60
Ptolemaic dynasty, 147-50, 156, 167-68
Pylos, palace, 223, *Plates 289-90*
Pyramid Texts, 93
Pythius of Priene, 348

Qasr el Sagha, temple of (near the Faiyum), 93-94
Qaw el Kebir, tombs at, 112, 114

Radedef, 90; tomb complex of (north of Giza), 90
Ra-Harakhte, 115-16, 158-59
Ramesses II, 130, 132, 135, 159; court of, Temple of Amenhotep III, Luxor, 135, *Plate 217;* mortuary temple of, Thebes, 132, 158-59; pylon of, Temple of Amenhotep III, Luxor, 115, 135, 158, *Plate 216;* rock temple of, Abu Simbel, 159, *Plates 220-25*
Ramesses III, 132, 147; court of, Temple of Khonsu, Karnak, *Plate 208;* mortuary temple of, Medinet Habu, 121-22, 147, 158-59, *Plates 218-19;* temple of, Temple of Amon-Ra, Karnak, *Plate 194*
Ramessid dynasty, 120, 132
Residential Palace, Pasargadae, 65, *Plate 126*
Rhamnus, acropolis and fortress walls, 303, 326, *Plate 404;* Nemesis, temple of, 303
Rhampsinit, 174
Rhoikos, 228, 233, 235
Roman architecture, Greek prototypes for, 349-50, 354, 358, 366-67, 372, 379-80
Royal Mausoleum, Ur, 19, 22, *Plate 36*

Sabni and Mekhu, rock-cut tomb of, Aswan, 104, 110, 150, *Plate 171*
Sacred Lake: Dendera, 183, *Plates 240, 245;* Karnak, 130, *Plate 193*
Sacred Way: Acropolis, Athens, 332, *Plate 389;* Apollo, sanctuary of, Delphi, 334, *Plate 448*
Sahura, pyramid complex of, Abusir, *Plates 168-69*
Sais, 167
Samos, Hera, sanctuary of, 228, 233, 326, 332, 335-36, 342, 362, *Plate 299;* Hera III, temple of, 228, 233, *Plate 300;* Hera IV, temple of, 277, *Plate 301;* stoa, 335, 342
Saqqara: Herneith, tomb of, 80-81, *Plates 143, 145;* niched tomb, 81, *Plate 144;* Weserkaf, pyramid of, 90, 102; Zoser, King, mortuary precinct of, 80-81, 84, 118-19, 155, *Plates 146-55*
Saqqara, North, *see* Saqqara
Sarcophagus of the Mourning Women, Archaeological Museum, Istanbul, 354, 370, *Plates 466-67, 497*
Sardis, Artemis Cybele, temple of, 350, 360, 362, *Plates 484-87*
Sargon, 19
Sargon II, 37; royal palace of, Khorsabad, 37-38, 40, 51, 60, *Plates 71-72, 76, 100;* citadel, 38, 60, *Plates 72, 75*
Schliemann, Heinrich, 29

Scopas, 304, 308, 350, 354; frieze by, Mausoleum, Halicarnassus, 350, 354, *Plate 329*
Sebennytos, 167
"Secret Cistern," Mycenae, *Plates 286-88*
Segesta: Doric temple, 326, 349, *Plates 369, 441, 462-63;* theater, *Plate 433*
Selinus, 249, 251, 253-60, 270, 275, 335, 342; Temple C, 253, 267, 332, 342, *Plates 343-46;* Temple D, 342; Temple E (Hera), 260, *Plates 347-50;* Temple F, 260, 267; Temple G (Apollo or Zeus), 260, 267; stoa, 335, 342
Senmut, 150, 156
Sennacherib, palace of, Nineveh, 43, *Plate 85;* reliefs from, 38, *Plates 78, 85*
Sesostris I, 188; mortuary temple of, Lisht, 112, 118; obelisk of, Heliopolis, 104, 115-16, *Plate 181;* "White Chapel" of, Temple of Amon-Ra, Karnak, 79, 116, 118, *Plate 182*
Sety I: cenotaph of, Abydos, 159-60, 167, *Plate 227;* temple of, Abydos, 159-60, *Plate 226;* residence of, Kantir, 159; influence at Karnak, 130
Shalmaneser, Fort, Nimrud, 38, *Plate 73*
Shalmaneser III, 43
Shara Temple, Tell Agrab, 16-19, *Plate 30*
Sicyonians, treasury of, Delphi, 334, *Plate 371*
Sinjirli, 52, *Plate 102;* citadel, 52, *Plate 103;* wall construction, 52, *Plate 105*
Sin temples, Khafaje, 16-19, *Plate 29*
Siphnians, treasury of, Delphi, 235, 367, *Plates 305-8, 310-11*
Sirenpowet II, Prince, rock-cut tomb of, Aswan, 114, *Plate 179*
Smyrna, 225-26
Solomon's Temple, Jerusalem, 58, *Plate 113*
Solon, 336-37
Sphinx Gate, Alaca Huyuk, *Plate 59*
Sumer, civilization of, 12-13, 15-16, 19-20, 22, *Plate 13*
Sunium, Poseidon, temple of, 303, 326, *Plates 399-403*
Susa, relief from, 65-68, *Plate 135*
Syracuse, 249, 251, 253, 260, 267; Athena, temple of, 267, 270; Euryale, fortifications of, 360, *Plates 475-77*
Syracuse (Ortygia), Apollo, temple of, 251, 253, *Plates 340-42*
Syro-Hittites, *see* Hittites

Taharqa, kiosk of, Temple of Amon-Ra, Karnak, *Plate 194*
Tegea, Athena Alea, temple of, 304, 350, 354, *Plates 406-7*
Telesterion, Eleusis, 318, *Plates 421-23*
Tell Agrab, Shara Temple, 16-19, *Plate 30*
Tell Asmar, 19, 22; Akkadian palace, 19, *Plate 31;* Gimilsin, temple of, 22-23, *Plate 37;* Governors, palace of, 22-23, *Plate 37*
Tell Atchana, 195; Niqmepa, palace of, 32, 52, 199, *Plate 66;* Yarimlin, palace of, 32, 52, 199, *Plate 65*
Tell Brak, "Eye Temple," 15, *Plate 21;* Naramsin, palace of, 19, *Plate 33*

Tell el Amarna, *see* Akhetaten
Tell Halaf, Kapara Palace, 52, *Plates 109-11*
Tell Rimah, 27, 43
Tell Tayanat, palace, *Plates 106-7;* temple, *Plate 107*
Teos, Dionysus, temple of, 348-49
Tepe Gawra, 13; temples, 13, *Plate 15*
Terrace of the Treasuries, Olympia, 249, 334, *Plates 333, 449*
Thasos, Silenus, gate of, 358, 360, *Plate 471;* Zeus, gate of, 358, 360, *Plates 472-73*
Theater: characteristics of, 323; Athens, Agora, 312; Dodona, *Plates 429-30;* Epidaurus, *Plate 432;* Priene, *Plate 431;* Segesta, *Plate 433*
Thebes, 110, 112, 121, 124, 127, 150, 195; Amenhotep III, palace complex of (West Thebes), 121-22; Djar, tomb complex of, 110, *Plate 172;* Ramesses II, mortuary temple of, 132, 158-59
Thebes, West, *see* Thebes
Themistocles, 283
Theodoros, 228, 233
Thermon, Apollo, temple of, 227-28, 249, *Plates 298, 331*
Tholos: Athens, 337; Delphi, *Plate 370;* Delphi (Marmaria), 350, *Plates 412-15;* Epidaurus, 350, 354, *Plates 416-20, 465*
Til Barsip, Assyrian palace, mural from, 40, *Plate 81*
Tiryns, palace: 223, 249, *Plate 281;* casemates, 223, *Plate 283;* fortification walls, 223, *Plate 282*
Tod, temple at, 114
Toprakkale, building models from, 51, *Plates 94, 95*
Troy, 23, 29; Levels I and II, 29, *Plates 49-50;* Priam's Treasure, 29; Level VI, 29, *Plate 51*
Tukulti-Ninurta I, 25; wall painting from palace of, Kar Tukulti-Ninurta, 27, *Plate 47;* ziggurat of, Assur, 25, *Plate 46*
Tuthmosis I, 116, 130, 150; chapel of, Temple of Hatshepsut, Deir el Bahari, 156, *Plate 189;* obelisk of, Temple of Amon-Ra, Karnak, 130, *Plates 202, 207*
Tuthmosis II, 150
Tuthmosis III, 120, 130, 135, 147; great festival hall of, Temple of Amon-Ra, Karnak, 120, 130, *Plates 198-201;* hall of annals of, Temple of Amon-Ra, Karnak, 119, 130, *Plate 196;* mortuary temple of, Deir el Bahari, 158, *Plate 174*

Ur, 16, 19-20, 22-23, 27, 60, *Plate 34;* Royal Mausoleum, 19, 22, *Plate 36;* ziggurat, 20, 22, *Plate 35*
Urartians, civilization of, 48, 51, 65
Uruk, 13, 15, 25; Eanna precinct, 15, *Plates 19-20, 22;* Kara-indash, temple of, 25, *Plates 42-43;* "White Temple": 13, 15, *Plates 16-18;* ziggurat of, 15, *Plate 18*

Velia, Porta Rosa, 358, 360
Vitruvius, 348-49, 358, 367, 375

Weserkaf, 90, 102; pyramid of, Saqqara, 90, 102
"White Temple," Uruk, 13, 15, *Plates 16-18*
Woolley, Sir Leonard, 20, 22, 60

Xanthos, Letoön, theater of the, 360; Nereids, monument of, 246-47, 349-50, 367, 370, *Plates 325-28*

Xerxes, palace of, Persepolis: 65, 68, 72, *Plates 128-34:* Darius I, audience hall of, 68, 72, *Plates 128-29, 132-33:* Hall of One Hundred Columns, 72 *Plates 128, 131:* sculpture from, 65, 68, 72, *Plates 133-34, 136:* tripylon, *Plates 128, 134*

Yarimlin, palace of, Tell Atchana, 32, 52, 199, *Plate 65*

Yasilikaya (Phrygia), "Midas Monument," 48, *Plate 91:* rock shrine of, *see* Bogazkoy

Zakro, 195-96, 210; excavations at, *Plate 276*

Zet, King, stele of, Abydos, 79-80, *Plate 140*

Ziggurat: 12-13, 20; Assur, 23, *Plates 46-47:* Choga Zambil, 65, *Plate 127:* Dur Kurigalzu, 23, *Plate 41:* Ur, 20, 22, *Plate 35:* Uruk, 15, *Plate 18*

Zimrilim, palace of, Mari, 23, *Plates 39-40*

Zoser, King, mortuary precinct of, Saqqara, 80-81, 84, 118-19, 155, 170, *Plates 146-55*

# LIST OF PHOTOGRAPHIC CREDITS

Aurelio Amendola, Pistoia: 342, 345, 348, 349

Bildarchiv Foto Marburg, Marburg/Lahn: 111, 140, 144, 156, 157, 168, 188, 189, 208, 227, 232, 235

British Museum, London: 13, 77, 78, 82, 83, 85, 86, 87, 88, 94, 95, 98, 99, 101, 104, 325, 329

Director General of Antiquities, Iraq Museum, Baghdad: 22, 25, 26, 27, 28, 41

Fotocielo, Rome: 352, 459

Hirmer Verlag, Munich: 35, 36, 179, 230, 231, 233, 248

Institut français d'archéologie, Istanbul: 91

Prof. Hans Wolfgang Müller, Irschenausen: 139, 145, 172, 194, 209, 228, 234, 246, 247, 249

Musée d'Archéologie, Marseilles: 461

Oriental Institute, University of Chicago: 38, 75, 80, 106

Antonello Perissinotto, Padua: 57, 58, 59, 61, 123, 126, 128, 129, 130, 132, 133, 134, 136

Josephine Powell, Rome: 90, 92

Francesco Quadarella, Agrigento: 468

Ezio Quiresi, Cremona: 353, 451

Saint Hugh's College, Oxford: 6

Service des Documentations Photographiques des Musées Nationaux, Paris: 40, 76, 81, 135

James A. Sinclair, Ltd., London: 12

Soprintendenza alle Antichità, Reggio Calabria: 364, 480

Staatliche Museen, Berlin: 16, 43, 118, 122, 498, 510,

Warburg Institute, London: 47